# Cooking for the Professional Chef

## Kenneth C. Wolfe

**VNR** VAN NOSTRAND REINHOLD COMPANY
NEW YORK · CINCINNATI · ATLANTA · DALLAS · SAN FRANCISCO
LONDON · TORONTO · MELBOURNE

Van Nostrand Reinhold Company Regional Offices:
New York   Cincinnati   Atlanta   Dallas   San Francisco

Van Nostrand Reinhold Company International Offices:
London   Toronto   Melbourne

Library of Congress Catalog Card Number: 76-17269
ISBN   0-442-29505-7

Manufactured in the United States of America

Published by Van Nostrand Reinhold Company
450 West 33rd Street, New York, N.Y.  10001

Published simultaneously in Canada by Van Nostrand Reinhold Ltd.

15 14 13 12 11 10 9 8 7 6 5 4 3 2

**Library of Congress Cataloging in Publication Data**

Wolfe, Kenneth C.
    Cooking for the professional chef.

    Includes Index.
    1. Cookery.   I. Title.
TX663.W84        641.5'72        76-17269
ISBN  0-442-29505-7

# Preface

Gourmet cooking, Commercial Food Service, or Quantity Food Preparation are specializations of vocational cooking. This text provides "how-to-do" knowledge and information to future skilled cooks and chefs. It considers dietary as well as production needs. Some of the concepts expressed here may seem revolutionary in relation to practices still held over from the past, but all information is based on provable facts and data.

A credentialed Culinary Arts instructor must help and supervise students to practice what they are going to learn, but thanks to this new structure, all cooking will become less complicated than expected. The contents of this book can be covered in one or two years of a college or trade school course, depending on class and lab hours.

Also, a working journeyman cook will find *Cooking for the Professional Chef: A Structured Approach* valuable in attaining new knowledge and skill. Consequently, a better position with greater earning power may become his.

Most American and European cuisine is based on a dominating Italian-French influence which has been virtually unchanged for hundreds of years. This book uses the sciences of nutrition, organic chemistry, microbiology, and especially thermodynamics to explain what happens during the cooking process. Through the new analysis, cookery has become much less complicated and difficult. It shows that only a few methods of cookery exist for those hundreds of preparations that differ only in semantics, sequence and details.

Cooking definitely has a structure. By understanding and applying this structure every student can become a skilled cook. Today's vocational cooking aims to efficiently prepare food without the guesswork of the past. To reach the level of *creative* chef, the student needs some talent and much experience.

The new cook of today must be aware of the nutritional and sanitary codes as well as of the gastronomic and economic needs of his trade. Cooking is the technique which presents edible food to mankind. To a certain degree, man is what he eats. Medical data prove that nutrition controls man's physical and mental well-being. To be effective and competitive, today's chef must replace old concepts with an understanding of modern cooking approaches.

The philosphers of all times have always acknowledged the physiological and emotional importance of cooking and considered a good cook to be an especially responsible and needed member of our society.

The author has a baccalaureate and a masters degree in Vocational Education. He is Chef-Instructor and Department Chairman of Culinary Arts at Contra Costa College in San Pablo, California. He teaches day and evening classes, as well as adult and high school lecture sessions. Mr. Wolfe is past president of the Chefs Association of the Pacific Coast, and has also been National Chairman of the Educational Institute of the American Culinary Federation. He holds the "Careme Medal" and is a member of Epsilon Pi Tau, the honor society of the professional occupational educator.

# Contents

# Section 1 Modern Cooking Technology

## Unit 1 New Approaches to Cooking Methods

*OBJECTIVES*

After studying this unit, the student should be able to

- Explain how heat changes food.
- List the substances which prevent food from burning.
- Name the five basic modern categories of cookery.
- List the cook's obligations to his occupation and to the consumer.

The modern cooking technology covered in the units of this text is based upon the definition of *cooking* as the heating of food to a certain temperature to make the food *edible* (eatable). The term *cooking* is also used to mean the preparation of food in general.

*NEED FOR HEAT EXPOSURE*

Heat breaks down the *cellulose* (fibers) of plant food and partly dissolves connective tissues in meat in order to increase tenderness. Heat evaporates water. It also fluffs starches, as in baked potatoes. Heat melts sugar, *caramelizes* it (changes its color to brown), and finally, *carbonizes* (burns) it completely. Heat breaks down, browns, and melts fats. As a result, heat changes the flavor and appearance of food. When enough heat is applied to food, it sterilizes the food by killing the bacteria. These physical and chemical changes tenderize food for easier chewing and digestion and sterilize the food to guard against bacterial infections.

*CATEGORIES OF THE PAST*

Cookbooks in general divide food into groups based on the menu sequence. Some of these groups are Appetizers, Soups, Fish, Meat, Poultry and Game, Vegetables, Salads, Egg Dishes, and Desserts. For each of these categories, many different cooking methods are listed. Sauces are subdivided by flavor and color. For

Fig. 1-1

MEAT, FISH, DAIRY, VEGETABLES, FRUITS

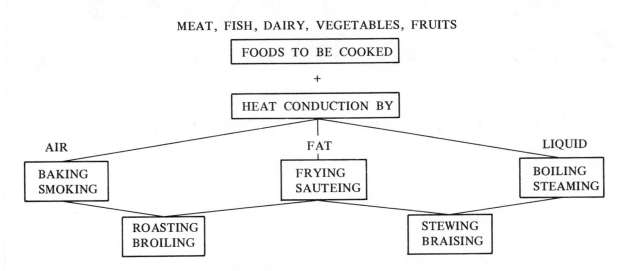

Table 1-1 The Five Basic Cooking Processes for all Foods

example, Auguste Escoffier (1847-1935) in his book *Culinary Guide* (viewed by many chefs as the final authority in cooking) listed two different tomato sauces. One sauce is made from tomatoes, meat stock, and bacon. The other sauce, intended for Lenten use (Sauce Tomate Maigre), is made without any meat or meat stock at all.

## A MODERN APPROACH

The modern categories of cooking deal with five techniques based on the actual cooking procedure rather than on the menu sequences. These categories all involve putting heat into food through a *conductor,* or carrier of heat. All cooking pots are heat conductors, as are frying pans and some other utensils. In addition to conduction, convection and radiation also transfer heat. *Convection* means that heat is carried by warmed air. *Radiation* means exposure to direct rays from an open flame.

Unprotected or unshielded food placed in a fire burns or *chars* (carbonizes) instead of being cooked. A shield must exist between the heat source and the food to be cooked. Regardless of the type of heat transfer, (conduction, convection, or radiation), the shields for foods are air, liquid, and fat.

The five categories of cooking based on actual cooking procedure are

1. **Dry Hot Air.** Cooking in hot air is called convection cooking or baking. When small quantities of fat are added, the process is called *roasting.* When the heat radiates from an open fire, the process is called *spit roasting* or *broiling.*

2. **Liquid or Water.** The cooking of foods in liquids is known as *boiling* (simmering) or *steaming.* Other liquid methods are *poaching* and *pressure cooking.*

Fig. 1-2

3. **Browning in Hot Fat.** This type of cooking is divided into groups depending on the amount of fat used. The process may be called *flip frying, pan frying, griddle frying, deep frying,* or *pressure deep frying.*

4. **The Combination.** In this method, food is exposed to all three previous categories in a sequence or even together in the same pot. This process is commonly known as *stewing, braising, pot roasting,* or *fricasseeing.*

5. **Extraction of Liquefiable Foods.** This method uses the by-products of foods which have been simmered in liquids. When the foods so cooked are the main result, such as boiled chicken or boiled beef, the liquid is called *broth.* When the food and flavor value of otherwise unusable meat, fish, and vegetable leftovers is extracted by a slow simmering or steeping method, the liquid is called *stock.* When a starch ingredient is added to these liquids, the results are soups, sauces, and gravies.

### Caramelizing Starches

Long ago, someone realized that browned food has a better taste. Today many foods are browned before being finally cooked.

Only the dry or fat cooking methods result in browning; moist methods do not. The desirable browning results from caramelization of *carbohydrates* which are present in various amounts in all plant food and animal blood. Browning also occurs through the breakdown of fats, a first step toward burning. This explains why steaks which contain a large percentage of fat and blood brown easily on the broiler or in the pan, whereas the lean white meats of veal, skinless chicken breast and fish have to be dipped in flour or other starches before frying to become browned.

The temperatures needed to brown carbohydrates and fats are higher than the temperature needed to boil water in an open container, 212° Fahrenheit (F.). Beef fat starts browning at 225°F., while other fats need temperatures of 300°F. Sugar caramelizes at about 300°F.

### Tenderization Through Moisture

Moist cooking methods are used in the preparation of dry plant foods and old, tough meat with little fat content to avoid overbrowning and the resulting burnt taste. The connective tissues in meat are unrefined *gelatine.* The older the animal, the tougher the tissue. To tenderize this tissue, hot water is needed to dissolve the gelatine.

Moisture in a food is often used as a measure of whether or not a food is edible. Food which is too dry or dehydrated must be reconstituted by the addition of water or other liquid to make it edible. The moisture content of food is used as an indication of its juiciness. In general, the juicier a food, the better it tastes.

### Caramelizing and Tenderizing Combined

The *combination* category of cooking first caramelizes food by frying or roasting it to obtain a more acceptable taste. Then it is tenderized by adding liquid (water) to complete the cooking.

### Liquid Food Extracts

The last category of cooking uses either a broth or a stock. A broth is the by-product of simmering food in water to which flavor ingredients, such as vegetables, herbs, and spices, have been added. The *leaching* (extraction) process of the water causes some flavor and many nutrients to be transferred from the food into the broth. The broth is simmered until the food it covers is tenderized, then it is strained and used primarily in the making of soups.

True stock is not the by-product of boiled food and must not be confused with broth. Stock is the result of simmering surplus bones, *sinews,* and *gristle* trimmed from raw meat. Various root vegetables, herbs, and spices are added to the stock to improve the flavor. Stock must simmer for many hours until all nutrients and flavors have leached out into the liquid. Stock is used for sauces, in gravies, and for the braising or combination method.

## COOKING OBJECTIVES

The objectives of cooking are based on the principles of nutrition and an obligation to the public. If cooks in service to the public neglect these objectives, then they have failed in their responsibilities. The objectives are

> *To satisfy the nutritional needs of the people served*
>
> *To preserve food quality and natural taste*
>
> *To consider the aesthetic needs of the public*
>
> *To utilize the variety of all foods available*
>
> *To uphold sanitary requirements of the food service industry*

## SUMMARY

The most significant action of all cooking is the carrying of heat into food. Modern cooking processes are based on the several ways in which heat enters food. Cookery uses three shields to protect foods from being charred or burned before they are cooked. The shields are *air, liquid,* and *fat.*

The modern approach divides cookery into five basic categories which are used for all foods to be cooked. In addition, the similarity of the chemical makeup of food results in a similarity of cooking methods. The immediate objectives of cooking or heat induction are to produce a change of flavor (caramelization), to improve digestibility (tenderization), and to prevent bacterial infection (sterilization).

Recognizing the modern approach of five basic categories makes all cooking easier to understand and accomplishes the cook's obligation to nutrition and to the public he serves. Applying this modern approach makes the student realize that the many existing food dishes from all over the world are based on only five cooking methods, several main ingredients, and a variety of flavor-giving additions.

### DISCUSSION TOPICS

1. What happens when foods are exposed to heat?
2. Why are food service workers called Sauce Cooks, Roast Cooks, Pastry Cooks, etc., but never Salad Cooks?
3. What does the modern approach to cooking mean?
4. Does cooking in foreign countries use the same basic categories as the ones introduced in this unit?
5. What is the difference between broth and stock?
6. What are some reasons for food to be inedible?
7. What is the nature of caramelizing or browning?
8. Does the cook's vocation have a greater obligation to the public than most other occupations?

### SUGGESTED ACTIVITIES

1. Define the following terms:

   a. Conduction
   b. Convection
   c. Radiation
   d. Sterilization
   e. Caramelization
   f. Nutrition
   g. Carbohydrates

   h. Aesthetics
   i. Roasting
   j. Leaching
   k. Broth
   l. Stock
   m. Dehydrated

2. Look at three books with a traditional menu sequence, and compare them to each other.

3. Interview a food service worker and ask his opinion of the five techniques as a basis for categories of cooking procedures.

*ACHIEVEMENT REVIEW*

A. Complete the following statements:

1. Cooking changes the flavor of food through the process of browning known as _____.

2. Cooking by moist heat is used mainly to tenderize food and to prevent it from _____.

3. Cookbooks usually divide food into groups based on the _____ sequence.

4. Many chefs consider the final authority of cooking to be _____.

5. Cooking pots and frying pans are heat _____.

6. Shields used to prevent burning of foods are fat, air, and _____.

7. Baking or dry heat cookery can also be called cooking by _____.

8. The by-product of boiled food is called _____.

9. The connective tissues of meat are unrefined _____.

10. In the combination method of cooking, food is tenderized by the moist method after the frying or roasting has achieved a certain _____.

B. Read each question carefully and completely before answering it. Select the best answer.

1. Most people of Western civilization prefer meat which is
   a. baked
   b. browned
   c. steamed
   d. unsalted

2. To get a brown crust on a fried chicken the meat has to be dipped first in
   a. butter
   b. flour
   c. milk
   d. egg whites

3. Beefsteaks brown very well because they contain
   a. protein and water
   b. unrefined gelatine
   c. blood sugar and fat
   d. vitamins and minerals

4. When food is put into an open fire it will
   a. overcook
   b. burn or char
   c. toughen
   d. redden

5. Of the following, the one which does *not* occur when food is exposed to heat for a sufficient time is
   a. sterilization of bacteria
   b. tenderization of muscles
   c. changes of flavor
   d. increase of vitamin value

6. At what approximate temperature does sugar begin to caramelize?
   a. 212°F.
   b. 225°F.
   c. 300°F.
   d. 400°F.

7. The following name which is *not* used to describe the combination method of caramelizing and tenderizing is

   a. poaching
   b. braising

   c. fricasseeing
   d. stewing

C. Answer the following in your own words.

   1. List the five basic modern categories of cookery. Briefly describe each one.

   2. List the cook's obligations to his occupation and to the consumer.

# Unit 2 Various Food Service Establishments

## OBJECTIVES

After studying this unit, the student should be able to

- Outline the continuous growth of the hospitality industry.
- Name at least twelve different food service establishments.
- Describe the bonds between international and American restaurant cuisine.
- Identify cook ranks in English as well as French terminology.

## MEANING OF FOOD SERVICE

Food service establishments are business concerns which serve freshly cooked food directly to consumers. These businesses produce and also retail the product. The two functions are rarely found together in other industries. Therefore, food service establishments are divided into different parts: 1) the service part, called the *front of the house,* 2) the food-producing kitchen part, called the *back of the house,* and 3) the office or business administration part.

Workers in each one of these groups have had a different training background and perhaps have some class consciousness. This class consciousness may be a source of friction between the staff members. Such friction must be avoided in order to have a successful business.

Today's schools and training methods try to unify these groups. Groups are being trained together, and each person is aware of the difficulty of the others' work. All have a great responsibility. It is stressed that working together has more advantages than competing against each other.

## HOSPITALITY INDUSTRY OF TODAY

Food service has a long and colorful history. Cookshops and taverns in England were mentioned in literature as early as the twelfth century. In time, cookshops became restaurants, and taverns became hotels. These two concepts dominated the hospitality field until recently. Then the motels appeared with "no service — no food" approach. This was designed to make traveling cheaper for the customer. The new concept seemed very competitive to hotels at first, but the "no service" policy did not last. The hospitality industry is still based on the same principles as ever. Changes in traveling and transportation modes brought the city hotel concept to the forefront again. Motels became more hotel-like and a newer concept, that of the "drive-in" motorhotel, is now widely accepted.

Restaurants in the United States have gone through changes during the last half century. At first, they were "full service" restaurants and served breakfast, lunch, and dinner. Then

Fig. 2-1 The setting up of a luncheon buffet, made and served by a culinary arts class.

7

they were divided into special groups serving different foods to different customers at different meal times. The new trend of the restaurant field is an economically necessary measure for the success of the business.

Full-service restaurants are still in operation. It is a hard task for the chef to supervise them. One working shift of seven and a half hours does not cover the service time open to the public. Second and third shifts have to be set up. This causes wasteful overlaps of working hours. For this reason, the full-service restaurant is gradually disappearing.

## MODERN AMERICAN CATEGORIES

Today, only large city hotels maintain dining rooms, luncheon rooms, grillrooms, coffeeshops, bistros, banquet facilities, and room service. Therefore, a hotel remains the most interesting working place for the young cook.

The new branches of the hospitality industry are found in the many types of specialized food serving places. Specialty houses include dinner, steak, fish, and spaghetti houses; French, Italian, German, and other ethnic restaurants; luncheonettes, sandwich counters, hofbraus, and delicatessens. All have a limited food selection and short service hours. In addition, there are summer and winter resorts, camps, ships, airlines, trains, hospitals, institutions, canteens, catering companies, and industrial cafeterias.

### A LISTING OF DIFFERENT FOOD SERVICE ESTABLISHMENTS

HOTELS

SHIPS

FULL-SERVICE RESTAURANTS

| | EMPLOYMENT AREAS FOR THE CHEF AND COOK | |
|---|---|---|
| CANTEENS | | LUXURY RESTAURANTS |
| CATERERS | | REGIONAL RESTAURANTS |
| HOFBRAUS | | ETHNIC RESTAURANTS |
| LUNCH COUNTERS | | DINNER HOUSES |
| DRIVE-INS | | SEAFOOD HOUSES |
| HAMBURGER STANDS | | STEAK HOUSES |
| CHUCKWAGONS | | SPAGHETTI HOUSES |
| SMORGASBOARDS | | COFFEESHOPS |
| BISTROS | | CAFETERIAS |
| TRAINS | | CAMPS |

RESORTS

HOSPITALS

INSTITUTIONS

**Table 2-1**

## REGIONAL DIFFERENCES IN CUISINE

A regional style of cooking emphasizes the best native food products of a region. Regional cuisine also develops a special style of cooking suitable to climate and consumers. Lobsters, oysters, and seafood from New England's shores are famous. New England is also well known for heavy dishes, such as baked beans and chowder, which are preferred in the colder climates. Florida and California abound in fruits and vegetables; their seafood is served mostly in salad mixtures. Because of the humid climate, seafood preparation in

Louisiana places great emphasis on the use of more spices, many of them hot. In addition, state labor laws, union locals, and socio-economic levels are responsible for other differences. When moving to another state, it is wise to accept a position where local working habits and cooking differences can be learned.

### INTERNATIONAL CUISINE

The style of cooking practiced in most American restaurants is called the International Cuisine of the Western world. The term *Western world* applies to the people of Western civilization. Asians and Africans have their own styles of cooking and eating.

It must be emphasized that the *cuisine* (style of cooking) of continental Europe is strongly influenced by the Italians and the French. The immigrants from Europe brought along their customs and achieved a mixing of the various cuisines by selecting the best that each group

Fig. 2-2 Instructor, (left) demonstrating garde-manger techniques on a Lobster en Belle Vue.

had to offer. Then the increase in travel and in the export and import of foods made the restaurant cuisine basically the same all over the world. Because of this newly developed structure, the cooks and chefs of today are able to choose many areas and foreign countries in which to practice their craft.

### SKILL LEVELS AND RANKS

Skill levels and ranks go hand in hand. In industry, elevation in rank comes as a reward for service. Students must be aware that skill alone, even when matched with professional knowledge, is not enough to be promoted. Personality, reliability, and honesty are qualities just as important. A good business sense, a capability for public relations, and a cool head are as important in a chef as his top culinary performance. The shortage of good chefs is so great that many establishments are satisfied with a chef whose business sense is greater than his culinary know-how.

The graduated student, ready for a cook's job, becomes integrated into the working process. He decides which way to go. He may become a skilled master chef or he may be satisfied with a job that offers money and social comfort with less demands on knowledge and skill.

Fig. 2-3 Culinary art student and student chef preparing food.

Fig. 2-4 Student chef using a modern vertical speed cutter to make Pate Maison (homemade liver and meat pate).

Fig. 2-5 Chef-Instructor of a Culinary Arts class (center, tall hat) helping students with buffet (Garde-manger) work.

| CHEF DE CUISINE | EXECUTIVE CHEF |
|---|---|
| SOUS CHEF | SOUS CHEF |
| CHEF DE PARTIE | STATION CHEF |
| PREMIER COMMIS | STATION COOK |
| DEUXIEME COMMIS | COOK'S HELPER |
| TROISIEME COMMIS | COOK'S HELPER ASSISTANT |

**Table 2-2 FRENCH RANKS OF A COOK'S BRIGADE**

For the Executive Chef, experience as a Chef Garde-manger, Second Cook, Banquet Chef, or Sous Chef is important. But for a Head Chef's job in the average restaurant, experience as Pantry or Broiler Man, Station Cook or Second Cook is enough. As a working chef in a special type of restaurant, partial knowledge of cookery could well meet the requirements.

Kitchens, like other production facilities, are divided into sections or work stations. This way of organizing speeds up production and improves the quality of cooking. In vocational cooking, all kitchens use either the French style work station division or an American adaptation of it. The crew of chefs, cooks, bakers, butchers, and helpers who work under the Executive Chef (Chef de Cuisine) is called a *brigade*. Some cooks like specialized work and rarely change from one station to the other; others prefer more variety and experience and make it a point to change stations often. Stations seldom have more than three cooks under one Station Cook (Chef de Partie). If there is more work than they can handle, the station is subdivided. For example, one section of the Sauce Cook's work may be given to one or two new cooks called Saute Men. The new subdivided Saute Station pan fries (sautes) all dishes made to order. Other Sauce Cooks perform certain duties. All Sauce Cooks help with the preparatory work. Preparation for orders served later is very important for the efficient functioning of a kitchen. In chef's terms, the phrase, *mis en place* is used to describe this preparatory action. Cooks with the title Chef de Partie, Chef Saucier, Chef Rotisseur, Chef Entremetier, and others are department heads and rank next under the Sous Chef.

Large city hotels and ocean liners use the French type division. The American adaptation is for smaller establishments or those on a cheaper level. Two or three stations are combined and the work is supervised by one chef. This approach creates the Second Cook who is often a combination of Sous Chef, Saucier, Entremetier, and Potager. The American adaptation is also responsible for the Short Order Cook, a rather unique position for the coffeeshop type establishment. A Short Order Cook, as the name implies, cooks only

| Large Hotel or Passenger Liner | Medium Restaurant | Small Restaurant |
|---|---|---|
| Executive Chef | Head Chef | Chef |
| Day Chef (Sous Chef) | Night Chef | Broiler Man |
| Night Chef (Sous Chef) | Second Chef | Pantry Man |
| Banquet Chef (Sous Chef) | Broiler — Short Order Man | |
| Second Cook | Pantry Man | |
| Chef Garde-manger | Steamtable - Fryman | |
| Station Cook | | |
| Broiler Man — Short Order Man | | |
| Cook's Helper — Fryman | | |
| Steamtable Man — Carver | | |
| Pantry Man | | |
| Pastry Chef | | |
| These rank tables will not be exactly the same in different states or areas. They are influenced by union classifications and management preferences. | | |

**Table 2-3 AMERICAN RANKS OF COOKS' BRIGADES**

| French Style | English Name | American Station or Rank Equivalent |
|---|---|---|
| Saucier | Sauce Station Cook ⎤ | Sauce Cook ⎤ |
| Poissonier | Fish Station Cook ⎦ | ⎢ Second Cook Station |
| Potager | Soup Station Cook | Vegetable Cook ⎦ |
| Entremetier | Vegetable and Egg Station Cook | |
| Rotisseur | Roast and Broiler Station Cook | Broiler—Short Order—Breakfast Cook |
| Garde-manger | Cold Pantry Cook ⎤ | Salad and Sandwich Pantry Cook |
| Buffetier | Buffet Carver Cook ⎦ | |
| Patissier | Pastry Station Cook | Pastry and Dessert Pantry Cook |
| Tournant | Relief | Swing Shift Cook |

**Table 2-4  KITCHEN DEPARTMENT OR STATION DIVISION**

"fast" foods in portion sizes. He does not produce cooked foods such as soups, sauces, stews, and roasts. In contrast, Skilled Cook implies that a cook has been trained to work every station of a large kitchen. He knows all working procedures and skills. After enough years of experience, he will become Executive Chef or Head Chef.

## CHARACTERISTICS OF GASTRONOMIC CULTURE

*Gastronomy* is the art and science of good eating. In its wider meaning, it adds the art of serving and the art of cooking to the art of dining. Gastronomic culture develops best in affluency, but it also requires respect for the preciousness of food. Gastronomic culture is a part of general culture. Several important factors of a medical, nutritional, or religious nature influence this culture. Publicity from pressure groups selling their own products results in the formation of eating and food buying habits, thus creating a gastronomic culture. The study of gastronomic culture could reveal why specific dishes can or cannot be found on public menus in certain areas. It could explain why an upsurge in vegetarian dining, milk consumption, or a new food trend comes into existence. For the cook, the chef, and the restaurant operator, it is absolutely necessary to have some understanding of gastronomic art and culture.

| AMERICAN RANKS AND CORRESPONDING SKILL LEVELS | |
|---|---|
| Executive Chef | Master Chef and Administrator |
| Day Chef — Night — Sous Chef | Skilled Chef, Department Head |
| Banquet Chef — Chef Garde-manger | Master Chef |
| Second Cook | Skilled Cook |
| Station Cook | Skilled Cook |
| Broiler — Short Order Man | Semi-skilled Cook |
| Pantry Man | Semi-skilled Cook |
| Cook's Helper — Fryman ⎤ | |
| Steamtable — Carver ⎢ | Unskilled Labor |
| Vegetable Helper ⎦ | |

| FRENCH STYLE RANKS AND CORRESPONDING SKILL LEVELS | |
|---|---|
| Chef de Cuisine | Master Chef and Administrator |
| Sous Chef | Master Chef |
| Chef de Partie | Master Chef or Skilled Cook |
| Premier Commis | Skilled Cook (5 years minimum experience) |
| Deuxieme Commis | Skilled Cook Cook (1-5 years experience) |
| Troisieme Commis | Skilled Cook (first year after apprenticeship) |

**Table 2-5  RANKS AND CORRESPONDING SKILL LEVELS (AMERICAN AND FRENCH)**

## NEEDS OF TOMORROW

The growth of the food service industry and the increase in the number of its customers are evidence that more skilled cooks are needed. Eating away from home is an increasing trend. Statistics from many sources show a constant growth in the manpower needs of the food service industry.

When precooked convenience food was introduced, many experts forecasted the use of this type of food would revolutionize the restaurant industry. People were expected to cook at home instead of eating in restaurants. This forecast has not come true.

Restaurant customers of the last few years have indicated a need for fresh cooked food, "gourmet" food, or luxury fare in appropriate settings. For his part in this trend, the young cook must take his professional learning seriously. He must acquire manual skill, theoretical knowledge, work experience, and the personality characteristics needed to get along with coworkers. As soon as he succeeds, his future will be a bright one.

## SUMMARY

The large and powerful food service industry of the United States still grows rapidly. Operators have learned to stay solvent and independent. They know how to manage themselves. The techniques and styles of restaurant cuisine are uniform or closely related. Regional differences exist, and are caused by climate, supply, and other factors. General American restaurant cookery is part of the International Cuisine of Western civilization. Continuous needs for more skilled manpower are projected. The skill levels required in the United States are not as high as the ones Europe demands from the trained continental chef.

Culinary Art is a part of Gastronomic Culture, which pertains to dining as well. Knowledge about gastronomy is not an immediate necessity for the young cook. It is important for the student to be aware of its existence and to plan to learn about it during his work experience. Tomorrow's needs imply that the cook's future is secure, and food service will not be a field where automation can take over, as it has done with other vocations.

The higher the skill levels attained, the more secure a chef's future will be. Master chefs are not apt to be replaced. But Steamtable Men or Fry Cooks, who have not developed characteristics of reliability, may very easily lose their jobs when times are hard. As long as customers clamor for good food, which they will do for a long time to come, skilled cooks will be promoted to higher ranks with higher salaries and better fringe benefits. After all, it is unlikely that there will be a substitute for eating.

### DISCUSSION TOPICS

1. What factors should influence the choice of employment?
2. What are the strengths and the future of service industries?
3. Why is there a trend toward specialty restaurants?
4. What are the differences in skill levels of American and French cooks?
5. What is a master chef?
6. What is advertising's influence on the food buying of restaurants?
7. What is gastronomic culture?

### SUGGESTED ACTIVITIES

1. Define these words:

   a. bistro
   b. cuisine
   c. gastronomy
   d. gastronomic culture
   e. mis en place
   f. brigade
   g. caterer
   h. short order cook

2. Field trips to various food service establishments, such as

   a. city hotel
   b. large restaurant
   c. hospital or institution

3. Invite a city hotel chef for lecture or question and answer session in regard to his responsibilities.

4. Dinner-field trip (if possible) to luxury restaurant or hotel, banquet style.

5. Determine regional influences on cuisine in your area.

## ACHIEVEMENT REVIEW

A. Read each question carefully and completely before answering it. Select the *best* answer.

   1. Which one of the following is a full service restaurant?

      a. ship's dining room       c. nationality restaurant
      b. dinnerhouse              d. luxury restaurant

   2. Which of the following would be likely to need a French type cook's brigade?

      a. luxury restaurant        c. steakhouse
      b. hospital                 d. passenger ship

   3. Which one of these needs the highest skill level?

      a. Broiler — Short Order    c. Garde-manger
      b. Night Chef               d. Second Cook

   4. Which one of these chefs is likely to supervise the largest brigade?

      a. Head Chef                c. Banquet Chef
      b. Executive Chef           d. Day Chef

   5. Which one of these cooks is likely to have the least skill?

      a. Broiler Man              c. Steamtable Man
      b. Pantry Man               d. Troisieme Commis

   6. Which one of these establishments is likely to serve breakfast, lunch, and dinner every day?

      a. coffeeshop               c. caterer
      b. resort hotel             d. bistro

B. Match the English descriptions in the left column with the terminology in the right column.

   | | |
   |---|---|
   | Soup Cook | 1. Garde-manger |
   | Pastry Cook | 2. Buffetier |
   | Relief Cook | 3. Saucier |
   | Cold Pantry Cook | 4. Poissonier |
   | Fish Cook | 5. Rotisseur |
   | Buffet Cook | 6. Potager |
   | Roast Cook | 7. Entremetier |
   | Sauce Cook | 8. Patissier |
   | Vegetable and Egg Cook | 9. Tournant |

C. Answer the following in your own words.

   1. Outline the continuous growth of the hospitality industry.

2. Describe the bonds between international and American restaurant cuisine.

3. Why are more skilled cooks needed?

4. Name twelve different food service establishments.

5. List the following in order, from most to least skilled:

   a. Deuxieme Commis, Chef de Partie, Troisieme Commis, Sous Chef, Chef de Cuisine.

   b. Executive Chef, Station Cook, Station Chef, Sous Chef, Cook's Helper.

# Unit 3  Cooking as Art, Science, and Craft

*OBJECTIVES*

After studying this unit, the student should be able to

- Describe the origins of cooking.
- Identify the sciences which create food technology.
- Name the areas where artistic talents in cookery can be applied.
- Explain why apprenticeship has lost its usefulness.

The roots of cookery reach back to the dawn of mankind. The need for food is one of the few things early man and modern man have in common. Some forms of cooking started with man's earliest history.

*ORIGINS OF COOKERY*

The beginning of cookery and storing of food greatly influenced the growth of civilization. Man's first cooked food may have been meat burned in a forest fire. After he was freed from foraging day by day, he had time to think, experiment, and progress.

First records of cooking go back many thousand years, but contemporary Western cookery emerged about two hundred years ago. At that time Monks in cloisters made great contributions to Culinary Art.

Cooking at all times depended on the supply of food and the amount of technical knowledge. In certain geographic regions, special dishes were prepared because the raw materials for them existed there in abundance. By the same token, other foods were unknown or unavailable because of the lack of fast transportation.

Cookery has developed through trial and error. Some people showed talent while working with food, but others did not. As a result, cookery evolved into an art which was handed down from mothers to daughters and from masters to apprentices.

Culinary Art slowly changed from art to craft and from craft to science. More recently, chefs, scientists, and other members of the food service industry became research-minded. They have gained better opportunities to experiment and to communicate. Research results became stepping stones to more research and there was a discovery of new knowledge and skills. Food preservation grew into food processing and food processing became Food Technology. Culinary Art, influenced by Food Technology, developed into Culinary Technology. Medical Art prodded by Gastronomic Art spawned the sciences of dietetics and nutrition.

*LOUIS PASTEUR*

Louis Pasteur (1822-95), the famous French microbiologist, known to the world as the healer of rabies and inventor of inoculation, is the actual Father of Modern Food Technology. His research into fermentation,

**Fig. 3-1**

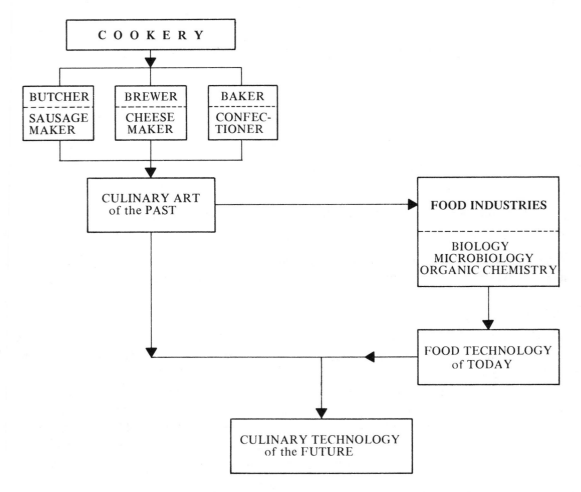

Table 3-1 COOKERY'S CONVERSION TO CULINARY ART AND TECHNOLOGY

pasteurization (a sterilization process named after him), and bacteriology paved the way for modern food preservation. His discoveries initiated the change from Culinary Art and Craft to the Culinary Art and science of today.

## FOOD PRESERVING TECHNOLOGY

Dehydration (or sun drying), salting, and smoking have been known to mankind as means of food preservation for thousands of years. It was not until 1809 that Francois Appert discovered by chance that food, sealed in airtight containers and boiled in water for a considerable time, became immune against spoilage. Thus, the canning process was created. Appert never understood the causes of his discovery; years later Louis Pasteur found them. From then on food preservation became an industry and grew to a powerful force. During these early times, cooks and master chefs, chemists and biologists banded together, and the discoveries of these groups became Food Technology. The new industry continued to employ scientists and

Fig. 3-2

chefs in the search of better methods and new products. All this, in different ways, was beneficial to Culinary Art, and thus, to Culinary Technology.

## COOKING TECHNOLOGY AND CULINARY ART

Cooking Technology is the part of Culinary Art that explains why meat roasted in the oven gets brown and changes its texture, or why the color of vegetables changes during cooking. The more a cook knows about the technology of cooking, the better he can create wholesome products.

The cooking of foods serves many different prupuses. Sanitary nutrition is one of the most basic aims. This is where the knowledge of cooking technology is imperative. But other factors must be considered too. Feeding, eating, or dining are different emotional and cultural levels of food intake and they, too, have to be satisfied.

As a result, a part of Culinary Art will stay art, and this is where the cook should apply his artistic talents. Technology, cooking by formula, is applied by a technician, but craftsmanship includes the artistic vein. It is the talent to please people by creating food that is nutritionally sound and appetizing. The final criterion is that the food must be exciting and tasty to the palate.

## DIFFERENT LEVELS OF CRAFTSMANSHIP

All these factors create different levels of craftsmanship. Art, Culinary or otherwise, is a value judgment; so is taste; they are formed by environment and habit. Craftsmanship is recognized universally as being functional. Craftsmanship without artistic talent is acceptable, but food prepared by artistic talent alone without the functionality of craftsmanship is barely tolerable. Craftsmanship includes all that a good chef should stand for. It is a reflection of his work.

## ARTISTIC INFLUENCES

The chef as a creative artist is in a difficult position. Like the commercial artist, he has to arouse the buying impulse of the consumer, satisfy it, and make him want to come back again soon.

Many creative chefs have established their own little restaurants with a personal touch. Their food is mostly of ethnic origins. Their restaurants are styled in a unique way. They express themselves gastronomically. A few of these restaurants are famous all over the world.

On the other hand, the Head Cook of a large establishment may be feeding hundreds of customers per day. He may work for an institution where the audience is captive. This chef must evaluate his customers and find out what they consider attractive, valuable, and tasty. The chef must adjust his artistic presentation to the level of his customers.

Some chefs misunderstand that in the first place they are to prepare edible food. They are not in competition with artists who create permanent but inedible works of art. Most customers who consistently return to the same restaurant do so for the food. "The proof of the pudding is in the tasting" goes an old saying.

## APPRENTICESHIP

Earliest recorded apprenticeships date back to antiquity, with the early Greeks and Romans.

To the English, it has been known since the eleventh century. Apprenticeship was one of the first forms of organized learning, and it retains some usefulness until today. As part of the labor system, it grew and changed whenever the conditions of the working men changed.

In modern times many countries, especially the Central European leaders of Culinary Art,

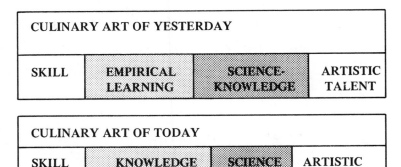

| CULINARY ART OF YESTERDAY | | | |
|---|---|---|---|
| SKILL | EMPIRICAL LEARNING | SCIENCE-KNOWLEDGE | ARTISTIC TALENT |

| CULINARY ART OF TODAY | | | |
|---|---|---|---|
| SKILL | KNOWLEDGE | SCIENCE | ARTISTIC TALENT |

Table 3-2

turned toward a trade school education. With the full-service restaurant fading away and the emergence of the specialty restaurant, apprenticeship could not teach all phases of cookery. Trade schools not only teach everything that pertains to cookery, but they also offer supplementary education in many fields such as chemistry, microbiology, and business.

Work is divided into "thinking units" and "doing units". The thinking unit develops through academic learning. The doing unit develops better by practical learning. Learning by doing is an established fact. Apprenticeship which is closer to learning by looking and copying than by practice does not give the wide scope of theory, background, and understanding that a good school does. Even the best establishments are output-centered. Quantity and speed to them are more important than quality and understanding. For the bright young student cook of today, a good trade school offers the best vocational education.

## SPIRAL OF PROGRESS

A hungry man eats everything that is available and edible and then gets to like it by habit. When supplies become plentiful, his appetite gets jaded. He searches for new taste sensations, and eats more selectively. As soon as he gets used to these foods, they become everyday fare. In his search for the new, he is finding the old again. There is very little really new in the world of food. Cooking has made the least number of contributions to the technology of man. Today's preference has gone back to meat broiled over an open fire as it was done thousands of years ago. The only change is that the hand which turned the spit has been replaced by an electric motor.

## SUMMARY

Recorded food history goes back only several thousand years. It can be assumed that cooking meat over an open fire was the first form of cookery.

Cooking is subject to the availability of supplies and develops accordingly. Early in its past it became an art, later a craft. It was taught for hundreds of years through the system of apprenticeship, and only recently through trade schools.

Louis Pasteur became the father of modern Food Technology. The new Food Technology was conceived by the close bond of food knowledge, organic chemistry, microbiology, and cookery. In turn, the research done by food technologists uncovered more knowledge pertaining to Culinary Art, and in this way helped to change it to Cooking Technology.

Although a part of cookery has changed to technology, some of the "art" parts will always remain. It is a difference of talents which causes cooks to become great chefs.

Today, disregarding progress and a better understanding of nutrition, man still eats what he likes and the popularity of the steakhouse indicates that meat cooked over an open fire, as the oldest form of cooking, is also the most popular one.

### DISCUSSION TOPICS

1. What are the influences which created cooking technology?
2. What is a cook's place in the food processing industry?
3. How does the chef show artistic expression?
4. What type of cooking was done by early man?
5. Predict the future of cooking technology, and justify your prediction.
6. Compare the relationship between apprenticeship and trade schools.

### SUGGESTED ACTIVITIES

1. Define these words:

   a. technology          c. craftsmanship
   b. apprentice

2. Field trip to a cannery.

3. Field trip to a food production plant.

4. Visit a microbiology lab.

5. Arrange for demonstration of simple food chemistry test.

6. Show a film or photos from Culinary Art Show.

7. Field trips to the kitchen of a luxury establishment, if possible.

8. List school library books which refer to history and origin of cooking.

## ACHIEVEMENT REVIEW

A. Complete the following statements:

1. One of the earliest forms of cookery was the exposure of meat to the open _____ .

2. The beginning of food storage and cookery spawned the beginning of _____ _____ .

3. Chefs must restrict their artistic endeavors to materials which are _____ _____ .

4. The inventor of the canning process was a French confectioner by the name of _____ .

5. A special sterilization process of food called pasteurization was invented by _____ .

6. Culinary Art became more science-oriented due to tremendous progress in _____ .

7. One of the oldest forms of organized learning is the _____ .

8. The two branches of science that contributed to food technology are _____ _____ and _____ .

B. Read each question carefully and completely before answering it. Select the *best* answer.

1. Which one of these sciences has not contributed to food technology?

   a. organic chemistry        c. biology
   b. inorganic chemistry      d. microbiology

2. The development of Culinary Art was dependent on the availability of

   a. microwave ovens          c. refrigeration
   b. raw food supplies        d. food technologists

3. Which influence has changed the Culinary Art of yesterday to the Culinary Technology of today?

   a. empirical learning       c. food technology
   b. equipment improvement    d. food and drug administration

C. Answer the following in your own words:

1. Describe the origins of cooking.

2. Name the areas where artistic talents in cookery can be applied.

3. Briefly describe the stages in the development of Culinary Technology from its assumed beginning (early man finding some burnt meat) up to today.

# Unit 4 Sanitation and Safety

## OBJECTIVES

After studying this unit, the student should be able to

- Explain the importance of sanitation to food service.

- Identify causes of bacterial contamination.

- Name the processes used to keep food safe.

- Explain uses of food warmers and hazards.

- Point out the dangers of a commercial kitchen.

- List rules for preventing accidents.

Sanitation and safety are not isolated bits of information used from time to time. The awareness of sanitation and safety must start at the moment the cook arrives at his station and continue until the end of the work shift. Sanitation and safety are related and must be integrated into the work of every day.

Sanitation is practiced to prevent health hazards to customers. Safety is practiced to avoid injuries, not only to oneself but also to workers and customers as well.

## WHAT SANITATION MEANS

Sanitation is applied cleanliness to all the chores of a kitchen. Sanitizing raw food, cooked food, utensils, dishes, areas, and humans also means cleaning, washing, cooking, pasteurizing, sterilizing, and refrigerating. Sanitary, originally a Latin word, is used to assert that everything related to the health of a living being is handled in a safe way.

A sanitarian is an officer of a local or federal health department who is charged with supervising all health rules and regulations. For example, the rule of no smoking in kitchens is supervised by the local health department.

## AREAS OF SANITATION

The practice of sanitation together with common sense will make a food service establishment safe for its customers. Dirty dishes, rest rooms, work stations, pantries, hand tools, doorknobs, and human beings are the transmitters of microorganisms, also called bacteria.

## BACTERIAL GROWTH

Bacteria, or microorganisms, are everywhere except in a medically sterile environment. They are not visible to the naked eye, but can be seen through a microscope. Some bacteria are harmless, some are helpful (yeast), and some are dangerous. Food areas are ideal places for bacteria to multiply. Bacteria need food, warmth, and moisture. If conditions are right, these microbes grow at a very fast rate and can reach the point of danger quickly. In a public food establishment, there are many people who may have come into contact with possible contaminations. Then, by becoming infected themselves, they could continue this dangerous circle endlessly.

## PERSONAL GROOMING

The first area of concern is personal hygiene. A food service worker coming from home can be carrying harmful bacteria to his work. This could start a vicious circle of infections. Some personal hygiene habits have to be observed. A bath and clean garments, especially undergarments, are a must for every day. A

clean shave for men, with short cut and clean hair, or a hairnet for longhaired persons are also very important. Trimmed, clean fingernails and clean hands are another must. Washing of one's hands every time after
switching from one working process to the next or when the rest room is used is a habit to be formed. No
smoking on the job is one rule which is also helpful to the worker. The wearing of a clean uniform goes
without saying, and in some instances, aprons have to be changed twice per shift. More specific rules of the
place of employment can be added to this.

## PREVENTIVE CLEANING

The term cleaning is understood by all civilized people. But there also exist different standards of cleanliness. Two persons cleaning identical objects may not achieve the same level of cleanliness. Every person
considers himself clean, but one's own standard may not reach an acceptable minimum level. Food service
workers must accept guidance and supervision by their superiors and follow exactly all rules and regulations.

Since dirt might not be visible, it does not imply that looking clean means to be clean all the way. Preventive sanitation includes the systematic scheduled cleaning of all facilities, tools, and equipment in operation.

Dishwashing is also an important cleaning process. Water, chemicals, and heat are combined to sanitize
tablewares before they are used again. If this is not done properly, cross contamination from one customer
to another could occur. The actual cleaning comes from the dishwashing compound combined with the
mechanical action of pressure spraying the wash water. The tableware is clean, but the detergent may have
left a harmful residue. To wash this residue off, a final waterspray of not less than 180°F. is required by the
public health department. Cooler water might bring new bacteria from the outside to the clean dishes. The
dishwashing room is an important part of all food service establishments.

The pot-washing area is essential, too. If an improperly cleaned container is used to store cooked food,
contamination could ultimately occur. Cooks do not usually wash pots, but sometimes they have to clean
a needed utensil. This is one example of why it is necessary for students to understand every work level
of a food service establishment.

## STERILIZATION THROUGH HEAT

Sterilization means making ineffective or killing most microorganisms. Exposure to sufficient heat
kills bacteria. Length of time and amount of heat necessary vary for different organisms. The heating of
liquids, like milk, juices, beer, wine, etc. to 140°F. for thirty minutes is called pasteurization; it is effectively used in food manufacturing plants. Food establishments lack the time to use this process. They
sterilize by using boiling water. When boiling starts, it is certain that water has reached a temperature of
212°F. A few minutes of exposure to this heat will make everything safe and sterile. This explains the
reason for reaching the boiling point whenever cooked food is prepared or reheated.

| SOME PERSONAL GROOMING RULES |
|---|
| 1. Wear clean clothes going to shift and clean uniform on shift. |
| 2. Never appear unkempt or unshaven at work. |
| 3. Cover long hair with hairnet, apply only a little makeup. |
| 4. Keep fingernails short and clean. |
| 5. Avoid body odors, bad breath, and too much perfume. |
| 6. Do not overdress, especially when a uniform is not required. |
| 7. Change undergarments frequently. |
| 8. See doctor immediately at signs of illness. |

**Table 4-1**

*KEEPING FOOD "SERVICE-READY"*

Food warmers are pieces of equipment found in every food establishment. They are called "bain-maries" (French for steam table). Some examples are thermotainers, quartz lamps, heated compartments, and dry heat servers. The purpose of these is to keep precooked food service-ready at a minimum temperature of 140°F. At the same time, food must be prevented from drying out and shrinking, or from becoming watery, overcooked, and mushy.

The guidelines to this service-readiness are in the understanding of minimum acceptable food quality. Then, maximum time spans for keeping food hot can be established.

The following rule cannot be repeated too often.

> Food warmers must not be used to warm up any precooked food, refrigerated from a previous day.

All foods have to be cooked or reheated to the sterilization point before they can be placed in the food warmer.

The heat span from 70°F. − 140°F. is a dangerous one for foods in a kitchen. Bacteria multiply fast in this temperature range. Pasteurization uses 140°F. of heat for thirty consecutive minutes to sterilize food without destroying too many vitamins and nutrients. At 130°F., many bacteria, such as salmonella, still multiply. If food from the refrigerator (average temperature 45°F.) is put into a 140°F. warmer, it will take hours before it becomes pasteurized. During this slow warmup, food could spoil and cause food poisoning when served.

*REFRIGERATION OF FOOD*

Cooked or perishable raw foods are stored in temperatures ranging from 34°F. − 45°F. They are then called refrigerated. Walk-in refrigerators are room-like areas of various sizes with shelves. Reach-in refrigerators resemble boxes with doors or drawers. The air in these refrigerated units is circulated (moved by fan), cooled, and also humidity controlled. As pointed out previously, moisture encourages bacterial growth, but in dry air this growth is retarded. On the other hand, dry air will dehydrate stored food faster. To prevent this, different humidity ranges are kept. Fruits and vegetables need more moisture than meat; dairy products need the least moisture.

Sanitary refrigeration is essential to food service. Containers must be covered. All stored goods must be at least six inches from the floor. Special meat units may have additional antibacterial blue light. Thermometers to check the temperature range are installed so that they can be read from the outside. Thermostats are used to maintain an even temperature.

Most walk-in units are powerful enough to hold even hot foods and refrigerate them

**IMPORTANT TEMPERATURES IN THE KITCHEN**
(in degrees of Fahrenheit)

|  |  |
|---|---|
| 212°F. | Water boils at sea level, sterilization of bacteria after short exposure. |
| 205°F. | Starches coagulate (cook). |
| 195°F. – 185°F. | Simmering of water. |
| 180°F. | Sterilizing rinse spray of dishwasher. |
| 170°F. – 150°F. | Egg and meat proteins coagulate (cook). |
| 150°F. – 140°F. | Keeping food "service-ready" in food warmer. |
| 140°F. | Pasteurization begins, time span of exposure thirty minutes. |
| 140°F. – 70°F. | Danger zones for fast bacteria multiplication. |
| 70°F. – 50°F. | Normal kitchen temperature range in which bacteria will slowly multiply under right conditions. |
| 45°F. – 40°F. | Vegetable and fruit refrigeration. |
| 40°F. – 34°F. | Meat, dairy, and cooked food refrigeration. |
| 33°F. | Melting of ice. |
| 32°F. | Freezing of water. |
| +10°F. – 0°F. – -10°F. | Deep freezer storage. |

**Table 4-2**

quickly. Older units may break down when they are overloaded with too much hot food.

Walk-in refrigerators must have safeguards to prevent a person's being locked in them by accident.

Deep freezers are also used. They are similar to refrigerators except that their cooling temperature ranges from -20°F. to +20°F. to keep food frozen solid.

All the rules of the public health department valid for refrigerators also apply to deep freezers. For refrigeration Dos and Don'ts, see Table 4-3.

The information in this unit is the minimum basic sanitation knowledge every foodhandler must have. Many counties insist on sanitation education for foodhandlers and a foodhandler's card is mandatory for every employee in their districts.

| REFRIGERATION DOS AND DON'TS |
| --- |
| 1. Check and be familiar with all safety devices of the cooler. |
| 2. Keep door closed at all times. |
| 3. Do *not* impair flow of cool air through stored objects. |
| 4. Do *not* store food directly on the floor. |
| 5. Change open canned food to a different container before it is refrigerated. |
| 6. Use clear plastic wrap to cover container. |
| 7. Do *not* store liquids in containers above eye level. |
| 8. Clean up any spilled food or water immediately. |

**Table 4-3**

Food service workers carry great responsibilities. Carelessness results in the food poisoning of people. The public has a right to be protected. Food service workers should take pride that they are competent.

## DANGERS IN THE KITCHEN

Kitchens, like all manufacturing plants, have mechanical and physical perils to which workers are exposed. Six of the most common areas of danger are listed:

1. Hazards such as colliding with other persons or objects, and slipping over spilled liquids, vegetable peels, oil spots.

2. Electric-mechanical equipment with the danger of shocks caused by short circuits.

3. Personal hand tools, such as knives, cleavers, forks, and needles.

4. The handling of boiling liquids, such as sauces, stocks, soups, or hot fat. This demands know-how, a sure grip, and often physical strength.

5. Heat sources such as ovens, ranges, griddles, steamers, deepfryers, and broilers which may cause painful burns. In many cases, carelessness with one of these is the reason for the burning down of a whole establishment.

6. Walk-in refrigerators and walk-in deep freezers. Frequent exposure to low temperature may cause damage to a worker's health. Accidental locking into a deep freezer could become fatal.

Nobody wants accidents, but they do happen. Statistics show that the majority of all accidents are caused by carelessness. This means that a worker, either ignorant or thoughtless, has failed in his responsibilities. The accident-prone worker is easily found. He is a person not interested in his job. He might despise work, have a chip on his shoulder, or might lead a troubled life. For whatever reasons a worker is not attentive on the job, no excuses exist. Work is an exchange action. A person does his job in order to get paid. In exchange, he earns money. Decent pay can only be expected for work done to a given standard. If standards of responsibility are achieved, accidents will be reduced. By realizing that accidents are caused by carelessness, workers can avoid them.

## PREVENTION BY COMMON SENSE

Common sense means the making of intelligent decisions in situations not expected or foreseen. It means to relate a previous experience to a new situation.

Some causes of accidents which could be avoided by using common sense are listed:

1. Playfulness, horseplay, and practical jokes.

2. Using defective, unsafe equipment which is not reported immediately and not repaired.

3.  Handling hot cooking utensils without proper protection for hands.

4.  Using a meatgrinder without a stomper.

5.  Cleaning electrical equipment which is not disconnected.

6.  Failing to replace safeguards after cleaning of food machinery.

7.  Knives carried incorrectly with their blades pointing up.

8.  Trying to catch knives falling down from a table.

9.  Lifting heavy objects without a good footing.

10. Spilled liquids which are not wiped up immediately.

11. Trying to extinguish grease fires without a $CO_2$ fire extinguisher.

12. Tasting food in the mixer while the machine is still in use.

13. Lighting a gas oven and forgetting to keep the door half open until all burners are on.

14. Leaving utensils on floors.

15. Handling new equipment without learning instructions first.

## SUMMARY

Sanitation and safety awareness are part of a student worker's daily routine. Cleanliness and personal hygiene help to safeguard the health of customers and coworkers. Since kitchen conditions are conducive to bacterial growth, there is need for constant preventive cleaning. The importance of the dishwashing operation is stressed. The pasteurization at 140°F. and sterilization at 212°F. of food are some of the safeguards.

The use of refrigeration prevents short time spoilage, but may allow food contamination, if storage is extended. A knowledge of the kitchen temperature tables is essential for every cook.

Accidents can be minimized, when workers act and behave in a mature manner. Accident proneness is a state of mind.

The observation of posted rules, the learning of regulations, and the use of common sense are the best ways to avoid accidents. The food service newcomer has to accept sanitation and safety. Sanitation is a safeguard to health. Safety is the awareness of avoiding all mechanical-physical perils to which food service workers are constantly exposed.

### DISCUSSION TOPICS

1.  How important is sanitation on every working level?

2.  How can bacterial growth be avoided?

3.  Why is personal grooming important?

4.  Should a preventive cleaning schedule be supervised?

5.  Do cooks practice sterilization of food?

6.  Are food warmers an asset or a liability?

7.  Are kitchens more dangerous today than yesterday?

8.  Are there really accident-prone persons?

9.  What is common sense?

10. How can accidents be prevented?

### SUGGESTED ACTIVITIES

1.  Define the following:

    a. sanitation
    b. sterilization
    c. hygiene
    d. safety

2. Inspect kitchen machinery for cleanliness.

3. Use yeast in an experiment as an example of how fast "good" bacteria multiply.

4. Observe a set-up food plate in a food warmer for different time spans. Then discuss the observations.

5. Make a plan (blueprint) of the school's walk-in refrigeration unit and try to improve the layout.

6. Make posters and invent slogans in regard to dangers in the kitchen.

7. Keep a table of statistics indicating daily how many days have passed without accidents.

*ACHIEVEMENT REVIEW*

A. Complete the following statements:

1. A chef's daily work must always include safety awareness and _____.

2. Bacteria multiply fastest when they have food, warmth, and _____.

3. Preventive cleanliness is imperative to food sanitation, because kitchens are conducive to bacterial _____ _____.

4. Most accidents are the result of someone's _____.

5. Strict observation of posted rules is the best accident prevention method next to the use of _____.

6. The final rinse of a dishwasher must have a minimum temperature of _____.

7. Bacteria which are everywhere, except in a sterile environment, can only be seen with a _____.

8. An integrated part of personal grooming is personal _____.

9. In kitchens serving the public, it is not legal to _____.

10. Preventive sanitation calls for cleaning and sterilizing in a method that is called _____.

B. Read each question carefully and completely before you answer it. Select the *best* answer.

1. Good refrigeration retards food spoilage, because

   a. bacteria cannot multiply fast without warmth
   b. it deprives bacteria of food
   c. it kills bacteria completely
   d. it prevents contamination of food

2. A falling knife should not be

   a. used without resharpening it first
   b. picked up, unless one knows the owner
   c. caught in the air while falling
   d. used without pasteurizing it first

3. Pasteurization is a sterilization process at a temperature of

   a. 100° Fahrenheit          c. 140° Fahrenheit
   b. 120° Fahrenheit          d. 160° Fahrenheit

4. Cooks sterilize most food they prepare through

   a. refrigeration            c. salting
   b. pasteurization           d. boiling

5. Food warmers are needed because

    a. serving time exceeds the period in which food stays warm by itself
    b. they are a good way to warm up leftover food
    c. restaurant patrons like to be served hot food
    d. they reduce labor costs

6. When water starts to boil, it has reached a temperature of

    a. 208° Fahrenheit         c. 216° Fahrenheit
    b. 212° Fahrenheit         d. 220° Fahrenheit

C. Match the degrees of temperature in the right column to the corresponding areas in the left column.

| | | |
|---|---|---|
| Freezing point of water | 1. | 205°F. |
| Boiling point of water | 2. | 185°F. – 195°F. |
| Pasteurization for 30 minutes | 3. | 180°F. |
| Meat, dairy storage | 4. | 212°F. |
| Vegetable and fruit storage | 5. | 140°F. – 150°F. |
| Final spray of dishwashing machine | 6. | 140°F. |
| Cooking (Coagulation) of starches | 7. | 70°F. – 140°F. |
| Safe food warmer range | 8. | 40° – 45°F. |
| Fast bacteria multiplication range | 9. | 34°F. – 40°F. |
| Simmering range of water | 10. | 32°F. |

D. Answer in your own words:

1. Name and describe the processes used to keep food safe.

2. Explain the uses of food warmers and the hazards of their use. Name one instance where a food warmer should not be used.

3. Name 5 dangers in a commercial kitchen.

4. List 10 rules for preventing accidents.

5. Explain why personal grooming and hygiene are important.

# Unit 5  Manual Skills and Modern Technology

*OBJECTIVES*

After studying and practicing this unit, the student should be able to

- Explain the reasons for cutting food.
- Identify food cuts of different shapes and their corresponding names.
- Draw a rough sketch of a magnified knife blade.
- Identify four basic knife groups.
- Explain the need for speed tools.
- List common machinery used in kitchens.

Unit 3 has pointed out that work can be separated into "thinking units" and "doing units". For thinking efficiently, the mind must be trained. For doing efficiently, manual skills must be acquired.

## SKILLS NEEDED

The cook needs only a few manual skills and all of them are simple. Doing techniques are divided into blocks, such as flipping a pan, stirring in a pan, mixing in a bowl, and pouring liquids from one container to another. Other doing techniques are the lifting of pots and pans, moving them, using knives, forks, spatulas, whips, larding needle, or vegetable peelers. Turning over hot objects with the help of simple tools is another example of a doing technique. The beginner needs time and practice to master these skills safely and efficiently.

## MANUAL DEXTERITY

Four different ways of cutting can be recognized. Therefore, there are four basic knife groups. The first and most common way of cutting is with the chef's knife, also called a French knife. For this, the food is placed on a cutting board, held with one hand, and the knife is used with the other. The slicing motion of the knife and the correlated holding down and moving motion of the second hand need extensive practicing.

The second way of cutting is with the paring knife. The trimming (paring) is done in the air. The object to be trimmed is held in one hand, the knife used with the other. Peeling an apple is a good example.

The third way of cutting is carving, which is visualized as cutting with a slicing motion. For cooked food, variously shaped slicers are used either in a horizontal or a vertical way.

The fourth way of cutting is the seaming of raw meat. This is done with the same motions, except with steak knives or scimitar-shaped butcher knives. The boning knife is used to bone, separate, disjoint, and skin meat or fish ready for cooking.

The best way to learn these cutting skills is to watch several cutting demonstrations. Such

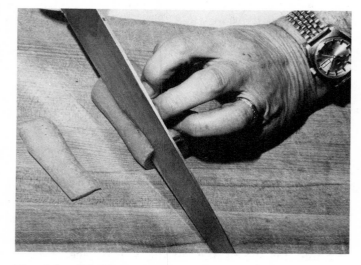

Fig. 5-1  CUTTING TECHNIQUES: The tip of the chef's knife slides backward and forward on the board. During the forward movement, the knife is pressed down on the food to be cut. The other hand holds the food. The palm of the hand rests on the board, fingernails are in line with the knife blade, the fingers act like a vise to keep the food in place.

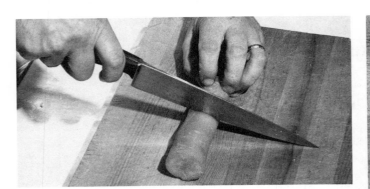

**Fig. 5-2 CUTTING WITH THE CHEF'S KNIFE: Cutting a peeled carrot into equal sections.**

**Fig. 5-3 Cutting the sections into slices**

demonstrations are most important, and, with enough practice, students will learn to master this necessary skill.

When a new skill is to be learned, the learner must only concentrate on mastering the proper techniques and disregard speed completely. Many students, in their eagerness for speed, sacrifice quality for quantity. The worker is then never able to produce quality because he only learned fast, sloppy habits. If quality is stressed from the beginning, speed will come later.

## OBJECTIVES OF CUTTING

There are important reasons for the cutting of food. Raw meat is cut up for the separation of edibles from inedibles, and for faster, better, and easier cooking. Cooked food is cut for easier serving and eating. Raw food is cut uniformly, so that in each lot each piece has the same shape and same size. This allows food, cooked in one batch, to be done at the same time. The smaller raw food is cut, the shorter will be the cooking time. Another reason for cutting food is that it can be placed in containers and molds for serving and storing.

Special terms identify the various shapes into which food is cut. Some terms vary with geographic locations. In general, one group includes slicing and shredding while another includes cubing-dicing, mincing, and chopping. Luxury cuisine uses mostly French terms of identification. Slicing has no specific size. It is only a given shape. It can be visualized best by a slice of bread, a slice of cheese, a slice of meat, or a sliced tomato.

Shredding means the cutting of leaf vegetables into strips, such as shredded lettuce, cabbage, and so on. It is here that the French term of julienne is applied. Shredded cabbage would be translated as a julienne of cabbage. American culinary terminology also refers to a julienne of ham,

**Fig. 5-4 Cutting slices into julienne**

**Fig. 5-5 Cutting julienne into brunoise**

SUMMARY OF PURPOSE OF CUTTING

Professional cooks have many names for cutting foods into various shapes. Exact cutting by hand or mechanical means is important and serves the following purposes:

a. Mixed sizes of food are reduced to the same size and shape resulting in a shorter cooking time.

b. Various shapes add to eye appeal and give the impression of variety.

c. Eating and chewing is made easier by precutting.

d. Cutting shortens cooking time. Less cooking time saves vitamins, nutrients, flavor, and working time.

e. Cutting vegetables neatly and fast is the trademark of a good culinary craftsman.

**Table 5-1**

Culinary terminology accepts many French terms to describe certain shaped cuts. Some of these shapes and names are used for vegetables as in "Mirepoix", "Fermier", and "Paysanne". Names like "Julienne" and "Brunoise" are applied to all foods cut into the particular shape.

*Julienne*: A common way of cutting, but the sizes vary. Strips may range from 3/4 inch to 2 inches in length and from 1/16 to 1/8 inch in width. Julienne is a noodle shape.

*Brunoise (fine dice)*: A fine cut, resembles mincing, consisting of tiny cubes of about 1/8 inch side length.

*Medium Cube (med. dice)*: A cube, approx. 1/4 inch side length.

*Large Cube (large dice)*: Same as above, but approx. 1/2 inch side length.

*Mirepoix*: A larger, inexactly cubed cut of about one inch in length, applied as name to root vegetables.

*Fermier (Farmers)*: A slice, approx. 1/2 inch square and 1/16 to 1/8 inch thick.

*Paysanne (Peasant)*: A triangular slice, 3/4 inch base and 1/16 to 1/8 inch thick.

**Table 5-2  DETAILED CUTTING TERMINOLOGY**

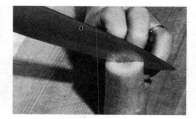

Fig. 5-6 Quartering sections of a carrot for paysanne and fermier

Fig. 5-7 Carrot quarter sections are cut into small trimmed slices (paysanne or fermier)

Fig. 5-8 (upper left to lower right:) cubes, square slices, finest cubes (brunoise), julienne, minced onions, triangle trimmed slices.

**First vertical cuts**

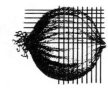

**Second vertical cuts**

Materials Needed:
8- or 10-inch stainless steel cook's knife
Chopping board or chopping surface.
Peeled onions.

Introduction:
Handling a knife is one of the most important skill characteristics a cook has to acquire.

Workmen are judged by the way they handle their tools and show their manual skill.

All mechanical aids have to be cleaned after every use, therefore the fastest way of mincing small quantities of onions, is still using the knife.

### ATTENTION:  KEY POINTS

1. SAFETY FIRST, check your hand as well as knife blade position constantly.
2. Realize that top of the onion refers to the onion's position while still in the ground.
3. Watch and study sketches as well as real onion. Visualize your steps before starting to cut.
4. Cut very slowly until process is understood, speed will come later.

*STEPS*:

1. Cut the onion in half from top to bottom.
2. Align onion half on the board. Onion's bottom side to your left.
3. Use left hand to press onion to the board.
4. Apply first vertical cuts about one sixteenth of an inch apart, across 2/3 of onion but leave the left end of the onion uncut.
5. Apply two parallel horizontal cuts of the same direction and depth as before. (If step 5 seems too complicated omit it until later.)
6. Apply second vertical cuts about one sixteenth inch apart, at a 90 degree angle to the first cut. Onion will fall apart by itself after this final cut has been applied.

**Table 5-3  HOW TO MINCE ONIONS**

A. The first vertical cuts are applied across 2/3 of the onion, about 1/16 inch apart. The root end of the onion stays uncut to hold all together.

B. The first of two horizontal cuts, (parallel) in the same direction as before, is applied.

C. Next the final vertical cuts, at a 90° angle to the first vertical cuts, leaves the onion minced.

D. If a still smaller size of minced onions is needed, the preminced onion can be chopped finer.

E. The root end is not cut any further, but used as a "mirepoix" for stockpot, soups or sauces.

**Fig. 5-9 ONION MINCING TECHNIQUES**

cheese, or vegetables, whenever a stick shape ranging from one inch to three inches in length and 1/16 to 1/8 inch in thickness is required.

The words cubing and dicing are interchangeable and used by personal preference. The size is referred to as 1/8, 1/4, or 1/2 inch cube or dice.

Mincing or chopping are the terms used for a very small cube-like shape. Cooks also mince with a meat grinder or with a knife. It is similar to chopping.

Chopping may also imply the use of a cleaver. Only bones are chopped with a cleaver. Edible foods are chopped with a knife.

## PERSONAL TOOLS

Knives are the most important hand tools of the cook. Every craftsman's work performance depends greatly on the quality of his tools. Cooks buy and use only high quality knives. Quality has its price, and good knives are expensive. Modern cooks use stainless steel knives. Carbon steel knives oxidize when in contact with acid fruits or vegetables. Then they discolor, smell, and look unappetizing. Stainless steel knives last longer and are sharper than carbon steel knives.

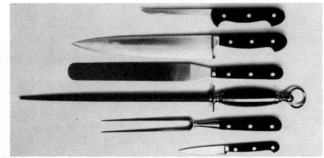

Fig. 5-10 The Cook's Basic Tools: (top to bottom): 6" boning knife, 10" chef's knife, palette knife, sharpening steel, chef's fork, paring knife.

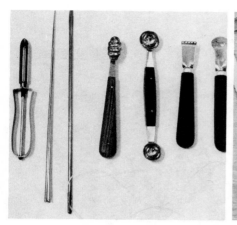

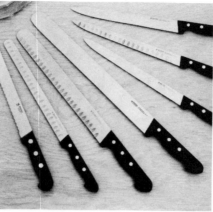

Fig. 5-11 Additional basic tools: (left to right) asparagus or potato peeler, larding needle, trussing needle, fluted oval vegetable cutter, two sized potatoball cutter, lemon zester, lemon or vegetable scorer (decorative).

Fig. 5-12 Various slicers: (left to right) serrated slicer (breadknife), fluted narrow slicer (turkey, ham), fluted wide slicer (roast beef), straight-edged heavy slicer, three pointed slicers for diverse uses.

Fig. 5-13 (top to bottom): light meat cleaver, 6" chef's fork, 8" sandwich slicer, 6" sandwich slicer, 4½" paring knife, and 3½" paring knife.

The edge of a knife blade put under a microscope will resemble a saw with irregular teeth. As a result, all cutting, regardless of the type of knife used, is done in a sawing-slicing motion; pressing a knife straight down will not cut properly at all.

## Basic Knives

Basic knives fall into the following four groups:

1.  The Chef or French Knife has a blade length from 6 to 14 inches. It is sharply pointed, and the height of the blade near the handle should be at least 1 1/2 inches. It is used in a swinging motion, with the point of the knife seldom leaving the board while cutting. The material to be cut lies on a smooth, flat, straight board or table top.

2.  The Paring Knife is a small knife with a blade length from 3 1/2 to 4 1/2 inches. It is also called a vegetable or fruit knife. The food cut with this knife is hand held.

3.  The slicer is a straight and long knife with a blade from 10 to 16 inches. It can only be used in a sawing motion. The food which is cut has to be held in a secured position. Slicers are now available with serrated or fluted (Granton type) blades. They are selected by personal preference.

4.  Butcher and boning knives come in various sizes for different uses. They are mostly scimitar (sword) shaped and are handled differently from other knives. Cooks use them for the cutting of raw meat or fish. They are also known as steak knives. A short, sharp, thin bladed, pointed knife from 5 to 6 1/2 inches long is used for boning or seaming of meat. They are called boning knives and may have flexible blades and safety handles.

## TOOLS FOR SPEED

The ability to produce is the motive of our time. The higher salaries of today are earned by a higher work output. This increased

Fig. 5-14 (left to right) Chef's knives in three different sizes, boning knife and serrated utility slicer.

Fig. 5-15 (left to right) Five different shaped boning knives, two steak knives (scimitar-shaped butcher knives), skinning knife.

Fig. 5-16 Semiautomatic electric food slicer

Fig. 5-17 Electric meat saw

Fig. 5-18 Commercial meat chopper (grinder)

output was made possible by speeding up preparations (mostly cutting) and reducing cooking time.

The demand for speed tools brought better, faster meat slicers and vegetable cutters. Blenders are used for salad dressings and sauces, and the greatest work saver is the (Hobart) horizontal speed cutter. For example, the making of mayonnaise (homemade in many quality-conscious establishments) in a regular mixer would take half an hour of work. The same quantity of mayonnaise made in a speedcutter takes five minutes.

Reduction of cooking time was made possible by the use of pressure steam equipment, new fryer models, and a new approach to cooking in general. Vegetable cooking times are cut in half, and tender meats of today make long stewing obsolete.

Fig. 5-19 Abrasive potato peeler with water flush

### Standard Machines

The machines used in food service, in spite of the general technical progress, have not changed as much as one might expect. The

Fig. 5-20 Medium-sized food mixer with automatic timer

Fig. 5-21 Horizontal speed cutter, more advantageous than the Buffalo chopper

Fig. 5-22 One gallon commercial blendor

Fig. 5-23 Decoratively cut potatoes: Parisienne (left), fluted Stachys shaped potatoes (right)

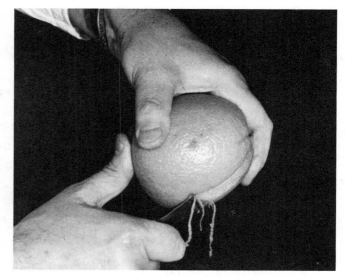

Fig. 5-24 Using the citrus zester on an orange

mechanical equipment of a kitchen consists of meat grinders (choppers), meat slicers, meat saws, meat tenderizers, meat patty molders, blenders, buffalo choppers (outdated), speed or horizontal food cutters, and mixers. More modern ovens include convection ovens, rotation ovens, and smoke ovens. Relatively new are automatic deep fryers, pressure deep fryers, pressure steamers, speedy steam kettles, and microwave ovens. In Culinary Art just as in computers, the automated equipment is only as good as the person behind the machine.

The principles of food machinery have remained simple, with just the models changing from time to time. The machines are designed for the average worker and can be handled easily by reading the instruction manual. No special training is needed to use them. Keeping the machines clean after every use is the important thing for a student to keep in mind.

## USING TECHNOLOGY

Culinary procedures have been changed since the machinery has been improved. Some machinery has brought semi-trained people into the kitchens. Previously, cooks had to be physically strong for all the lifting, pouring, straining, and cutting. Today, most of this work is done with mechanical help. As a result, the number of female cooks has increased.

By choosing certain foods and using modern machinery, one cook today can easily cook food for 1000 persons in a few hours. To do this, ten times as many man-hours were needed only a few years ago. It is unlikely that food service will be affected by automation as much as many other vocations. Emphasis must remain on the service part of the food industry. People are traveling and eating away from home in larger

Fig. 5-25 Zester and orange zeste

Fig. 5-26 Using the decorative scorer (strip peeler) on a lemon

Fig. 5-27 Decorative lemon slices

numbers. Eating establishments which give good service and good food for a proper price are the ones that have more customers each year.

## SUMMARY

Despite mechanical progress, manual skills are still needed. It takes more time to use a machine and clean it again, than to cut certain foods by hand.

Knives remain the most important hand tools, and the cook must learn to master them effectively. Proper food cutting before cooking is of importance to the total preparation.

For faster communication at work skilled cooks and chefs use their own kitchen terms based on the French language.

Although models have improved, the basic designs of kitchen machinery have remained the same for many years. Automation will not affect the cook's job security, if he has acquired skill, knowledge, and a service-minded attitude.

### DISCUSSION TOPICS

1. What are the safety aspects in the use of hand tools and machinery?
2. Why is the use of terminology in the field of occupational work important?
3. What are the reasons for selecting, buying, and maintaining personal tools?
4. Why is there a need for manual skills, despite the progress in sophisticated kitchen machinery?
5. Why should food be cut into comparatively uniform shapes?
6. Why is quality more important than quantity in productions by manual skill?

### SUGGESTED ACTIVITIES

1. Define the following words:

   a. seaming
   b. carving
   c. paring
   d. julienne
   e. brunoise
   f. mirepoix
   g. fermier
   h. paysanne
   i. zester

2. Demonstrate safe knife handling.
3. Demonstrate and practice shredding using chef's knife.
4. Demonstrate and practice peeling and carving fruits using paring knife.
5. Demonstrate and practice peeling (potatoes, squash, asparagus, etc.) with vegetable peeler.
6. Demonstrate and practice slicing (French bread with serrated slicer, cold cuts with straight blade, etc.)
7. Demonstrate and practice parsley chopping with chef's knife.
8. Demonstrate and practice the cutting of various vegetable shapes: Julienne, fine slice, small dice, medium dice, large dice.
9. Demonstrate and practice the seaming and cutting of meat for stew with the butcher knife.
10. Demonstrate and practice the boning and disjointing of a chicken with the boning knife.
11. Demonstrate and practice onion mincing the professional way (see diagram).

12. Demonstrate safe handling and cleaning of common kitchen machines:

a. meat grinder

b. mixer

c. meat slicer

d. blender

e. steamer or steam-kettle

f. pressure steamer or steam-kettle

g. speed cutter or buffalo chopper

## ACHIEVEMENT REVIEW

A. Complete the following statements:

1. All knives should be used in a slicing type motion, because a magnified knife edge resembles a _____.

2. Speed tools reduce general preparation time and increase worker's _____ _____.

3. Thin, uniformly cut ham strips for a chef's salad are identified in French kitchen terminology as a ham _____.

4. Chances are good that well-trained cooks will not be affected by the progress of automation, provided the emphasis of their work is on _____.

5. The most common type of knife used for cutting vegetables is called a _____ _____.

6. A beginning student, while cutting, should disregard speed and emphasize that he is able to produce _____.

B. Read each question carefully and completely before answering it. Select the *best* answer.

1. The cutting of vegetables before cooking serves many purposes, but does not

a. reduce cooking time

b. preserve more vitamins

c. make them cook uniformly

d. make them easier to serve

2. Shredding cabbage for cole slaw means

a. to quarter and wash a head of cabbage

b. to cut cabbage into a Julienne of cabbage

c. to cut cabbage with a buffalo chopper

d. to cut cabbage into medium chunks

3. A Brunoise of celery for a chicken salad means

a. to mince celery finely

b. to cut celery into cubes approximately 1/8 of an inch long

c. to cut root celery into 1/4 inch cubes

d. to mince celery with the meat grinder

4. The best expensive chef knives are made from stainless steel because

a. stainless steel can be sharpened fast

b. stainless steel is unbreakable

c. stainless steel is non-oxidant and rustproof

d. stainless steel outlasts carbon steel three times

5. While cleaning a meat slicer one must make certain that

a. only cold water and a clean towel is used

b. the machine is taken apart properly

c. the electric current is unplugged or disconnected

d. only a weak detergent solution is applied on the rotary blade

6. The most suitable tool to peel oranges would be

   a. a potato peeler
   b. a paring knife

   c. a decorative peeler
   d. a short boning knife

C. The left column lists food items to be cut or prepared. Match them with tools or machinery from the right column.

| | |
|---|---|
| French bread | 1. Straight regular slicer |
| Oranges | 2. Electric slicer |
| Italian Salami | 3. Serrated slicer |
| Asparagus | 4. Steak knife |
| Shredded lettuce | 5. Boning knife |
| Minced meat | 6. Paring knife |
| Disjointed chicken | 7. Meat grinder |
| Hot Roast Beef | 8. Speed cutter |
| Mayonnaise | 9. Potato peeler |
| Beefstew | 10. Chef's knife |

D. Answer in your own words:

1. Name and briefly describe the four basic knife groups.

2. List three reasons for cutting food.

3. Explain the need for speed tools.

4. List ten common machines used in kitchens.

# Section 2
# Methods of Cooking

## Unit 6  Cooking With Dry Heat

*OBJECTIVES*

After studying this unit, the student should be able to

- Explain the reasons for roasting and broiling.
- Identify meat cuts for broiling and roasting.
- Describe the theories of roasting.
- Explain the importance of recirculation.
- List common food holding times for the warmer.
- Identify different types of ovens and broilers.
- List the safety hazards of a broiler.

Cooking with dry heat was identified earlier as one of the five basic cooking methods. Dry heat is used in baking, roasting, and broiling. Baking and roasting use convection heat with additional conduction. Broiling uses radiation and less conduction. Since the general tenderness of meat improves constantly, dry cooking methods are becoming acceptable for a wider range of meat cuts.

### BAKING AND ROASTING

For better classification, the term baking should be used for the cooking of vegetable substance, such as cakes, pies, breads, or baked beans. The term roasting is used for the dry heat cooking of plain meats. An exception is baked ham, a term rooted in usage.

A turkey cooked by dry heat should be called a roast turkey, not a baked turkey. For meat wrapped in dough, as in "Beef Filet Wellington", or dough filled with meat, as in a "Beefsteak and Kidney" pie, the term baking is correct.

### REASONS FOR ROASTING

The term roasting applies to large pieces of meat (more than three portions) cooked by dry heat with only the addition of fat, salt, and spices. The roasting process is selected because it results in browning. Browning occurs through the caramelization of carbohydrates and fats present.

*Caramelization* is the term used to describe the change of sugar to caramel under the influence of heat. Caramelization is also sugar's last stage before burning. Sugar and starch are carbohydrates. Meat, mostly protein, has only a few carbohydrates in it. These are called glucose or blood sugar. Fat also browns and melts at the same time. With enough heat, both sugar and fat will burn completely.

Carbohydrates and fats, when browned, change flavor. This different flavor of browned food is preferred by a majority of people. In unit one, under *Caramelizing Starches,* it was explained that the minimum degree of heat needed for browning is 225°F. for beef fat and 300°F. for carbohydrates. Water in an open container boils at 212°F., changes into steam, and evaporates into the air. In other words, as long as water is present in a cooking process, the temperature can never be higher than 212°F. This explains why dry cooking processes, which are different from moist cooking processes, are used whenever the characteristics (tenderness, fat, and moisture content) of the food will allow it.

## FOODS FOR ROASTING AND BROILING

Not all meat cuts can be roasted. All those which can, are also excellent when broiled. Dry cooking methods do not dissolve, but only tenderize, most of the gelatines (called collagen) that hold muscle fibers together. When this collagen comes from animals of old age, the tenderization through roasting is not sufficient and the meat remains tough. For the meat of all young animals, dry cooking methods are very satisfying. Young animals are those raised for not longer than six months before they are processed.

Beef, mostly one or two years old, is divided into first and second cuts. First, or prime, cuts come from the full loin and part of the rib. These are all areas where the animal muscles are used the least. Prime cuts are used for roasts, steaks, chops, and cutlet. Not all the meat a butcher calls roast or steak can be cooked by dry heat. True beef roasts and steaks must come from prime cuts to be tender and juicy. Veal, pork, and lamb, as a rule, are young enough so that any part of the carcass may be roasted. In the poultry class, hens or fowl are too old, and only those marked roasters and fryers can be dry heat cooked.

## MEAT ROASTING THEORIES

The principles of roasting can be stated very simply: In roasting, large meat pieces are exposed to such a degree of dry heat that the center of the roast becomes just done and stays juicy. At the same time, the surface of the roast browns without being charred or dried out.

To roast meat efficiently, one must understand some theories of thermodynamics. Radiated heat rays are electromagnetic waves. As they strike a surface, the molecular action is increased and this moving action within the substance produces heat. Fast moving molecules cause high heat, slower ones cause less heat. As long as these rays continue, more heat is created. Heat has a unique characteristic. Unless completely insulated, it will always equalize itself with all the other substances with which it comes in contact.

In cooking, heat is transmitted by direct radiation (open fire), conduction (candle experiment), or convection (air currents). Try experiments shown in Table 6-1.

As soon as meat is exposed to heat, conduction transports the heat from the surface of the roast to the center of the roast. Heat creates its own equalization as long as new heat waves are directed against its surface.

If heat, directed against the surface of a roast, is more than 300°F., the caramelization of the surface takes place quickly. The meat is not able to conduct most of this heat toward the center. The heat will be concentrated on the surface. In other words, a roast exposed to more heat than its size can absorb will burn on the surface while the center remains cold.

## ESTIMATION OF ROASTING TIME

Brillat-Savarin, the great French food philosopher (1755-1826), made this statement: "Making the best sauce can be learned, but cooking the perfect roast is a talent." These words are still as true as ever. Many factors are involved. Everyone can learn to roast close to the "point", but cooks have to work out roasting techniques of their own. Different ovens, different

This experiment will help the student to visualize heat equalization by methods of conduction, convection, and radiation.

*Materials needed*:

One household candle, six inches of straight copper wire, not insulated.

*Procedure*:

1. Light candle.
2. Hold flat, outstretched palm of hand horizontally six inches away from flame. Wait one minute and see how much heat can be felt, if any at all.
3. Hold wire on end between thumb and forefinger. Stick other end into flame. Hold same position as before. Wait one minute or stop any time the wire gets too hot.
4. Hold flat palm of hand over the top of the candle flame, about six inches. Check the time it takes to make it too hot.

*Conclusion*

2. The candle flame has radiated heat into a 360° sphere, but radiation over a distance of six inches could not be felt.
3. Since copper is one of the best heat conductors, the heat of the flame is transmitted to the fingers.
4. The radiant flame is heating the air all around the candle, but the heated air becoming lighter than the cold air rises up high and dissipates into the surrounding air. This shows the principle of convection.

**Table 6-1 HEAT TRANSFER EXPERIMENT**

roasting pans, different meats with a different *marble* (visible fat veins), and different desired results need different individual approaches.

The following considerations can be used as a guide.

- Roasting time depends on the size, type, and geometric shape of the roast, as well as the heat degrees of the oven.
- Large roasts need lower heat for a longer time.
- Small roasts need higher heat for a shorter time.

Low heat for large roasts will reduce shrinkage, prevent burning and produce an evenly cooked good roast. Low heat for small roasts results in overcooking before browning has been achieved. This is also true for roasts with a geometrical shape which allows fast heat penetration.

Management and some chefs are often too concerned with *yield*. Yield means that the less shrinkage there is in a roast, the more portions there are to be sold. Shrinkage describes food weight loss during any cooking process. Enough heat melts fats and evaporates water. For instance, while frying bacon, the liquid fat burns away, or is at least separated from the lean. As a result, there is shrinkage in cooked bacon. For the sake of good cooking, it is more important to serve tasty food, than to gain a few more portions. Preparations must come up to expectations. If the browning has not occurred, the roast is not a roast, because it does not taste like a roast.

## RECIRCULATION OF JUICES

When a roast appears to be cooked, carry-over heat must be considered. The heat from the original source is stopped by removing the roast from the oven and from the pan, but the heat of this mass still needs to equalize within itself. Some heat will flow into the surrounding air and some will pass deeper to the center. More important, the meat juices will recirculate. This carry-over action of heat has to be considered while the roast is still in the oven. If a beef roast or a steak is cooked to medium, then removed from the heat source, carry-over heat will make it nearly well done.

On the other hand, a recirculation, also called setting time, is absolutely necessary. Warm meat juices and heat must equalize themselves within the roast, before carving should be attempted. A medium-rare beef roast, which is cooked to a 145°F. inside temperature and then cut in half without setting, will show a dry overcooked ring of meat beneath the surface and a nearly raw center. When the same roast is allowed to set for the juices to recirculate, a uniform pinkish red will cover the whole slice. The larger the roast, the more setting time must be allowed.

## WARMKEEPING AND CARVING

Setting time and warmkeeping are two different phases. Setting time is a must for a better roast, but warmkeeping after setting is a necessary evil to make the serving of roasts easier in a restaurant.

Various types of food warmers are used to keep cooked food "service ready". The larger the roast, the longer it can be kept warm without too much drying out. It is important to time the cooking so that only the shortest warmkeeping time is needed.

The handling of a roast, from the oven to the warmer, is done in the following order:

a. Take roast and pan out of the oven.

b. Remove the roast from the pan to a holding container.

c. Reserve the hot roasting pan, with all drippings, for gravy.

| Type of Roast | Weight | Setting Time | Holding Time |
|---|---|---|---|
| Rib of Beef | 25-30 lbs | 35-45 minutes | 2-3 hours |
| Boneless Rib Eye | 12-16 lbs | 20-25 " | 1-1½ " |
| Baron of Beef | 55-75 lbs | 55-75 " | 4-5 " |
| Striploin | 10-14 lbs | 15-20 " | ¾-1 " |
| Fillet of Beef | 6-8 lbs | 10-15 " | ¾-1 " |
| Rack of Lamb | 2-3 lbs | 5-10 " | ¼ " |
| Leg of Lamb | 6-8 lbs | 20-25 " | 1½-2 " |
| Loin of Pork | 7-10 lbs | 15-20 " | 1-1½ " |
| Leg of Pork | 12-18 lbs | 20-30 " | 1½-2 " |
| Roast Turkey | 25-30 lbs | 25-30 " | 2-2½ " |
| Roasted Capon | 4½-6 lbs | 10-15 " | ¼-½ " |

**Table 6-2  RECIRCULATION AND MAXIMUM WARMKEEPING TIMES FOR VARIOUS ROASTS**

Fig. 6-1 Slicing a boneless beef rib eye roast

Fig. 6-2 Carving a standing rib roast (beef)

d. Cool off the roast at room temperature, for the time needed according to its size.

e. Place the roast in the warmer (Bain-Marie) until it is to be carved.

Different types of restaurants use different serving techniques, which depend on their price levels. The best way is to cut each order, when needed. This is expensive and requires one more cook. Such expense would be reflected in the price on the menu.

Carving is not difficult. The cook needs sharp knives, a blueprint for the carving of specific roasts, and practice. He should understand that guests must be served appetizing and reasonably warm orders.

If at all possible, roasts should be cut so that the slice has a short *grain*. Grain is the visible structure of the meat fibers. The short grain is accomplished by holding the knife at a 90° angle against the fibers. Lamb or pork legs, ribs, loins, poultry, and fish are carved in distinct ways, either for the sake of appearance or for efficiency.

## BROILING VERSUS ROASTING

Broiling does to one portion of meat what roasting does to one piece (several portions in one) of meat. The same meat cuts and the same additions of salt, spices, and fat are used. The dry heat process of cooking is applied, but the convection heat (hot air) is replaced by radiated heat for a stronger impact. Regular roasting ovens maintain their highest temperature at about 500°F., but a good broiler may have up to 1200°F. heat output with some going as high as 1600°F.

A single steak is too small to be roasted in an oven. If it were placed in a 500°F. oven, the steak would be well done inside before getting a crust on the surface. For double or triple portion steaks, experienced cooks always use the broiler first and then the oven. The high broiler heat browns and marks the steak, then the oven finishes cooking it without burning the surface.

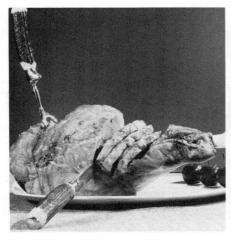

Fig. 6-3 Carving a leg of lamb, french style

Fig. 6-4 Slicing a center cut pork-loin (partially boned)

Fig. 6-5 Slicing (carving) the shank half of a baked ham

To become a good broiler cook, the student needs to understand these theories, have a cool head, and a strong sense of responsibility. Then, with a few demonstrations of how it should be done and a lot of experience, he attains this goal in due time.

The good broiler cook has knowledge and experience. The perfect broiler cook, like the perfect roast cook, has some added inborn talent.

## ADVANTAGES OF BROILING

Broiled foods are cooked when ordered. Cooking time for the largest steak is seldom more than twenty minutes. No precooking is needed and no cooked food is left over to spoil. A steakhouse keeps a refrigerator full of precut raw steaks and the cooks "fire" them when ordered. The command *fire a steak* means to cook pre-ordered food at this very moment.

Refrigerated meat keeps for days. Steaks can be counted and checked easily, and no elaborate cooking process is needed in their preparation. A steakhouse is an ideal setup for the restaurateur.

Customers, too, like fresh-made orders. A steak, ordered rare, assures the customer that he will not get any leftover warmed-up meat or some reconstituted convenience food.

Dieticians believe that broiled food is healthier than panfried or even sautéed food. Most of the fat drips off the meat, and even some of the juices are lost. Therefore, the caloric count for a broiled steak is lower than for the same steak sautéed.

A broiled meat dish, when done to perfection, is one of the finest dishes, even to sophisticated diners. Perfection means quality meat cooked as ordered, with only basic salt added, and the meat not burned. Food quality is much more visible in plain dishes than in fancy food combinations where everything is covered with sauces and garnishes.

## FOODS FOR BROILING

An experienced broiler cook can prepare almost any dish on the broiler. Obviously, some dishes are easier to handle than others. Since production is the watchword of the modern food service establishment, menus often contain those dishes which are easiest to handle.

A steak is the most popular meal in the USA. The Eastern US offers rib, spencer, and Delmonico steaks in addition to the full loin cuts which are used in all their variations on the West coast. A boneless sirloin strip steak is called a New York cut steak. Regional differences in names are common, but the specific cuts used are the same all over.

Lamb chops in a variety of cuts and shish kebabs are next in popularity. Then pork, often as Satays (spiced skewers of meat), chicken, and turkey steaks follow. From the waters come salmon, halibut, swordfish, fresh tuna, bass, lobsters, langustes, prawns, scallops, and abalones. Another group of foods to be broiled includes the offals, such as liver, sweetbreads, and kidneys. As a basic rule of what to broil, it can be said:

- Fat meats and firm seafoods are preferred for taste and ease in handling.
- Vegetables are very rarely cooked on the broiler.

Lean pieces of meat can be larded. Small pieces, such as chicken livers, prawns, or scallops can be lined up on skewers for easier handling. There are few limitations for the creative and interested broiler cook.

## MISUSED TERMINOLOGY

In most of the states of the USA, broiling is the accepted term for dry heat cooking by radiation. In other English speaking areas, the word grilling is used. The "Grillroom" is a restaurant serving food only from the grill. "Mixgrill" is the internationally accepted name for a combination of lamb meats and offal cooked on the broiler. A grill (or grille) is an open grating similar to the type used for grilling meat. Many cooks use the term grilling, whenever they mean griddling, which is a commercial form of pan frying. To avoid misunderstanding, it is important to check out the local usage of the term.

## DIFFERENT HEAT SOURCES

Broilers are made in many shapes, forms, and models. Most of them are gas fired, and are lined with special fire bricks to reflect and concentrate the heat. Electrical broilers for commercial use are not very popular. Gas or electric broilers are easier to handle and to keep clean than the charcoal broilers. Gas or electric broilers have fewer fire hazards, since their heat can be regulated faster. For overall customer appeal and flavor, nothing can beat the old fashioned charcoal broiler. It is basically the oldest unchanged piece of equipment still in use. The charcoal broiler, used properly, produces beautiful food and is highly regarded by the eating public.

## EMOTIONAL IMPACT

Charcoal broilers, like all things Western, remind people of America's pioneer days and have great emotional appeal with the American public. They look simple, giving the impression of something natural. They produce pleasant, appetizing smells. Their fire looks romantic, and they do produce a more flavorful meal, especially if hickory or maple coal is used. Real charcoal broilers are mostly used today in speciality houses. Sometimes, the business is even centered around this broiler.

These facets make the Steakhouse a very popular type of eating establishment. Many franchises and food service chains, which specialize in only broiled food have come into existence. They are trying to take the fullest advantage of the broiler's emotional appeal.

## HEALTH HAZARDS IN CHARRING

The burning of organic substance results in a residue of carbon or coal. It is obvious to most people that coal is neither healthy nor food. However, there are many uninformed restaurant guests who believe that a steak charred on the surface and raw on the inside is a sophisticated way to eat. But these guests who order their food charred are only hurting themselves. It is more dangerous to the public that many untrained or uneducated broiler cooks take extreme delight in broiling with flames burning high. Some even pour grease on the coals to get this fiery effect. This practice is a health hazard to the unsuspecting diner. The majority of the public trusts the chefs who cook for them. They are not aware that a cook even unknowingly would do something harmful to the diner's well-being. It has been proved that burned organic matter is *carcinogenous* (cancer inducing) to mice and humans. Common sense alone should stop such disgusting and unprofessional broiler handling.

## SAFETY HAZARDS

Broilers have a container to collect the fat drippings of the broiled meat. Hot fat, even in small quantities, is a fire hazard. This is especially true if the fat is close to an open fire. Drip pans of broilers must be checked and emptied routinely. Most fires in destroyed restaurants have started at a carelessly handled broiler. The danger factors on broilers are overheating, sloppy working habits, and too much fat left on the raw meat. A cook, if he is working nervously, can easily burn himself. First aid kits and $CO_2$ fire extinguishers must be within the reach of any broiler cook. Broiler cooks, chefs, and managers should post rules of what to do in emergencies. Fire drills at regular intervals should be held.

Charcoal broilers need more care and attention than gas or electric broilers, but the greatest danger to any broiler is a careless, irresponsible cook.

## BROILING AS AN ART

Broiling is a good example of why Culinary Art is unlikely to change totally to Culinary Technology. Some parts of art will always remain. A variety of factors defies attempts to establish a formula for broiling the many existing dishes. Every cut of meat, even from the same animal, has a different distribution of fat within its fibres. Each cut also has a different density of muscles and a different geometric shape. All of these are factors in heat conduction. More variables exist from one animal to the next. These are breed, age, feeding and the method of slaughtering. Such variables change the fat percentage and its distribution, the conformation (shape) and the water (blood) content of each piece of meat. The size of the steak and the customer's own concept of doneness also vary. For instance, it has been concluded by meat researchers that consumers who live west of the Rocky Mountains accept broiled or roasted meat about one step higher than the customers of the Midwest. A steak, considered rare in the Midwest, is considered medium rare in the West. There is also the recirculation and holding time. Broiler cooks often have to allow for the time it takes the diner to eat.

## SUMMARY

Cooking with dry heat is one of the oldest but still one of the most desirable ways to cook. According to dieticians and nutritionists, baking, roasting, and broiling are better than other forms of cooking. Baking to the cook is not as important as it is to the baker. The cook's baking is mostly called roasting, which implies the presence of fat. Only tender meat cuts can be dry heat cooked. Meat roasting as well as other forms of cookery can be analyzed in relation to thermodynamic laws which explain what actually happens. Large roasts should cook at low heat for a longer time, but smaller roasts need higher heat for a shorter cooking time. The importance of recirculation and the necessary evil of the food warmer is explained. Broiling has advantages to the customer as well as to the restaurateur and is similar to roasting. The terms grilling, broiling, and griddling are sometimes mixed up. There are a variety of different broiler models for different heat sources available.

### DISCUSSION TOPICS

1. Should flavor and looks of a roast be sacrificed to provide yield?

2. What are the advantages of the short order restaurant to customer and operator?

3. What are the types of broilers and how are they used for different purposes?

4. Do emotions influence the food selections of customers?

5. Does barbecuing or broiling have to be a health hazard?

6. Why did Brillat-Savarin consider roasting and broiling a real talent?

7. Why is the broiler cook with all these responsibilities not considered a skilled master chef?

8. By what means should the broiler cook develop his concepts of medium, medium rare, and rare meats?

9. Could a good meat thermometer be used to establish the exact degree of doneness of every steak or roast?

10. What are some possible causes of fire in a kitchen and how can fire be prevented?

### SUGGESTED ACTIVITIES

1. Define the following words:

   a. collagen
   b. recirculation
   c. offal
   d. carcinogenous
   e. mix grill
   f. conformation
   g. to fire a steak

2. Demonstrate the handling of various oven types.

3. Demonstrate the handling of all three broiler types: gas, electric, and charcoal.

4. Make a recirculation test. Broil two equal steaks cut in sequence. Cut one immediately, and the other one after setting.

5. Demonstrate steak cooking on a broiler, and emphasize grillmarks.

6. Demonstrate the handling of $CO_2$ extinguisher. Have a fire drill.

7. Demonstrate fish cooking on the broiler.

8. Demonstrate the cleaning and maintenance of the broiler.

9. Demonstrate the handling of a meat thermometer on differently shaped roasts.

10. Measure the actual heat in various parts of an ordinary commercial roasting oven and compare it to the thermostat.

11. Perform experiment in heat transmission. (Table 6-1).

## ACHIEVEMENT REVIEW

A. Complete the following:

1. Dry heat cooking processes are also called baking, roasting, and _____ .

2. A distinct roast flavor can only be achieved after the roast has been _____ _____ .

3. When a turkey is cooked by the dry heat method, it should be called _____ _____ .

4. A baked ham is cooked by the method of _____ .

5. The term grilling is used in many English speaking countries to imply _____ _____ .

6. A charcoal broiler appeals to the customer's _____ .

7. Burned organic substances are unhealthy and have lately been referred to as _____ .

8. The most practical heat source for a broiler is _____ .

9. Variable meat factors are some of the reasons why broiling is likely to remain an _____ .

10. A cook's concept of a rare steak and a customer's concept of a rare steak may not be the _____ .

11. A San Franciscan might order a steak rare in Omaha and find it cooked to _____ .

B. Read each question carefully and completely before answering it. Select the *best* answer.

1. Cooking with dry heat is also called
   a. radiation          c. dehydration
   b. conduction         d. pasteurization

2. All of these conventional ways of cooking are dry heat methods with the exception of
   a. broiling           c. roasting
   b. frying             d. baking

3. Broiled food is preferred on many a diet, because it
   a. tastes better              c. is comparatively fatless
   b. maintains more calories    d. is easier to digest

4. A beef rib roast of about 28 pounds weight has a recirculation of
   a. 10 minutes         c. 30 minutes
   b. 20 minutes         d. 40 minutes

5. To achieve the purpose of roasting, a
   a. small roast needs high heat, short cooking time
   b. small roast needs high heat, long cooking time
   c. large roast needs high heat, long cooking time
   d. large roast needs high heat, short cooking time

6. Placing a "service-ready" roast into a food warmer, means to
   a. transfer it immediately from oven to warmer
   b. let it set at kitchen temperature for some time
   c. chill it off in the refrigerator to reduce carry-over heat
   d. keep the roast under the desired degree of doneness

7. The browning or caramelization of sugar needs a minimum temperature of
   a. 250° Fahrenheit          c. 300° Fahrenheit
   b. 275° Fahrenheit          d. 325° Fahrenheit

8. Lean white meats contain less blood than dark meats and have therefore
   a. less protein             c. less glucose
   b. less flavor              d. less eye appeal

9. The decisive factor for the cooking time of a roast is
   a. untrimmed weight         c. geometric shape
   b. fat content of meat      d. percentage of bones

10. In broiling, the heat transfer method used is called
    a. forced air circulation  c. contact heating
    b. intensified conduction  d. direct radiation

11. The boneless Sirloin steak is also called
    a. Delmonico Steak         c. Boston Steak
    b. New York cut Steak      d. Spencer Steak

12. The probability of starting a fire through a broiler is *not* reduced by
    a. trimming the excess fat off meat
    b. emptying the drip pan routinely
    c. having a $CO_2$ extinguisher within reach
    d. guarding against overheating

13. Broiling is not suitable for cooking tough meat, because dry heat
    a. does not soften collagens sufficiently
    b. tenderizes the fat (marble) of meat only
    c. burns the increased glucose of tougher meat
    d. dehydrates meat completely

C. Match the words of Column I with their most fitting counterparts of Column II.

| *Column I* | | *Column II* |
|---|---|---|
| Grilling | 1. | visible fat veins |
| Baked Ham | 2. | touch heat transfer |
| Recirculation | 3. | unrefined gelatine |
| Radiation | 4. | broiled lamb meats |
| Convection | 5. | boneless Sirloin steak |
| Bain-Marie | 6. | Steakhouse |
| Carbonizing | 7. | Food warmer |
| Conduction | 8. | heat from open fire |
| Carcinogenous | 9. | broiling |
| Mix Grill | 10. | setting time |
| New York Steak | 11. | airheat equalization |
| Glucose | 12. | charring |
| Collagen | 13. | slicer |
| Grillroom | 14. | cancer-inducing |
| Carving knife | 15. | blood sugar |
| Marble | 16. | roasted smoked pork leg |

D.    Answer in your own words:

1.    List the possible sources of fire in the kitchen and ways to prevent a fire from starting.

2.    Describe the theories of roasting.

3.    Explain the importance of recirculation.

4.    List the meat cuts that are generally broiled.

5.    List the meat cuts that are generally roasted.

# Unit 7  Cooking With Moist Heat

## OBJECTIVES

After studying this unit, the student should be able to

- List the plain moist heat cooking methods.
- Explain the need for boiling.
- Describe the sight recognition of boiling temperatures of water.
- Explain the differences between steaming, boiling, and simmering.
- Explain the reasons for shrinkage.

Cooking with moist heat, one of the five basic cooking methods, is known as simmering, boiling, or steaming. The term poaching, which is sometimes used, comes from the French verb "pocher". It is applied only to fish or eggs simmered in water or liquid.

## REASONS FOR BOILING

In unit 1, reasons for cooking food submerged in liquid or surrounded by steam (boiling) were listed. All foods can be cooked in water, if it is so desired. In the past, most foods had to be cooked with moist heat in order to become edible. Now, fewer meats need tenderization through moisture. Boiling of meats is not popular anymore, especially in the United States.

The boiling of meat provides a by-product called broth. True chicken soup cannot be made without first boiling a chicken to produce the broth.

Foods preserved by salting, dehydration, or a combination of both, need water to become edible. Water desalts and reconstitutes these foods. Corned beef, pastrami, smoked meats, and Smithfield ham are good examples of meats which need water. Some cereals and legumes, such as dried beans and peas also need water to become edible. Moisture is added whenever the preparation of a dish needs a soupy or liquid consistency.

## HEAT CONTROL THROUGH WATER

Water is an excellent and uniform heat conductor. Its approximate temperature can be easily seen. Before the invention of the thermometer, this was helpful in the control of heat. Today, heat is measured by more exact methods and "simmering" means water heated to 185°F. – 195°F. Little bubbles of air rise from the bottom of the cooking pot and burst on the surface of the water.

When the temperature of simmering water is raised, splashing bubbles are created and this is called a rolling boil. This action indicates that the highest temperature of 212°F. has been reached.

When a temperature of 212°F. is maintained, the rolling boil continues, water transforms to steam and disappears into the air. The temperature of steam is slightly higher than that of the boiling water. The escaping steam can be channelled through baskets filled with food, thereby creating the steam cooking process. All this applies to sea level only. At higher altitudes, the pressure is lower and less heat is needed for a rolling boil or steam. Cooking times, then, must be adjusted accordingly; that is, slightly longer.

Of these three different visible heat levels, simmering is the slowest and steaming is the fastest. The rolling boil is harmful to the cooking of vegetables and tender proteins. The strong movements break up or cook apart all but the toughest foods.

The rolling boil is useful only for the cooking of "pasta", or paste. Paste is the generic name for starchy food made of flour, water, salt, and sometimes eggs, which is shaped into types of noodles, spaghetti, macaroni, shells, vermicelli, and others. Paste items are dried and have to be re-hydrated or reconstituted in water in order to become edible. Flour, a starch, needs 200°F. to be thickened. Simmering does not have enough heat. Steaming does not provide enough liquid to swell up dried starch and make it edible. Here, the rolling boil is useful.

## The Nature of Boiling

Boiling is a process of cooking food in water. The action of osmosis must be considered when food is boiled. Osmosis is the tendency of fluids to equalize their saturation level with other fluids whenever possible.

Blood contains salts (taste). Therefore, a salt level exists in meats. If raw meat is covered with unsalted water, osmosis will equalize the salt of the meat, leaving it without flavor. For this reason, all foods which are to be boiled must be simmered in pre-salted water.

Vegetables contain up to 80% water in which their taste-providing substances (salts) are dissolved. Hence, vegetables cooked in unsalted water lose their taste through osmosis in the same way. The conclusion is that all boiled foods must have a given salt content in their cooking liquids in order to prevent the complete leaching of flavors and taste.

The more a student knows about boiling, the easier it will be for him, as a cook, to prepare good food. The more a student understands about the nature of heat, the composition of foods, and their interactions, the better his cooking will become.

A cook who is using good boiling techniques makes certain that the pre-salted cooking liquid is never above the simmering temperature. Temperature control is necessary. Cooks can watch the fine bubbles coming to the surface. A thermostatic control set at 195°F. is even better. The extra minutes of cooking time will be well spent in return for a superior quality.

## Less Need for Boiling

Food service establishments today have less need for boiling than in the past. The American customer does not favor boiled meat. In colder climates, boiled meat is liked better than in warmer climates. Europeans still like boiled meats, but they too, prefer steaks and roasts if the quality of the meat is improved.

*Objective*:

Cook the same type of potatoes by four different boiling methods and find the difference of handling, yield, and quality. Conclude which method seems to be the best.

*Materials needed*:

Four batches of four potatoes each, of the same kind, size, and weight; salt.

*Utensils needed*:

A pressure steam cooker, a potato steamer (both either commercial or household types); two identical pots, large enough to hold potatoes in a layer; a paring knife, four time clocks.

*Procedure*:

1. Wash all potatoes, place one batch into each of the two pots.
2. Add salt, cover them with boiling water and bring to re-boil immediately.
3. Keep one pot on simmering, the other on a rolling boil; set timers for estimated cooking time.
4. Handle remaining batches the same way but in the two steam cookers.
5. Cook by estimated time or manual inspection until done. Record cooking time of each batch.
6. Drain each batch when ready. Cool, peel, and taste.
7. Compare for the following: time, sogginess, firmness, remaining shape, weight loss, taste. Record on Table 7-2.
8. Compare data. Weigh advantages against disadvantages. Make a conclusion to which method seems to be the best.

Table 7-1 POTATO BOILING EXPERIMENT

|  | Time | Sogginess | Firmness | Kept Shape | Taste |
|---|---|---|---|---|---|
| PRESSURE STEAM |  | 1. |  |  |  |
|  |  | 2. |  |  |  |
|  |  | 3. |  |  |  |
| LIVE STEAM |  | 1. |  |  |  |
|  |  | 2. |  |  |  |
|  |  | 3. |  |  |  |
| ROLLING BOIL |  | 1. |  |  |  |
|  |  | 2. |  |  |  |
|  |  | 3. |  |  |  |
| SIMMERING |  | 1. |  |  |  |
|  |  | 2. |  |  |  |
|  |  | 3. |  |  |  |

Table 7-2 COMPARISON TABLE

Live crabs must be boiled for the sake of efficiency, but lobsters need not be boiled. On the East coast, the broiled lobster has replaced the boiled lobster in popularity. Prawns, shrimps, and mussels come frozen or even cooked. Meat tenderness has increased so much that broiling and roasting have become the preferred ways of preparation. Corned, smoked, and cold meats — used mostly as sandwich fillings — are supplied precooked.

Food processing plants using thermostatic controls are very efficient in controlling shrinkage. Restaurant operators feel that it is better to buy precooked foods even though they are higher priced to buy.

### SIMMERING IS BEST

Simmering creates a light movement of the water only and its degree of heat is best for cooking most foods, except starches. In the past, simmering was used only for eggs without shells and fish. This was called poaching. Hence, the terms still in use are poached eggs and poached fish. Simmering is also best for meats because it cooks proteins without toughening them. Simmering is best for vegetables because the water does not evaporate much and the flavor and nutrients are retained. The vegetable water should also be used.

### ADVANTAGES OF STEAMING

Steam is hotter and therefore, cooks faster than simmering or boiling. It does not have the forceful actions of the rolling boil and it does not break foods apart. In addition, less water is used than in submerged simmering. Therefore, less vitamins, nutrients, and flavors are leached (washed) out. Since live steam disappears into the air, little condensation occurs, and there is no broth. Steaming is advisable for cooking potatoes and other root vegetables which do not discolor. Steamed vegetables do not have to be drained after cooking. This saves time and accidental mishandling. For the cooking of meats or fowl, steaming is not too advantageous, since it makes no broth. Heat over 190°F. makes proteins and albumins (egg whites) tough and chewy.

#### Steam Under Pressure

A pressure steam cooker consists of pressure proof compartments where live steam builds up. The temperature increases with every pound of pressure. Most pressure cookers generate up to fifteen pounds of pressure which, in turn, produces 250°F. moist heat. The increased heat reduces cooking time from 40-50%. Obviously, overcooking is a greater possibility and pressure steam cookers must be watched very closely.

Potatoes, a starchy vegetable, need 200°F. to coagulate the 20% starch content. When the inside temperature of the potato reaches 200°F., the water in the cell structure simmers and breaks the cell open which, at the same time, cooks the starch. Using live steam (212°F.), the time needed to achieve this might be thirty minutes. A pressure cooker generating 250°F. cooks the same potato in fifteen minutes. Heat of 212°F. needs thirty minutes to transfer 200°F. to the center of the potato. But heat of 250°F. needs only fifteen minutes to do the same.

Accidental overcooking by only 15% of the time needed may completely ruin some foods. Many foods cooked in pressure cookers keep their qualities only if they are timed correctly. The real advantage of the pressure cooker lies in its ability to cook most green vegetables and even·small cut potatoes (Parisienne potatoes) in a few minutes, assuring freshly cooked vegetables all the time.

### REASONS FOR SHRINKAGE

Shrinkage is the loss of weight occurring to all foods during any cooking process. This loss could be considerable, up to 30% of the trimmed weight. The fattier the meat, the more fat melts during cooking even before browning. Meat contains an average of 60% water and some of this water will merge with the cooking liquid. If meat is cooked to an inside temperature of 200°F., the blood (water) in its cells will flow out. It is the same reaction that happens during the dry cooking process, but there, the juices (water) evaporate. The hotter the cooking temperature, the greater is the shrinkage.

Overcooked meat loses fat, most of its juices and, as a result, also loses its flavor and texture. Overcooking is the greatest destroyer of taste and nutritional value. It also causes considerable shrinkage of the portion size.

## SUMMARY

Cooking with moist heat is known best as boiling, but for best results, with the exception of boiling pasta, the cooking liquid should only simmer.

Poaching is simmering, but this term is applied only to eggs and fish. Moist cooking methods are used to dissolve collagen in the meat from older animals. Other reasons for moist cooking are the desalting and rehydration of dried, cured, or smoked foods. Fine bubbles on the surface of heating water is a sign that a simmering temperature between 185°F. and 195°F. has been reached. The rolling boil shows that the water is at 212°F., boiling water changes to steam and, if not collected for further use, disappears into the air. This temperature guide is set for sea level only.

The use of live steam is preferable to a rolling boil. The more gentle steam does not break up vegetables or tender foods as much as the rolling boil.

Pressure steaming produces higher temperatures than 212°F. and cooks foods faster, saving nearly 50% of the cooking time.

Shrinkage is the loss of weight through cooking. The hotter the cooking temperatures, the greater the loss of fats and juices (blood, water). Meats boiled at the minimum temperatures needed for the coagulation of proteins have little shrinkage, but accurate thermometers or thermostats must be used.

Boiling, as a cooking method, develops a different taste, which is liked by many people through habit, especially by those who live in a cold climate.

### DISCUSSION TOPICS

1. Why are boiled meats liked better in some areas than in others?

2. Are pressure steam cookers helpful for a continuous supply of freshly cooked vegetables?

3. Should a chef be more concerned about taste, quality, or yields?

### SUGGESTED ACTIVITIES

1. Define the following words:

   a. osmosis
   b. saturation
   c. shrinkage
   d. leaching
   e. pasta
   f. albumins
   g. simmering

2. Perform the potato boiling experiment. (Table 7-1)

3. Demonstrate pasta cooking (film, if available).

4. Estimate, as well as measure, temperatures of water from simmering to boiling.

5. Demonstrate the handling of a pressure steam cooker.

6. Demonstrate the handling of a live steam cooker.

7. For a review on boiling, reread unit 1, page 3.

### ACHIEVEMENT REVIEW

A. Complete the following:

   1. Poached fish or eggs on the menu implies that these foods were _____ .

   2. The rolling boil is a good method for the cooking of _____ .

   3. The gentle action of steaming has a temperature high enough to coagulate starch; it is the best way of boiling _____ .

   4. In meat cookery, one reason for shrinkage is the melting of _____ .

5. Water, used for the boiling of foods, has to be salted in order to prevent the loss of flavor by _____.

6. Foods, preserved by salting, need to be cooked in water, to become _____ _____.

7. When the temperature of simmering water is increased, it will change to ____ _____.

8. Steam under pressure generates more heat, therefore cooks _____.

B. Read each question carefully and completely before answering it. Select the *best* answer.

1. Potatoes are cooked best in the pressure steam cooker, because

   a. the rolling boil may cook them apart
   b. simmering needs too long a cooking time.
   c. the pressure steam cooker does not break them up
   d. the live steam cooker changes their taste

2. Simmering generates heat from 185°F. - 195°F. which is enough to cook these foods except

   a. chicken          c. eggs
   b. fish             d. spaghetti

3. The rolling boil can reach a maximum temperature of

   a. 208° Fahrenheit      c. 216° Fahrenheit
   b. 212° Fahrenheit      d. 220° Fahrenheit

4. Small potatoes which need 30 - 35 minutes of cooking time in a live steamer, are cooked in a pressure cooker under 15 pounds of steam pressure in

   a. 7 - 10 minutes       c. 15 - 18 minutes
   b. 11 - 14 minutes      d. 19 - 22 minutes

5. A Virginia Ham, soaked in cold water overnight, will lose some of its salt through the process of

   a. rehydration          c. osmosis
   b. coagulation          d. moisturizing

6. Shrinkage reduces the weight of food while it cooks. To prevent unnecessary shrinkage, meat is boiled best

   a. without salt         c. in live steam
   b. at 15 pounds of pressure   d. by simmering at 190°F.

7. Without a thermometer, the simmering of water can be recognized by

   a. fine air bubbles coming to the surface
   b. big air bubbles coming to the surface
   c. the splashing and steaming of the pot
   d. the gradual disappearing of the water

C. Answer in your own words:

1. List the reasons for boiling food.

2. List the four moist heat cooking methods.

3. Explain the reasons for shrinkage.

# Unit 8  Cooking in Fat

## OBJECTIVES

After studying this unit, the student should be able to

- Explain the difference between pan frying and sautéing
- Describe the difference between pan frying and deep frying
- Identify three different coatings for food
- Demonstrate the flipping of food in a skillet
- Explain why a "Beef Stroganoff" is called a sauté dish

Cooking in fat, commonly called frying, is listed in unit 1 as one of the five cooking techniques. This fast cooking method is used for dishes made to order or "a la carte".

## DISTINCTIONS OF FRYING

Frying can be grouped into pan or deep frying on one hand, and sautéing or flip frying on the other. In deep frying, the cooked food is separated from the cooking fat. In sautéing, fat is absorbed as part of the preparation. Students must learn to be aware of this great distinction between frying and sautéing. Originally all frying was done in skillets on the top of the stove. The modern deep fryer and the griddle were developed as a result of the increase in restaurant business. As pointed out in unit 6 on dry heat cooking, the griddle is sometimes called a grill. Students should be well aware of this difference.

## FOODS TO BE COOKED IN FAT

Foods to be cooked in fat, either deep fried or sautéed, must be tender before they are fried. The size of the food is of importance, also. Sauté dishes should be cut evenly in small pieces. One portion at a time is the largest piece of food cooked by the deep frying method. Examples are one pork chop, one veal cutlet, one quarter of chicken, and one portion of fish. Fish and seafoods can be either deep or flip fried. All tender or prime cuts of meat and poultry may also be cooked by either method. The food selection is similar to that for broiling.

Vegetables may be cooked by deep frying or sautéing, but cooks prefer to blanch or precook some vegetables for a different appearance and flavor. An example is the difference between home fried potatoes and cottage fried potatoes. Slices of browned potato pieces are served under both names. The home fried potatoes are boiled "in the jacket" (unpeeled) first, peeled, cooled, sliced, and then re-fried in a skillet with a *good fat* such as butter. In this case, the sautéing process is used, and in some areas home fried potatoes are called "sauté potatoes". For cottage fried potatoes, raw potatoes are peeled, sliced and sautéed in a skillet with a *good fat* such as butter, until they are done. This may need up to 20 minutes of sautéing time, with the skillet covered in the beginning, in order to prevent the drying out of the potatoes. The emphasis for both preparations is on *good fat*, since the fat becomes a part of the dish and is not separated from the potatoes after the cooking.

An example of another way of cooking potato slices is shown by potato chips. They are made by slicing raw peeled potatoes uniformly, then deep frying them in very hot shortening or deep frying fat until they are done, brown and crisp. Here the potato is separated from the frying fat after cooking. The result is startling since the same raw materials were used. The difference is caused simply by surrounding the potatoes with more intense heat through the same conductor.

## DEEP FAT FRYING

Pan fried food and deep fried food preparations are similar in theory. Pan fried food is only half sub-merged in fat, while deep fried food is fully submerged in fat. Frying fats which are heated to 350°F. add the browned taste to the cooked food.

The deep fryer uses a large quantity of fat, and reheats and uses this fat over and over again. The steam and flavor of the food escape into the fat of the fryer, changing the original composition of the frying fat.

While the first batches of food in a kettle of fresh frying fat come out tasty and golden brown, the next batches are not of the same high quality. The food accepts the flavors of previously cooked food from the fat. This results in the loss of appetizing browning ability and adds an undesirable taste.

The old-fashioned pan frying process, where food is half submerged in fat, lets steam and volatile oils escape into the air, thus keeping the fat cleaner than in the deep frying process. Since a much smaller amount of fat is used per batch of food, the fat can be strained immediately after each use and saved for other purposes. In better restaurants, the fat is used only once, and then discarded.

Pan frying uses more fat and is less economical, but gives better quality food. The deep fryer fries faster, reuses the same fat over and over again and reduces food costs. From a quality point of view, pan frying is preferred.

### Coatings for Deep Fried Foods

Except for all types of french fried potatoes, deep fried foods have a coating. The coating is usually a mixture of starch, eggs, and liquid. Depending on how these three ingredients are used, the coating is referred to as a batter, an eggwash, or a breading. Fish and chips are a good example of deep frying in a batter. A southern fried chicken represents fried food which is coated only. A veal cutlet is usually breaded. (How to handle breading and batters is explained in detail in section 3, unit 15). Food is coated before deep frying for the safeguarding of the frying fat, the protection of natural food flavors, a better golden browned appearance, and additional caloric value. The coating also acts as a shield between the fat and food. It absorbs some of the food flavor and juices on the inside and prevents the intrusion of frying fat into the food from the outside.

### Modern Deep Frying

The use of the modern deep fryer has become a mixed blessing to culinary art. Scientists concerned about nutrition know that proper diet is the key to the well-being of all humans. They are opposed to the concept of modern deep frying. Commercial deep frying is based on the principles of fast cooking and reuse of the frying fat. This combination causes the breakdown of the fats used. The breakdown of fats is the same as the burning of fats. Deep fried food absorbs more of the burned fat than there should be in anyone's diet. Young people can eat large quantities of french fries and other fried foods without feeling ill effects at the time. Burned fat causes ulcers and other medical problems. Any burned matter is carcinogenous (cancer-causing). Persons who eat too much deep fried food sooner or later have medical bills. Nutritionists see the dangers, but their voices are not heard.

Deep fried foods can be handled easily by unskilled labor. Modern deep fryers have timer controlled pop-up devices. Precut, prebreaded and precooked frozen food is available everywhere. Skilled chefs are not needed to fry whatever is ordered.

## FAST FOOD OPERATIONS

The fast food service establishments of today work mostly with griddle and deep fryer. They feature breaded fried items rather than batter fried items. Breading can be done in advance. Prebreaded food can be stored under refrigeration until it is used. Dipping into batter must be done at the very moment before frying. It takes additional time and this food is much more difficult to handle than breaded or even coated food.

## FLIP FRYING OR SAUTÉING

Sautéing falls into the realm of the skilled cook. The term sautéing comes from the French word sauté. It implies that the food in a skillet is not turned with a spatula while the skillet is on the stove. The pan is flipped in such a way that its contents fly through the air, turn over and fall back into the pan. This is fast and efficient work for small quantities, and it keeps food in an attractive shape. Sautéing food is considered as one of the best ways of cooking by connoisseurs (people knowledgeable about food). Chinese cuisine, which has a great reputation for taste and nutrition, is based almost entirely on sautéing. The Chinese call it stir-fry cooking in a wok. Sauté cooking applies to all foods, if they are tender from the start. All foods that can be broiled or deep fried can also be sautéed.

### A Sauté is not a Stew

A sauté made of meat, poultry, or fish and vegetable might look like a stew and even taste like a stew, but it is not made like a stew. Sautés are made when ordered, and they are made from choice raw materials. Stews are cooked in advance to use up secondary cuts and tough foods. Sautés have names like "Beef Stroganoff", "Emincée de Veau á la Suisse", "Gypsy liver" or veal kidneys sauté. They are made by the sautéing technique. The food which gives the dish its name and the appropriate garnish are sautéed freshly, then finished with a previously made sauce.

A sauté made to order should be compared to the cocktail made by a bartender. For Beef Stroganoff, a julienne of raw fillet meat is sautéed quickly, then pre-sautéed sliced mushrooms and shallots are added. The combination is finished by the addition of some brown sauce and sour cream. Emincée de Veau á la Suisse consists of sliced veal leg, onions, brown sauce, fresh cream, and white wine. The Gypsy Liver is equal to a Beef Stroganoff with liver replacing the beef fillet. The preparation for all meat sautés is the same. A sauté dish retains the flavor of fresh cooking (like a steak) and the quality of a previously made sauce. Cookery that is called French Luxury or Gourmet cuisine is actually sauté cooking at its finest.

### USING THE GRIDDLE

Griddle or grill cooking is a form of commercial sauté cooking. The disadvantage is that all meat juices are lost. It also resembles broiling and many restaurants with insufficient facilities substitute a griddled steak for a broiled one. Griddles are efficient and fast for short order work. This makes them very popular in coffeeshops and restaurants with breakfast service. Hotcakes, pancakes, griddle cakes, eggs, bacon, ham, steaks, hamburgers, and grilled sandwiches can be made on it all at the same time.

The griddle, like the deepfryer, is not equipment for quality work. It has its place when quantity and speed production are important. Griddle cookery, like deep frying, has been abused by unskilled and untrained workers. The quality conscious cook can easily use a griddle with satisfying results if he keeps it clean.

### SAFETY HAZARDS OF COOKING IN FAT METHODS

Fats when overheated burn and become combustible. An electric deep fryer will explode into flames if it is overheated. Obviously, fat fires are dangerous and difficult to bring under control even with a $CO_2$ fire extinguisher. Pan frying on the open range has dangers, too. Overflowing fat is apt to catch fire and the confusion following such an incident multiplies the dangers. The only true prevention of an accidental and serious fire is common sense and maturity on the part of the cook. (See tables 8-1 and 8-2.)

### SUMMARY

Cooking in fat, or frying, is one of the five basic cooking methods. It includes sautéing and deep fat frying. In sautéing, a small quantity of good fat is mixed into the dish. In deep fat frying, the food is separated from the larger amount of fat after cooking.

Deep frying today is mostly done in commercial deep fryers. Deep fried food must be at least half submerged in the frying fat. Nutritionists consider deep frying undesirable, but fast food operators enjoy the profit-making characteristics of the process. Not all deep fried food is bad. The commercial deep fryer allows for considerable abuse, and too few conscientious chefs are trying to avoid these abuses. The frying and sautéing processes can be applied to all foods that are tender and need only a short cooking time. Deep fried foods have to be coated first. One of the more popular methods of coating is called breading. Sautéing

| *PAN FRYING* | *DEEP FRYING* |
|---|---|
| Using a skillet or pan on the top of the range with enough fat to float the foods to be cooked. | Using a piece of equipment consisting of a kettle with drain valve, heating elements, fry basket, and control panel. |
| *SAFETY RULES* | Most fryers have electric elements, but a few are still gas fired. |
| Do not fill skillet more than half with fat. Keep skillet in a safe position on the range. Do not leave skillet on fire unattended. | *SAFETY RULES* |
| | Do not leave control knobs over 325°F. when fryer is unattended. |
| Do not put wet foods into hot fats. Fat will foam, spill and catch fire. Do not overheat fat. | Do not depend on automatic features alone; they may misfunction. |
| Do not start frying until all necessary utensils like skimmer, carrier for finished food, etc. are on hand. | Do not put too much food into basket at one time. |
| | Do not put wet food into basket at any time. |
| Overheated fat can be cooled off by adding more cold fat. | DANGER MOMENTS AT THE FRYER ARE NOT WHILE FRYING, BUT WHEN FILTERING OR CHANGING FAT. |
| | Before draining kettle, make certain all controls are off. Do not turn heat on unless elements are completely covered with fat. |
| | Automatic deep fryers are set to work with a full kettle of frying fat. Make certain fat is filled to the proper level to prevent overheating. |

**TABLE 8-1  SAFETY PRECAUTIONS FOR PAN FRYING AND DEEP FRYING**

(flip frying) is one of the finest cooking methods the skilled cook has at his disposal. Sautéing preserves the taste and texture quality of freshly browned meat (like steak) and adds the quality of a separately made sauce. Sauté cooking is done mostly for "gourmet cooking" and in Chinese cuisine and accounts for the freshness, taste, and nutritional values these cuisines have to offer.

A griddle can be considered a large stationary skillet, used for frying foods in a small quantity of fat, similar to broiling. To the quality-concerned chef, griddling of food is not as good as broiling or sautéing. As a fast all around method, griddling is useful to the breakfast and short order cooks. Cooking in fat has many safety hazards. All students and cooks must be completely familiar with the handling of equipment and precautions which have to be observed.

Have a tight fitting heavy cover for the skillet; in case fat catches fire, cover the burning skillet tightly. This method will shut off the oxygen supply to the fire and suffocate it immediately. It is the best way to extinguish small grease fires in a skillet.

This method is also used when a sauté pan catches fire during flip frying over the open flames.

*IN THE CASE OF SPILLED FAT BURNING ON THE RANGE TOP*

A. Shut off exhaust fan to prevent exhaust catching fire.

B. Shut off all gas burners which still feed the flames.

C. Suffocate flames with salt, baking soda, old rags or sand when available. Do not use water as it will spread the flames more. Do not use sugar or flour. Carbohydrates burn.

FAMILIARIZE YOURSELF WITH THE EMERGENCY REGULATIONS OF THE ESTABLISHMENT. KEEP CALM. DO NOT PANIC. *NEVER START YOUR WORKING SHIFT* WITHOUT CHECKING TO SEE THAT THE $CO_2$ EXTINGUISHER OF YOUR STATION IS IN REACH AND USABLE.

**TABLE 8-2  PAN FRYING**

## DISCUSSION TOPICS

1. What are the advantages of pan frying?
2. How bad, nutritionally, is deep fried food?
3. What is considered a fast food operation?
4. What are the characteristics of a sauté?
5. What are the differences in griddle, grill, and broiler?
6. How do the safety aspects of a grill compare to that of a broiler?

## SUGGESTED ACTIVITIES

1. Demonstrate flipping and pan frying on suitable pans and skillets.
2. Demonstrate the handling of the deep fryer including filtering and changing of fat.
3. Demonstrate the safety features of the modern deep fryer.
4. Demonstrate flipping of food in a skillet, using the proper skillet and raw beans or other suitable materials.
5. Have a fire drill.
6. Demonstrate the use of the griddle and its cleaning procedure by using the grill stone.

## ACHIEVEMENT REVIEW

A. Complete the following:

1. In deep frying, the food is separated from the frying fat after the cooking, but in sautéing the fat is _____ .
2. Originally deep frying was done in pans on top of the _____ .
3. Increased coffee shop business developed the use of the griddle instead of the
   _____ .
4. Foods usable for one of the cooking in fat method variations must be
   _____ .
5. In a commercial deep fryer, fat is reheated and reused many _____ .
6. Coating improves the deep frying of foods with the exception of various types of _____ .
7. Fast food service establishments work mostly with griddle and _____ .
8. Nutritionists believe that the best diet is not _____ .
9. Modern deep fryers have pop-up devices which are controlled by _____ .
10. Sautéing, unlike deep frying, falls into the working performance of the skilled
    _____ .
11. "Beef Stroganoff", made correctly, belongs to the group of preparations made by the method of _____ .
12. An electric deep fryer with faulty controls could overheat and burst into
    _____ .

B. Read each question carefully and completely before answering it. Select the *best* answer.

1. Restaurants using commercial deep fryers almost exclusively are called:

   a. commercial kitchens     c. coffee shops
   b. fast food operations     d. seafood restaurants

2.  The term pan frying implies that food is

    a. cooked in a commercial deep fryer
    b. floating in fat while frying
    c. coated with a batter before being fried
    d. sautéed in butter or olive oil

3.  The making of cottage fried potatoes can be analyzed as follows:

    a. raw potatoes peeled, sliced, deep fried
    b. raw potatoes peeled, sliced, sautéed, half the time covered
    c. boiled potatoes peeled, sliced and sautéed
    d. boiled potatoes, peeled, sliced and deep fried

4.  Foods to be sautéed should be first

    a. cut into a uniform size
    b. washed well before cooking
    c. dipped into a batter
    d. breaded like a veal cutlet

5.  Deep fried foods are coated for all the listed reasons except one:

    a. for a better browned crust
    b. for retaining more meat flavor and juices
    c. for protecting the frying fat
    d. for quicker frying

6.  Fat, in a deep fryer controlled by a thermostat, which has been heated over and over again

    a. stays constantly fresh
    b. keeps fried foods especially crisp
    c. develops an off flavor
    d. will never taste burned

7.  Sauté cooking is the most used method in

    a. Italian cookery        c. Southern type cookery
    b. American cookery     d. Chinese cookery

8.  A griddle in a coffee shop is ideal for the making of

    a. home fried potatoes     c. breakfast steaks
    b. hotcakes                  d. Beef Stroganoff

9.  How safe an electric deep fryer is depends on

    a. the thermostatic controls
    b. the presence of a $CO_2$ fire extinguisher
    c. the maturity and common sense of the attendant
    d. the quantity of fat used

10.  Nutritionists say that deep fried foods are not as healthy as broiled foods because

    a. deep fried food is not cooked long enough
    b. deep frying destroys more vitamins
    c. deep fried food absorbs too much burned fat
    d. deep fried food does not provide enough calories

C.    Answer in your own words:

1.    Explain the difference between pan frying and sautéing.

2.    Describe the difference between pan frying and deep frying.

3.    Identify the three different coatings for frying food.

4.    Explain why a "Beef Stroganoff" is called a sauté dish.

# Unit 9 Caramelizing and Tenderizing Combined

*OBJECTIVES*

After studying this unit, the student should be able to

- Explain the reasons for using the combination method of cooking.
- Define the differences in the terms stewing, braising and pot-roasting.
- Explain the basic procedures of the combination method.
- Identify the most practical meat cuts for the combination method.
- Describe the similarity of cooking for all terms in use.

Caramelizing and tenderizing combined is the fourth of the basic cooking methods which are listed in unit 1. The combination method, as it is called, makes tough meats digestible and tasty. The moist heat method is applied for tenderization. At the same time caramelization is added to give the meat a more acceptable taste.

## DEFINITION OF OLD TERMS

Stewing, braising, and pot-roasting are the three ordinary terms used to describe the combination method. Different terms are used in order to distinguish between the sizes of meat pieces used in this combination method.

*Stewing.* Stewing means the slow cooking together of foods in a closed pot. A little juice and fat are used, which creates a sauce. For stews, pieces of meat are cut so small that several pieces together are needed to make one portion. The term "stew" always implies cut-up pieces of mixed food like meat or poultry as well as some fish and vegetables.

*Braising.* Braising describes exactly the same cooking process as stewing. For braising, food is cut in a single portion size. There are braised steaks, pork chops, or short ribs, but not stewed ones. Braising comes from the French work "braiser", meaning the same as stewing. It is used on English language menus to avoid the implied meaning of the word 'stew'. In some restaurants, "Braised Beef" could mean any piece of beef cooked by the combination method.

*Pot-Roasting.* Pot-roasting also describes the stewing process. A large piece of meat with many portions in it is cooked the same way. By saying 'roasted in the pot', it is implied that large pieces of meat have been stewed.

*Fricasseeing.* Fricasseeing is a French term which implies that the same combination method has been used on cut-up portion-size white meat. Only a veal fricassee, a chicken fricassee or a turkey breast fricassee exist. This term is never used with beef, lamb, or venison. In restaurants with French influences, a chicken stew is likely to be called a chicken fricassee.

## MODERN TERMS

A beef carcass does not consist of fillet and sirloin exclusively. Secondary meat cuts are offered to the customers in a variety of forms. In America, different terms are used to avoid the word 'stew', which unfortunately sounds cheap to a lot of customers. Potted steak, Casserole of Beef, Swiss Steak, Sauerbraten, and Burgundy Beef, are some of the terms better accepted. They are in addition to stew, pot roast, and braised meat.

## BASIC PROCEDURES

As stated in unit 1, the combination method of cooking uses three other methods of cooking. For example, a pot roast is started by the dry heat cooking method. When the meat is browned, stock or water, herbs, spices, and browned, flavor-giving vegetables are added. The container is then covered and simmered slowly on top of the range (i.e., roasted in the pot) or remains in the oven at a low temperature, covered or uncovered, until done.

Braised steaks are pan-browned or griddle-browned, transferred to a suitable container and then finished the same way as the pot roast. Meat stews are started like sautes but after the liquid has been added, they are simmered continuously until the meat is tender. A "stew", made of white meat and vegetables, without tomatoes, in a white sauce, is called fricassee.

## SELECTION OF MEAT CUTS

Progress in meat breeding has resulted in more tender meats. Pork, veal, lamb, poultry, and fish do not need the combination method to become tender. If a lamb, chicken or veal stew is made, it is done by preference or ignorance. Preference may be from habit, but it is ignorance when the difference between a saute and a stew is not known. Moisture is needed to tenderize many cuts of beef. These come from the chuck or shoulder and the rump. Chuck meat, which has to be well trimmed in order to make it free of gristle and sinews, is commonly used for stews. Rump meat from the outside or bottom round and the knuckle are used for Swiss steaks and pot roasts. (Meat or butcher terminology is explained in section 3, unit 11.) When selecting meat cuts, it must be remembered that *all* meat cuts could be used for the combination method. Choice becomes a matter of price, labor needed to trim, habit, and personal preference.

### Differences and Similarities

The main difference is the size of the pieces into which meat is cut up. A bottom round can be cut as a stew, a steak, or be left whole as a pot roast. The cooking is done by the same method, the same garnish of green peas, carrots, cauliflower, brussel sprouts, and mushrooms is added to the sauce. The same spices and herbs are used. Another difference is the cooking time. Stew and steak will cook faster (smaller cut, faster heat penetration) than the roast. When served, the three dishes will be named Beefstew Jardinier, Braised Steak Jardinier, and Potroast Jardinier. In the last instance the dish might be called Beef Jardinier. Jardinier is the French word for gardener and the reference is to the added garnish of fresh vegetables, supplied by the gardener. For lamb stew jardinier, lamb replaces the beef, and for Chicken Fricassee Jardinier tomatoes are avoided in order to keep the ivory color of the sauce.

## CONCLUSION AND NEEDS

Combination cooking developed as an improvement of boiling which had been necessary to make tough meats edible. Its use today and for the future becomes less and less necessary. Overall meat quality has improved and continues to do so. The combination process is used for tender meats by habit and preference only. For example, it is more economical and tastier to sauté chickens and finish them with a garnish and premade sauce than to make chicken stew in advance. The stew may have to be kept warm for hours (thereby reducing its quality) and there may be a large quantity of wasted leftovers. With food prices constantly on the rise, food costs are more important than ever.

Since few cuts in each beef carcass are suitable for roasting, true roasts are highly priced. Carcasses contain more pounds of the cheaper cuts, such as beef roast, chuck roast, cross rib roast, and rump roast. The combination method is the only way to prepare tough but tasty and nourishing beef cuts. Section 3, unit 11 explains the differences between various meat cuts. On many menus, pot roast is called beef roast. This distinguishes it from "roast beef", in which the emphasis is on roasting, the dry heat cooking method. "Beef roast" implies that a quantity of beef meat has been cooked in one piece before being carved and served.

The terminology used at present differentiates between sizes of various meat cuts, colors of the sauce, and ways of serving. A stew, served in the same container in which it was cooked, becomes a casserole. A braised steak, cooked and served in a fireproof china casserole with a cover, is called a potted steak. Americans are more steak and roast conscious than most other nations. Stewed meat does not have great appeal to the majority of restaurant patrons, and fancy terminology is used to avoid any thought of a stew.

## SUMMARY

Caramelizing and tenderizing combined is called the combination method. Other well known terms are stewing, braising, and pot-roasting. Presently each of these terms implies a limited application, referring to the size of the meat pieces and the looks of the dish instead of the preparation method. Students and young cooks should remember that all these terms describe the same working procedure. All these various names have developed through time and the mixing of different cultures. All basic cooking procedures of the combination method are the same, regardless of names and ingredients used. The student who has learned to master the basic technique of making a good stew, can apply the same technique to all the preparations listed in section 4, units 22, 23, 24, and 25.

The combination method pre-browns food, preserves the drippings and adds vegetables, spices, and liquid. This mixture is simmered slowly together until tender, creating its own sauce while cooking. Only tough foods *have* to be braised for tenderization. Tender foods are sometimes braised by habit and taste preference. Dinner houses with large menus are economically better off if they prepare chicken sauté instead of a chicken stew.

## DISCUSSION TOPICS

1. Is a stew by any other name also a stew?
2. What are the similarities and advantages of stews and sautes?
3. What are the differences between Roast Beef and Beef Roast?
4. Why are stews not preferred in restaurants?
5. Are there economic differences between broiled steaks and Swiss steaks? If so, what are they?

## ACHIEVEMENT REVIEW

A. Complete the following:

1. The combination method uses moist heat to tenderize and adds flavor by _____ .

2. True roast cuts from beef are used for steaks and roasts, secondary beef cuts are used for _____ .

3. The difference between Burgundy Beefstew and Burgundy Pot Roast is in the _____ .

4. Most people believe stew is meat that has been _____ .

5. Meat stews are started like sautés, but finished by _____ .

6. Pot roasts must simmer a long time to become tender but first they have to be _____ .

7. Combination cooking or braising has emerged as an improvement of _____ .

8. The combination method is not only used by economic necessity, but also by habit and _____ .

9. Chicken fricassee is a stew where tomatoes have been _____ :

10. Many people like stews at home, but in restaurants they prefer steaks and _____ .

B. Read each question carefully and completely before answering it. Select the *best* answer.

1. Which of the following preparations is not a pot roast?

   a. Sauerbraten        c. Beef Stroganoff
   b. Beef Jardinier     d. Burgundy Beef Roast

2. Which one of these steaks is served without sauce?

   a. Potted Steak       c. Braised Steak
   b. Broiled Steak      d. Swiss Steak

3. To be used in a beef stew, chuck meat has to be

   a. well trimmed      c. spiced
   b. cooked             d. tenderized

4. Pot-roasting implies a large piece of meat, browned first and finished by

   a. roasting in the oven
   b. griddling until tender
   c. boiling in the soup pot
   d. simmering in a little juice

5. The cooking time for Swiss Steak is

   a. shorter than for beef stew
   b. the same as for beef stew
   c. the same as for pot roast
   d. longer than for pot roast

6. Which of the following types of meat is suitable for fricasseeing?

   a. Veal      c. Lamb
   b. Venison    d. Beef

7. For a chicken fricassee Jardinier which of the following ingredients has to be omitted ?

   a. Green peas      c. Tomatoes
   b. Carrots         d. Mushrooms

8. Meat for a lamb stew has to be cut to such a size that one order consists of

   a. one slice      c. two pieces
   b. two slices     d. four to six pieces

C. Match the terms listed in Column I with the best corresponding terms of Column II.

| *Column I* | *Column II* |
|---|---|
| Braising | 1. Trimmed Chuck |
| Swiss Steak | 2. True Roast |
| Pot Roast | 3. Veal stew with no tomatoes |
| Beef Casserole | 4. Veal stew with tomatoes & vegetables |
| Beef Roast | 5. Stewing |
| Red Wine Beef Stew | 6. Sauerbraten |
| Veal Fricassee | 7. Potted Steak |
| Stew meat | 8. Bottom Round |
| Veal Stew Jardinier | 9. Pot Roast |
| Raw pot roast | 10. Secondary cut |
| Beef fillet | 11. Burgundy Beef Stew |
| Chuck Roast | 12. Beef stew |

D. Answer in your own words.

1. Explain the basic procedures of the combination method of cooking.

2. Define the differences between stewing, braising, and pot-roasting.

3. Identify the most practical meat cuts for the combination method of cooking.

# Unit 10  The Extraction of Liquefiable Foods

*OBJECTIVES*

After studying this unit, the student should be able to

- Explain flavor extraction.
- Define Broth and Stock.
- Identify different stocks.
- Explain the need for roux.
- List four groups of soups.
- Explain the making of cream soups.

The fifth and most demanding cooking process is the extraction of liquefiable foods. Listed in unit 1, this is commonly known as the making of stocks, soups, gravies, and sauces.

## INFUSION AND EXTRACTION

Tea leaves brewed with boiling water become an infusion. The liquid tea has been extracted. The leached out leaves became valueless. Soluble solids can be taken from most foods in a similar way.

Cold water poured over food and brought slowly to simmering extracts more nutrients and flavors than does boiling water when poured over food. When one is cooking for flavor extraction, food is started with cold water, but for the retaining of flavor in boiled foods, hot boiling water is used to start the simmering.

## BROTH, THE BY-PRODUCT OF SIMMERING

To boil a chicken, it is covered with boiling water. Salt, herbs, spices and vegetables are added and it is kept simmering until tender. By osmosis (equalization properties of the water), flavor from vegetables, herbs, and spices is transferred to the chicken and vice versa. At the end of the cooking, all flavors are mixed together. Some flavors stay in the chicken, some are in the vegetables and the rest are in the liquid. Nutrients, such as proteins, vitamins, and minerals are also present in the chicken, vegetables, and liquid. The chicken has lost some of its food value, but the cooking water has gained much food value. It has become a broth. After the tender chicken is removed from this broth, then the broth is strained, defatted and used for the intended purpose. Depending on the ratio of water to chicken and vegetables used, the broth could be weak, normal or very strong. Other broths such as beef, fish, or vegetable, are made in exactly the same way.

## STOCK, THE USE OF TRIMMINGS

Stock is an extraction similar to broth. Instead of using valuable raw chicken, the leftover raw chicken bones, skin and giblets are used. The same process, with the same vegetables, spices, and herbs is used. After starting in cold water, the bones and trimmings are simmered from 2 to 8 hours, depending on the bones used. When it seems that all the flavor has been extracted from the bones, the liquid is called stock. The stock is handled like broth. The names of the bones used give the name of the stock yielded. For example, chicken bones yield chicken stock, beef bones yield beef stock, fish bones yield fish stock (also called court-bouillon) and so on. The ratio of bones and trimmings to the water, the additional vegetables, herbs, and spices, and the length of simmering are the factors responsible for taste and strength of the stock.

### Different Basic Stocks

The bigger a kitchen, the greater is the variety of stocks which could be made. Depending on the needs of the menu, chicken stock, white meat stock (mixed), brown meat stock, and sometimes even fish stock are available. All stocks except brown stock, are simmered from raw bones. Brown stock gets its color from

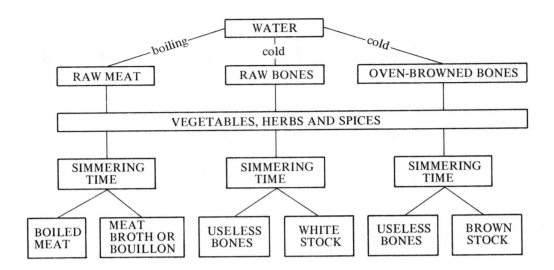

**TABLE 10-1 BROTH AND STOCK FLOW CHART**

the pre-roasting of bones which are then simmered. Tomatoes may also be added. General meat stocks are usually mixed. Beef, veal, pork, and poultry bones are used together. Lamb has too strong a flavor to be used in this way. Fish stock is made mostly in fish restaurants, but many general food establishments make it once in a while.

### Usage of Stock

Escoffier, the famous classical chef of modern times, insisted that the quality of all cooking depended on the quality of the stocks made. This is only partially true because today's cooking trends are toward a sauce-less cookery. Freshly cooked vegetables and tender fast-cooked meats need less of the flavor addition which a good sauce gives to many dishes. Brown meat stock is used to make basic brown sauce which is called Espagnol. It is also used to make pan gravy, which is called "jus de viande", and the meat glaze called "glace de viande".

White stock is used for most soups and for the ivory colored basic white sauce, called veloute. When meat and poultry bones are not mixed, chicken veloute, veal veloute, and others can be made and used for special purposes. Fish stock is white and is used for a basic fish sauce called fish veloute, as well as for the making of seafood dishes and soups.

## CHANGING STOCK TO SAUCE

Making a perfect sauce was considered by many people as the most difficult of all the cooking procedures. Today, culinary technology has analyzed what makes a sauce and most difficulties disappeared. Sauces based on starch are made from water with a flavor (called stock), a thickener made of starch (flour), and fat. The quality of a sauce is judged by flavor, texture, and color. These are value judgments. Flavor depends on the quality of the stock, flour, and fat used. Texture depends on the ratio of starch to fat and liquid. Color depends on the ingredients and their handling.

Starches most often used are all-purpose flour and cornstarch. Some chefs use potato, rice, or arrowroot flour as the starch. For quality cookery, all-purpose flour is mixed with fat, heated, and fried lightly. This mixture, called *roux,* is added to the stock and simmered for a short while. This procedure changes stock to a sauce.

**Fig. 10-1 Heavy-duty stockpot with faucet.**

Other cooking styles do not mix fat and flour into a roux. Starch, which has been stirred into some cold water, is added to the simmering stock. In this procedure the sauce has a different texture and taste.

### The Use of Roux

Roux is an essential ingredient to French-Continental cookery. Roux is used directly and indirectly for nearly everything that French-Continental Cuisine produces.

Roux is made from any *good* fat (as in sauteing), and the approximate equal weight of flour. Frying over low heat or in the oven is done in three stages. These are white, golden, or brown, depending on the color of the sauce wanted. Roux can be made once a day or once a week. It keeps for a long time if kept under proper refrigeration and if the correct fat is used. The ratio of roux to liquid governs the texture of the sauce. Roux is also used for soups, gravies, and all the dishes made by the combination method.

### PAN GRAVIES OR "JUS"

Gravies should be pan gravies or be called sauces. Gravy means a thinly textured liquid substance with a strong flavor of roasted meat. Gravy, the by-product of a roast, is made of coagulated meat juices (blood) diluted with a little brown stock and then thickened with a small

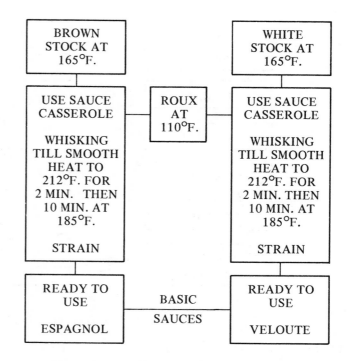

**TABLE 10-2 CHANGING STOCK TO SAUCES WITH ROUX**

**Fig. 10-2 Light sauté pan to make roux**

amount of cornstarch. Gravy must be much thinner than a sauce. Gravies and sauces, often made from the same ingredients, are as different from each other as "Cottage Fried Potatoes" are from "Potato Chips" (see section 2, unit 8 - Sautéing). Gravy is equal to the French "Jus de Viande", called "jus" for short. Restaurants specializing in roast prime ribs of beef often use the French term instead of the misused word gravy and mark their menus "Roast Prime Rib of Beef au Jus". The other characteristic of good pan gravy is that after setting for a short time, fat drippings and meat juices separate like a salad dressing.

### SOUPS

Soups are extracted or dissolved nutrients from meat, fish, and vegetables. These are made into a liquid food dish which is eaten with a spoon. The liquid for making them may be water, stock or milk. There are clear soups, thickened soups, puree soups and speciality soups.

*Clear Soups Made From Broth*. Strained chicken or beef broth is called bouillon. When served in a bouillon cup without any garnish it is called "Bouillon en tasse". When cooked rice and chopped chicken meat are

$$\frac{1 \text{ CUP FAT}}{\text{HEAT } 160°F.} + \frac{1½ \text{ CUPS FLOUR}}{\text{HEAT } 160°F.} + \frac{\text{WHISKING STIR}}{\text{HEAT } 195°F.} \times \frac{5 \text{ MIN.}}{\text{HEAT } 210°F.} \div \frac{\text{OFF}}{\text{HEAT } 75°F.} = \frac{\text{ROUX}}{110°F.}$$

**TABLE 10-3 ROUX-MAKING CHART**

| | | | |
|---|---|---|---|
| BROTH | IN CUP | = | BOUILLON EN TASSE |
| STRAINED | FINE NOODLES | = | VERMICELLI SOUP |
| BOUILLON | WIDE NOODLE + CHICKEN MEAT | = | CHICKEN NOODLE SOUP |
| MORE BEEF MORE SIMMERING EGG WHITES | RICE + CHOPPED CHICKEN | = | OLD FASHIONED CHICKEN BROTH |
| CLARIFICATION FILTERING | FINE NOODLES | = | CONSOMMÉ VERMICELLI |
| | IN CUP | = | CONSOMMÉ EN TASSE BEEF TEA |

**TABLE 10-4  FLOW CHART OF CLEAR SOUPS**

added, it becomes "Old-fashioned chicken broth". Bouillon served with fine noodles is called vermicelli soup. With wider noodles it is called beef or chicken noodle soup. A tasty bouillon is appetizing when served at the beginning of a meal and it can be varied with a great number of garnishes. In the past, bouillon and consommé were considered important because they brought important meat proteins to old people who had lost their teeth.

*Consommé and its Clarification.*  Consommé, a tasty soup essence, is made by simmering lean beef meat and vegetables with herbs and spices in already made bouillon. The bouillon thus becomes doubly strong. In England, this soup is called Beef tea. While a consommé simmers, it clarifies itself. Raw egg whites are added to the still cold bouillon to aid in clarification. When heated to the simmering point, the egg whites coagulate (gather together) and attract additional protein impurities from the bouillon. The egg white and the impurities float as foam to the top of the consommé and are removed after simmering. Consommé is served in the same manner as bouillon.

*Soups Made With Roux.*  Soups thickened with roux are made of meat, fish, and vegetable stock, with an optional garnish. For texture improvement, rich cream can be added. A thickened chicken soup which has been improved with cream is called "Cream of Chicken Soup". It is made the same way a chicken veloute sauce is made, and the cream is added just before serving. The difference between chicken sauce and chicken soup is in the texture. The soup should be thinner than the sauce.

Soups thickened with roux are made from protein food and vegetables combined. Roux is added to soup in the same manner as it is to a sauce. Garnish and cream are optional.

*Pureed Soups.*  Purees can be made from most food substances. Meat puree and vegetable puree are very common. Fish puree is sometimes made for special preparations. Puree soups contain a high percentage of food pulp which is used to bring out the flavor and provide texture in place of the roux. Some starchy vegetables change to puree easily. These include potatoes, split peas, lentils, beans, and some fresh vegetables such as cauliflower, spinach, and tomatoes. A chicken puree soup, called "Potage a la Reine" is made with white chicken meat puree, some roux, and some cream. Puree soups made of starchy vegetables rarely need additional roux, if the vegetable pulp is sufficient. Puree soups, like

Fig. 10-3 Heavy-duty soup or stockpot

other soups, are mixtures of meat and vegetable stocks. Sometimes they have a garnish, and the addition of cream is optional. Popular puree soups are made from green or yellow split peas, such as the green "Potage St. Germain" from France, the yellow "Habitant Pea Soup" from Canada's Quebec and the various pea soups made with ham, bacon, and sausages from continental Europe.

*Speciality Soups.* These are substantial soups which originated from soupy kettle stews. Today they are used as lunch dishes, and in the wintry East, special soup restaurants sell them over the counter at lunch time. These soups are full of calories and a bowl is a meal in itself. Speciality soups come from many parts of the world.

Speciality soups may be made from a semi-clear liquid, or from one thickened with puree or roux. They have a rich starch or protein garnish to provide the necessary filling. Although they come from different cultures, their preparation procedures are as simple as any other soup.

The USA has produced the Boston Clam Chowder, the Philadelphia Pepperpot, and the Louisiana Chicken Gumbo. Some European speciality soups are Marmite (France), Minestrone (Italy), Gazpacho (Spain), and Borscht (Russia). When speciality soups representing different regions are prepared, the young cook should be sure that the soup retains as much of its national or regional character as possible.

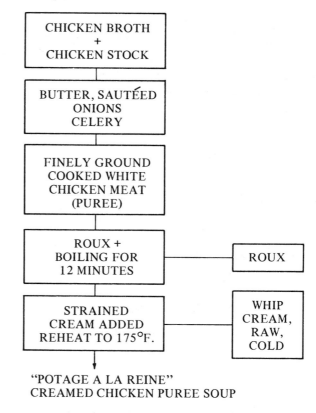

"POTAGE A LA REINE"
CREAMED CHICKEN PUREE SOUP

**TABLE 10-5 POTAGE A LA REINE, A DELUXE SOUP**

## COOKING TECHNIQUES FOR LIQUIDS

Escoffier's dictum that the quality of cooking depends on the quality of the stock made, is very important for the soup and sauce cook. Section 1, unit 2 explained the importance of the second cook, or the saucier, whose job it is to prepare liquid food. Culinary technology has found ways to simplify many procedures. The "key points" listed here will help the student to make excellent soups and sauces in a short time.

---

**ATTENTION: KEY POINTS FOR WORKING WITH STOCK**

- Trimmings, bones, and vegetables must be fresh and clean.
- Use enough bones, meat, and vegetables to have the correct water-food ratio.
- Cold water extracts better than hot water.
- The slower and longer the simmering, the better the broth.
- Liquids must be kept refrigerated in non-oxidizing containers.
- Stored liquids must be rotated.

---

**ATTENTION: KEY POINTS FOR WORKING WITH ROUX**

1. Roux should be added to liquid for better texture control.
2. For mixing, the roux should be lukewarm and the liquid should be about 170°F.
3. A whisk should be used to work roux into liquid.
4. The sauce casserole used is very important; it must be low, wide, made of a heavy gauge material and not warped.
5. The approximate ratio of roux to liquid for sauces is 1½ to 2 cups of well fried roux to one gallon of liquid.
6. Sauce must come to a rolling full boil and then continue to bubble for 10-15 minutes.
7. When sauces become too thick, they should be diluted with stock.
8. For keeping sauces hot, uncovered, a buttered paper on the sauce's surface will avoid a dried out skim.
9. There is no substitute for fresh whipping cream.
10. Garnishes for soups and sauces are better when sauteed in butter first.

## SUMMARY

Sauce and soup cookery is a more demanding skill than some of the other cooking techniques. The base of all sauces, gravies, and soups is stock and broth. Stock is an extraction from meat bones and trimmings. Broth is the by-product of simmering food for consumption. Cold liquid has more dissolving ability than hot liquid. When several foods simmer together in broth, osmosis and water equalization properties interchange flavors from one food to the other. Lamb bones which have a strong flavor must be kept separate when stock or broth is made.

The most used basic white sauce is called veloute. The most used brown sauce is called espagnole. French-Continental cuisine uses roux, an equal weight mixture of fat and flour fried over low heat, to thicken cooking liquids. The making of roux and sauce demands exactness of work and some artistic touch, since the quality of sauce is a value judgement.

Popular soups from all over the world have been interchanged from country to country. Speciality soups have colorful names and remind patrons of faraway places. Cooking techniques for extracting liquid foods have been analyzed and improved by culinary technology to such an extent that soup, sauce, and liquid food cookery is no longer really difficult.

## DISCUSSION TOPICS

1. Is Escoffier's dictum, that the quality of cooking depends on the quality of the stocks made, still true today?
2. What is the difference in sauces made with roux and sauces made with the starch-water mixture?
3. What might be the difference between kitchen-made stock as compared to convenience stock base?
4. What is the importance of pan gravy?
5. What is the importance of soups and what is their historical role?

## SUGGESTED ACTIVITIES

A. Perform the following:

Infusion - Extraction comparison

- Soak 1 teaspoon of tea leaves in one cup of cold water overnight.
- Brew one cup of tea with one teaspoon of leaves, cool it off.

Compare the results

B. Perform the following:

1. Make a roux of 2 tablespoons of oil and 3 tablespoons of flour and fry on lowest heat until roux bubbles.
2. Take it off the heat and cool for 5 to 10 minutes.
3. Add 2¼ cups of hot water, approx. 165°F., whisk it smooth and bring mixture to a boil.
4. Wait for a rolling boil, keep whisking, reduce heat to bubbling and continue for 10 more minutes.
5. Take mixture off the burner, strain through a tea sieve, check for lumps. Examine this tasteless water sauce for texture smoothness, flow, and looks.

## ACHIEVEMENT REVIEW

A. Complete the following:

1. Broth, as the by-product of food simmered for eating, should be started with water that is _____ .

2. Meat stock, which is extracted food from bones into water, should be started with water that is _____ .

3. A chicken simmered in water loses more food values than a chicken roasted in the oven. The missing nutrients are found in the _____ .

4. To make a mixed meat stock, all conventionally used bones are used with the exception of _____ .

5. For brown stock and sauce, meat bones have to be _____ .

6. Stocks or other liquids are changed to sauces through the addition of _____ .

7. The quality of a sauce is judged by its flavor, color and _____ .

8. Properly made roux is heated and fried _____ .

9. Making sauces with roux is the style of the _____ cuisine.

10. The important part of making pan gravy is the inclusion of _____ .

11. Soups are a form of liquid food, because nutrients from meat, fish, and vegetables have been _____ .

12. A tasty strained chicken broth when garnished with fine noodles is called _____ .

13. The additional ingredient which helps to clarify consomme is _____ .

14. Consommé, which is a strong, deeply colored clear meat broth, is appropriately called _____ .

15. It is believed that speciality soups have originated from soupy _____ .

B. Read each question carefully and completely before answering it. Select the *best* answer.

1. Stock or broth, regardless of how it was started, should continuously
   a. boil for several hours
   b. steep for several hours
   c. simmer for several hours
   d. steam for several hours

2. Common sense should indicate that bones used for stock making should be
   a. cut as small as possible
   b. cut as large as possible
   c. split lengthwise only
   d. left as they are

3. Not all raw foods can be used to extract flavor. From the ones listed, which is the most *un*likely to be used?
   a. Ham
   b. Eggs
   c. Bacon
   d. Potatoes

4. French-Continental cooking thickens most of its sauces with a mixture of
   a. rice starch and water
   b. potato flour and cream
   c. all purpose flour and fat
   d. cake flour and milk

5. Roux is used to thicken many food preparations, but not
   a. tomato sauce
   b. beef stew
   c. cream soup
   d. liver sauté

6. Roux is a mixture of measured fat and flour in the following proportions:
   a. 1 cup fat + 1 cup flour (volume)
   b. 1 cup fat + 2 cups flour (volume)
   c. 8 oz. fat + 12 oz. flour (weight)
   d. 8 oz. fat + 8 oz. flour (weight)

7. The clear meat soup with the greatest amount of meat extract in it is called
   a. Beef Tea　　　　　　　　c. Beef Broth
   b. Beef Bouillon　　　　　　d. Vermicelli Soup

8. To make consommé, bouillon is not only clarified by egg whites but also flavor improved with
   a. more vegetables　　　　　c. tomato puree
   b. additional meat　　　　　d. more spices

9. Chicken cream soup is made of chicken stock, roux and
   a. Whipping cream　　　　　c. Chicken giblets
   b. Chicken meat puree　　　　d. Rice or Noodles

10. Puree soups made from starchy vegetables like split peas or dried legumes are not made with
    a. strong meat stock　　　　c. roux or cornstarch
    b. vegetable and meat garnish　d. herbs and spices

11. All of the listed regional speciality soups are American except
    a. Clam Chowder　　　　　　c. Pepperpot
    b. Minestrone　　　　　　　d. Chicken Gumbo

12. Speciality, puree, and thickened soups have substantial food value and by comparison to sauces should be
    a. heavier　　　　　　　　　c. spicier
    b. richer　　　　　　　　　　d. thinner

C. Match the speciality soups of Column I with the geographic areas of Column II.

| *Column I* | *Column II* |
|---|---|
| Minestrone | 1. Boston |
| Pepperpot | 2. Canada |
| Borscht | 3. Spain |
| Potage St. Germain | 4. Louisiana |
| Clam Chowder | 5. Philadelphia |
| Gazpacho | 6. Italy |
| Chicken Gumbo | 7. Russia |
| Habitant Pea Soup | 8. France |

D. Match the food terminology of Column I with the English names of Column II.

| *Column I* | *Column II* |
|---|---|
| Espagnol | 1. Meat extract |
| Bouillon | 2. Fine noodle soup |
| Jus de Viande | 3. Chicken essence |
| Veloute | 4. Fish stock |
| Court Bouillon | 5. Brown sauce |
| Beef Tea | 6. Strained broth |
| Potage a la Reine | 7. Pan Gravy |
| Glace de Viande | 8. White meat sauce |
| Chicken Consomme | 9. Chicken puree soup |
| Vermicelli soup | 10. Beef essence |

E. Answer in your own words:
   1. Describe roux and its use.
   2. List the four groups of soups.
   3. Describe how cream soups are made.

# Section 3 Handling of Foods Before Cooking

## Unit 11 Meat and Poultry Supplies

### OBJECTIVES

After studying this unit, the student should be able to

- Explain the chef's need for butcher knowledge.
- Describe the change of quality control.
- Identify the reason for meat inspection.
- List the first five meat grades.
- Explain the need for portion control.
- Compare meat cuts to cooking methods.
- Discuss different phases of portion control.

### MEAT AND POULTRY SUPPLIES

Meat and poultry, the most expensive food materials used in food service operations, are supplied by *purveyors.* They are specialists in the semiwholesale jobbing of meat and poultry to hotels, restaurants, and institutions. Purveyors handle everything from meat on the carcass to frozen steaks and from smoked meats to precooked hamburgers. Most meat and poultry items today are available in convenient forms, such as portion-controlled, processed, semicooked, or frozen. Food service operators can choose to handle fresh meats or to buy all their needs processed and frozen or precooked.

### THE CHEF-BUTCHER

Chefs must have enough knowledge of meat and poultry handling to be efficient. The selection of fresh food is a decisive factor to the finished product. Many chefs feel that personal handling of these supplies is of the greatest importance. They are proud of their special ways of trimming, cutting, and boning meat before it is cooked. Some food service establishments do all their own meat cutting and portioning on the premises. They do not use frozen supplies even in emergencies. Other places prefer a minimum of fresh meat handling and depend entirely on portion-controlled supplies. Whatever the choice, chefs must have enough meat know-how to supervise both of these operations.

### QUALITY SELECTION

Only half a century ago, chefs would go to the markets at the break of dawn and select the meats which they considered to be the best available. This judgement was the only grading available, and it was perfected over many years of personal experience.

Today there is compulsory federal and state meat inspection and voluntary meat quality grading. Meat inspection approves the wholesomeness of the meat, whereas meat grading standardizes the quality of meat. The U.S. Department of Agriculture (U.S.D.A.) stamps a round mark with a number on all carcasses. The number identifies the slaughterhouse and the inspectors. (See Fig. 11-1.) A shield-like stamp is used to indicate the grade range of the meat. These grades are Prime, Choice, Good, Standard, Commercial, Utility, Cutter, and Canner. Purveyors

Fig. 11-1 Meat inspection stamp. U.S.D.A. approval of wholesomeness only.

TABLE 11-1a BEEF GRADING STAMP, IN-DICATING USDA AFFIRMED QUALITY.

and retail meat markets handle most of the first five grades. The last three are reserved for the manufacture of meat products. Without federal inspection and grading, meat purchasing would still be very difficult and time consuming for the average chef.

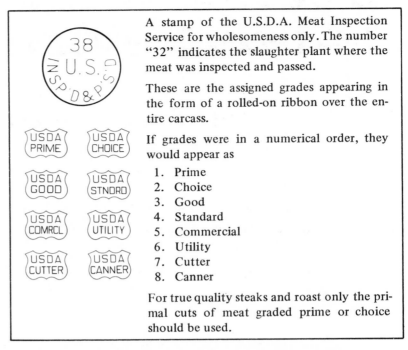

A stamp of the U.S.D.A. Meat Inspection Service for wholesomeness only. The number "32" indicates the slaughter plant where the meat was inspected and passed.

These are the assigned grades appearing in the form of a rolled-on ribbon over the entire carcass.

If grades were in a numerical order, they would appear as

1. Prime
2. Choice
3. Good
4. Standard
5. Commercial
6. Utility
7. Cutter
8. Canner

For true quality steaks and roast only the primal cuts of meat graded prime or choice should be used.

TABLE 11-1b INSPECTION AND GRADING STAMPS

## IDENTIFICATION OF MEAT CUTS

Not all parts of a slaughtered animal, especially of the bovine family (ox, cow), have the same characteristics. Tenderness, juiciness, and flavor of meat vary. These depend on which muscles have been exercised and the amount of fat (marble) deposited between the meat fibers. Although the whole animal is graded "Prime", the difference in usability of various parts is considerable. Experienced chefs and butchers do not always agree with regard to a selection of meat cuts.

The ordinary coffee shop or restaurant uses a wide variety of steaks, roasts, pot roasts, stews, hamburgers and cold meats. The meat purveyor and the chef use a standard meat terminology, without reference to the intended use of the meat. The National Meat Board encourages the nationwide use of this terminology since grading is also on a national basis. Standard terms avoid misunderstandings. The most common terms can be found and studied in tables 11-2a and 11-2b.

## MEAT SELECTION AND COOKING METHODS

The establishment of a quality standard of tenderness and flavor for the individual preparations of a kitchen is the duty of management and the chef. For this purpose, the chef must know which cuts of meat

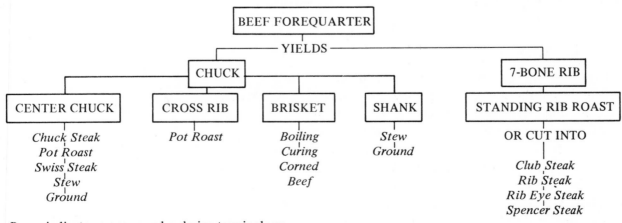

Boxes indicate purveyor and ordering terminology
Italics indicate preparation or kitchen uses of the jobber cuts

TABLE 11-2a BEEF FOREQUARTER IDENTIFICATIONS

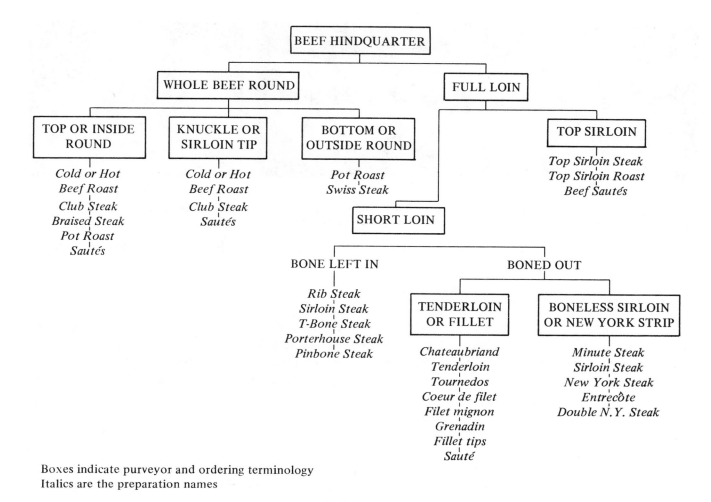

Boxes indicate purveyor and ordering terminology
Italics are the preparation names

**TABLE 11-2b BEEF HINDQUARTER IDENTIFICATION**

to use for a specific preparation. There is no choice for a New York, Fillet, T-Bone or Top Sirloin Steak. The names on the menu establish the meat cuts to be used. For brochettes, sautés, stews, roasts, and cutlets, a choice of suitable meat cuts must be made. This choice is based on price, clientele, and the reputation to be maintained. First cuts differ from secondary cuts in cost and characteristics. Secondary cuts should be used instead of a first cut only if the quality is adequate. Chefs have different opinions of what is a better or a good enough cut for a certain preparation. Chuck (the squared-off forequarter) is primarily used for stews and ground meat by most chefs. Beef-round (the center part of the hindquarter) is generally used for braised steaks, pot roasts, cold roast meats and club steaks. Beef loin and Beef rib (see table 11-2), both first cuts, are used for steaks, prime roasts, brochettes, and quality sautés like "Beef Stroganoff". However, prime chuck meat, when properly *seamed* (cut along the natural divisions), can be used for many speciality dishes with great advantages.

## *MEAT REFRIGERATION AND STORAGE*

Considering the high price of meat, nothing must be wasted. Waste results from over-ordering or over-preparation. Purveyors need orders big enough to compensate for the high cost of delivery. For this economic reason, meat is ordered only once or twice per week. A smooth running and profitable establishment must have enough refrigerated space. The chef must match deliveries with production schedules. For example, defrosting time must be considered for the large whole turkeys used today. For items in short supply, ordering must be done far in advance of the use time. When the delivery arrives, it must be checked in. Meat inspection only makes sure that the meat was wholesome when slaughtered. The chef's responsibility is to be sure that it is still wholesome when delivered. Items received must be checked against items ordered, and weight must also be verified. Fresh meat must be unpacked, refrigerated, and placed on marked shelves to avoid misuse by untrained help. Old stock must also be checked for freshness, and

Fig. 11-2 Portion-controlled rib steaks sliced on a meat saw.

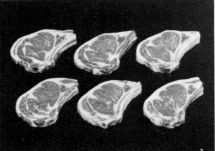

Fig. 11-3 Portion-controlled rib steaks as supplied by the purveyor.

Fig. 11-4 Portion-controlled machine slicing of a boneless rib eye steak.

then rotated. All this is the responsibility of the chef or of the cook-butcher whom he assigns to do this work.

### PORTION CONTROL

Uniform size of each order is necessary for any successful food operation. The customer receives full value for the price paid. The operator is sure that estimated and actual food costs are the same.

Portion size is influenced by many factors. One is the caloric value of food, or the need of the average customer to satisfy his hunger. There are sales prices and customs of the region. A customer in the Midwest is used to larger steak and potato orders than in a coastal city. In addition, other factors are the image which the establishment wants to create, the sex and age of average customers, and the actual preparation method.

A 4-ounce boneless and breaded fried pork chop, served with tomato sauce, will look larger and have more calories than a 6-ounce bone-in broiled pork chop, served with applesauce. Orders served a la carte should be larger than orders served on the dinner. When a 14-ounce untrimmed New York Steak is served, the meat appears large if it is compared to the potato and the vegetable. The same steak, trimmed of fat and gristle to about 11 ounces, looks daintier when compared the same way. After eating the untrimmed steak, if the customer realizes that 30% of his steak could not be eaten, there is a definite psychological effect. From the trimmed steak, he leaves only 10% fat, or even nothing at all. The trimmed steak is not only more satisfying, but also less of a fire hazard while it is cooking. (See unit 6, Safety Hazards.) Young cooks should be prepared to accept counsel before deciding on portion sizes.

Portion control starts with raw food at the buying level, continues through the cooking process (see unit 7, Shrinkage and Yield), and ends with carving and serving. Portion control applies to ALL foods served in a food service establishment.

### Portion-Controlled Supplies

Hamburger patties are the ideal food for portion control. Ground meat is used. There are no leftover trimmings.

| | Weight in Ounces Small | Weight in Ounces Large |
|---|---|---|
| Minute Steak | 8 | 10 |
| Fillet Steak | 6 | 10 |
| Tournedos | 6 | 10 |
| Coeur de Filet | 6 | 10 |
| Filet Mignon | 6 | 10 |
| New York Steak | 12 | 16 |
| Sirloin Steak | 12 | 16 |
| Entrecote | 12 | 16 |
| Loin Strip Steak | 12 | 16 |
| T-Bone Steak | 14 | 18 |
| Porterhouse Steak for 2 | 22 | 28 |
| Chateaubriand for 2 | 16 | 20 |
| Beef Brochette | 5 | 7 |
| Beef Saute | 4 | 7 |
| Boneless Cutlet | 4 | 6 |
| Porkchop, breaded | 4 | 7 |
| Porkchop, broiled, single | 7 | 9 |
| Porkchops (2), broiled, each | 5 | 6 |
| Lambchops (3), frenched, each | 2.50 | 3.25 |
| Scallopine (3), each | 2 | 2.75 |

Meats reasonably defatted and trimmed

**TABLE 11-3 APPROXIMATE RAW MEAT WEIGHT FOR VARIOUS MEAT PORTIONS**

The patty is machine molded. It has exact weight to the quarter ounce. One patty is just like the next. This accounts for the popularity of hamburger chains and franchises. From a food control point of view, there is no difference between selling meat patties or selling ice cream bars.

It is much more difficult to portion control a regular steak. The weight, shape and fat content of one piece of meat is never exactly the same as the next. If a 12-pound trimmed New York strip is bought, in theory, it means that 16 trimmed 12-ounce New York steaks could be cut from it. The average yield will actually be 15 or more likely 14, or even only 13. If the 12-pound strip were machine cut into 16 equal-sized steaks, some of the steaks would be better than acceptable (very well trimmed),

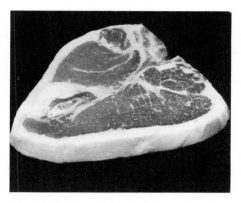

Fig. 11-5 T-bone steak, also referred to as porterhouse steak

but others would be totally unacceptable (too much fat and skin) for customer satisfaction. Portion-cut steaks supplied by the meat purveyor are about 90 to 95% acceptable. The price per pound for portion-cut meat is so much higher than the price for uncut meat that portion-controlled buying of steaks does not result in real savings.

Grading by size of chickens is a real advantage. Poultry is purchased *eviscerated* (completely cleaned) within a range of 2 ounces. This means that a chicken graded as a 1½-pound size may weigh from 23 ounces to 25 ounces. A 1¾-pound chicken may weigh from 27 ounces to 29 ounces. Breast or leg quarters of chickens can also be purchased. These may even be stuffed. All are within one ounce of specifications.

Portion-controlled raw supplies are available for chickens, steaks, chops, cutlets, scallopine, brochettes, chopped steaks, and meat patties. True portion control begins after the cooking of roasts, stew, and others.

### FROZEN MEAT AND POULTRY

The freezing of food began for the purpose of mass feeding in times of war and emergencies. Development was continued for the purpose of being helpful to the consumer. Soon it was found that the freezing of meat and poultry never became a convenience to the consumer. It was a convenience only for the producer. The freezing and necessary extra handling of food reduces its quality. This can be proved with a large fresh steak which has been cut in half. Wrap and freeze one half. Cello wrap and refrigerate the other half. After three or four days cook both halves at the same time in exactly the same way and compare. The results speak for themselves. Housewives who are interested in good food have found the difference between a frozen and a fresh chicken. Frozen raw supplies of meat and poultry are a convenience to the producer and a quality loss to the consumer.

### SUMMARY

Meat and poultry are the most important and expensive food products in the USA. These can be purchased at different levels of preparation and for different prices. The food service management must decide what to buy. Whatever foods are bought, chefs must know about the total preparation process in order to make correct judgements. Quality levels are defined, measured, established and maintained. Meat cuts are selected according to menu and preparation needs. Ordering or specifying selection and quantity is another of the chef's responsibilities. Chefs establish and maintain food costs. Therefore, the total handling of food from purchase selection to receiving to storage to rotation and use must be the chef's concern. The Chef might establish portion size policy together with the management. The enforcing of portion control, checking yields and costs, and keeping customer satisfaction are the reasons for the chef's position.

Portion-controlled supplies, either fresh or frozen, are new to the market. A food service establishment is in an unusual position: to its supplier, it is a consumer; but to its guests, who are the true consumers, it is the producer. The use of frozen meat and poultry raw products is a convenience to the producer and a quality loss to the consumer. The chef and the management of the food service establishment must make many joint decisions.

## DISCUSSION TOPICS

1. What are the advantages of open market buying?
2. Why do chefs need butchering skills?
3. Can meat quality be defined?
4. Why is there a need for meat inspection?
5. Why is there nationwide meat grading?
6. What are the benefits of portion control?
7. Is frozen meat a blessing?

## SUGGESTED ACTIVITIES

View films available from National Meat Board.

View films available from Beef and Lamb Council.

Field trip to a slaughterhouse.

Field trip to a wholesale butcher (Purveyor).

Field trip to a meat freezing plant.

View demonstration on "Meat Identification", using wall charts.

Field trip to a supermarket meat counter.

Field trip to a wholesale poultry house.

## ACHIEVEMENT REVIEW

A. Complete the following:

1. Food service operators today can use supplies which are precooked or _____ .
2. Chefs have special ways of boning meat before it is _____ .
3. Meat inspection before and after slaughter for wholesomeness is _____ .
4. Not all parts of a beef animal have the same _____ .
5. All beef meat can be subdivided into prime cuts and _____ .
6. For a first class steak, the meat is not only a primal cut, it is also graded _____ .
7. The checking in of delivered meat is the responsibility of the _____ .
8. Since meat has a high food cost, its ordering must be strictly according to _____ .
9. Portion control benefits the customer as well as the _____ .
10. Portion control assures that the same value is given to each _____ .
11. Portion size is related to total caloric value of the food served. Therefore, of importance is the food's _____ .
12. Portion size policy is established by the Chef and _____ .
13. The freezing of poultry and meat must be considered as a convenience to the _____ .

B. Read each question carefully and completely before answering it. Select the *best* answer.

1. Although a chef must have butcher skills to a certain degree, he need not be able to

   a. cut up a whole beef round    c. skin a calf

   b. bone a chicken    d. make veal meat balls

2. To select meat quality in the past, the chef had to depend on his experience. Today he is greatly assisted by
   a. Fair Trade Laws
   b. The Federal Health Department
   c. The U.S. Department of Agriculture
   d. The Department of Health and Welfare

3. Meat ordering is the chef's responsibility but does not include
   a. placing orders in time for delivery
   b. specifying quality standards
   c. estimating his need
   d. selecting meat at the market

4. Portion control is an important tool to a profitable operation and means
   a. reducing the size of steaks when meat is high priced
   b. adjusting selling price of cooked food to purchase price of raw food
   c. keeping each portion of food constantly to the same size
   d. watching that all customers are getting served before food runs out

5. An untrimmed steak may look 30% larger than the same steak trimmed. Still, customers prefer the trimmed one because
   a. it fits better on the plate
   b. it is easier to chew and digest
   c. it is all meat, no trimming left
   d. it has a better taste

6. Which one of these meat grades does not belong to the first four?
   a. prime          c. standard
   b. good           d. commercial

7. Meat that is graded prime has
   a. more nutritional value     c. less fat per pound
   b. tenderness and flavor      d. better digestibility

8. Primal cuts of prime meats are expensive and are not used for the preparation of
   a. roast top sirloin     c. German Sauerbraten
   b. roast rib of beef     d. Porterhouse Steak

9. The grading of whole chickens to size has become so exact that fluctuations are not more than
   a. one ounce per chicken     c. three ounces per chicken
   b. two ounces per chicken    d. four ounces per chicken

10. For most dishes portion control begins after the cooking process, but not for
    a. Roast beef     c. Beef stew
    b. Pot roast      d. Swiss steak

C. Match the Beef Grades of Column I with the numbers of Column II.

| Column I | Column II |
|---|---|
| Choice | 1. First |
| Good | 2. Second |
| Prime | 3. Third |
| Canner | 4. Fourth |
| Commercial | 5. Fifth |
| Standard | 6. Sixth |
| Cutter | 7. Seventh |
| Utility | 8. Eighth |

D. Match the preparations of Column I with the *average* portion weight of Column II.

| Column I | Column II |
|---|---|
| Filet Mignon | 5 ounces |
| Sirloin Steak | 6 " |
| Minute Steak | 8 " |
| T-Bone Steak | 9 " |
| Chateaubriand | 14 " |
| Porterhouse Steak | 16 " |
| Boneless Cutlet | 18 " |
| Beef Brochette | 25 " |

E. Answer in your own words:

1. Explain the chef's need for butcher knowledge.

2. Describe the change of quality control.

3. Identify the reasons for meat inspection.

4. Discuss the different phases of portion control.

# Unit 12  Fish and Shellfish

*OBJECTIVES*

After studying this unit, the student should be able to

- List the different kinds of edible seafood.
- Name the area of origin of some of the seafood.
- Explain about fish cooking methods.
- Identify processed fish specialties of the world.
- Name the important principle in the handling of shellfish.
- Explain the need for fish butchering.
- Describe some hazards of frozen fish products.

## *ANALYSIS OF SEAFOOD*

Seafood, which implies food from the sea, is the term used for all edible fish and shellfish. There are salt-water, freshwater, and migratory fish. Shellfish can be divided into crustaceans and mollusks. Some of the crustaceans are lobsters, prawns, shrimps, crabs, and crayfish. Some of the mollusks are edible clams, oysters, scallops, and squid.

Fish is high in nutritional value and very low in fat. Fish is easy to digest, but shellfish is not. Seafood must always be absolutely fresh. It has a very short storage time. Because of the improvement in freezing techniques, frozen seafood is shipped to all areas of the country. Most seafoods eaten are not raised on fish farms. They are game fish which have developed certain characteristics of the place where they live. Therefore, seafood from one region is often thought to be superior to seafood from another region.

## *REGIONAL EMPHASIS*

The true lobster, with claws, lives only in the cold waters of the North Atlantic. The eastern areas of America and Canada feature lobster restaurants where this crustacean is king.

Spiny lobsters, also called *langustes* or rock lobsters, have no claws, look like giant shrimps and are caught in the warmer waters off California and Mexico. There is a great difference in meat texture and flavor between the spiny and Atlantic lobsters. The "Maine Lobsters" from New England and the Canadian waters are considered to be the best.

The same regional differences are true for crabs, prawns, shrimps, oysters, and the various kinds of fish. There are many seafood restaurants in and near coastal areas. They promote the best native seafood of their regions. Some of these seafood areas have developed special preserving processes, such as marinating or smoking. The native catch, combined with the special processing, has often become famous all around the

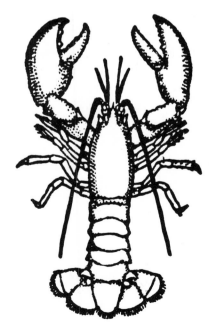

**Fig. 12-1 "Maine Lobster"**

world. These products are listed under appetizers on restaurant menus. They should be well known to both chefs and gourmets.

## PROCESSED FISH SPECIALTIES

Smoked salmon, a true delicacy, can be made from any fresh salmon. The best ones come from Scotland, Germany, and Nova Scotia. The best sardines in olive oil come from Portugal and southern France. Herring, pickled or marinated, are special to Sweden and Germany. The best smoked herring, also known as kippers, are from Scotland and Germany. Smoked haddock, or Finnan haddie, comes from Scotland and Nova Scotia. Pickled eel is a specialty of Commachio, Italy. The most expensive of all the preserved fish delicacies is *Caviar*, or the slightly salted roe of a sturgeon. The best liked ones are of Iranian or Russian origin. Russia, Scandinavia, and some of the other colder countries produce a large variety of cured, brined, pickled, and smoked fish for their own local use. The delicacies mentioned here are only a few of those that are available from all over the world.

## FISH PREPARATION

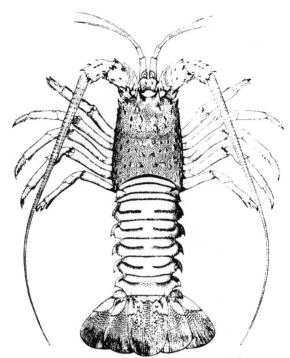

Panulirus interruptus, Randall. (p. 780.)
Drawing by H. L. Todd, from a specimen obtained on the coast of California
**Fig. 12-2    The spiny lobster or rock lobster (Languste), from the Pacific Ocean. (Smaller than natural size.)**

Many of the same cooking methods used for meat are also used in preparing seafood. Because seafood is very tender, prolonged cooking methods are not needed. Since it is a brittle food, it should be handled in portion sizes. Seafoods, because they are very lean, are most popular if deep fried or sautéed. They can also be broiled or poached. Fish stews, or whole braised fish, in the sense of the combination method, are rarely made. A well-accepted, original French sauté method for fish is called a la "Meunier". Flour-dusted fish pieces are sautéed in butter until done and then sprinkled with chopped parsley and a few drops of lemon juice. Freshly browned butter is poured over this dish before serving. Fish broiling is well accepted for salmon steak, halibut steak, swordfish steak, seabass, red snapper, and cod. All fish with coarse-textured flesh allow for rougher handling, such as in broiling. Fish with fine-textured flesh, such as sole, sanddab, and trout are better pan fried or poached.

Cooking a whole fish by baking or roasting is never done commercially. It is messy and has no advantage to taste or handling. A whole fish for display at a buffet is boiled (simmered) or poached. For the moist cooking of fish and shellfish the same principles apply as explained in section 2, unit 7. Fish cooking has no different rules. Prevention of overcooking is very important since fish is a pure *albumin* (protein such as in eggwhite) — a food which only toughens and dries out when exposed to too much heat. Fish must always be fresh, and no fish odor should be present. There is much difference between fresh and freshly defrosted fish. Shellfish, if unfrozen, must be alive until seconds before cooking. Oysters and clams, eaten on the half shell (raw), are still alive when they are eaten. For additional assurance of freshness, they are served on crushed ice. Due to the chemical makeup of seafood, toxic changes could take place if the shellfish were not frozen or cooked immediately. Grading for fish quality does not exist. USDA or local Health Department inspectors check the fish processing plants for general cleanliness and freshness of the product. The quality of fresh fish is easily found by looking at the color and firmness of the flesh and the absence of any fishy smell. Some fish buyers also look at the redness of the gills and the shine of the fish eyes. Pale color and dullness indicate that the fish is not fresh.

## EDIBLE CRUSTACEANS

Crustaceans enjoy a great popularity in the Western world. The giant frozen Alaskan King Crab is distributed on a nationwide basis. This delightful crab meat is now available cooked and frozen in a variety of packaging sizes.

Fig. 12-3 Alaskan King Crab

Fig. 12-4 Blue Crab, from the Atlantic

The East coast has "Blue Shell Crabs" and "Soft Shell Crabs", which are blue crabs after they have shed their shells. "Dungeness Crabs" are found on the West coast. They are larger than blue crabs but smaller than king crabs. Crabs are available live or cooked and frozen. When cooled and frozen, they are sold as crab meat. Crab meat in cans is overcooked and inferior to the frozen food. Soft shell crabs are not boiled, they are only pan fried or sautéed to order.

American Lobsters, with claws, are a specialty from New England to North Eastern Gaspe in Canada. Lobsters are boiled alive and may be eaten either hot or cold. An excellent preparation is live broiled lobster, an American specialty. "Lobster Americaine" on the other hand is a true French specialty. For Lobster Americaine or "Amoricaine", as it is properly spelled, a live lobster is chopped in about 8 or 10 pieces. It is sautéed immediately in butter with some fine chopped onions, shallots, parsley and tomatoes, then deglazed with brandy and white wine and finished, with a cover, for a few minutes more.

Live, Pacific spiny lobsters, or langustes without claws, are handled like "Maine Lobsters" but usually they can be bought cooked and frozen.

Shrimps and prawns are distinguished by size. The very small ones, called shrimps, are available cleaned and cooked, either canned or frozen. The various larger sizes are called *prawns*, although they belong to the shrimp family. They are available semi-cleaned and raw frozen (shell on) or fully cleaned, peeled, deveined, and raw frozen. The most common preparation for prawns is deep frying. They are also boiled for "Shrimp Cocktail" and "Shrimp Louis". In better restaurants, they are sautéed or broiled on skewers.

### EDIBLE MOLLUSKS

The edible mollusks, popular in the USA, are oysters, scallops, various clams, mussels, and squid. Oysters, especially on the East coast, are eaten raw on the half shell, but they can also be fried, sautéed or poached. Clams are eaten the same way, or they may be used in soups (Clam chowder), sauces, or as a garnish in fish dishes. Scallops are preferred fried in the USA; the most popular French preparation is poached with white wine and cheese, known under the name of "Coquille St. Jacques". Scallops are known in Europe as "St. Jacobs mussel" or the "Pilgrim's Shell", because pilgrims returning from the Holy Land pinned the shells on their robes, as a proof that they were there.

Abalones, from the Pacific, are large mollusks with scallop-like meat. They are popular in the Far East and with Americans from the West Coast. Americans eat abalones fried, sautéed, and broiled; but in the Far East, they are preboiled in water, sliced when cold, and then used in various ways.

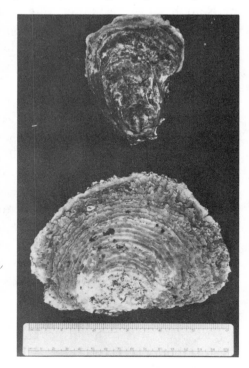

Fig. 12-5 Top: American Oyster, Bottom: European Oyster, planted in Maine.

Fig. 12-6 Atlantic surf clams

Fig. 12-7 Calico Scallop shell

Squid, also known as Calamari, are fried, sautéed, and sometimes even boiled, stuffed and finished in the oven.

## FISH BUTCHERING

*Fish butchering* means the cleaning, filleting, skinning, and cutting of raw fresh fish into portions or cookable pieces. Some years ago, larger food establishments in coastal areas had their own fish cooks and fish butchers. In smaller establishments, fish is handled by the meat butcher or the cook designated to do this type of work. Today only seafood specialty restaurants do their own fish butchering. Many Americans were never forced for economic reasons to live on fish as their main protein source. They are unwilling to even taste fish. The main reason is the fear of choking on a fish bone. Every chef who handles fish must see to it that fish portions are as boneless as they can be. The butchering of fish on the job and the serving of fish without bones will help the customer to overcome his fears. Commercial fish boning places emphasis on speed and the least amount of trimmings. This is not as good as having the fish butcher fillet and portion fish according to his needs and the standards of the establishment.

It is the fish butcher's job to make fish ready for cooking. Like the meat butcher, he is also responsible for the ordering and storage of his supplies. His fish refrigerator should be set for about 34°F. and should have good air circulation. He should only use stainless tools and utensils to handle and store raw fish.

Fig. 12-8 Alaskan Weathervane Scallop (edible part)

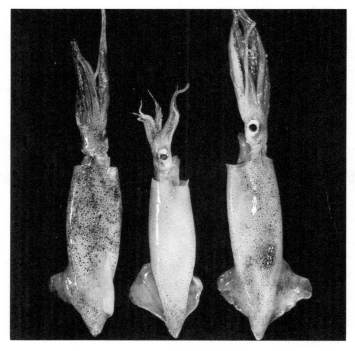

Fig. 12-9 Squid

## THE FILLETING OF A WHOLE SALMON OR OTHER SIMILAR SHAPED FISH, AND ITS CUTTING INTO SERVING-SIZED PORTIONS

Fig. 12-10 A whole Pacific Silver Salmon, as purchased from the seafood supply house. The fish is only gutted.

Fig. 12-11 With kitchen shears or the butcher knife, all the fins are snipped off.

Fig. 12-12 The head is cut and separated from the body. The head can be used for fish stock.

Fig. 12-13 The headless fish, laying on its side, is cut in half lengthwise along the spinal fish bone. Fresh firm fish is easy to fillet. A fish stored in the refrigerator for several days, becomes soft and difficult to handle. If freezing of raw fish is unavoidable, it should be frozen after cleaning, filleting and portion cutting.

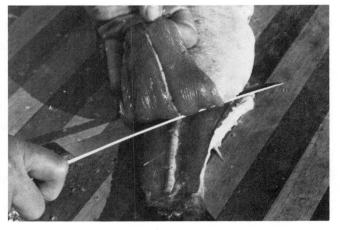

Fig. 12-14 After the top side of the fish (fillet), which should be boneless, is set aside, the remaining fish is turned over so the other fillet can be removed. Depending on the fish butcher's dexterity (left handed or right handed) one side is cut from the head end toward the tail, whereas the other side from the tail end toward the head.

(continued)

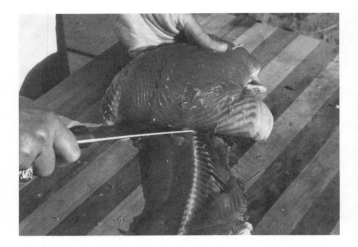

Fig. 12-15  The cut is continued in the same manner until the second fillet can be set aside as before.

Fig. 12-16  If the long rib bones around the belly opening of the fish have been cut off the carcass by mistake, they are removed from the inside belly of the fish. Excessive belly flap and ragged ends are trimmed off.

Fig. 12-17  For skinning the trimmed sides, the skin side is laid on a flat working surface and a narrow-bladed butcher knife is inserted between skin and flesh. While one hand holds the knife in place with a firm grip, the other hand pulls the skin, which is held by the tail, slowly back. The knife edge presses the skin firmly against the board at an angle of about 30°. The pull on the skin must be slow at first. This skinning method avoids the loss of flesh and can be done in seconds.

Fig. 12-18  The fillet is scored lightly. Scoring in this instance means to make shallow, parallel slashes at an angle following the pattern of the flesh. The score marks cut through the remaining skin ligaments and prevent the contractions (curling up) of the fish pieces during the cooking process.

Fig. 12-19  Finally, the portion-cut pieces are ready for cooking.

# PREPARING PORTION-SIZED FLATFISH, SUCH AS BRILL, PLAICE, DAB, AND SOLE, FOR THE COOKING PROCESS

Fig. 12-20 Flounders, portion-sized or smaller. Generally accepted food fish are the Brill, Plaice, Dab, Lemon Sole, and Sole. There are, of course, many regional names for the same fish. All of these fish are handled raw in the same manner.

Fig. 12-21 The head is cut off.

Fig. 12-22 The visible fin plus about ½" rim off the body must be cut away. This ½" consists of additional fish bones, which are hard to remove when the fish is cooked.

Fig. 12-23 The tail is trimmed away.

Fig. 12-24 With a small paring knife, the dark outer skin is initially separated from the whole flesh. Then it is pulled back by hand. The other fish side, which is white, does not need to be skinned on portion-sized fish.

(continued)

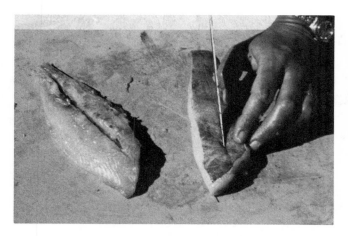

Fig. 12-25 Two incisions, one to the left side and one to the right side of the bone are made. Be certain not to make the cuts all the way or the fillets will fall apart during the cooking. A second cut, following the first, changes the plain cut into a pocket. The unskinned side is handled the same way.

Fig. 12-26 After all four pockets have been cut, the fish will open easily and is ready to be cooked. The pockets allow faster cooking and make the "table boning" very easy.

## HANDLING OF FROZEN SUPPLIES

Fish, more so than meat, is available frozen in many different ways. Stuffed, processed and precooked fish cutlets, fish sticks, fish balls, paupiettes and many other items are on the market, ready to be deep fried when needed. Customers for this kind of seafood are the fast food operators, some institutions, and all those places which do not have qualified help available. In general, most fish today must be purchased frozen. Only big port cities, with their seafood reputation of the past, are still able to get some supplies of fresh fish. Frozen fish comes in many packages: large 50-pound blocks of imported halibut and cod, 5- and 10-pound packages of domestic fish fillet, individual frozen (I.Q.F.) whole fish fillets, and portion-cut fish steaks graded to size.

Shellfish comes in all sizes from all parts of the world. Most common are raw South African and Australian rock lobster tails in the shell or as meat. Also raw are the frozen prawns, which come mostly from Mexico and Louisiana. Prawns come from India, Thailand, Japan, Hong Kong, Chile, Denmark, and many other places, too. Some of these supplies are of a quality which is below any standard of acceptance. Some look good while still frozen but have off-tastes and poor textures when they are cooked.

To depend on the supplier for a quality judgement is risky. First, there is no government grading standard for frozen seafood. Second, in a frozen product the final quality can only be checked after the food is cooked and eaten. To test quality, there is no substitute for eating.

One of the most common problems with frozen fish is that the move from one cold storage to the next may not be fast enough. Foods get partially thawed, and then are refrozen automatically when properly stored again. The USDA is very aware that a transit problem of frozen food exists. A pamphlet of the Agricultural Research Service ARS-74-14 called, "Taking Product Temperatures in Frozen Food Cases" is available and will help buyers to check deliveries before acceptance.

A large amount of water expands during freezing and breaks the cell walls of fish. When it is defrosted, the water oozes out, and the portion size shrinks. Frozen fish dealers suggest that fish should be cooked while it is still frozen. This does not really change anything, except that cooking takes longer and the water oozing out is not seen. A cook should handle frozen fish the way management wants him to handle it. Whatever he may do, the results, in most cases, are inferior to fresh fish. Raw shellfish freezes better than regular fish. Processed or precooked fish handles better than raw frozen fish. A huge difference in quality is found among the many available kinds of fresh and salt water fish. This is because of the origin of the raw fish, as well as its processing, storing, and handling in transit.

## SUMMARY

Seafood, a term for live edible food taken from the waters, is high in nutritional value and low in fat. Seafood must be used absolutely fresh. It has a much shorter storage time than meat. For this reason, most seafood available today is frozen. The same species of fish taken from different regions show a considerable difference in taste and texture. Processed fish and seafood specialties originating in various countries are known and appreciated all over the world.

Fish cookery is the same as general cooking procedures, except that long cooking times are not needed. All shellfish must be kept alive until it is cooked. Oysters and some clams are eaten alive from the shell. Crustaceans are well accepted by the public and considered a specialty. The king of the crustacean is the American lobster, with langustes, crabs, and shrimps being close in popularity.

Fish butchering means doing the same thing to fresh fish that a regular butcher does to meat. It is an important job, very necessary for any food establishment interested in providing the best seafood for its customers.

A large variety of fish and fish products are available in the form of convenience foods. Most of them are ready to be deep fried but some are precooked to such an extent that only reheating is needed. In many areas, fish and shellfish are only available in a frozen form. Transporting and distributing fresh unfrozen salt water fish to some faraway inland area is too expensive and difficult.

No grading standards exist for frozen seafood, which means that fish buyers have to check carefully before committing themselves to large quantities. For fresh fish, no standards of grading are needed. Fish quality is self-evident by looks, touch, and smell. In general, raw shellfish freezes better than raw fish. A great quality margin exists for frozen salt water fish, depending on the origin of the raw fish and the applied freezing and handling procedures.

## DISCUSSION TOPICS

1. Why are fish cooking methods the same as most cooking methods?

2. Are live oysters really a delicacy?

3. Is it good business practice to eliminate the fish butcher?

4. Why must shellfish be cooked alive?

5. Has frozen fish more merit than frozen meat?

6. What are the reasons for regional quality differences?

7. Will fish be the future protein source of the world?

8. Do seafood restaurants have a tradition?

## SUGGESTED ACTIVITIES

1. Define:

   a. smoking
   b. pickling
   c. seafood
   d. languste
   e. paupiette
   f. mollusk
   g. caviar

2. Take a field trip to a fish processing plant or fish dealer.

3. Visit a gourmet section of a food store to look for processed and imported food specialties.

4. Demonstrate the handling of live lobster and crab.

5. Demonstrate the handling of frozen whole lobster.

6. Visit a fish counter of a supermarket to view fresh and defrosted fish.

## ACHIEVEMENT REVIEW

A. Complete the following:

   1. Fish is high in nutritional value and very low in _____.

   2. Fish is easy to digest; shellfish is _____.

3.  For health reasons, shellfish before cooking must be _____.

4.  Most fish eaten is classified as _____.

5.  The true lobster exists only in the waters of the _____.

6.  Spiny lobsters, or langustes, come from waters off _____.

7.  Clams, oysters, and squid are classified as _____.

8.  Lobsters, crabs, and prawns are classified as _____.

9.  A method to process fish specialties is _____.

10. Finnan Haddie, originally from Scotland, is a fish that has been _____.

11. Sturgeon roe, slightly salted, is called _____.

12. Kippers, a breakfast food, are smoked _____.

13. For tender seafood, the cooking time must be _____.

14. Fish that can be broiled are only those with flesh that is _____.

15. When eaten, iced oysters on the half shell are still _____.

16. The quality of fresh fish is judged by looks, touch, and _____.

17. Blue shell crabs are native to the _____.

18. Dungeness crabs are native to the _____.

19. King crabs are native to _____.

20. Abalones are native to the _____.

B.  Read each question carefully and completely. Select the *best* answer.

1.  Which of the following is *not* a shellfish?

    a. shrimp            c. haddock
    b. scallop           d. prawn

2.  Which of these mollusks are often eaten raw?

    a. abalones          c. oysters
    b. squid             d. scallops

3.  Which of these cooking methods is rarely used on fish?

    a. pot-roasting      c. boiling
    b. broiling          d. frying

4.  Many people who do not eat fish are afraid of

    a. fish poisoning        c. fish indigestibility
    b. fish bones            d. fish preparations

5.  Quality of fresh fish is judged by

    a. a grading stamp       c. its origin
    b. packaging label       d. looks and smell

6.  Smoked salmon is produced best in

    a. Sweden            c. Scotland
    b. Italy             d. France

7.  Which one of these cooking methods is *not* common for lobster?

    a. a la meuniere         c. broiled
    b. a l'Amoricaine        d. boiled

8. Which of the following is *not* a crustacean?

   a. languste                    c. prawn
   b. scallop                     d. crab

9. Which of the following is *not* a fish preservation method?

   a. curing                      c. barbecuing
   b. smoking                     d. pickling

10. Tender and brittle fish is handled better when

    a. frozen                     c. processed whole
    b. portion cut                d. preblanched

11. Which of these fish steaks does not belong to the group?

    a. Halibut steak              c. Trout steak
    b. Salmon steak               d. Seabass steak

12. Crabs from different regions are of different sizes and have flesh of different textures. Which crabs are the biggest?

    a. Softshell crabs            c. West coast crabs
    b. East coast crabs           d. Alaskan crabs

C. Match the seafood dishes in Column I with the geographic area of their origin in Column II.

| *Column I* | | *Column II* |
|---|---|---|
| Lobster Amoricaine | a. | Far East |
| Broiled Lobster | b. | West Coast |
| Pickled Eel | c. | USA |
| Sardines in olive oil | d. | East coast |
| Raw oysters | e. | France |
| Fried Scallops | f. | Scotland-Nova Scotia |
| Abalone sautéed | g. | Portugal |
| Abalone boiled | h. | Italy |
| Finnan Haddie | i. | Russia |
| Pickled Herring | j. | Sweden |
| Caviar | | |
| Coquille St. Jacques | | |

D. Answer in your own words:

1. List the different kinds of edible seafood.

2. Name the important principle in the handling of shellfish.

3. Explain the need for fish butchering.

4. Describe some hazards of frozen fish products.

# Unit 13 Produce Knowledge

*OBJECTIVES*

After studying this unit, the student should be able to

- Describe the different produce packing units.

- Explain the precleaning of vegetables before storage.

- Explain produce storage procedures of a commercial kitchen.

Earlier units stress that the ordering and storage of perishable food belongs to the work frame of the chef. If the importance of a food were judged by the volume used, produce would take the first place. Rarely is a meat or fish dish made where at least some vegetables are not a necessary part of the preparation. The common vegetables used in cooking are seldom marked on the menus or seen on the plates of food served. Vegetables require handling, storage, cleaning, and often more care than meat or fish.

*PACKAGING INFORMATION*

Vegetable suppliers to commercial kitchens call themselves produce dealers. Their stock consists of fresh or frozen vegetables and fruits, eggs, and sometimes synthetic nondairy cream products. Like meat suppliers, they are semiwholesalers and use special terms for the ordering of their goods. This packaging information is essential to the chef for meeting his food costs.

*Tomatoes*

The price for tomatoes is quoted per *lug* (box). A lug is a flat wooden crate holding a standard weight quantity of tomatoes. A lug, marked "5/5", contains 5 rows of tomatoes each way, a total of 25 tomatoes in one layer. Tomatoes of this size need two layers to fill a lug, or a total of 50 tomatoes. The label "6/7" means 42 tomatoes per layer. Since they are smaller, 3 layers are needed to fill one lug. This makes a total of 126 tomatoes, as compared to 50 tomatoes of the same weight, for the same price. Obviously, there is a big difference in portion size and cost. The largest tomatoes available are "5/4", and the smallest are "7/8". A few other produce items, such as peaches and pears, are packed in the same way.

Packaging is standard because produce comes from the same commercial growing areas and is sent nationwide. At the height of the season, produce may be packed loose, especially for immediate local use. This means it will be uncounted, of different sizes, and all in the same box. The box has the same weight as the standard lug. Loose packed items are cheaper in price, but not always cheaper in yield. Odd sizes do not allow portion control and loose packaging damages the content.

A number marked on the produce box shows the individual size of the content. The lower number indicates the larger size of the fruit or vegetable inside, while the upper number stands for the smaller size.

*Onions*

Onions are available in yellow, white, or red. Basically these are the same, with just a minor taste difference in sweetness or sharpness. They are packed in 50- or 100-pound sacks, graded as medium, large, and jumbo sizes. Green onions and leeks are sold in bunches (12 bunches equals 1 bundle). Shallots and pearl onions, which are small boiling onions, are supplied in 5-pound bags. Storage should be in a cool, dry place to prevent sprouting. Only leeks and green onions need washing. All others are peeled dry, often in advance, and kept in clear plastic wrap, under refrigeration, until needed.

*Garlic.* A special flavor-giving vegetable, garlic has a heavy smell much like onions or shallots. It is sold loose by the pound but otherwise handled like onions.

90

## Potatoes

Potatoes are of American origin, and were introduced to the rest of the world by Sir Walter Raleigh. These are now the staple starch of the Western world. Baking potatoes are of a late crop, large and oval in shape. Their skin is rough and they are called "Russets" or "American #1". They are of the Idaho type and considered the best potato in the world. They are size-graded from 6 to 12 ounces and are available in 50-pound boxes or 100-pound sacks. They are also available at a cheaper price as irregular #1 or #2 "Field-grade" (bruised).

Boiling or salad potatoes are new or first crop potatoes and have a smooth skin and irregular shape. They are mostly of the "White Rose" or "Red Rose" variety and are packed in 50-pound boxes.

## Root Vegetables

The most common root vegetables are carrots. Some others are parsnips, celery roots, turnips, radishes, and beets. They all need cool, humidity-controlled storage. They are packed in sacks or boxes from 25 to 100 pounds. Radishes and beets, with the greens still on, come in bunches.

## Mushrooms

The cultured fresh mushrooms sold in the USA are called "Champignon" and are considered essential by most chefs. Mushrooms are quite expensive. They are grown on mushroom farms and are often distributed by them directly. The smallest packed unit is a 2½-pound open cardboard basket. Fresh mushrooms are

| | | |
|---|---|---|
| ARTICHOKES | carton | count #18 to #36 |
| ASPARAGUS | crate | 30 lb. ½/15 lb., grass, med. large, jumbo |
| AVOCADOS | flat | count #12 to #18 |
| BEANS, green | carton | loose, 30 lb. |
| BRUSSEL SPROUTS | carton | loose, 30 lb. |
| BROCCOLI | carton | 24/1 lb. bunches |
| CABBAGE, red | carton | loose, 40 lb. |
| CABBAGE, white | carton or sack | 40 lb. |
| CARROTS | sack | 25 lb., 50 lb., 100 lb. |
| CAULIFLOWER | crate | count 12, 16, 18, 24 |
| CELERY | crate | 24 stalks, (bunches) |
| CHARD | carton | 24 bunches, of about 1 lb. each |
| CHIVES | bunch | 12 bunches = 1 bundle |
| EGGPLANTS | crate | 30 lb. loose |
| GARLIC | bag | 5 lb. - 10 lb. loose |
| LEEKS | bunch | 24 bunches in 1 carton |
| LETTUCE | carton | 24 heads |
| MINT | bunch | 12 bunches = 1 bundle |
| MUSHROOMS | basket | 2½ lb. per basket; 12 baskets = 1 carton  30 lb. |
| OKRA | loose | _____ |
| ONIONS | sacks | 50 lb., 100 lb., med., large, jumbo |
| PARSLEY | bunch | 12 bunches = 1 bundle |
| PARSNIPS | sacks | 25 lb., 50 lb. |
| PEARL ONIONS | bag | 5 lb. |
| POTATOES, Russet | sack | 100 lb. graded 8 to 10 ounces |
| POTATOES, Russet | carton | 50 lb. graded - 4/6, 6/8, 8/10, 10/12 oz. |
| POTATOES, Field | sack | 100 lb. ——— |
| POTATOES, Salad | carton | 50 lb. ——— |
| RADISHES | bunch | 12 bunches = 1 bundle |
| ROMAINE | crate | 24 heads |
| SCALLIONS | bunch | 12 bunches = 1 bundle |
| SHALLOTS | bag | 5 lb., 10 lb. |
| SPINACH | bunch | 24 bunches to 1 carton |
| SQUASH, summer | carton | 30 lb. loose |
| SQUASH, yellow | per lb. | loose |
| SQUASH, zucchini | lug | 30 lb., loose |
| TOMATOES | lug | sized, by layers, 5/4 largest — 6/8 |
| TURNIPS | per lb. | loose |
| WATERCRESS | bunch | 12 bunches = 1 bundle |

**TABLE 13-1 FRESH VEGETABLE PACKING INFORMATION**

moist, heavy, and snow white, with a typical raw mushroom smell. When they are only a few days old they lose the good appearance and flavor. Their storage is difficult because the right humidity range is so important. Many chefs precook mushrooms as soon as they are delivered because they keep better when cooked.

### Other Vegetables

*Artichokes.* Artichokes are packed in cardboard boxes, with the number showing their size. Number 18 is one of the largest, and 36 is one of the smallest graded artichokes. The very small artichoke hearts are sold by the pound, loose or in boxes.

*Asparagus.* Asparagus is packed in special conical crates to protect the tips. They weigh 30 pounds. The asparagus thickness is shown on the crate by the imprint of "grass" (the thinnest), medium, large, or jumbo. A cheaper second grade with crooked stems is called *crooks.*

*Cauliflower.* Cauliflower comes in crates by head count. The lowest number is the largest size.

*Broccoli.* Broccoli is tied into bunches of about 1 pound each. Usually 2 dozen are in a crate.

All vegetable packing falls into the same pattern. As soon as the student understands how the most commonly used products are handled, he will become familiar with the rest in a short time. The basic packing information given in table 13-1 will help the young cook to understand vegetable ordering.

### VEGETABLE RECEIVING

Vegetables are just as perishable as meat, fish, or dairy products. Some vegetables are expensive and easily damaged. Deliveries are checked against the order sheet and the invoice. Each item is checked for weight, count, specifications, damage, and visible freshness. As soon as the delivery is accepted, storage begins.

### Lettuce

Romaine lettuce is packed with 24 heads in one large wooden crate. This lettuce has many soiled unusable outer leaves. For better storage and space-use, the lettuce is prewashed and stored in nonoxidizing (nonrusting) containers, under refrigeration. Iceberg, Boston, Butter, Limestone, Endive, and other types of lettuce are packed in cardboard boxes and should be handled the same way.

### Vegetable Precleaning

Precleaning of bulky leaf vegetables saves space and helps to keep the *reefer* (short for refrigerator) clean and sanitary. Precleaning and orderly storage allow for better checking of stock on hand. It also makes

---

*Equipment Needed*

Double vegetable sink, garbage disposal unit, running water, paring knife, colanders, storage containers.

*Procedure*

1. Stop up sink without disposal. Fill with cool water.
2. Open wooden crate carefully (watch for sticking out nails).
3. Remove heads of lettuce from crate, one by one, and cut off the end of the stem.
4. Remove loose, bruised or bad looking outer leaves and throw them into disposal.
5. Put trimmed head into first sink, now filled with water.
6. Repeat this with other heads of lettuce until all are soaked.
7. Clean up other sink, run all the refuse through garbage disposal.
8. While lettuce is still in deep water, take each head into one hand, holding stems with three or four fingers.
9. Move lettuce rapidly up and down in the water for quite a few seconds (10-15 times) to loosen dirt.
10. Check each head by inspection. If clean, lift it out of the water, shake out and put into cleaned other sink for drainage.
11. Drain water of first sink and clean it. Notice residue of sand and dirt accumulated at bottom of sink.
12. Fill first sink with clean cool water again.
13. Repeat steps #5, 6, 8, 9.
14. Check heads again, lift out of water, shake out and put on colanders for better drainage.
15. Transfer to nonoxidizing container, cover with plastic wrap or wet towel, place in cooler.

**TABLE 13-2 CLEANING AND WASHING ROMAINE LETTUCE**

the shelf-life of the produce longer. Spinach, chard, turnip greens, celery, and many others belong to the leaf vegetable group and should be precleaned, except for cabbage. Parsley, watercress, and mint have to be washed, soaked for a while, and then stored with the leaves up cut-flower style in a pail with water, so they will not become limp. The standard procedure for Romaine lettuce cleaning (table 13-2) should be used in cleaning of all leaf vegetables.

## VEGETABLE STORAGE

Clean vegetables such as tomatoes, mushrooms, artichokes, asparagus, broccoli, cauliflower, carrots, and parsnips are stored in their original containers. These must be opened, and the covers and nails must be re-moved. Containers must be easy to reach in order to prevent damage to the contents by impatient helpers. All goods have to be stored in the same areas on shelves at all times. This avoids the confusion of not finding what is needed. Stock must be rotated after each one is inspected for freshness, not just by its arrival date.

### Food Value Retention

Produce should not be kept in water needlessly. Cold water leaches out all the vitamins and nutrients which are valuable to the diet. The habit of storing peeled or cleaned vegetables in cold water to prevent a change in color should never be allowed.

### FRUITS

Nearly all commercial kitchens use at least some fruits in their daily operations. In California, oranges are often used for decorations. Lemons or apples are used for cooking in Western Cuisine. Where breakfasts are served, grapefruits, melons, berries, and bananas should be in stock. Fresh fruits in restaurants are used for pastry baking and desserts, to add to other dishes, and to be served as either plain fruits or in salads. Fruit popularity depends on the supply and geographic region. In fruit-growing states like Florida and Hawaii, buffet tables at breakfast, brunch, lunch, and dinner are full of fresh, nicely presented fruits. In areas where fruits are expensive, the displays are much smaller. Fruits, supplied by the produce dealer, are handled in the same way and by the same people as the vegetables. Soft fruits without a protective peel, like berries, do not keep as well in storage as those with a peel that protects them. Green fruits keep much better than ripe fruits, but have to be ripened in a warm place for one or two days before they can be used. Fruit terminology, table 13-3, is used to avoid misunderstandings and speed up ordering.

| | | |
|---|---|---|
| APPLES, specify: Delicious — yellow, red; Pippin, McIntosh, Jonathan's, etc., etc. | carton | count #72 (large) — #96 (small) |
| APRICOTS | lug | 30 lb., loose packed, med. & large |
| BANANAS | carton | 40 lb., ½/20 lb. & single "hand" |
| BERRIES | flat | 12 baskets, about 1 lb. each |
| CANTALOUPES | crate | count #45 (smallest) |
| CRANSHAWS | crate | count #4-5 biggest, (seasonal) |
| CHERRIES | lug | 30 lb. loose packed, med., large |
| GRAPEFRUITS | carton | count, #36 (largest) — 64 |
| GRAPES | lug | 30 lb. specify: Muskat, Thompson, etc. |
| HONEYDEWS | crate | count #36 (smallest) |
| LEMONS | carton | select, med. |
| MANGOS, Hawaii | box | count, 8 to 12 (large) |
| MANGOS, Mexico | flat | count, 18, 24, 36 |
| NECTARINES | lug | sized; 6/8, 6/7 |
| ORANGES | carton | count, #42 (largest) — 64, 72, 88, 96 |
| PAPAYAS | box | count, 6 — 10 large |
| PEACHES | lug | sized, 6/8, 6/7 |
| PEARS | lug | medium to large |
| PINEAPPLES | flat | count 4, 5, or 6 |
| PLUMS | lug | 30 lb. loose |
| WATERMELONS | per lb. | individual pieces |

**TABLE 13-3  FRESH FRUIT PACKING INFORMATION**

## FROZEN PRODUCE

Every vegetable and nearly all fruits are available frozen. Frozen produce has the advantage of being fully cleaned, cut up, and preblanched. It is a great time saver for the cook. Fresh frozen green peas are a real convenience and give very good quality to the consumer. They are accepted by nearly all chefs in the USA. For other vegetables, and especially for fruits, the ratio of acceptance varies and depends on the quality level of the establishment. The decision to use frozen vegetables for the sake of convenience, rests with the management. Some of the new chain-type restaurants have designed their facilities in such a way that no space for fresh vegetable handling and storing was included.

The institutional trade handles frozen vegetables in 2½- or 3-pound packages, with 30 pounds to one box. Frozen peas, corn, beans and some others are also supplied loose in 20-pound boxes and are cheaper. Frozen fruits are packed by different companies with little standardized packing. The frozen food distributors will gladly inform the new cook what is available.

## SUMMARY

Produce consists of fresh vegetables and fruits supplied by the produce dealer. He also carries fresh eggs, frozen produce, and nondairy cream products. The daily use of vegetables for side dishes or as part of total cookery is quite large. There must be enough storage and handling space for the quantities needed.

Produce, some of it more expensive and perishable than meat, is packed in a special way. This assures size and weight specifications and easier handling and storage. Cooks must have knowledge of produce terminology to speed up ordering and avoid misunderstandings. Different vegetables or fruits use different size descriptions and packing methods.

Cooks must also be fully aware of the looks of good and fresh produce. It is the chef's duty to receive and check the ordered supplies. Received deliveries are placed under refrigeration as soon as possible to prevent unnecessary loss of quality. Some vegetables have to be precleaned before storage to save space in the refrigerator and help keep it clean. Proper storage retains food value, which is the ultimate reason for cooking. Fruits, which are handled like vegetables, come from the same supplier. Frozen produce is gaining more popularity, not for its better taste, but for the convenience of needing less labor. Management must make the decision between cooking for their own convenience or for producing a variety of quality food for the public.

### DISCUSSION TOPICS

1. Why do produce dealers and purveyors use their own terminology?
2. Is a produce container chosen at random or for reasons?
3. Are food costs and packing information related?
4. Why is there a need for the organized storage of perishable foods?
5. What are the pros and cons for using frozen vegetables?

### SUGGESTED ACTIVITIES

1. Define: crate, lug, carton, flat, box, grass, champignon, crook, nonoxidizing.
2. Write out a produce order.
3. Practice washing romaine lettuce.
4. Inspect a vegetable walk-in reefer.
5. Take a field trip to a produce market.
6. Take a field trip to a supermarket produce section, for the purpose of identifying fresh vegetables.
7. Check invoices and deliveries.

*ACHIEVEMENT REVIEW*

A.   Complete the following:

1.   Rarely is a meat or fish dish made without _____.

2.   Vegetables and fruit suppliers call themselves _____.

3.   Packaging should prevent fruits and vegetables from _____.

4.   Tomatoes are packed in lugs and their "count" is based on _____.

5.   Like purveyors, produce dealers use a special ordering _____.

6.   Size specifications of fruits and vegetables are needed for _____.

7.   Some vegetables are expensive and also easily _____.

8.   Most produce, like meat, fish, and dairy goods are _____.

9.   Precleaning before storage saves valuable refrigerated _____.

10.   Food freezing has grown to such a scope that nearly all different varieties of vegetables are _____.

B.   Read each question carefully and completely. Select the *best* answer.

1.   On incoming produce deliveries, purchase orders and goods must correspond to assure the

   a. quality of the produce ordered
   b. pricing of the produce ordered
   c. freshness of the produce ordered
   d. specifications of the produce ordered

2.   The containers which hold commercially packed tomatoes are called

   a. cartons                  c. crates
   b. lugs                     d. bags

3.   The use of frozen vegetables is on the increase because

   a. they are better tasting      c. they need less preparation
   b. they retain more vitamins    d. they provide greater variety

4.   Without efficient vegetable cleaning facilities, a large restaurant cannot serve with their dinners

   a. french fried potatoes        c. buttered spinach
   b. fresh fruit salads           d. tossed salad greens

5.   Asparagus is packed in a conical shaped crate because it

   a. is easier to handle          c. protects the stem
   b. protects the tip             d. is the cheapest way of doing it

6.   Potatoes for baking are bought graded to assure that

   a. they have a shorter baking time
   b. they provide automatic portion control
   c. they are of the best quality
   d. they can also be used for salads

7.   A produce dealer sells food to institutions on a

   a. come-and-get-it basis
   b. delivery, but retail price basis
   c. semiwholesale basis
   d. portion-controlled basis

8. Onions to be cleaned do not need washing except

   a. the small boiling ones        c. shallots
   b. scallions                     d. the large yellow ones

9. Prepeeled onions are best kept in the reefer by

   a. soaking them in cold water
   b. wrapping them in clear plastic
   c. covering them with a damp towel
   d. using stainless steel pans only

10. A modern refrigerator where unwrapped food is stored should have shelves
    and containers which are

    a. nonoxidizing material
    b. aluminum for best conduction
    c. easily reached and handled
    d. moveable and easy to clean

C. From the terms in Column I, choose the one that is used for each produce item in
   Column II. Each letter may be used more than once.

   *Column I*                      *Column II*

   A. Sacks                        1. Apples
   B. Crates                       2. Avocados
   C. Bunches                      3. Artichokes
   D. Cartons                      4. Apricots
   E. Flats                        5. Berries
   F. Lugs                         6. Carrots
                                   7. Cabbage
                                   8. Cauliflower
                                   9. Cherries
                                  10. Chives
                                  11. Eggplants
                                  12. Grapes
                                  13. Leeks
                                  14. Melons
                                  15. Mangos
                                  16. Onions
                                  17. Parsnips
                                  18. Pineapples
                                  19. Plums
                                  20. Potatoes, fieldgrade
                                  21. Radishes
                                  22. Romaine
                                  23. Salad Potatoes
                                  24. Scallions
                                  25. Watercress

D. Answer in your own words:

   1. Describe the cleaning and washing of Romaine lettuce.

   2. Compare the storage of vegetables with the storage of fruits.

# Unit 14  Eggs and Dairy Goods

*OBJECTIVES*

After studying this unit, the student should be able to

- Explain why dairy and egg products need extra storage care.
- Explain the quality grading of eggs.
- List the graded sizes and weights of eggs.
- Classify cheeses of the Western world.
- Establish the reasons why chefs need quality in dairy products.

Eggs and dairy goods are one more group of perishable foods used in cooking. Eggs have no relation to dairy food. They are perishable and often used with dairy goods. The milkman who delivers to institutional kitchens will supply eggs on request.

## EGGS

Eggs may have been man's best protein source since the dawn of history. Today they are needed in all styles of cookery. Their price is still reasonable in the USA. Other countries have much higher prices. Eggs are fragile, very perishable and possibly salmonella carriers. *Salmonella* is a bacteria that causes most of the common foodborne illnesses, such as upset stomach and food poisoning. Salmonella can be found everywhere, but they are nearly always on poultry products. Continuous refrigeration of these goods is a necessity. Careless, or not cold enough, storage will create dangers to health. This applies to raw eggs, with or without shells, and dishes with raw or partially raw yolks in them.

### Grading of Eggs

Grading of eggs is for wholesomeness, quality, and size. The difference lies in their freshness. All eggs sold commercially come from the same type of chicken (leghorns). The chickens are formula fed to control the thickness of the shell, the color of the yolk, and to fight infectious diseases. The freshest eggs are graded AA, the rest A, and all those with blemishes or cracks on the outside, but still wholesome, are graded B. Grade B eggs, because of the cracks, should only be used in baking, where full sterilization through heat can take place. Only the best and freshest AA should be used if the eggs are to be used raw, or only partly cooked. Fried eggs, "sunny-side up", are only partly cooked. The yolk stays raw. Mayonnaises or buttercreams

---

Eggs for institutional supply are packed 15 dozens to one box. Each box contains 7 corrugated egg trays for protecting eggs. In between are 6 layers of 30 eggs each.

Eggs are graded into 6 sizes:

| Grade | Weight per dozen | Grade | Weight per dozen |
|-------|------------------|-------|------------------|
| JUMBO | 30 ounces | MEDIUM | 21 ounces |
| EXTRA LARGE | 27 ounces | SMALL | 18 ounces |
| LARGE | 24 ounces | PEEWEE | 15 ounces |

*Quality Grading USDA Standards*

AA = US Fresh Fancy          A  =  US Grade A          B = US Grade B

The three quality grades are based on the storage potential and actual freshness on day of inspection. When grading for AA Fancy and US Grade A, all cracked eggs at the time of inspection are removed and added to the Grade B.

**TABLE 14-1 EGG GRADES AND WEIGHTS, QUALITY GRADING**

contain raw egg yolks. Warm egg sauces like "Hollandaise" or "Sabayon" are raw since they are heated to 125°F. or 130°F. This prevents curdling. (Hollandaise, sect. 4, unit 16, Sabayon, sect. 5, unit 28).

Egg sizes are graded by U.S.D.A. standards. The largest size is called Jumbo, then Extra Large, Large, Medium, Small, and Peewee. Bigger eggs give a better yield. Peewees are used in pantry and buffet work for decorative looks rather than nutritional value. Breakfast restaurants have become famous for serving fresh jumbo eggs on fried, poached, and boiled egg orders. For scrambled eggs or omelettes, smaller ones may be used without changing the portion size.

## DAIRY PRODUCTS

### Milk

Fresh milk is pasteurized and homogenized, then distributed in a great variety of containers for many different purposes. Milk in food establishments can be resold as a table beverage or used for cooking. The chef handles the milk. In cooking, milk is used for soups, sauces, and desserts. Sauces made from milk often become parts of other dishes. When real milk is used (instead of the lately popular nondairy milk substitutes), the freshest and richest milk is best. Rich milk has a high butterfat content. Fresh milk sours easily and has to be stored as close as possible to a 34°F. temperature. Milk is heated or scalded in a double boiler, with controlled temperature to prevent boiling over. When milk boils over, some of the milk is lost. Milk will often scorch when heated over an open heat source. The scorched milk cannot be used. Milk, stored too long, could become infected by bacteria. Souring cannot be tasted at this point, and the milk will curdle when heated. In milk that *curdles*, the milk separates into water and milk solids. Many chefs have changed to milk substitutes because curdling of milk happens more often now than it used to do. It may take a long time to transport milk from cow to consumer. The USDA checks food service establishments to be sure milk is of good quality. Coffee shops and fast food services, where milk is made into milk shakes and soft ice cream, are checked most often.

*Cream.* Luxury cuisine uses much cream in its cooking. In milk that is not homogenized, the lighter butterfat rises in the container. It is taken off and called *cream*. After the cream is taken off the milk, the rest is called *skim milk*. Cream is classified by its butterfat content. *Whipping cream,* also called heavy cream, has between 30 and 40 percent butterfat. *Manufacturing cream,* which is whipping cream in three-gallon cans, can be handled at a cheaper price. *Commercial,* or coffee, cream has a 20 percent butterfat content. *Half and half* has 14 percent and is mostly used for coffee. *Sour cream* with 18 percent is a favorite with baked potatoes and in salad dressings.

Milk products are not graded for quality, like meat and eggs. They are classifed by butterfat content. The wholesomeness of milk products is assured by U.S.D.A. supervision during processing. The standards

| | CREAM, HEAVY WHIPPING | CREAM, HEAVY FRESH | CREAM, MANUFAC- TURING | CREAM, COFFEE | HALF & HALF | CREAM, SOUR | MILK |
|---|---|---|---|---|---|---|---|
| Container sizes: | 1/2 pint, pint, quart | 1/2 pint, pint, quart | 3-gallon | pint, quart, gallon | pint, quart, gallon | 1/2 pint, pint, quart, gallon | 1/2 pint, 1/3 pint, pint, quart, gallon |
| Uses: | Pastry | Supreme sauce | Supreme sauce | Supreme sauce | Cream sauce | Salads | Cream sauce |
| Uses: | Fruit salads | Sauce refinement | Sauce refinement | Sauce refinement | Cream soups | Dressing | Custards |
| Uses: | Beverage topping | Cream soups | Cream soups | Cream soups | Chowder | Vegetables | Chowders |
| Uses: | | | | | Oyster stew | Special sauces | Baking |

**TABLE 14-2 MILK AND CREAM IN COOKING**

for milk products are regulated by state laws. Products of some dairies have a butterfat content which is higher than the state laws require. For quality cookery, dairy products should have a high fat content and be absolutely fresh. The quality of a cream sauce is directly related to the quality of butter, milk, and cream used for it.

*Butter.* In French-Continental cuisine of the Western world, butter is used for its ability to give flavor. In areas where vegetable oils are not common, butter is ranked first among animal fats for easiest digestibility. There is no substitute for true butter flavor. There are substitutes for the nutritional values of butter, but they are only substitutes. The Western world, outside the USA, places more value on milk products (butter, cream, and cheese) than on milk itself. Butter and cream cannot be replaced in French-Continental cuisine, without losing the quality this cuisine demands. A certain superiority of the best French cooking in France can be related to the superiority of the dairy products available there.

Butter, when not fresh, develops an off taste and becomes rancid. In the USA, butter marked and sold as "sweet" is mislabeled and meaningless. Salt is added to butter to increase the storage time. Unsalted butter is better than salted butter. Salted butter absorbs more water. The light rancid taste caused by overstorage is not easily found with the salt flavor. Unsalted butter is available in most parts of the USA, but for a much higher price than regular butter. The milkman who delivers dairy goods supplies butter. It is packed in ¼-pound cubes, in 1-pound bricks, and in 50-pound blocks. He also supplies unsalted butter if it is ordered.

*Cheese.* *Cheeses* are fermented milk solids and have been a food source for several thousand years. They are now accepted in most parts of the world. Some large population groups, such as the Chinese and those influenced by their culture, refuse to eat what they call "spoiled milk". Natural cheese is made under 400-500 different names. Like cooking, cheese making is classified into a few basic groups. Beginning procedures of cheese making are alike. Only the finishing processes are slightly different. All cheese making has three factors that vary: a) the kind of milk, b) the microorganism used for coagulation, and c) the aging-curing factor. Most cheeses are made of cow's milk, but a few are made of sheep or goat's milk. Some strange cheeses, not sold in the USA, are made of milk from buffaloes, llamas, mares (female horses), reindeer, yaks, and zebras.

*Classification of Cheeses.* About 18 varieties of cheeses can include all the others. The more general classifications are hard cheeses, semihard cheeses, and soft cheeses. Nutritional values of cheese are high. Caloric value varies with the butterfat content, which can be from 5 to 75 percent. Natural cheeses for table and cooking use have a range from 30 to 50 percent butterfat. Some of the excellent French triple cream cheeses may have 80 percent. Most hard cheeses are used only for cooking. They can be grated before use, or kept pregrated in a cool, dry area for quite some time. Soft and semihard cheese must be refrigerated for storage. When it is to be used at the table, cheese is taken out of refrigeration and warmed up at room temperature for a few hours before serving. Temperatures for cheeses and red wines, which often go well together, should be about 68°F. The cheese groups listed on table 14-3 are classified under the best known names of their types.

| HARD | | SEMIHARD | | SOFT | |
|---|---|---|---|---|---|
| | | | | Cured | Fresh |
| PARMESAN | CHEDDAR | FONTINA | BLUE | BRIE | CREAM |
| Parmesan | Cheddar | Fontina | Danish Blue | Fromage de Brie | Cream |
| Reggiano | American | Bel Paese | Roquefort | Camembert | Neufchatel |
| Romano | Cheshire | Port Salut | Gorgonzola | Liederkranz | Boursin |
| Sardo | Tillamook | Reblochon | Stilton | Schloss | Gervais |
| | | Teleme Jack | | Coulommiers | Cottage |
| | Swiss | Monterey Jack | | Breakfast | Ricotta |
| | Gruyere | Oka | | | |
| | Edam | | | | |
| | Gouda | | | | |

**TABLE 14-3 CHEESE TYPES IN GROUPS UNDER THEIR MOST POPULAR NAMES**

| SOUPS | SAUCES | VEGETABLES EGGS PASTA FISH MEAT | SALADS | SNACKS CANAPE SANDWICH CHEESE PASTRY | PASTRY BAKING |
|---|---|---|---|---|---|
| grated | grated | sliced grated | creamed | grated sliced creamed | creamed |
| Parmesan Romano Sardo Cantal | Cheddar Tillamook Parmesan | Swiss Jack Mozzarella Cheddar Romano Parmesan Provolone | Roquefort Gorgonzola Stilton Blue Brie Camembert | Cheddars Blue Brie Fontin Cream Choice | Cottage Cream Ricotta |

How to use them: very hard and dry – grated, semihard – sliced, soft – creamed.

**TABLE 14-4  CHEESES COMMONLY USED FOR COOKING**

*Cooked Cheese Dishes.* In cooking, cheese can be mixed into a preparation or can be sprinkled on as a topping. It can be used in slices to cover a surface. Then it melts and browns under heat. The browned cheese crust, with an appetizing smell, is called "au gratin" or sometimes "gratinate". Cheese is usually made into a cheese sauce first (Sauce Bechamel + cheese = Sauce Mornay) then used to cover the food in a dish. Cheese can be mixed into food as a binder for baking, or stirred into a finished risotto. Whenever cheese is used, the cheese flavor is expected to be noticed. Smoother and tastier sauces, as well as lighter and fluffier browned crusts are made from cheese with higher butterfat content. The selection of cheeses to use is a value judgement of the chef or the consumer. A grilled cheese sandwich, a cheeseburger, a cheese soufflé and custard cheese combinations are classified as cheese dishes. Food preparations and corresponding cheeses to be used are listed in table 14-4.

*Uncooked Cheese Dishes.* These are food combinations in which cheese is neither heated nor melted. The plain cheese sandwich can be changed into a "Gourmet" treat by using different breads, a variety of cheeses, and some better ways of presentation. The American luncheon dishes of Cottage Cheese and Fruits, or Fresh Fruit Salad with Cottage Cheese and dressing are standard on most lunch menus. There are cocktail cheese canapes and appetizers, celery sticks with cheese fillings, fruits with cheese filling, cheese cream desserts, and the famous blue cheese or roquefort salad dressings.

Countries which export cheese often sponsor cheese recipe contests to find new ways of using cheese. Cheese has a place in many regional and other food preparations, and at the end of a fine dinner. A preparation named "Alla Italian" is not necessarily covered with parmesan cheese. Some of the leading cheese names for table use are listed in table 14-5.

## SUMMARY

The last group of perishable foods consists of eggs and dairy goods, both of them supplied by the dairy truck or what is commonly called the milkman. Milk, milk products, and eggs have to be continuously re-

| HARD CHEESES, Sliceable | SEMIHARD CHEESES | BLUE VEINED CHEESES | FERMENTED SOFT CHEESES | FRESH SOFT DOUBLE CREAMED |
|---|---|---|---|---|
| Tillamook Swiss Gouda | Bel Paese Fontina Port Salut Reblochon | Stilton Roquefort | Fromage de Brie Camembert Coulommiers | Boursin Gervais |

For a display, cheeses are served in their original packaging, so the brands are visible. Only cheeses with the best reputation should be presented.

**TABLE 14-5  AFTER DINNER CHEESES FOR A CHEESE BOARD (Buffet or Table Service)**

frigerated. They are easily infected with bacteria. Eggs, as chicken products, may be potential salmonella carriers. Salmonella, the feared bacteria of kitchens, are responsible for most of mankind's food-borne illnesses. Fortunately, they are seldom fatal but still bothersome. The USDA checks and supervises egg distribution and grading, as well as milk and dairy standards. The sanitary handling of milk in food preparations or as a beverage to the customer, is the responsibility of the chef. The USDA is in charge of inspecting milk distribution facilities, and frequent checks on milk handling equipment are common. The USDA, as a federal agency, is completely independent of the local health inspector. In fresh milk products, as compared to cheese, freshness is a part of quality. The other part is butterfat content. Cream sauces or cheese dishes can never be better than the quality of the dairy products used. Butter, the most important milk product, is important in French-Continental cookery. There are substitutes for butter's nutritional values, but not for its characteristic flavor. Unsalted butter is superior to salted butter. Cheese, made from the best part of milk, has been known to mankind for several thousand years. It is not accepted by all the people of the world as food. In China it is considered 'spoiled milk' and is not eaten. About 400 to 500 different cheeses exist. Cheese making, like cooking, can be classified and reduced to a few simple processes. In high class restaurants, cheeses are not only used for cooking but also for table service as a final course. Cheese has an important place in the cuisines of the Western world. Caution should be used in the promotion of cheese-combination dishes if they have doubtful culinary value.

## DISCUSSION TOPICS

1. Is egg grading a valid indication of freshness?

2. Is it economical to buy smaller eggs, when shelled eggs by the cup are required?

3. Do cooks have to be concerned as much about salmonella as chefs and managers?

4. Why is milk pasteurized and homogenized?

5. Was it necessary for chefs to switch to nondairy cream products?

6. Why is unsalted butter not generally used in the USA?

7. To which section of cooking could cheese making be compared?

8. Does butter really have an irreplaceable characteristic?

## SUGGESTED ACTIVITIES

1. Define the following: curdle, skim milk, homogenize, pasteurize, ricotta.

2. Film presentation on dairy farming.

3. Film presentation on a dairy plant.

4. Film presentation of cheese making.

5. Field trip to a dairy plant.

6. Field trip to a cheese factory.

7. Participate in cheese tasting, with a follow-up essay discussing the differences.

## ACHIEVEMENT REVIEW

A. Complete the following:

1. Eggs are an excellent and inexpensive source of _____.

2. Salmonella, a food-borne bacteria, is responsible for many food-borne _____ _____.

3. Continuous refrigeration of dairy goods is a _____.

4. Egg grading as AA, A, B, is essentially a grading for _____.

5.  Mayonnaise contains egg yolks that are _____.

6.  A fried egg "sunny-side up" is technically _____.

7.  Today's milk is pasteurized and _____.

8.  Milk is not only easily soured by bacteria, but reacts unfavorably when incorrectly heated. When this happens, it is said that the milk is _____.

9.  In French-Continental cuisine, butter is used for its easy digestibility and _____.

10. Butter substitutes can only replace the value butter has to _____.

11. Coagulated milk solids, molded and cured, are sold under the name of _____
    _____.

B.  Read each question carefully and completely before answering it. Select the *best* answer.

1.  Eggs graded for size are *not* given one of the following names:

    a. peewee                c. jumbo
    b. country               d. medium

2.  Eggs graded for freshness and wholesomeness are *not* stamped

    a. AAA                   c. A
    b. AA                    d. B

3.  The egg size called Jumbo should weigh, by the dozen,

    a. 36 ounces             c. 30 ounces
    b. 33 ounces             d. 27 ounces

4.  Manufacturing cream, which is cheaper in price than whipping cream, has a butterfat content of about

    a. 42%                   c. 26%
    b. 34%                   d. 18%

5.  Skim milk is milk without a normal content of

    a. calcium               c. butterfat
    b. milk solids           d. vitamins

6.  The minimum butterfat content of whipping cream is regulated by

    a. USDA                       c. dairy industry
    b. Public Health Department   d. state law

7.  Cheese is sold under close to 500 names. The number of basic groups is only about

    a. 22                    c. 18
    b. 20                    d. 16

8.  In the general classification of cheeses one group *not* included is

    a. fermented             c. semihard
    b. soft                  d. hard

9.  The law requires that all milk products sold commercially are

    a. homogenized           c. sterilized
    b. pasteurized           d. osterized

10. One of the best known hard cheeses is

    a. Mozarella               c. Fontina
    b. Parmesan           d. Port Salut

C. Match the egg grades in Column I with the weights listed in Column II.

| *Column I* | *Column II* |
| --- | --- |
| Large | 1. 15 ounces |
| Peewee | 2. 18 " |
| Jumbo | 3. 21 " |
| Medium | 4. 24 " |
| Extra Large | 5. 27 " |
| Small | 6. 30 " |

D. Match each cheese in Column I with its closest relative in Column II.

| *Column I* | *Column II* |
| --- | --- |
| Cheddar | 1. Gervais |
| Parmesan | 2. Liederkranz |
| Edam | 3. Gorgonzola |
| Port Salut | 4. Reggiano |
| Stilton | 5. Tillamook |
| Camembert | 6. Oka |
| Neufchatel | 7. Gouda |

# Unit 15 Breading and Coating with Batter

*OBJECTIVES*

After studying this unit, the student should be able to

- List the reasons for breading.
- Identify breading ingredients.
- Describe the breading process.
- List the steps of the breading sequence.
- Define various batters.
- Explain the deep frying of batter-covered foods as compared to breaded foods.

The necessity of coating deep fried foods was explained in unit 8 in the paragraph "Coatings for fried foods". Raw potatoes contain starch and water and do not need coating. The most important and most widely used coating is breading.

## BREADING

*Breading* is the term for coating portion-sized or smaller pieces of raw or precooked food with flour, egg, and bread crumbs before frying them in hot fat. Frying is a fast cooking process which does not tenderize tough food. Some foods must be preboiled and cooled, then breaded and refried to the order, when needed.

For frying, fat is heated to a minimum temperature of 325°F. Starch, which is in all coatings, cooks near 200°F. Thus, food covered with starch can be exposed to frying heat for only a short time, without getting too brown. This is why tender foods can be cooked from the raw stage, but tough foods are tenderized first by boiling.

Breading might have started to use up leftovers. Food has always been considered precious, and bread is symbolic for food. It is never wasted or thrown away. Leftover stale bread was made into crumbs and its best use became the breading of today.

---

*Purposes of Breading:*

1. Breading keeps food juicier, therefore, better tasting.
2. Breading adds nutritional values to food.
3. Breading gives a better look to fried foods.
4. Breading uses up leftover bread.
5. Breading preserves the original food taste by acting as a shield against the frying fat.
6. Breading permits the refrying of leftover cooked foods.
7. Breading changes many foods into finger food, as snacks and appetizers.

---

Breading can be done in advance. Breaded raw or cooked food can be kept under refrigeration or frozen. These are two important advantages as compared to plain flour or batter coating.

Breading is used on all meats, fish, shellfish, many vegetables, and even a piece of swiss cheese or a hard boiled egg can be breaded, fried, and served as a specialty.

The term 'breading' originally meant that bread in the form of crumbs was used as coating. Chefs liked the better looks, taste, and handling of breaded foods, so they experimented and replaced bread crumbs with similar or fancier products.

*Ingredients Used.* Today a variety of crumbs are used. Cheapest and most common, but not best, are cracker crumbs. French bread crumbs, at a high price, are available from French bread bakeries. The efficient chef makes his own crumbs from all leftover and dried white bread. For special quality breading, he uses French bread without crust. For unusual effects and taste, cornmeal (gritty) can be used. Luxury cuisine uses ground, unsweetened coconut and grated white or brown almonds. Raw, well-beaten eggs, sometimes diluted with water, milk, or oil are used to keep the crumbs stuck to the food. A trick of the trade, but unknown to many food service workers, is the use of all-purpose flour to prevent the egg from peeling off the food while it is frying.

### Breading Process

Breading not done in the proper sequence becomes a waste of time and material. It also results in messy, unsatisfactory food.

The sequence of breading described in these paragraphs is a manual process for one right-handed cook. Food processing plants use different types of conveyor belts, machines, and automatic sifters, but the principle of breading and its flow of work remains unchanged.

*Utensils.* The most practical utensils are two large flat standard steamtable pans and one 12 to 18-inch stainless steel bowl. One pan is filled with sifted all-purpose flour, and the other pan is filled with sifted bread crumbs. A few pounds are put in each pan according to the quantity of food to be breaded. Well-beaten eggs go into the bowl.

*Setup.* On a large enough working table, the items to be breaded are placed at the left end. Next to them are the pan with the flour, the bowl with the well-beaten eggs, and then the pan with the bread crumbs. On the right end of this line is a sheet pan for holding the breaded food.

*The Breading Process.* Certain steps must be followed for breading. If the items to be breaded are pork chops, the actual breading is as follows:

1. The left hand picks up one single pork chop (*without* the help of the right hand), and dips both sides into the flour.
2. Extra flour is shaken off the chop, still with the left hand only, and the chop is dropped into the egg, to be covered fully with egg. The *left hand* picks the chop out of the egg, drips off the extra egg and drops the chop into the bread crumbs. At this time it must be emphasized that the hand which touches flour and egg must never touch the bread crumbs. If it does, big lumps of gluey breading mass will stick to the fingers of the left hand and make proper and clean breading impossible.
3. The left hand goes immediately back to the raw pork chops and repeats the whole process.
4. At the same time as the left hand goes back, the right hand (which must be dry and clean) covers the chop with crumbs and pats them on, making sure that all parts of the meat are properly covered.
5. The right hand lifts out the chop, shakes off any extra bread crumbs, and places the breaded chop flat on the sheet pan.

*Storage of Breaded Foods.* Although breaded foods are ready for immediate deep or pan frying, they have to be stored at least for the length of the service period. If the foods are not sold, they are kept until the next day. To prevent them from sticking together, breaded items must be laid out neatly, in rows, on a flat pan that has been dusted with bread crumbs and is completely dry. If possible, the sheet should be covered with paper towels or butcher paper. Breaded foods must never be stacked, unless frozen. For short periods during service, two layers with paper in between would be acceptable. There should be enough air circulation through the breaded items to prevent a loss of quality and any sticking together of the food. Too long a storage time is not advised. If breaded food has to be frozen for later use, then the freezing should be done with food in single layers on sheets of waxed paper. When frozen solid, the food can be stacked in a box, with paper between. After it is wrapped in plastic, it can be kept frozen for only a few weeks.

### BATTER FOR FRYING

Flour mixed with liquids is called batter as long as it stays in a liquid or semiliquid state. Usually batter has the consistency of a sauce. Most batters are improved with egg yolks, egg whites, or whole eggs, and

**Materials needed for about 20 orders of Filet of Sole or food similar in shape:**

9 pounds fresh fillet of sole
2 pounds all-purpose flour
2 pounds bread or cracker crumbs

2½ cups well-blended eggs
1 ounce of oil or water

A.  **The lineup from left to right:**

Trimmed fish for 20 portions, salted moderately on both sides.
One standard steam table size pan with flour.
Another pan of the same size with the crumbs.
Eggs blended with oil in a 12" stainless bowl.
A dry, 18" x 24" bake sheet, covered with butcher paper.

B.  **The Breading**

1.  Pick up only one piece of fish with the left hand, dip both sides of fish into flour. Shake off surplus flour.
2.  Drop fish completely into egg bowl. Pick up fish with *left hand* and strip off surplus egg by using the side wall of the bowl.
3.  Drop fish, flat and straight, into the middle of the bread crumbs, but do not touch crumbs with the left hand.
4.  With the *right hand* cover fish with crumbs. Pat them on.
5.  Lift the crumb-covered fish carefully. Do *not* tear the breading. Shake off extra crumbs. Place fish flat on the baking sheet.
6.  Repeat these phases until all pieces of fish are breaded.

There must be *no* overlap of hands. If the hand used for flour and eggs gets into the crumbs, the fingers will get "breaded" instead of the food. Each hand has its own function. As soon as these movements are coordinated and controlled, the speed of working should increase. With practice, the breading of 20 food orders should take about 10 minutes.

C.  **Cleanup**

1.  The cook washes and dries his hands thoroughly.
2.  He moves the breaded food to a refrigerator.
3.  He refrigerates the leftover eggs for further use, or discards them.
4.  He sifts the flour and puts it into a clean container for storage.
5.  He sifts the bread crumbs and puts them in a clean container.
6.  He shakes out sifter and returns it to the storage.
7.  He returns all utensils and materials to proper storage.
8.  He wipes the working table clean with a wet towel.
9.  He washes his hands again and reports to the chef that he is ready for the next assignment.

**TABLE 15-1  A COMPLETE WORK CYCLE FOR BREADING**

contain baking powder or yeast. Batter-fried foods have a completely different appearance, texture, and taste than the same foods breaded. To use batter is a culinary variation, not an economic one.

*Batter Handling*

Food which has been dipped into batter must be fried immediately to prevent the batter from running off the food. This makes batter less practical to handle than breading. Another pitfall to batter frying in a commercial deep fryer is the fact that deep fryers use baskets to hold food. Batter-dipped food which is dropped into the frying basket sinks to the bottom while the batter is still raw. Then it sticks to the wire of the basket. When the cooked food is moved, the crust breaks open. The food gets greasy and soggy and the purpose of the batter frying is lost. To prevent this, food must not be dropped directly into the hot fat. It must be held by hand, with half of the food covered with hot fat for several seconds, until the outer crust forms. Thus, the deep frying of batter-coated food takes too much time and is often wasteful.

*Batter Uses.* Many foods fried in batter are called fritters, such as apple fritters and banana fritters. In French terminology, little rolls of cooked, chopped food, bound together with some sauce are called *"Cromesquis"*. These are similar to "Croquettes" (see section 4, unit 20, Croquettes) because both are made the same way and deep fried. But croquettes are breaded and cromesquis are batter covered. The most well-known of the foods fried in batter are the English "Fish and Chips" and the Japanese "Tempura". Both are a combination of fish and vegetable, dipped in batter, and fried to order. All foods fried in batters must be served immediately or they will lose appearance and texture.

**GENERAL RULES FOR ALL BATTERS**

1. Dry ingredients are sifted and mixed well.
2. Wet ingredients are blended together.
3. COMBINE DRY INGREDIENTS WITH 2/3 OF THE WET MIXTURE TO A SMOOTH PASTE WITH-OUT LUMPS.
4. When smooth, add the remaining liquid slowly.
5. Whip until sauce-like thickness is reached.
6. Put all batters, except those with yeast, under refrigeration from 3 hours to overnight.
7. Stir before use, and test with a small amount of food first.

───────────────── ATTENTION: KEY POINTS ─────────────────

- Reread "Batter Handling" (unit 15) before frying.

- Batter will only stick to food while frying if the food is completely dry.

- The best method is to dip all food into flour, as for breading, before dipping it into the batter.

**SIMPLE BATTER (Common for Fish and Chips)**

Ingredients needed for about 20 orders:

3 cups all-purpose flour
1/2 cup cornstarch
2 teaspoons salt
2 teaspoons baking powder
3 egg whites, half whipped
1 cup cold water
3/4 cup to one cup additional cold water

*Procedure:* See general rules for all batters.

**WINE BATTER FOR FRUITS AND DESSERTS**

Ingredients needed for about 20 orders:

3 1/2 cups of all-purpose flour.
2 teaspoons of baking powder.
2 teaspoons of sugar
1 teaspoon salt
4 whole well-beaten eggs
3/4 cup of dry white wine
additional: 1 cup white wine

*Procedure:* See general rules for all batters.

**BEER AND YEAST BATTER (For meat and fish specialties)**

Ingredients needed for about 20 orders:

3 1/2 cups all-purpose flour
1/2 teaspoon sugar
1 teaspoon instant dry yeast
4 egg yolks
12 ounces stale warm beer

When combined as usual, put batter in a warm place (85°F. to 90°F.) for about one hour, or until batter has doubled. Punch down and dilute with 3/4 to 1 cup of additional beer to desired thickness. Add 1 teaspoon of salt. Batter is ready for use, or may be kept under refrigeration to slow yeast growth.

*Additional Procedure:* See general rules for all batters.

**TABLE 15-2**

*Various Batters.* The simplest batter consists of a pan of flour and a bowl of eggwash. *Eggwash* is the term for beaten eggs diluted with liquid and used for various coatings. A good mixture is made of one part beaten whole egg and one part rich milk. The procedure is similar to breading except that bread crumbs are not used. The sequence for this simple dip is flour, eggwash, flour, and then into the hot fat to fry. A better crust-producing dip is flour, eggwash, flour and eggwash once more. Then it goes into the hot fat for frying. Many chefs have developed their own special variations.

*True Batters*

True batters are made in many variations. The liquid can be different: water, milk, buttermilk, sour cream, wine, beer, or a combination of these. The flour is mostly all-purpose. Rice, corn, or even potato starch is often added. The ratio of flour to liquid has a wide span and by adding whole eggs or parts of them, many different batters can be created. In addition, to control the crispness and desired outcome of the food, *leavening* agents (baking powder and yeast) are used in addition to or instead of the eggs. The contents of a batter depend on the intentions of the chef. Wine and egg batters are often used for fruit fritters. Beer and yeast batters are more often used for the heavier meat and fish preparations. Batters can be changed as the cook wishes.

## SUMMARY

The term breading is used to describe the coating of portion-sized or smaller pieces of raw or cooked food with flour, egg, and bread crumbs. Bread crumbs are an economical leftover use of stale bread, which should never be wasted. The purposes of breading are many: better appearance, better acceptance, and improved nutritional value. Luxury cuisine uses ground coconuts and almonds instead of the more common crumbs. Cracker crumbs, which are cheaper, are often substituted for real bread crumbs. Every kitchen should have enough leftover bread to make crumbs. Understanding the correct sequence and lineup of the breading process saves time and produces better food. Breading is very convenient for the fast food operator, since it can be done in advance and the deep frying is not complicated. Plain or fancy batters can be used to cover various deep fried foods. Batters are more time consuming to handle and not as convenient as regular breaded food. The plainest method of using a batter is similar to breading. Eggwash, diluted well-beaten egg with an equal quantity of milk, is used instead of pure egg, and no bread crumbs are used. The food is merely dipped into the flour, thereby creating a batter. For a crisper batter, food can be dipped once more into eggwash before it is deep fried. True batters are premade and consist of water, milk, wine or beer, flour, eggs, and baking powder or yeast. All-purpose flour is used most often. In special recipes, rice, corn or potato starch can be added to the batter. Most fruits and vegetables fried in batter are called fritters. The most widely known dish made with batter is the English "Fish and Chips".

## DISCUSSION TOPICS

1. Why was breading introduced as a cooking method?

2. Why are there different batters for different uses?

3. Does breading have quality differences?

## SUGGESTED ACTIVITIES

1. Define: leavening agent, eggwash, tempura, butcher paper.

2. Examine samples of different crumbs. Distinguish cracker from bread crumbs.

3. Watch the demonstration of breading by one cook.

4. Practice breading and its proper lineup.

## ACHIEVEMENT REVIEW

A. Complete the following:

1. Food coated with batter just dropped into the deep fryer basket has the tendency to get _____ .

2. The cheapest bread crumb substitutes are _____ .

3. Breading keeps food juicier, therefore _____ .

4. Breading means coating food with flour, egg, and _____ .

5. For fancy breading, luxury cuisine uses sometimes brown _____ .

6. A piece of swiss cheese, as a special dessert, can be _____ .

7. The breading process can be applied to all tender _____ .

8. Batter frying is not as convenient as breading. It consumes more _____ .

9. Fruits fried in batter are called _____ _____ .

10. The best known English dish in the USA is made with a batter and is called

_____ .

B. Read each question carefully and completely before answering it. Select the *best* answer.

1. The correct lineup for breading meat is

   a. meat, flour, crumbs, eggs    c. meat, flour, eggs, crumbs
   b. meat, crumbs, eggs, flour    d. meat, eggs, flour, crumbs

2. The finest bread crumbs are chef-made in the kitchen from

   a. leftover dried toast    c. leftover dried french bread
   b. leftover dried bread    d. no-crust dried french bread

3. Which of the following cannot be substituted for bread crumbs in breading?

   a. cracker crumbs    c. ground almonds
   b. cracked wheat     d. ground coconuts

4. Which of the following could *not* be used as the liquid for batter?

   a. oil     c. milk
   b. wine    d. water

5. Only small pieces of food can be coated for frying because

   a. the deep fryer has a size limitation
   b. deep fried food should be used for finger food
   c. big pieces would use too much fat
   d. too long frying time would burn the coating

6. Which one of these foods is most likely to be fried in a wine batter?

   a. corn fritters       c. chicken croquettes
   b. banana fritters     d. fish and chips

C. Answer in your own words:

1. List as many reasons as you can for breading food.

2. Briefly describe the breading process.

3. Compare the use of batter to the use of breading. (Ingredients, procedure, usage).

4. List the ingredients for beer batter.

# Section 4 How to Cook Typical Food Dishes

## Unit 16 Deep Frying and Pan Frying

*OBJECTIVES*

After studying this unit, the student should be able to

- Identify foods which can be fried.
- Demonstrate the deep frying of fish in a batter.
- Demonstrate the pan frying of breaded pork cutlets.
- Analyze and cook one order of southern fried chicken.

Deep frying and pan frying are a part of cooking in fat, as discussed in section 2, unit 8. This unit explains the frying of food in hot fat, whether it is done in a pan or in a commercial deep fryer.

There is one most important difference between frying and sautéing. Fried food must be separated from the cooking fat and served as dry as possible. Sautéed food has the small quantities of good fat mixed into the finished dish.

*PROCESS REVIEW*

Pan frying and commercial deep frying stay within a heat range of 325°F. to 375°F. Any mild fat, which can be heated to these temperatures without burning, may be used. The degree of temperature needed for frying limits the frying time. A relatively high temperature can only be applied for short cooking times and to small pieces of food. Frying at 325°F. produces nearly 50% more heat than boiling water at 212°F. It therefore cooks faster. The use of frying temperatures lower than 325°F. is not practical because

- the coating would wash off
- the fat would penetrate the food, and make it greasy
- very little browning would occur

Cooking without moisture does not tenderize tough food. Therefore, only tender raw or precooked foods can be fried.

The chef must select the correct size and quality of foods he wants for fast frying. Only portion-sized or smaller, tender, moist food pieces can be fried. Either breading or batter coating must be used as a shield between food and fat.

| | |
|---|---|
| 1. | Keep fryer hot only when necessary. |
| 2. | Keep fat at 375°F.; no hotter. |
| 3. | Strain or filter fat as often as possible. |
| 4. | Keep fried foods crisp and greaseless. |
| 5. | Frying is a fast food process. Food should be fried just before serving. |
| 6. | Do not place wet foods in a deep fryer. |

**TABLE 16-1 SOME KEY POINTS FOR DEEP FRYING**

Deep fried foods are well done. Therefore, frying needs less skill than broiling, and is done by fry cooks who are still on the lowest level of the chef ranks. They must apply all the principles of cooking to frying. Food could be dried out and browned too much. There is no excuse for doing an imperfect job.

## FOOD PREPARATIONS

All fried foods are to be served fresh and dry. In some luxury restaurants, fried food is served on doily papers (lace) or napkins to be sure of complete greaselessness.

Fried foods are served with lemon wedges or sauces. The choice depends on the chef and the customs of the area.

Seafood, in most areas, is served with tartar or remoulade sauces. If no sauce is indicated on the menu, lemon wedges are served. Fresh whole parsley is used to create a more appetizing eye appeal. Warm sauces served with fried foods may be tomato sauce, white cream, or supreme sauces.

---

The following process can be used for all food items which are fried in batter.

1. The prepared food portions are salted and dipped in flour.

2. A small bowl with batter is in the left hand of the fry cook, who is standing close to the fryer.

3. The prepared food is taken with the right hand, put into the batter, then lifted out; extra batter is wiped off on the side wall of the bowl.

4. The cook dips 3/4 of the food piece into the fat. If the whole piece were dropped into the basket, the soft batter would wrap itself around the wire basket and stick when fried. The food must be hand held for 10 to 15 seconds until the batter develops some crust.

5. The food now is dropped all the way into the basket. The process is repeated with other pieces of food.

6. Most fried foods will float to the top after about 3 to 4 minutes. Doneness depends on the type of fried food. The first order should be checked carefully by breaking it open in the middle. The average frying time can then be set correctly.

7. The cooked food is lifted out of the fryer and put on a paper towel to drain. It must be served immediately.

---

**Fish and Chips.** Fish and Chips are deep fried fish in batter, served with french fried potatoes, and some malt vinegar on the side. Any fish fillet can be used, but codfish and haddock are most popular.

**Fillet of Sole Orly.** Fillet of Sole Orly is the French version of Fish and Chips. As the name implies, only fillet of sole can be used. Instead of the vinegar, tomato sauce is served on the side. The french fries may be served, omitted, or substituted.

**Smelts.** Fried Breaded Smelts are cleaned smelts, which are salted, breaded (see unit 15), and then fried to the order.

**Prawns.** Fried Breaded Prawns are raw peeled and deveined prawns, 36/40 or larger, split open along the vein and *butterflyed*. They are salted, breaded and fried like smelts.

**Seafood.** Fried Oysters, Scallops, Squid, or any other suitable seafood is handled the same way. It may be either breaded or batter fried.

**Southern Fried Chicken.** Southern Fried Chicken is made using small spring chickens (1-1 1/4 lb.), which have been disjointed and salted. A type of batter is chosen and the chickens are fried at 325°F. until done. Often pressure deep fryers, broasters, are used for this preparation. Broasters reduce the cooking time. Southern fried chicken is garnished with honey, corn or banana fritters and french fries. It is often served in a basket.

**Viennese Fried Chicken.** Viennese Fried Chickens are similar to southern fried chickens, but breading is used instead of the batter. The raw chicken livers and the preboiled gizzards are included with the fried chicken. It is served dry, with lemon and fried parsley.

*Breaded Pork Cutlet.* The cutlets are cut from the pork leg, the boneless loin, or the "Boston" butt. They are pounded and stretched with the flat side of a cleaver, salted, breaded, and pan fried to the order.

*Wiener Schnitzel.* Wiener Schnitzel is like a pork cutlet but is cut from the leg of dairy veal. The true Wiener Schnitzel is served dry, garnished with lemons and parsley.

*Schnitzel a la Hollstein.* Schnitzel a la Hollstein is a Wiener Schnitzel garnished with anchovies, capers, and hard boiled chopped egg in addition to the lemon.

*Veal Cutlet Parmigiana.* Veal Cutlet Parmigiana is a breaded veal cutlet, pan fried, topped with a slice of cheese and cooked until a brown crust forms. The cheeses used include Mozarella, Swiss, Jack, and Parmesan. A light tomato sauce is served underneath the cutlet or in a side dish.

*Chicken Croquettes.* About 2 pounds of chopped cooked chicken is mixed with 1 cup of simmering sauce (such as veloute) and brought to a boil. This mixture is seasoned, tightened with 2 or 3 egg yolks, spread on a baking sheet, cooled, and then shaped into cylinders of 1 - 2 1/2 inches. These rolls are deep-cooled or half frozen, then breaded, and fried to the order.

Croquettes can be made of any mixture of leftover food. Sauce and egg yolks are needed to keep them together. There are seafood, meat, and vegetable croquettes. The combinations and garnishes reflect the taste of the chef.

---

**ATTENTION: KEY POINTS**

- Fried food should always be golden brown and crisp. Either breaded or in batter, this food should have a light, fluffy appearance.
- Sauce is never poured over fried food. It is served underneath or in a side dish.

---

## SUMMARY

Deep frying and pan frying are a part of cooking in fat. The main characteristic of frying is separation of fat and food after the cooking. Fat is preheated to $325°F. - 375°F$. If lower temperatures are used, the food loses its coating, gets greasy, and may not brown properly. Due to the fast browning of the starchy coating in high heat, foods can only be kept in the fryer a short time. As a result, food has to be suitably small or thin to become well-done in the same time it takes to brown.

The most popular fried foods are chicken, fish, veal, pork, and vegetables. Sometimes tough vegetables are preboiled before they are browned and crisped by frying.

### DISCUSSION TOPICS

1. What are the coatings in which foods can be fried?
2. How are frying fats selected?
3. Is deep frying a hazard to health?
4. Is pan frying a hazard to health?
5. How is a fried product kept crisp?

### SUGGESTED ACTIVITIES

1. Define: butterflyed, fillet, croquette, garnish, broaster.
2. Bread and fry a serving of "Viennese Fried Chicken".
3. Deep fry an order of "Fish and Chips".
4. Prepare a "Veal Cutlet a la Parmigiana".
5. Demonstrate the pan frying of breaded pork cutlets.

*ACHIEVEMENT REVIEW*

A.  Complete the following:

1.  Cooking in fat is subdivided into sautéing and _____ .

2.  All fried foods should be served _____ .

3.  For the frying process, the size of food must be _____ .

4.  For "Fish and Chips", the fried fish is coated with _____ .

5.  Breaded fried prawns are made from prawns that are peeled, deveined, and

_____ .

6.  Croquettes are made of leftover food that has already been _____ .

7.  All fish is tender enough to be _____ .

8.  "Viennese Fried Chicken" is always _____ .

9.  A "Veal Cutlet Parmigiana" is a breaded veal cutlet with _____ .

B.  Read each question carefully and completely before answering it. Select the *best* answer.

1.  A typical Southern Fried Chicken should be served with

a. tartar sauce          c. parsley
b. honey                 d. lemon wedges

2.  Chicken croquettes made from leftover cooked chicken meat have a cylindrical shape and are

a. dipped in batter         c. breaded
b. covered with crackermeal d. dipped in flour and egg

3.  The best temperature range for frying is

a. 225°F. to 275°F.      c. 325°F. to 375°F.
b. 275°F. to 325°F.      d. 375°F. to 425°F.

4.  Using a commercial deep fryer for batter-dipped food is more time consuming than frying breaded foods because

a. the batter needs more time to cook
b. the batter could stick to the wire of the fry basket
c. batter-dipped foods cannot be precoated and stored
d. batter can be fried in lower temperatures only

# Unit 17  Roasting of Meat and Poultry

## OBJECTIVES

After studying and practicing the content of this unit, the student should be able to

- Establish the doneness of a roast by use of a meat thermometer.
- Prepare a given piece of meat for roasting.
- Identify bones and unnecessary meat parts to be removed before roasting.
- Select matching pans for roasts.
- Explain the importance of washing and salting of roasts.
- Establish the approximate roasting time of differently shaped roasts.

Section 2, unit 6, explained cooking with dry heat, specifically roasting. Unit 16 will explain the practical applications of roasting techniques for meat and poultry.

## PROCESS

The cooking of meat in dry heat, with fat only, is called *roasting*. Roasts do not need added water. The steam which comes from the water content of the roast must evaporate quickly. A low rimmed pan without cover is best for this. Meat properly roasted has a brown crust, but it is not dried out. It is juicy and tender, but not overcooked.

Roasts are like steaks in many ways. The same meat cut is used, with the same ingredients, and with the same cooking principle. The only differences are the degrees of temperature and the cooking time. A roast is first cooked and then carved. A steak is first cut and then cooked. Any roast, like any steak or chop, is only as tender as the raw meat quality will permit.

## ROASTING TIMES AND TEMPERATURES

The greatest error in roasting is to accept the popular Time-Tables formula based on the idea that total roasting time at a given temperature equals some number of minutes per pound times the number of pounds. Table 17-1 shows how little meaning there is to this principle.

Roasting time depends on the kind of meat, its size, its geometric shape, and the heat of the oven. Large roasts need slower heat for a longer time. Smaller roasts need higher heat for a shorter time. Low heat for huge, fat roasts reduces shrinkage. Low heat for lean young roasts increases dryness, causes slow caramelization and results in a lower quality. Roasting needs temperatures from 325°F. to 500°F. Ovens need preheating. Empty ovens, preheated to 400°F., drop in temperature by 20% to 320°F. as soon as the door is opened and the cold roast placed in it. Roasts must be started with a high beginning heat and then reduced after 10 or 15 minutes. Heat must be regulated for a balanced result because the brownness of the roast is important to appearance and taste.

Experienced roast cooks do not use meat thermometers to check the doneness of a roast. Their guidelines are a combination of looking at a roast and its drippings, its shape, the oven heat, the cooking time already past, and the application of finger pressure to the meat. For the young cook, it would be wise to use his own quality meat thermometer as a substitute for experience. Table 17-2 provides a temperature scale for roasting. Thermometers are inserted into the center of the roast. Proper handling of them is the key to satisfactory results.

## ROAST PREPARATIONS

The preparation of a piece of meat for roasting depends on the meat itself. The objective of roasting is to provide appetizing, tasty, juicy, hot, easy to eat slices of meat, which are carved to the order. For this

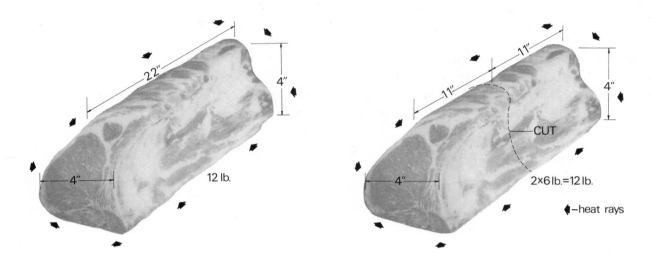 

**A FALSE FORMULA**

A widely accepted formula for total roasting time is weight times minutes per pound.

*Example:*

1 whole pork loin weighs 12 pounds. Cooking time: 30 minutes per lb. Total cooking time: 12 lbs. x 30 minutes per lb. = 360 minutes or 6 hours.

*Logical Conclusion:*

One half of the same pork loin weighs 6 pounds. Total cooking time: 6 x 30 minutes = 180 minutes or 3 hours. *Roasting time for half of the same loin = 3 hours.*

The falseness of this accepted formula is shown by the following diagram.

**HEAT PENETRATION DIAGRAM FOR THE ROASTING OF A PORK LOIN**

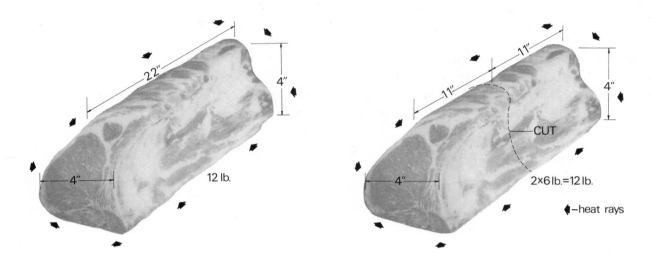

Heat rays strike and penetrate food uniformly. For a piece of food 4" in diameter, a penetration of 2" will carry heat to the center.

Of importance is the shortest distance from the outside to the center. 11" or 22" of length make no difference at all.

*Conclusion:*

HEAT RAYS IN A CONVECTION OVEN ARE EVERYWHERE AND WILL CONDUCT HEAT OVER THE SHORTEST DISTANCE.

FOR EACH SPECIFIC KIND OF MEAT OR FOOD, GEOMETRIC SHAPE, TRIM, AND FOOD MATERIAL (FAT, MEAT, BONE) ARE THE DECIDING FACTORS FOR DONENESS. Weight is not a factor.

**TABLE 17-1**

A meat thermometer of good quality must be used in the proper way. The sensitive tip of the thermometer is inserted into the center of the roast a short time before the roast is thought to be ready. The degrees of Fahrenheit listed reflect the degree of doneness no matter what kind of meat is used.

Carry-over heat and setting time (recirculation of juices) vary with the size of the roast (see table 6-1), and must be included. Depending on the roast, the retained heat (carry-over heat) during setting time will increase the final reading by about 10-15°F.

140°F. = rare or blood rare          155°F. = medium or medium rare          175°F. = well done

**ATTENTION: KEY POINT**

A roast, taken out of the oven at 130°F. + a 10° increase (equalization from the outside to the center) will be rare. But if removed at 140°F. + 10-15° increase during setting, the roast will be medium or medium rare.

**TABLE 17-2 THE USE OF A MEAT THERMOMETER**

result, the extra fat must be cut from the roast. Too much fat cover, which will not be eaten, prevents the lean meat from becoming crusty and brown. The extra fat also does not permit the penetration of the seasoning. This results in a double loss of taste. Too many drippings may fry the lower part of the roast and make the preparation of gravy difficult. Sinews, gristle, and loose pieces of meat, which would only burn, must also be removed. Bones stay in, if they will not obstruct the carving. They are good for heat conduction to the center of the roast. But such bones as *aitchbones* (hipbones), *chine bones,* (backbones), and shoulder blades should be removed without needless cutting of the meat. A roast with too many cuts will not stay as juicy and will fall apart when sliced. Roasts are not tied with strings to fake the appearance of one piece of meat, as is done at the retail counters of the supermarkets. String is used to hold extra fat in place or to improve the shape of the meat or poultry.

The selection of a properly fitting roast pan is very important. The rim should be lower than the meat so that the steam can escape. A heavy material will give better heat conduction and distribution. The pan must be only 2-3 inches larger than the roasts that are in it. If a pan is too large, the drippings will spread and burn before they are made into gravy. A pan with a high rim has more condensation than evaporation of steam and the result is closer to a pot roast.

The chef must decide if and how fat has to be added to the roast. Roasts that have enough fat of their own can be started dry at a lower temperature, until enough drippings have collected in the pan. Later the heat is increased. For average trimmed meats, the pan and the surface of the roast have to be oiled lightly. If the meat is truly lean, bacon, salted pork, or plain fat is added.

*Larding.* Strips of bacon or salt pork are put into lean meat with a larding needle. It is a common method for game birds and venison.

*Barding.* Slices of fat or bacon are tied over lean meat to protect it from drying out.

Washing is not needed when the meat is clean. Meat cuts delivered by the supplier can be used as they come. Sometimes soggy paper sticks to the meat and has to be removed.

### Salting and Seasoning

Some chefs do not salt meat before cooking because they claim that the salt does not pass into the roast; it draws out the juices and slows browning. Other chefs claim that the right way of salting does allow the salt to pass into the meat, and that there is no delay in the browning. If juices might be lost, which is doubtful, the taste and flavor of properly salted meat make up for everything which could have been lost. The proof, of course, is to make two identical roasts the two different ways and test them at the same time. The skilled chef knows the right way to salt. A ready roast, wetted and salted on its meat parts (not the fat covers) 30 to 60 minutes before roasting, will be much better than the unsalted one. The wetness dissolves the salt, which osmosis and capillary action suck into the roast.

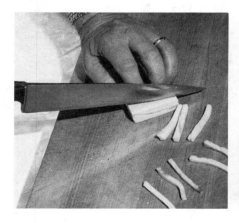

Fig. 17-1 Fat bacon or salt pork cut into Lardons. Approx. size 3/16" x 3/16" x 1 1/2"

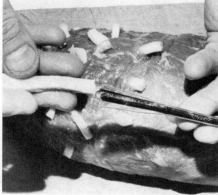

Fig. 17-2 The lardon is inserted into the larding needle

Fig. 17-3 When the larding needle has gone through the meat, the end of the lardon is held with one hand, while the other hand pulls the needle through.

Spices and herbs are used as a result of the chef's value judgement:

Dark meat, like beef, lamb, and venison, accepts pepper.

Pork, which is rather bland, goes well with garlic, lemon zeste, caraway, and some herbs.

Lamb can use garlic in addition.

Veal (dairy veal) and poultry are often seasoned with herbs such as oregano, thyme, basil, sage, and marjoram.

Roasting the continental way uses Mirepoix, which is added at the last quarter (or 25 minutes) of the roasting time. *Mirepoix* consists of onions, carrots, celery, and parsnips, cut into cubes of one inch. This root vegetable mixture improves the flavor of the gravy and also adds some flavor to smaller pieces of meat such as chicken, beef fillet and rack of lamb.

## *ROASTING OF BEEF*

Beef, for a la carte or banquet use, is roasted medium-rare to rare unless it is specified differently in advance. Roasting should be timed so as to reduce the time for warm keeping. This makes a better roast. During setting time (see table 6-2), the gravy should be made. If string was used, it is removed now, before the carving starts. General seasoning for beef is salt, pepper and sometimes paprika. Except for the ribs of beef, all beef roasts need a little fat in the roasting pan to cover the bottom and some fat brushed over the lean parts.

*Fillet of Beef or Beef Tenderloin.* This is the most expensive and most tender of all the beef roasts. It is served mostly at banquets or preordered parties. The warm-keeping time is limited. The average fillet weighs from 6 to 8 pounds and can be roasted fully trimmed or partly trimmed. For elegant presentation, it is trimmed to the silver skin and the lean surface is larded. The trimmed fillet tastes better, and the salt can pass into it easier. The crust is edible. Total roasting time for the trimmed fillet is about 25-30 minutes at 475°F. to 500°F. The untrimmed fillet needs about 45-55 minutes at 450°F. It may serve 12-15 guests.

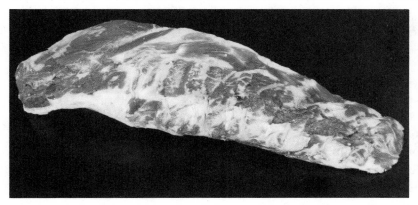

Fig. 17-4  Whole beef tenderloin (fillet), with fat partially on for roasting.

Fig. 17-5  A whole boneless strip loin, ready to be roasted.

*Strip Loin.* The New York strip, sirloin strip, or "Contre Filet Roti" is another expensive and excellent roast. Strips may weigh from 12 to 18 pounds. The flank tail should be trimmed close to the "eye". The back strap along the featherbones is removed. Any extra fat cover is trimmed off. Average total roasting time is 50 to 65 minutes at 375°F. to 400°F. It is best to roast the strip on a bed of bones on a rack. The yield is 18-26 orders.

*Top Sirloin.* This is not practical for a commercial roast. It is expensive and has an uneven yield because of its structure. It is roasted like the strip loin.

Fig. 17-6  Whole top sirloin, too irregular for portion control cutting but liked by many chefs for its flavor.

*Knuckle or Sirloin Tip.*  This is the least expensive beef roast. It is used for cold cuts, sandwiches, and cold plates. It weighs from 8 to 11 pounds. It has a better yield if trimmed and cut in half, lengthwise. The two halves are started in a skillet like a steak and finished in the oven at 400°F. for 25 to 40 minutes.

*Ribs of Beef.*  Ribs of beef is an American specialty. It is the main fare for many dinner houses or a "House of Prime Ribs". It is fairly expensive, not economic in yield, but the customers are paying the price. Ribs can be bought oven-ready, trimmed (more expensive), or as is. The chef who buys 'as is' and does a little extra work has a better roast and a much better food cost. An electric meat saw is used to cut portion sizes. Ribs of beef may weigh from 24 to 32 pounds, need trimming, and are roasted for 2 1/2 to 3 1/2 hours at 350°F. The roast stands on the rib bones, with the fat cover up. The use of a meat thermometer is advised. For large roasts, more recirculation time has to be allowed, and carry-over heat is significant. A roast is cooked to an internal temperature of 125°F. to be rare and it is handled as described in section 2, unit 6. "Cotes de Boeuf roti en Sel" is the Parisian way of cooking "Ribs of Beef". It is served from the cart and carved at the table. The trimmed ribs are put into a fitting, high rimmed roasting pan or a deep standard steam table pan. The roast is completely covered with a 2 inch layer of wet salt, which will bake into a hard crust. Coarse or kosher salt is moistened carefully first, then filled around and over the roast. The baking is done at 375°F. to 400°F. for about 3 1/2 hours or more. The crust becomes a part of the showy dish and is kept until carving. It acts as an insulation and carry-over heat must be considered. A thermometer is used to check for an internal temperature of 115°F. before removing the roast from the oven. About 50 - 60 minutes of "setting" must be allowed, which will bring the roast up to 140°F. for rare. This method of roasting is not recommended unless table carving can be done. There are no drippings to make a gravy.

## ROASTING OF PORK

Fresh pork is more popular in the rest of the world than it is in the USA. Nutritionally, it is better than beef. Pork fat has a lower melting point than beef fat (less stearin), and it is easier to digest. Analysis shows that it is equal to beef in comparative cuts except that it has no stored vitamin A, but more of the other

vitamins, such as thiamin. Pork meat is younger than beef, has a shorter cooking time, and all cuts can be roasted. For best flavor, proper salting is the first step. Rubbing in of lemon zeste, garlic, and caraway seeds also improves the taste.

Pork roasts are handled the same way as lamb or beef, except that pork has to be cooked nearly well-done. It should reach an internal temperature of 165°F., but never become dry. An internal temperature of 140°F. is enough to sterilize pork.

A pork roast has enough fat of its own, and can be started dry at low heat until enough of its own drippings are formed. The browning is done by increasing the temperature for the last half of the roasting time. The handling of gravy or jus is like other roasts.

Fig. 17-7  Knuckle or sirloin tip, untrimmed.

Fig. 17-8  Knuckle or sirloin tip, close trim.

Fig. 17-9  Ribs of beef, short cut.

Fig. 17-10  Ribs of beef, bone in, tied and oven-ready.

### Loin of Pork

Loin of pork is excellent in taste and portion control. Salt and some seasonings are necessary because pork is a bland meat.

A whole loin, untrimmed, should weigh from 14 to 16 pounds. It is cut into three parts: the main center cut (more expensive when bought by itself), the butt-end, and the rib-end. The center cut must have the chine bone removed, but the ribs stay as they are. The rib-end is boned completely, or only the chine and the blade tip are removed. The butt-end is best when boned completely. The fillet can be removed and used differently, or it can be tied back into the boned butt-end. Extra fat is removed.

**Fig. 17-11  Loin of pork, center cut rib cut view.**

Roasting time depends on the width of each part, not the length of the loin. Center cuts are cooked from 1 hour to 2 1/4 hours, at 350°F. The butt or rib ends may need 15 minutes longer. The portion yield is about 1 order each 8 ounces of raw trimmed meat.

### Leg of Pork

Leg of pork is also called a fresh ham. It is roasted with the skin still on only when it comes from young animals. The roasted pork skin, called "crackling", is a delicacy. Average weight of legs is from 14 to 18 pounds, with a portion yield similar to the loin. Salt curing, more than the smoking of a ham, changes a raw pork leg into a tasty ham. To prepare the ham, the aitchbone is removed first, then the leg bone is cut from the shank bone. The leg bone is removed whole, without cutting the leg open. The lean inside meat is seasoned with salt and the outside skin remains saltfree. The skin must be *blanched* in water (simmered) to become tender before it is changed into crackling. This is done by placing the leg skin side down on a low rack in a high rimmed roasting pan. The pan is half filled with boiling salted water and the skin side of the leg is simmered for half an hour. When done, the blanched skin of the leg is *scored* with a small sharp knife. The cuts should be parallel and about one fifth of an inch apart. The cuts are across the width of the leg, the same way as the leg is to be carved later. One inch of the blanching liquid is put in a roasting pan. The rest is added to the general stock or is kept for making gravy later. The leg, with the skin side up, is put into the pan of blanching liquid. No salting or basting is done to the scored skin. Initial roasting is at 325°F. for about 3 hours, then the heat is increased. For better browning, another 30 to 60 minutes is added. Total cooking time is 3 1/2 to 4 hours at an average temperature of 350°F.

### Boston Butt

Boston butt is a squared, trimmed pork shoulder. The blade bone and the shoulder bone are removed. The Boston butt is handled like the rib-end roast and is like it in texture.

### ROASTING OF VEAL

Meat known as veal by standards of continental cuisine, comes from calves 10 to 12 weeks old which have been fed only milk and a few added eggs. This type of veal is sold in the USA under the name of dairy veal. It is expensive and very hard to get. As soon as calves feed on grass or other vegetable solids, the meat changes. Until the calf has reached the age of at least one year, the meat is neither veal nor beef in quality. Dairy veal is very tender, lean white meat with a pinkish tint. The visible fat is white and firm. Whole legs, shoulders, loins, and saddles can be roasted with excellent results.

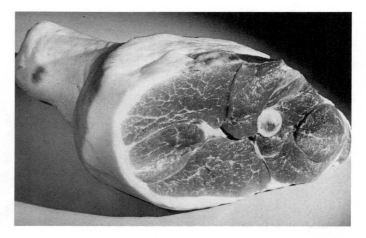

**Fig. 17-12  Leg of pork or fresh ham. Here the butt half was cut off. Roasting the whole leg gives a better presentation.**

### Leg of Veal

Leg of veal is made only for preordered parties in luxury restaurants because it is in short supply, has a high price, and needs much skill for its preparation. Trimming is like that for the pork leg, with the aitchbone and leg bone removed hollow. Veal legs have no fat or skin. The outside of the leg is larded or barded. Oil, butter, or pork lard is added, and frequently basting is advisable. Veal weight and quality are irregular. Leg sizes may vary from 7 to 16 pounds. Heavier legs should not be roasted whole. Roasting temperatures are from 325°F. to 350°F. for 55 minutes to 2 1/2 hours. Internal temperature of the roast when removed from the oven is 155°F. Mirepoix is added for the last 25 minutes of roasting.

Fig. 17-13  Leg of veal, short cut. The top of the leg can be larded; for table carving the bone is left in.

### Loin of Veal

Loin of veal is boned like a pork loin except that the center cut and rib end stay in one piece. Larding or barding is difficult, but the rest of the preparation is the same as for the leg of veal. Cooking time can range from 40 minutes to 1 3/4 hours, depending on its size.

### Saddle of Veal

Saddle of veal is the name given to the two trimmed loin ends, not split in half, of a small animal. A saddle of veal (called "Selle de Veau" in French) is a special party dish, carved at the table by the headwaiter, or in the kitchen by the chef and put back on the carcass for serving. It can be served plain, just as the loin, or roasted to rare, then finished in one of several fancy ways. Barding is often advisable for a saddle, which is handled and roasted like a loin. A steel rod is stuck through the spine to prevent curving of the saddle while roasting.

### ROASTING OF LAMB

Lamb, a dark meat, is roasted to medium (the English way). A lamb, even smaller than a calf, has much visible fat. Lamb fat has a peculiar taste, is hard to digest (high melting point because of the high lanolin content), is disliked, and should be trimmed as much as possible. The leg, the racks, and the saddle are popular roasts. Basically, they are roasted like beef, and garlic is used as additional seasoning.

### Leg of Lamb

Leg of lamb is not too often found on regular dinner house menus. It is used more often in better luncheon rooms, staff cafeterias, and hospitals. Lamb quality in the USA is better than in most parts of the world. Legs weigh from 5 to 8 pounds. They can be boned like a veal leg or roasted "bone in", French style, with only the aitchbone removed. Roasting time is 1 1/2 to 2 hours at 350°F. to 375°F. to an internal temperature of 150°F. Mirepoix is used for a better gravy.

### Rack of Lamb

Rack of lamb, unlike the leg, is found on the menu of nearly every French style restaurant. It is made to the order for two. The racks are center cuts from the loin, with 7 ribs and often

Fig. 17-14  Leg of lamb, bone in for table carving

frenched. To *french* means that meat from the flank end of the rib is completely removed. During roasting the meat shrinks and the bare bone sticks out. The racks are trimmed, after being frenched. Their trimmed weight is from 1 1/2 to 2 1/2 pounds. Racks are roasted to the order, for 18 to 25 minutes to rare, at 475°F. The bare bones are covered with aluminum foil in order to prevent burning. A skillet is used as a roasting pan.

### Saddle of Lamb

Saddle of lamb looks like a saddle of veal. It is also a favorite de luxe dish for four in expensive French style restaurants. The steel rod through the spine is used for roasting at 400°F. for 25 to 30 minutes.

## ROASTING OF VENISON

Venison is the generic name for the meat of deer, elk, moose, and other game. Only young animals are good for roasts. The meat is tougher than beef. Legs, saddles and racks are larded and aged for roasting. The meat must be well trimmed. All fat and skin, like the silver skin of a beef fillet, must be removed to the bare dark flesh. Salt, pepper, paprika, juniper berries, herbs and other spices are used, and the seasoning can be strong. Saddles, double racks, or both together in one piece, are kept straight by a steel rod through the spine. They are roasted to medium at 450°F. from 20 to 35 minutes. Venison from older animals, not well hung, and therefore tougher, should be prepared in some other way.

A leg of venison, trimmed like a leg of lamb, must be skinned, larded, and well seasoned. It is roasted at 350°F. for 1 1/2 to 2 hours. The meat thermometer can easily be used.

## ROASTING OF POULTRY AND GAME BIRDS

Poultry and game birds include all kinds of birds from the popular and common turkey to the seldom available wild pheasant. All previously discussed roasting information applies to this group.

### Turkey

Turkey has two kinds of meat, white and dark. They are of different appearance, taste, and tenderness. The modern way of roasting this meat is to cook them separately for different lengths of time and temperatures.

**TURKEY SETUP FOR MODERN ROASTING**

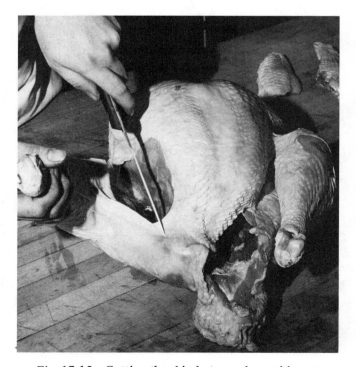

Fig. 17-15a  Cutting the skin between leg and breast

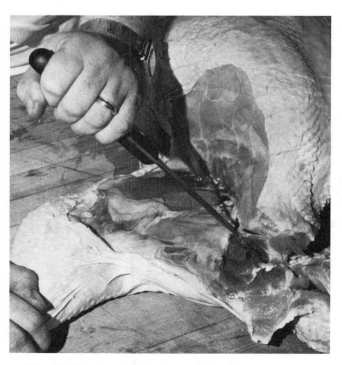

Fig. 17-15b  Severing leg in the joint from the carcass

(continued)

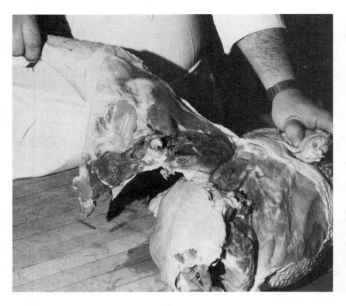

Fig. 17-15c  Pulling off leg from carcass.

Fig. 17-15d  Scoring between drumstick and hip joint to prevent the leg from stretching during roasting.

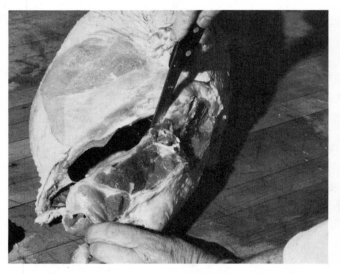

Fig. 17-15e  After both legs are removed, the back is prepared for separation from the carcass.

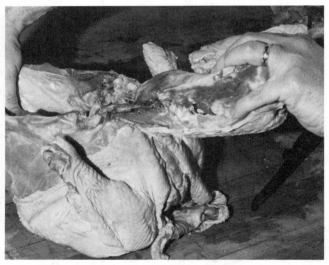

Fig. 17-15f  Backbone is snapped back and pulled off.

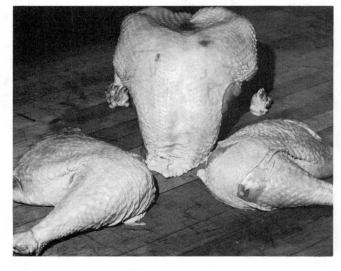

Fig. 17-15g  Remaining three main parts of the turkey.

Fig. 17-15h  Turkey is set up for roasting in a pan.

Boning a roast turkey for machine slicing is needed to get greatest yield. Carving from the carcass is only done in view of the customers. In the back of the house, machine slicing for portion control is the rule. If an electric slicer is not available, and the turkey is hand sliced, preboning will increase the yield.

*Materials Needed:*

1 roasted turkey          1 baker's or kitchen table, wooden top          1 6-inch boning knife

*Instructions:*

The legs:

1. Separate 2 drumsticks with the attached hips from the carcass.
2. Loosen ligaments of the drumstick and pull out as carefully as possible.
3. Cut on inside angle of the leg, close to drumstick bone and hip bone. Separate largest piece of dark meat in one whole chunk.
4. Cut remaining meat off hip bone.
5. Slice remaining meat from drumstick.
6. Repeat on second leg.
7. Collect all dark meat and put away for later use.

The breast:

1. Disjoint wing bone from collar bone with a few clean cuts, taking as little meat away as possible.
2. Repeat on other side of breast.
3. Set breast on its hollow opening, with neck part up and keel bone facing toward you.
4. Make one cut along one side of keel bone, from the center of neck opening to the tip of the breast.
5. Make one cut along the wishbone to the center of neck opening. This will connect with first cut.
6. Pull whole breast loose, use left hand for pulling, help with right hand and boning knife.
7. Repeat on right side.
8. Put 2 boneless breasts away for later use.
9. Clean the rest of the carcass of meat for hash, salads, soups, etc.

**TABLE 17-3  HOW TO BONE A ROAST TURKEY**

The breast of a large Tom (25-30 lbs.), separated from the legs but still on the carcass, cooks in about 2 1/2 hours at 325-350°F. The breasts are placed in the pan so as to improve the heat circulation. The tip of the breast bone is at the bottom of the pan. The fat and skin-covered throat part sticks up into the air. This new position makes the breast self-basting and prevents it from drying out. The drumsticks and hips are placed in another roasting pan, skin side up, roasted at the higher temperatures of 350-375°F. for the same time. This results in well done, tender and tasty dark meat, with crisp skin.

*Equipment Needed:*

Electric Meat Slicer          Standard Steam Table Pans          Portion Control Scale

*Instructions:*

1. Bone and skin a roast turkey into two breasts, 2 thighs and 2 drumsticks. Wrap in plastic film and chill in refrigerator thoroughly.
2. Slice all dark meat against grain on about No. 12 setting. Move carriage with right hand, catch falling slices with left hand.
3. Divide meat in 1 1/2-ounce heaps and lay them out in a standard steam table pan 3 x 4 rows, 12 orders.
4. Put boneless breast into meat slicer skin side up, bone side resting on slicer carriage, neck end toward slicer blade.
5. Leave control knob on No. 12, move carriage and catch falling slices as in step 2.
6. Divide sliced white meat into 2-ounce orders. Place on top of previously set up dark meat.
7. When pan is full, cover with wax paper, place in refrigerator until ready to use.
8. When ready to use, pour 1/4 inch of stock over pan, cover, and heat pan slowly on top of range until very hot. *CAUTION* – Overheating will toughen meat.
9. Bring out to steam table. Keep meat at 140°F., covered.
10. Keep hot gravy separate. Sauce only when ordered.

**TABLE 17-4  COFFEE SHOP STYLE TURKEY SLICING, PORTIONS CONTROLLED**

Chickens are oven or spit-roasted. Roasting chickens have two basic sizes: 1 3/4- to 2 1/4-pound chickens for 1/2 chicken per order, and 2 1/2- to 3-pound chicken for a 1/4 chicken to be served. Chickens are *trussed* (legs are bound tightly to body) with a large needle and twine. It makes them look more appetizing and they are easier to carve after roasting. All chickens are well salted inside and out, oiled, and roasted at high heat. A 2-pound chicken is cooked at 475°F. for 50 to 60 minutes and a 3-pound one is cooked at 450°F. for 60 to 70 minutes. Chickens may be larded. Mirepoix is used and gravy is made. For spit-roasting, the instructions of the equipment manufacturer should be followed.

## THE TRUSSING OF CHICKENS FOR ROASTING

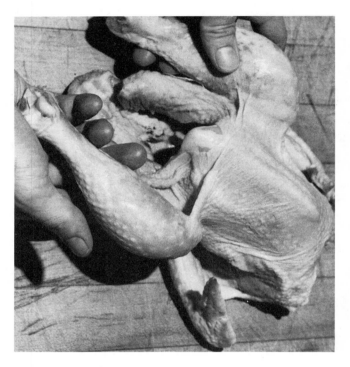

Fig. 17-16a  The cleaned chicken is pressed into shape.

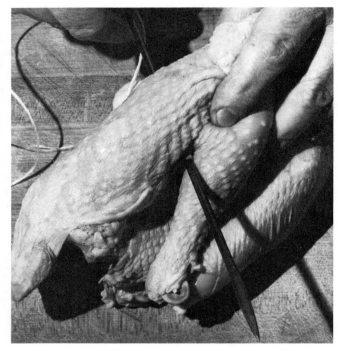

Fig. 17-16b  Trussing needle with string enters from the chicken's back and emerges between thigh and drumstick.

Fig. 17-16c  String is pulled through; the needle now pierces the chicken underneath the keel bone.

Fig. 17-16d  String is pulled through again; the untrussed leg is pressed against the body.

(continued)

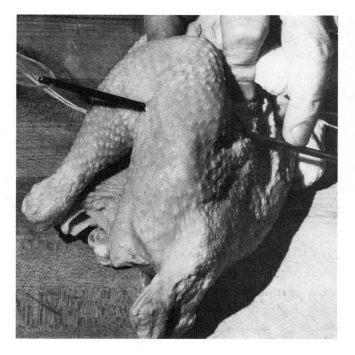

Fig. 17-16e  Now the trussing needle enters between drumstick and hip, and exits through back, close to the point where started.

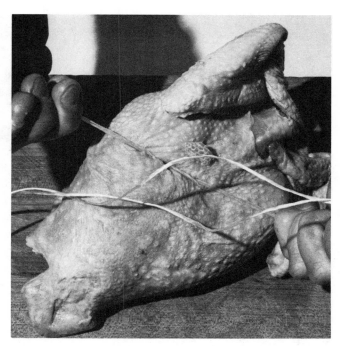

Fig. 17-16f  String is pulled tight and knotted securely.

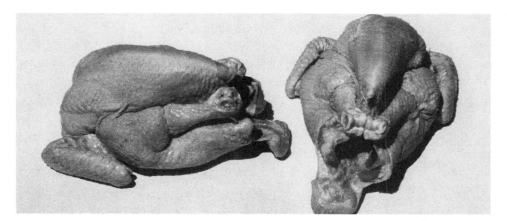

Fig. 17-16g  Trussed chickens ready to be roasted.

### Squab Chickens

Squab chickens are very small and available completely boned, from the inside, for stuffing. They usually weigh 3/4 to 1 1/4 pounds, and are roasted like chickens for only 20 to 25 minutes in a hotter oven, at 500°F.

### Pheasants

Pheasants are game birds. They are good only at the times of the year when they have fed on grain. Gourmets roast pheasants for the quality of their breast meat, which must be larded or barded. An herb bouquet of fresh sage, thyme, and basil can be stuffed into the cavity while roasting. They are roasted best in a skillet, with oil, at 500°F. for 15 to 18 minutes. If overcooked, they become tasteless and stringy. Farm raised, domesticated pheasants weigh up to 3 pounds, are clean and white, look like chickens, and are roasted like chickens of the same size.

### Ducks

Ducks are popular on dinner house menus. Peking duck, used in the USA, must be handled differently than the French Rouen duck, used in Europe. As a result, many of the French cooking methods are not too satisfying. Perhaps the best way to prepare this type of duck is spit-roasting on a charcoal rotisserie for about 3 hours. Under the bird, a drip pan with water will provide moisture and collect fat. A medium fire with the coals on the side, not under the duck, at approximately 325°F. will be enough.

Oven roasting will produce a good dish when the following guidelines are observed. Properly defrosted (24 hours under refrigeration) 4 1/2- to 5-pound ducks are well salted at least 2 hours before roasting. The salt should go into the cavity and underneath the skin of the breast. Sage, marjoram, and oregano are among the other seasonings which may be used. Use duck giblets, fat, and mirepoix to prepare a bed for the duck in the roasting pan. Add one inch of chicken stock. Place oiled duck, breast side down, on the bed, cover, and cook in 450°F. (preheated) oven for 30 minutes. Then take off the cover, and continue cooking 30 minutes more. The temperature may need to be reduced to 425°F. After one hour of total cooking time, turn the duck on its back and roast for 30 more minutes. If there are too many fat drippings, skim off as much as possible. Heat at 450°F. until the duck is browned in the total time of 1 1/2 hours. Remove from the oven, cool duck, and make gravy from the drippings as usual. As soon as duck is cool enough to handle, quarter it in the same way as a raw chicken would be disjointed, without cutting the carcass in half. Take off the drumsticks with hips and *oyster* (small muscle in part of the pelvis) first. Then make two cuts along the keel bone into the breast, with another at the neck along the wishbone to the wing bone. Grip breast and wing bone firmly and peel breast meat off the carcass in one piece. The four half-boned quarters are placed, skin side up, in a flat roasting pan, with a little stock at the bottom. Preheat oven to 500°F. Use the highest oven rack and heat duck for 6-7 minutes, until its skin is crisp without being burned. Serve with the crisp skin side up, with watercress, and a proper sauce and garnish on the side.

### Geese

Geese are seldom on restaurant menus in the USA but they are common in Central Europe. They are prepared like ducks. Even young geese weigh 8 to 10 pounds, and therefore, must be cooked at a lower temperature for about one hour more. Geese are often stuffed with sour apples or onions during roasting. Seldom are geese served the French way with fruit and wine sauces. They are plain roasted, au jus, and served with red cabbage or another hardy vegetable.

### SUMMARY

Roasting is dry heat cooking with the intent to evaporate some of the water content that all fresh meats have. To prevent the burning of the roast, time and heat are controlled. When meat (depending on type, shape, and desired doneness) is roasted, a ratio is created between time and temperature. Some pieces of meat are cooked better by increasing the heat and reducing the time. Other roasts may need less heat for a longer time. Every roast is different, even if it is the same type, size, and cut of meat as another.

The meat cut selection, boning, trimming, trussing, larding, and salting of the roast are very important preparation steps. All roasting principles and objectives are the same. The young cook is advised to use a meat thermometer (his own) until he gains experience.

Pan size must fit meat size. Fat to meat ratio should be the same. If the roast is too fat, some of it is trimmed off. If the roast is too lean, larding, barding, or oiling must be done. Dark meats are cooked medium or rare. White meats are cooked close to well done. Exceptions to regular roasting principles are ducks and geese. They are tenderized by moist cooking first and then browned.

At all times it must be remembered that roasting alone does not tenderize. Only moist cooking will do that. Meats to be roasted must be tender and young and must be true roasts from prime or choice graded animals. The age of the slaughtered animal in relation to its normal life span is important. Only high quality meat is roasted. For bringing out the flavor of a roast there is no substitute for proper salting.

### DISCUSSION TOPICS

1. Why do ready-cooked meats have such a high salt level?
2. Why is there a need for proper roast preparation?
3. Why is pork, with greater nutritional qualities than beef, less popular in the USA?
4. What are the advantages of modern turkey roasting?

### SUGGESTED ACTIVITIES

A.    Define: trussing, larding, rotisserie, disjoint, keel bone, saddle, rack, score.

B.    Teacher demonstrating and student practicing of

    1.    trussing and larding a roasting chicken.

    2.    trimming and roasting a beef tenderloin.

    3.    preparing and roasting a young pork leg.

    4.    frenching and roasting a rack of lamb.

    5.    preparing and roasting a goose or duck.

    6.    trimming, preparing and tying a Ribs of Beef roast.

### ACHIEVEMENT REVIEW

A.    Complete the following:

    1.    As a substitute for roasting experience, the beginning cook should use a _____ .

    2.    Bones of meats to be roasted are removed when they obstruct the _____ .

    3.    Too much fat cover prevents the edible meat from _____ .

    4.    Preparing the roast for the oven includes the selection of a proper size ____ .

    5.    When larding, bacon is added to the meat with the help of a _____ .

    6.    When barding, bacon is added to the meat with the help of a _____ .

    7.    The use of herbs and spices remains the chef's value _____ .

    8.    One-inch cubed vegetables added to the final stages of roasting are called _____ .

    9.    A New York strip, one of the finest roasts, is called in French _____ .

    10.    It is the salt more than the smoking that changes a raw pork leg into a tasty _____ .

B.    Read each question carefully and completely before answering it. Select the *best* answer.

    1.    Roasting has as its first objective

        a. the use of high heat for fastest browning
        b. the use of low heat to avoid shrinkage
        c. to achieve outside brownness and inside doneness at the same time
        d. to tenderize meat cuts which are too tough to be used as steaks

    2.    Trimmed lamb racks for double orders have

        a. 5 ribs              c. 9 ribs
        b. 7 ribs              d. 11 ribs

    3.    The roasting time of a saddle of veal as compared to a veal loin is

        a. much less         c. half again as long
        b. nearly the same     d. twice as long

    4.    A fitting roasting pan should be

        a. of nonoxidizing material     c. a little larger than the roast
        b. higher than the roast        d. much larger than the roast

5. Roasts should only be tied with strings for

   a. keeping the shape
   b. easier handling
   c. holding smaller pieces together
   d. making them look larger

6. Of the following beef roasts, the one with the shortest cooking time is

   a. "Contre Filet Roti"
   b. Roasted New York Strip
   c. Roasted Top Sirloin
   d. Larded Fillet of Beef

7. Of the following beef roasts, the one with the longest cooking time is

   a. Ribs of Beef roast
   b. Sirloin Tip roast
   c. Beef Tenderloin roast
   d. Strip Sirloin roast

8. A young, roasted pork leg, with the skin still on, is

   a. salted a day in advance
   b. roasted slowly for 5 hours
   c. blanched to tenderize the skin
   d. stuffed with "Mirepoix" for flavor

9. Ten pounds of raw, center-cut pork loin serves 16 orders and roasts for 2 1/4 hours at 375°F. When cut in half, serving only 8 orders, it roasts at 375°F. for

   a. 60 to 75 minutes
   b. 80 to 95 minutes
   c. 100 to 115 minutes
   d. 120 to 135 minutes

10. A calf, to qualify as dairy veal, is

    a. 2 1/2 to 3 months old and milk-fed
    b. 3 to 4 months old and corn-fed
    c. 4 to 5 months old and from a dairy breed
    d. 5 to 6 months old and formula-fed

11. Leg of lamb, a dark meat, is an   English   roast and generally served

    a. with mint jelly
    b. medium done
    c. well done
    d. larded or barded

12. Modern cooks realize that turkeys

    a. consist of different meat with different cooking times
    b. have to be preboiled before roasting to be tender
    c. have to be cooked hotter and longer than before
    d. have to be cooked very slowly at lowest heat

13. Game pheasants are only good when they

    a. are roasted slowly
    b. are stuffed with dressing
    c. have been fed on grain
    d. are roasted like chickens

14. Roast preparations done by chefs do not include

    a. larding or barding
    b. boning and trimming
    c. aging and tenderizing
    d. washing and salting

15. The most popular roast sold in American specialty restaurants is

    a. rack of lamb
    b. ribs of beef
    c. loin of pork
    d. saddle of veal

# Unit 18 Broiling to the Order

## OBJECTIVES

After studying and practicing this unit, the student should be able to

- Explain the objectives of broiling.
- Describe the sequence of steps for broiling a steak.
- Demonstrate the broiling of a meat dish.
- Identify the check point for doneness.
- List some foods, by their menu names, which can be broiled.
- Demonstrate the making of a Brochette.

Broiling, in some areas called grilling, is an important dry heat cooking method. It is an *a la carte* (cooking to the order) process, and the cook in charge is called short order cook or broilerman. Section 2, unit 6, discussed related broiling information in detail.

Broiling may be the oldest form of cookery. Today, it still gives mankind a great emotional and taste satisfaction. Broiling is known in every part of the world. Old-fashioned charcoal broilers, even plain wood burning ones, are still used often. Electric or gas broilers are faster and cleaner.

The principles of grilling are the same for all types of broilers. As long as the student remembers these few basic rules and principles, his broiling will become better and better after a short time of practice.

---

**BASIC RULES**

- Broiling is done by radiation and convected heat, but never by burning food over coals. Charred or burned meat is not the objective of broiling.
- Fats and liquids must not be allowed to drip on glowing coals or steel, causing flare-ups and scorched foods.
- Raw meats must be salted and oiled before broiling, but additional seasoning is by choice.
- Grill marks must show or the eye appeal is lost. Taste, in the case of broiled food, is less important than sight, aroma, and smell.
- Broiler must be clean at all times. It is done with a wire steel brush and old towels. The grease collection pan is emptied regularly.

---

THE THINNER THE STEAK, THE HOTTER THE FIRE, THE FASTER THE COOKING: THE SAME PRINCIPLES WHICH HAVE EXPLAINED ROASTING, RECIRCULATION OF JUICES, AND THE ACTION OF CARRY-OVER HEAT MUST BE APPLIED TO BROILING.

## BASIC HANDLING

The broiler is preheated before use. The grill bars must be hot enough to *sear* (scorch) the meat immediately at the first touch. When the bars are hot, they are scraped with a wire brush, then wiped clean with an oiled towel before the first order is made.

A coal shovel and stoker for charbroilers, a carbon dioxide fire extinguisher, a wire brush, towels, and the cook's personal tools are used for all broilers.

*Mis en place* (the French name for the work station setup) means that all that is needed for the menu at a given shift is lined up and ready to use. Warm service plates or platters, paper frills for lamb chops, doily papers, and napkins are as important as spices, herbs, salt, and pans of oil, bread crumbs and flour.

All foods must be trimmed, seasoned and oiled slightly before they touch the grill bars. White meats and fish are dipped in bread crumbs before they are oiled. Protein food with low blood content will show grill marks only if dipped in starch. Liver is dipped into flour to prevent oxidation. Liver cooked without flour discolors to a greenish tint and does not look appetizing. Vegetables, such as eggplants, zucchini, mushrooms and tomatoes are also dipped into bread crumbs so that some of the moisture is absorbed.

## ACTUAL BROILING

Foods on a broiler are moved or turned only when necessary. Grill marks, seared in by the hot grill bars, will become smeared if the food is moved. The searing is like a rubber stamp pressed on a paper. Food is first put at an angle of about 45° to the grill bar, and broiled for a quarter of the estimated cooking time. Then it is carefully lifted and turned 90°, still on the same side. After half of the total cooking time, the food is turned over, so that the grill marks are easily seen. The food item is then finished to the desired doneness. Constant turning from one side to the other, as some cooks do, adds to the cooking time, dries out the meat, and destroys the grill marks.

The French recognize only steaks which are cooked *saignant* (medium rare or bloody), or *bien cuit* (medium well). French customers realize that steaks should not be charred on the outside and cold inside (*blue* or *blood rare*). Neither should they be well done and dry. Cooking for the fine distinctions of medium to medium well or between rare and medium rare, is nearly impossible to do. It has happened that a steak, ordered rare, but cooked medium well, was returned by the customer with a serious remark that he only wanted a steak rare, not still bloody.

For meat, the best sign of its doneness is to watch for drops of blood-liquid to rise to the grill-marked face of the steak. When this happens the steak is rare inside and if taken off, the recirculation time and warmkeeping of several minutes will make it medium rare.

To obtain the best grill marks for a steak with an estimated cooking time of 6 minutes, follow the diagram.

a. 1st position, 1 1/2 minutes

b. 2nd position, + 1 1/2 minutes, to 3 minutes

c. 3rd position, + 1 1/2 minutes, to 4 1/2 minutes

d. 4th position, + 1 1/2 minutes, to 6 minutes

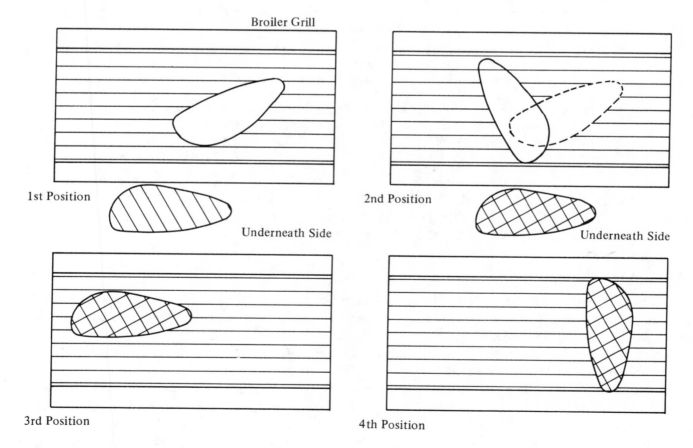

Broiler Grill

1st Position     Underneath Side

2nd Position     Underneath Side

3rd Position

4th Position

**TABLE 18-1 DIAGRAM OF STEAK ON A BROILER GRILL**

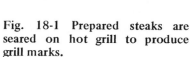

Fig. 18-1 Prepared steaks are seared on hot grill to produce grill marks.

Fig. 18-2 After about a quarter of the total estimated cooking time has elapsed, meat is lifted carefully and turned 90° in a right angle to the first marks.

Fig. 18-3 After the second quarter of the estimated cooking time, steak is turned over to show the side with grill marks. The steak is kept on grill to desired doneness.

> THE RISING OF THE BLOOD-LIQUID TO THE SURFACE OF THE ALREADY COOKED SIDE IS THE CHECKPOINT FOR THE COOK TO TAKE THE FOOD OFF THE FIRE.

## SPECIFIC PREPARATIONS

Although the principles of broiling are the same, there are small differences for some preparations. These differences are the key points of the trade, and learning them will help the beginning cook.

### New York Steak

New York Steak, also called Boneless Sirloin, Sirloin, Featherbone, New York Strip-Steak and Entrecote must have a thickness of 1 to 1 1/2 inches. It needs a slow fire and 5-8 minutes of recirculation time for a medium-rare steak.

### Minute Steak

From the New York Strip, the minute steak is sometimes called a "Lady's Cut Steak". It is 1/2 inch thick, at most, and it must be cooked very hot and fast, not more than 1 1/2 minutes per side. Only parallel grill marks are needed.

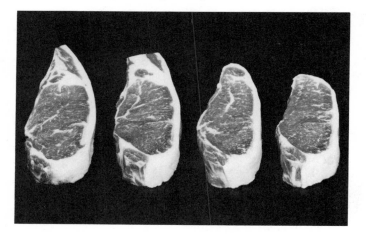

Fig. 18-4 New York cut, boneless sirloin steaks, from left to right: regular trim to complete trim.

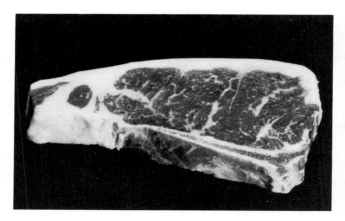

Fig. 18-5 New York cut steak with the featherbone left in.

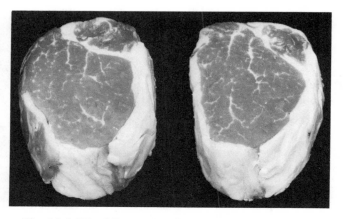

Fig. 18-6 Filet Mignon (Beef tenderloin), average trim.

Cross marks will overcook the steak. A too hot service platter, a slow server, or too much table warming service can easily make this thin steak well done. It should only be "fired" while the server is waiting to "pick up".

### Filet Mignon

Filet Mignon, also called "Coeur de Filet", is 1 1/4 to 2 inches thick, needs slow cooking and good recirculation time. It could be pounded lightly with a flat side of a cleaver if it is thicker than 2 inches. Cooking and setting time should be 8-10 minutes each.

Fig. 18-7  Tournedos (beef tenderloin), completely trimmed.

### Tournedos

Also called "Medallions" of Beef, Tournedos are Filet Mignons cut in half. They should be 3/4 to 1 1/4 inches thick and are cooked accordingly. They are served in pairs, on top of a *crouton* (round-cut buttered toast), with a sauce or garnish on the side.

### Chateaubriand

Chateaubriand is a fillet steak for two or three, carved at the table by the headwaiter. It is cut from the fillet head, then trimmed slightly and pounded to a 2-inch thickness. It is broiled like the filet mignon.

### Chops

Lamb chops (plain or frenched), Lamb Noisette (a boneless loin eye which looks like a filet mignon), English Mutton Chop (cut from a saddle of lamb, with the lamb kidney in the middle), and Pork Chops are all broiled the same way as Tournedos, New York Steaks, or Filet Mignons.

### Mixed Grill

Mixed grill is any group of grilled meats. Most popular are lamb chop grillades consisting of lamb chop, lamb kidney, liver, grilled bacon, pork links, and broiled tomato — served with french fries and watercress.

### Veal Steaks

Veal steaks are rarely broiled because dairy veal is very lean. They could be larded or barded and cooked on low heat without drying them out.

### American Grilled Chicken

American grilled chicken is a French dish, which uses a very young chicken or squab. After it is split open on the back, the keel bone, ribs and aitchbones are taken out. It is seasoned, dipped in bread crumbs,

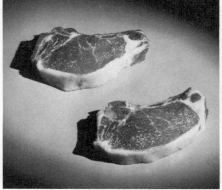

Fig. 18-8  Lamb Rib Chops, plain.

Fig. 18-9  Pork Rib Chops, trimmed.

Fig. 18-10  Pork Loin Chops

then oiled, pressed in a chicken rack, and broiled slowly for 12 to 15 minutes. Whole squab chickens are best for this preparation. It is served with bacon slices, grilled tomato, and shoestring potatoes.

### Chopped Steaks

Chopped steaks are often called minced sirloin or ground sirloin. These are cooked like any other beef-steak of the same size. They may be chef-made or machine-molded. These are portion-controlled up to an eight-ounce size.

### Fish Dishes

Fish dishes are handled like meat dishes. Fish is sometimes more brittle and will break easily. It should always be dipped in bread crumbs to absorb the wetness. Too much moisture makes them stick to the grill bars, destroys the markings, and breaks up the portion. Only firm-fleshed fish should be used. Fish should be cut rather short and chubby instead of thin and long. This makes it easier to handle. Fish must be well salted, and then cooked according to its thickness. Some of the most well known fish steaks are cut from halibut, swordfish, salmon, tuna, and seabass.

### Broiled Lobster

Broiled lobster is a specialty of New England and Eastern Canada. Live 1 1/2- to 2-pound lobsters are split in half lengthwise. The sack, with its sand, is thrown away. The *coral* (ovary) and other creamy parts are mixed with equal parts of fine french bread crumbs and clarified butter. Clarified butter is made by separating the butterfat from the water and milk solids after the butter has been melted and chilled. The shells of the claws are cracked carefully for easier cooking and eating. The empty shell of the lobster is filled with the coral mixture. The flesh of the tail and claws is lightly salted and brushed with a large amount of butter. The lobster, with the exposed side up, is placed on a baking sheet under a hot *Salamander* (broiler with overhead heat) for a few minutes. When it has started to brown lightly, it is moved to a 500°F. (or hotter) oven. It is finished in 8-10 minutes more. More butter is added. The lobster is served with clarified butter on the side, potato chips, and lemon wedges.

### Skewered Specialty Dishes from the Broiler

Pieces of well seasoned meat or fish may be put on a *skewer* (spit) with vegetables or fruits. These are broiled and served garnished. The best foods for this specialty are beef fillet ends, lamb, pork, ham, raw turkey, venison (game), beef liver, calves liver, kidney, chicken liver, lobster, scallops, oysters, and prawns. Some of the fillers can be bacon, ham, mushrooms, pepper, onion, eggplant, cherry tomatoes, squash, and pineapple. Spices, such as garlic, lemon, soy sauce, saffron, curry, basil, and thyme are used.

*Skewers* are spits of metal or wood. *Brochette* is their French name. Skewers often are in single-portion size, and are handled like a single steak. Beef and lamb are broiled rare or medium. Other foods are well done. Most of these specialties are still popular under their foreign names.

- *Shashlick,* of Russian origin, has lamb, seasoned with garlic and lemon juice, on the skewer with raw onions and thin pieces of lamb fat for flavor. This is charcoal broiled to medium and then served with coleslaw, dill pickles, pickled beets, and lemon sections.
- *Shish-kebabs* are Armenian-Turkish variations of the Russian Shashlick with red wine instead of lemon juice. Pilaf or risotto is used as a garnish.
- *Brochette Chasseur* (Beef tenderloin brochettes) is made of beef fillet ends.
- Fish-Kebab has oysters, scallops, or other fish and shellfish.
- *Satays* are an Indonesian specialty. Small wooden skewers are lined with curried and spiced raw chicken, pork or shellfish and then broiled.
- Spiced pork or beef meat balls, wrapped in bacon and broiled on skewers are of Eastern European origin.

There are countless ways of making brochettes. The meats, spices, vegetables, garnishes, and sauces may be changed. The taste of this dish is not improved when it is served on a flaming sword. This is strictly a showmanship antic and is not liked by the true connoisseur.

This step-by-step process is used for any brochette, shish-kebab or shashlick. Only the points stressed are important. The combining of meats, vegetables or fruits and their seasoning is a value judgement and reflects the taste of the individual chef. The skill, exactness, and speed of preparing this dish reflects the craftsmanship of the cook.

─── ATTENTION: KEY POINTS ───

Food on a skewer is cooked for the same time to the same doneness, therefore

- Food is cut to uniform thickness and size.
- Food on a skewer resembles a straight, even row.
- Food on a skewer is centered for balance.
- Food on a skewer needs a little space between pieces for heat circulation.
- Skewers are oiled before they are stuck through the meat.

*Material for 10 Brochettes (Meat wrapped with bacon)*

Trimmed Fillet Ends – 4 lb.
Thinly sliced bacon, 25 slices – 1 lb.
Mushroom caps, 1 1/2" diameter – 20 pieces
Sage leaves, fresh and large – 50 pieces
Garlic, fresh and squashed – 3 cloves

Olive oil, to be mixed with garlic – 1 cup
Stainless steel skewers, 8" long – 10 pieces
Salt and fresh ground pepper – to taste
Additional spices, optional
Vegetables, fruits for addition or change, optional

*Procedure*

1. Cut meat into 50 chunks of same size
2. Salt and pepper the meat
3. Mix with half a cup of the garlic-olive oil
4. Steam or blanch mushroom caps for 30 seconds
5. Cut onions into single leaf rectangles of 1/2 to 1 1/2 inches
6. Cut each bacon slice in half and line up in rows on the working table
7. Blanch sage leaves in boiling salt water for 2 seconds and place *one* in the middle of each 1/2 bacon slice
8. Place drained meat chunks in the middle of sage leaf
9. Roll up meat in bacon and sage leaf
10. Divide the 50 meat-bacon rolls into 10 portions of 5 each
11. Place one mushroom on the skewer by piercing it carefully from the top and sliding it to the ring end of the skewer
12. Pierce one onion piece and slide it next to the mushroom
13. Center the first meat piece, with the skewer piercing and holding the bacon end
14. Add second onion piece
15. Add second piece of meat, same way as before
16. Continue the lineup, to a total of 5 meat and 6 onion pieces
17. Use mushroom cap as the second end piece, with the top pointing outside
18. Continue until 10 brochettes are made
19. Place them on oiled bake sheet. Pour remaining olive oil over them
20. Keep refrigerated until broiling to the order

Unless ordered otherwise, they should be medium-rare, with good grill marks on the flat sides. They are taken off the skewer by the server in front of the guest. Sauces and garnishes are by choice of the chef.

**TABLE 18-2 MAKING OF BROCHETTES**

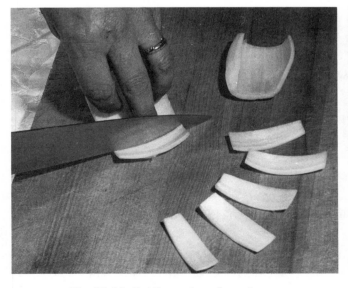

Fig. 18-11 Cutting onions for a skewer.

Fig. 18-12 Lining up of meat and onion pieces.

(continued)

Fig. 18-13 All food material for the same brochette must be the same size and lined up through the center.

Fig. 18-14 A finished, practical, meat brochette.

## SUMMARY

Broiling to the order is an important and popular form of a la carte cookery. Perhaps the oldest form of cookery, it has changed very little. Broiling means to cook by dry heat. Burning or charring of meat over the direct fire is not good for health and taste. All rules for roasting also apply to broiling.

All tender and fat foods broil well. The American public prefers steaks cooked this way. These are tender, portion sizes of meat which can be broiled rare, medium, or well done.

A brochette (French term for spit or skewer) is used to handle small meat or fish pieces for order. This means that 4, 6, or more pieces of food are held together on one spit. Meat on a skewer is like spit-roasting for one order.

It is most important for the student cook to learn and understand "the checkpoint to doneness". Overcooked broiled meat or fish preparations are not acceptable.

### DISCUSSION TOPICS

1. What are the advantages of a la carte cookery?
2. What is the importance of cooking steaks to the degree requested?
3. Could a meat thermometer be used on broiled steak?
4. Does a restaurant or a chef have any responsibility guiding customers to healthier foods (in regard to charring)?
5. Is the eye appeal of grill marks really important?
6. Why are the holding times for some steaks different than for others?

### SUGGESTED ACTIVITIES

1. Define: aitchbone, brochette, satay, mis en place, entrecote, tournedo.
2. Demonstrate handling live lobsters for broiling.
3. Demonstrate broiling a steak to identify the "checkpoint" of doneness.
4. Set up various brochettes of meat and seafood.
5. Practice the broiling of New York steaks.

6.  Practice the broiling of fillet steaks.

7.  Practice the broiling of chopped steaks.

8.  Practice the broiling of skewers of food rolled in bacon.

9.  Practice the broiling of white meats, such as pork or chicken.

Note:  Two students should work together. The first will broil the steak by himself. The second will use a stopwatch and record the cooking time between each turn. Setting time must also be included. The steak is then cut, compared to the desired result, and discussed.

## *ACHIEVEMENT REVIEW*

A.  Complete the following:

1.  Regardless of broiler type used, the principles for broiling are the _____ .

2.  Food from the broiler should not be _____ .

3.  In the broiler, fat from meats or seafood must not drip onto the _____ .

4.  Grill marks are a very important part of _____ .

5.  The grill bars of the broiler are cleaned best with a _____ .

6.  For a thin steak, the temperature of the fire must be very _____ .

7.  Before foods can be seared, the broiler must be very _____ .

8.  Food on the broiler is not turned _____ .

9.  The most popular broiler dish in the USA is the _____ .

B.  Read each question carefully and completely before answering it. Select the *best* answer.

1.  When watching a steak being broiled, a visual checkpoint appears when

a. the grill marks become visible
b. the first juice drops rise to the cooked surface
c. the fat rim of the steak is getting brown
d. the steak stops dripping juice

2.  A minute steak should have a thickness of

a. 1/2 inch                    c. 1 inch
b. 3/4 inch                    d. 1 1/4 inches

3.  A Chateaubriand (filet mignon for two or three) should be

a. 3/4 of an inch thick        c. 2 inches thick
b. 1 1/4 inches thick          d. 2 1/2 inches thick

4.  Mixed Grill could mean any combination of foods from the grill, but the most popular is a combination of

a. lobster, prawns, scallops, oysters
b. pork chop, bacon, wiener, french fries
c. lamb chop, liver, bacon, pork links
d. chicken, chicken livers, tomatoes, mushrooms

5.  A 10-ounce center cut of fillet, 2 inches thick and broiled is called

a. Chateaubriand               c. Tournedo
b. Coeur de Filet              d. Noisette

6.  Cooking a minute steak to rare will need

a. 3 minutes            c. 5 minutes
b. 4 minutes            d. 6 minutes

7.  A 10-ounce Filet Mignon, cooked to rare, will need

a. 5 minutes of cooking time
b. 7 minutes of cooking time
c. 9 minutes of cooking time
d. 11 minutes of cooking time

8.  The English Mutton Chop is a special cut from the

a. top sirloin          c. rack
b. saddle               d. loin

9.  The term "frenched" lamb chops implies

a. it has a bacon slice wrapped around
b. it is a lamb T-Bone
c. it has the rib bone scraped clean
d. it is a boneless chop

10.  A New England Broiled Lobster is

a. shelled raw lobster meat on a skewer, grilled
b. shelled cooked lobster meat on a skewer, broiled
c. a cooked half lobster, buttered and browned with grill marks
d. a live lobster split in half, cooked in salamander and oven

11.  Small pieces of beef fillet-ends placed on a skewer and broiler are called

a. Brochette Chasseur    c. Shashlick
b. Shish Kebab           d. Indonesian Satay

12.  Seafood, to be broiled easier, should have the characteristic of

a. tenderness            c. leanness
b. firmness              d. tastiness

C.  Answer in your own words:

1.  List the objectives in broiling.

2.  List some foods, by their menu names, which can be broiled.

3.  Describe the sequence of steps for broiling a steak.

# Unit 19 Sautéing — Griddle Frying

*OBJECTIVES*

After studying this unit, the student should be able to

- Explain the principle of sautéing.
- List suitable sauté fats.
- Demonstrate the sautéing of Fillet of Sole Meuniere.
- Describe the cooking of sautéed, deglazed foods.
- Demonstrate the cooking of Chicken Sauté with Mushrooms.
- List the names of four different chicken sauté preparations.

Sautéing (sometimes called Flip Frying) is a form of pan frying. Food is fried (sautéed) in small amounts of good fat which become a part of the finished dish. The general term *frying* should mean that food is cooked while floating in fat and then is separated from it after the frying is done. This theory was discussed in units 8 and 16.

## PROCESS REVIEW

Sautéing is the fast browning of tender foods in good fat, with the fat becoming a part of the cooked dish. Since it is a type of quality cookery, sautéing has become very popular. The fast sauté method is very good for the tender meats now available as a result of special breeding and feeding. In vegetable cookery, to keep both taste and nutrition, sautéing is best.

## SELECTION OF SAUTÉ FATS

Culinary Art standards of the Western World consider these fats tastier and healthier than others: olive oils, refined salad oils, butter, clarified butter, fresh pork fat, and, in some cases, chicken or goose fat. The fat is chosen to compliment the food cooked in it. Gourmet chefs, like the Food and Drug Administration, are very conservative in these choices. They go by the G.R.A.S. (Generally Recognized As Safe) list. This means that foods which have been eaten by mankind for thousands of years with no ill effects, are probably safer than many of the new, advertised foods which have not been checked or observed for many years.

## DEGLAZING

*Deglazing* means to use up the caramelized leftover juices that remain in a skillet after meat has been sautéed in it. It is done by adding a small amount of liquid to cook these juices loose. This can be done only if juices exist. When sautéing potatoes or buttered almonds, there can be no deglazing. The frying fat, preferably butter, is left in the potatoes or almonds. For fish a la "Meuniere", extra butter is browned in the skillet with the fish and then poured over it for serving. Again, deglazing can not be done. For freshly made meats served in a small amount of sauce, deglazing does take place. Beef a la Stroganoff is the typical

**Fig. 19-1 Frying pan or skillet, used for sautéing or flip frying**

*Ingredients needed for two orders:*

2 New York Cut Sirloin Steaks, 16 oz. each
3 tablespoons chopped shallots (substitute with
    finely chopped onions and garlic if shallots are
    not available)
1 ounce olive or other good cooking oil

2 ounces butter
1 ounce brandy
1/3 cup basic brown sauce (Espagnol)
1/3 cup Red Bordeaux wine
1/6 bunch cleaned watercress

────────────ATTENTION: KEY POINTS────────────

- Under correct conditions, as detailed below, the cooking time of a medium rare steak of this size is about 6 minutes.
- Medium rare is the best way to serve any steak for the best flavor, texture, and appearance.
- These 6 minutes of total heat exposure include the flambé time.
- If a steak, cooked exactly to medium rare, is covered with the hot sauce and left standing on the table for an additional 5 minutes, it probably will become well done.
- The term "correct conditions" applies to the following:
    - Quality grade of the meat itself (prime or choice)
    - Using the true boneless sirloin (New York cut)
    - The pounding of the steak to a 3/4-inch thickness. This loosens the fibres, that is, tenderizes it and, thus, reduces cooking time.

*Procedure:*

1. Trim excess fat off meat, and pound to the thickness of 3/4 inch. Score if necessary. Salt.
2. Leave brandy in original bottle, but have other ingredients measured.
3. Prewarm brown sauce.
4. Pour oil into heated skillet.
5. Put steaks in the pan.
6. Sauté on high heat (sizzling noise) for 40 to 60 *seconds.*
7. Reduce heat to approximately 375°F. and cook 1 minute more.
8. Turn meat over and continue to cook for 60 more seconds.
9. Add butter in small flocks around steak.
10. Add shallots to steak in the same way.
11. Swish around in pan, or stir, but not longer than another 60 seconds.
12. Pour brandy into the hot pan.
13. Let alcohol burn away. (For safety reasons, always have the cover of the pan at hand. In case fire gets out of control, smother it by covering the pan.)
14. Turn heat down to prevent burning of pan.
15. Remove steaks, to warm dinner plates.
16. Pour red wine into pan, bring to a boil.
17. Use spatula to stir simmering residue and loosen it from pan.
18. Add the brown sauce and whisk until smooth.
19. Ladle sauce over the steaks, not necessarily all of it. (Too much sauce on a plate makes a dish look cheap.)
20. Decorate plate and steak with watercress instead of parsley.

**TABLE 19-1  ENTRECOTE BORDELAISE**

example of both sautéing and deglazing. Other sauté dishes are referred to in unit 8, in the section, "A Sauté is not a Stew". Most deglazing is done with some wine or brandy first (called flaming), and then a suitable sauce is used as a follow-up. The making of sauces is discussed in unit 21. These are made before the sautéing is done.

## SAUTÉED FOODS WITHOUT DEGLAZING

Sautéing food without deglazing may mean that the food is served without any sauce, or with only the liquid which has been formed as the by-product of the process. An example of this is in the cooking of sliced or whole raw mushrooms. These are washed in slightly acid water, lifted out, and sautéed immediately. Because of the washing, there is more mushroom juice, which most chefs like to keep to prevent the mushrooms from drying out during storage. Raw carrots, asparagus, green peas, cabbage and many more vegetables may be sautéed in a covered skillet, in the same way as the mushrooms. In many areas, it is the custom to preboil vegetables, store them under refrigeration and sauté them, as needed, in butter.

Pasta, the name for all types and shapes of noodles, is produced in a dehydrated state. Pasta must be boiled in water first. In quality cookery, all pasta and most boiled vegetables are sautéed before serving. On a menu, Egg Noodles Sautéed in Butter simply means that butter was used for the sautéing instead of another fat.

Sautéing of meats without deglazing is a preparation in which food values and taste are wasted. It is of interest to note that many connoisseurs prefer sautéed and deglazed steaks instead of broiled steaks.

Fish a la "Meuniere" may be one of the most common fish preparations, with slight regional variations. A portion-sized fillet of any fish is salted, dipped in cream, then in flour (a simple way of coating) and sautéed in a small quantity of clear butter. When the fish is about 80% done, a small piece of fresh butter is added, browned, and poured over the fish before serving. Chopped parsley and a few drops of fresh lemon juice are added as a final touch.

## SAUTÉED, DEGLAZED FOODS

Raw, sautéed vegetables can also be deglazed. This is done by adding a small amount of veloute or bechamel sauce and some cream. These are then called creamed vegetables, for example, creamed spinach, creamed carrots, and creamed peas. Green peas can be sautéed with bacon, onions, and chopped romaine lettuce and then deglazed with some light veloute sauce. They are called "Petit Pois a la Francaise" or "Peas a la Parisienne".

Deglazed sauté dishes which look like stews, but are not stews, have been described in unit 8. By the same principle as in the examples given, chicken, lamb, or pork could be sautéed and deglazed with a sauce.

---

Sautéed pork chops are all made in the same manner, with a different final garnish. This step-by-step description of pork chops Hungarian style can be applied to any sautéed pork-chop preparation.

*Materials Needed for 6 Orders:*

6 single, portion-sized, center cut pork chops with full rib bone, chine bone removed
1 1/2 cups "Lesco" sauce (page 159)
1 tablespoon Hungarian paprika

1 1/2 cups sour cream with 1 tablespoon of flour stirred in
1 ounce oil
2 ounces fresh butter
1/2 teaspoon finely chopped garlic

*Procedure:*

1. Pound the pork chops to a thickness of one-half inch.
2. Salt them well; dip one side into flour.
3. Heat skillet very hot; pour in the oil.
4. Put all the chops in with the floured side down.
5. Sauté over medium heat until brown, about 2 minutes.
6. Turn chops over, (once only); continue sautéing for 2-3 minutes.
7. Reduce heat, lift pan, and drain off surplus fat.
8. Add butter to pork chops in the pan and brown the butter.
9. Add the garlic; sauté until garlic is golden brown.
10. Remove the chops, their first side (floured) up, to service plate.
11. Add paprika to the drippings.
12. Deglaze with the Lesco sauce.
13. Bring to a boil and add all the sour cream.
14. Bring to a full boil again, then simmer quickly into a smooth and velvety sauce.
15. Spoon over the pork chops and serve.

─────────── ATTENTION: KEY POINTS ───────────

- Pork chops must be cut with the full rib bone still in, then trimmed and pounded, to loosen the fibres for faster cooking.
- Meat must be salted well, while still raw.
- Sautéed (or roasted or broiled) meat should not be cooked super well done and thus dried out.

NOTE: Pork cooking techniques are not as developed in the USA as they should be. There are many wrong ideas about trichinosis. First, it must be taken for granted that only USDA inspected meat is used. Second, the old belief that 185°F. is needed to sterilize possible trichinas must be changed. New research has shown 140°F. to be enough for any necessary sterilization. Pork should not be eaten rare, although this could be safe. There is a long span between 140°F. and 185°F., which is super well done or dried out. Sautéed or grilled meat must not be overcooked to such a degree that it becomes tasteless, tough, and of little nutritional value. Third, there must be proper salting because pork is more bland than beef. An unsalted ham would not appeal to anyone, nor would unsalted pork chops be tasty.

**TABLE 19-2 HUNGARIAN PORK CHOPS**

Veal scallopini in different sauces are a favorite with all Italian restaurants in the USA. Scallopini are very simple to prepare. They can be true gourmet dishes, if all ingredients are of prime quality and are cooked right. Like other food preparations, garnishes or styles are interchangeable. Only the basic preparation is always the same. In some areas, scallopini are also called "Piccata".

Raw scallopini are pieces of dairy veal leg, with no sinews, gristle or fat, pounded to a 1/4-inch thickness. The weight per scallopini is about 2 ounces, 3-4 pieces to the order.

*Materials Needed for 6 Orders:*

18 veal scallopini , pounded, salted, and flour dipped  
2 ounces olive oil  
4 ounces fresh butter  

1/2 cup brown sauce  
3/4 cup Marsala wine

*Procedure:*

1. Heat skillet very hot, then pour in the oil.
2. Put meat into the pan quickly while shaking pan with other hand to prevent burning of the scallopini through uneven heat.
3. After sautéing them for one minute, turn them over and sauté one minute more.
4. Add the butter and brown quickly on high heat.
5. Turn heat down; remove scallopini to a dinner plate.
6. Deglaze the skillet with Marsala; cook drippings loose.
7. Add the brown sauce and reduce to a desired smooth texture; turn off heat.
8. Return the sautéed scallopini to the skillet, including the freshly accumulated drippings; mix well together.
9. Portion scallopini on platters, overlapping like shingles, and spoon just enough sauce over them to cover.
10. Garnish with whole parsley and serve.

--- ATTENTION: KEY POINTS ---

- Avoid a plate overfilled with sauce.
- Total sautéing time should be not more than 3 minutes.
- Never reboil a sautéed meat in the sauce.
- Serve immediately.

**TABLE 19-3 VEAL SCALLOPINI WITH MARSALA (Scallopini di vitello al Marsala)**

For instance, Chicken, Lamb, or Pork Curry can be made by using a curry sauce. An endless variety of meat sautés exists in the form of chops, Noisettes, Scallopini, Grenadins, and Entrecotes.

### Disjointed Chicken Sautés

Chickens can be sautéed in different sizes. Semiboneless chicken quarters are used most often. The leg quarter has the aitch and hip bone removed. The drumstick stays in, so as to preserve the chicken shape.

## A FAST WAY OF DISJOINTING AND BONING A CHICKEN

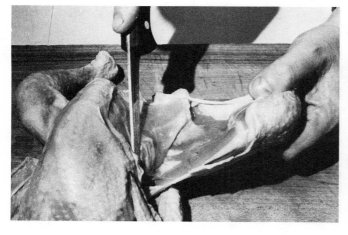

Fig. 19-2 The leg is pulled away from the carcass and the skin between hip and breast is cut.

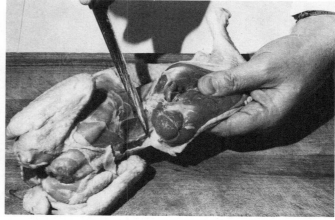

Fig. 19-3 The fleshy meat part on the chicken's back, the "oyster", is carefully loosened from the bone, the joint muscles are cut and the whole leg is pulled off the carcass.

(continued)

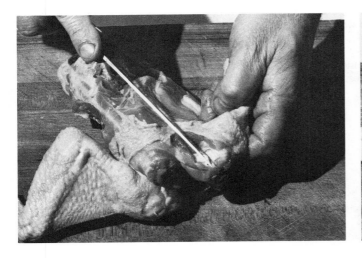

Fig. 19-4  The wing bone is disjointed from the collar-bone.

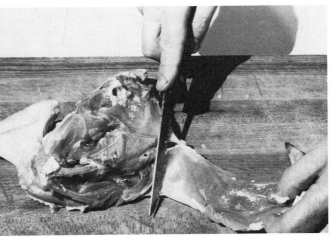

Fig. 19-5  The flesh is pulled off the carcass by gripping the wing bones and the heavier part of the chicken breast; the knife held in the other hand cuts the skin to prevent tearing, and helps to loosen the flesh from the bone.

Fig. 19-6  The wing is now removed (cut in the second joint) from the wing arm.

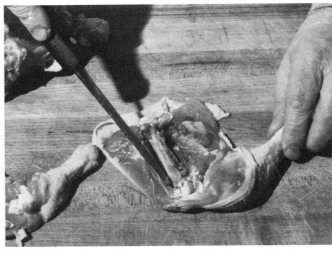

Fig. 19-7  The removal of the hip bone is optional.

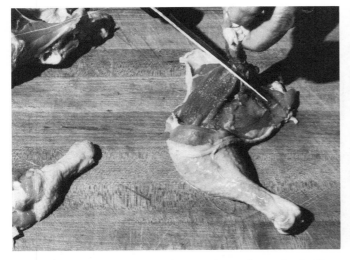

Fig. 19-8  The hip bone is boned out from the inside part of the chicken leg and carefully cut from the drumstick joint.

Fig. 19-9  The wing is scored underneath the joint on the inside, then snapped back.

(continued)

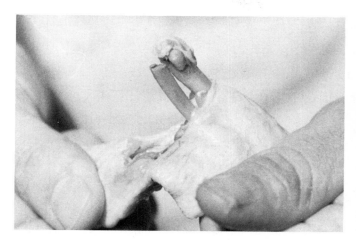

Fig. 19-10 The snapped back wing tip is pulled down half the length of the wing bone, then the tip with the bone end in it is cut off. Now the smaller of the two remaining bones is taken out.

Fig. 19-11 The various parts of a disjointed chicken: two semiboneless legs, two semiboneless breasts, two trimmed wings, and one boned carcass.

The breast, with the wing bone still attached, is peeled off the carcass. This boning results in semiboned and disjointed chicken quarters which still look like chicken when cooked. The boning of chickens must be learned by watching a demonstration and having additional practice.

Chicken, a very neutral tasting meat, blends well with many sauces, flavors, and garnishes. Thus, many different combinations of chicken sautés can be made.

Garnishes may be specially cut or shaped precooked vegetables, herbs, spices, meats, seafood, or whatever might be edible and decorative.

Following is a step-by-step instruction for the sautéing of disjointed chickens.

*Materials Needed for 10 Orders:*

| | |
|---|---|
| 5 small chickens (2 lbs. each), disjointed in 10 leg and 10 breast quarters | 1/4 lb. fresh butter |
| Garnish and basic sauces as indicated in each recipe | 1 cup flour |
| 1/4 cup salad or other oil | Salt |
| | 2 skillets, each large enough to hold all legs or all breasts |

*Procedure for Sautéing:*

1. Preheat oven to 375°F.
2. Salt chickens; dip skin side into flour.
3. Take first pan, put in 2 ounces of oil, then heat to smoking point.
4. Put all chicken legs, floured side down, into pan, shake pan, and reduce heat while doing this.
5. Increase heat, to sauté the floured side, until it is golden brown. *Keep pan moving.*
6. Turn each leg over.
7. Put pan with chickens into a pre-heated 375°F. oven.
8. Use second pan and repeat steps above with the breasts. *Work fast.*
9. After 15 minutes for legs and 10 minutes for breasts, the chickens are ready to be deglazed.
10. Chickens may be kept warm for 1-2 hours and finished when needed.

*Procedure for Deglazing or Finishing:*

11. Drain surplus fat from the pan. Chickens stay in the pan.
12. Return pan and chickens to a low fire. Add two ounces of fresh butter.
13. Melt and slightly brown butter.
14. Add clear liquid (wines, brandy, clear stock or cream) from recipe. Increase heat.
15. While doing this, turn each chicken piece once to assure that color and flavor from liquid are distributed evenly.
16. Reduce heat, remove chicken pieces to serving platter, and keep warm.
17. Add the remaining sauces. Use whip to stir into smooth liquid.
18. Simmer, (or boil) for 1 or 2 minutes, depending on existing and desired sauce texture.
19. If sauce is not smooth, but is full of burned residues, strain.
20. When sauce is smooth, add garnish. Wait until thoroughly hot.
21. Spoon just enough sauce over chicken for an elegant presentation.
22. Pour remaining sauce into sauce boat and serve on the side.
23. The finished chicken dish should be decorated with a little whole parsley or watercress, unless a different garnish is indicated.

*Chicken Sauté Preparation and Corresponding Garnish*

For each order approximately 3 ounces of finished sauce is needed.

*Chicken Sauté Sec.*  1 part red wine, 2 parts brown sauce. No garnish.

*Chicken Sauté Aux Marsala (Or Sherry or Port).*  Deglaze, as for "Sec" but change red wine to Marsala (Sherry or Port).

*Chicken Sauté With Mushrooms.*  Deglaze as for "Sec". Garnish: sautéed sliced mushrooms.

*Chicken Princess.*  1/8 white wine, 1/8 asparagus water, 1/4 veloute, 1/2 cream. Garnish: asparagus tips, green peas.

*Chicken Creole.*  1/4 red wine, 1/4 tomato sauce, 1/2 Spanish sauce. No garnish.

*Chicken Marengo.*  1/3 white wine, 1/3 tomato sauce, 1/3 brown mushroom sauce. Garnish: crayfish tails or a 1/2-ounce bay shrimp.

*Hungarian Chicken.*  1/2 sour cream, 1/2 paprika sauce. Garnish: sautéed bell pepper, onions, and tomato cubes.

*Chicken Jerusalem.*  1/3 white wine, 1/3 veloute, 1/3 heavy cream. Garnish: sliced Jerusalem artichokes (topinambour), chives.

*Chicken Raphael Weil.*  1/3 white wine, 1/3 veloute, 1/3 heavy cream. Garnish: sliced globe artichoke bottoms, sliced mushrooms.

*Chicken Chasseur.*  1/2 red wine, 1/2 brown sauce. Garnish: tomato cubes, sliced mushrooms, green onions.

*Chicken Sauté Italian.*  1/2 red wine, 1/2 brown sauce. Garnish: fried garlic, shallots, scallions, mushrooms, and tomato concasse.

*Coq Au Vin.*  2/3 burgundy wine, 1/3 brown sauce, a dash of sherry. Garnish: mushroom quarters, pearl onions, bacon lardons.

*Chicken Bombay.*  1/2 curry sauce, 1/2 cream. Garnish: diced green apples, papaya, tomato concasse on top of curry sauce, chopped parsley.

### Shellfish Sautés

Shellfish sautés can be made of raw or precooked seafood. Cleaned and frozen prawns, lobsters, and scallops should be sautéed from the raw stage. If cut properly, their cooking time is only minutes. Crab legs for sautéing are used, precooked only. Again, the same principles are used as in meat sautés.

*Lobster Newburg.*  Cut-up lobster meat is sautéed in butter. It is deglazed with 1/2 ounce dry sherry, 1 ounce bechamel sauce, and 2 ounces heavy fresh cream. Cayenne pepper and salt to taste are added.

*Crab Legs, "Bordelaise".*  Cooked, shelled crab legs are sautéed in butter with some fine chopped shallots. It is deglazed with 1/2 ounce brandy and 2 ounces brown-red wine sauce. Sprinkled with chopped parsley when served.

*Scampi Maximilian.*  Raw, peeled, deveined, butterflyed prawns (scampi are prawns from the Adriatic sea) are sautéed in clear butter. Then they are deglazed with 1 ounce dry white wine, 1 ounce heavy veloute sauce, 2 ounces of sour cream and 1/4 teaspoon of chopped dill weed.

*Prawns Creole.*  Raw, peeled, deveined, butterflyed prawns are sautéed in butter. They are deglazed with 1 ounce dry white wine and 3 ounces of Spanish sauce (creole sauce).

### GRIDDLE

A griddle may be thought of as a large stationary skillet, used only for short order cooking. The griddle has more disadvantages than advantages, however. The griddle is only excellent for the cooking of large quantities of hotcakes. Perhaps this was its original purpose. But when it is used as the instrument for all breakfast cookery, it is both wasteful and less than mediocre in its product. Meats are better cooked on a broiler. Pork links and bacon should be cooked in the skillet. The griddle easily dirties up during rush hours. It also needs much constant cleaning. Unlike the skillet, it cannot be brought to the sink and washed, nor can it be exchanged for another one.

## CONCLUSIONS

It must be emphasized that sautéing does not really mean the same as flip frying. Flip frying is the part of sautéing where small-cut ingredients are flipped into the air, then are caught in the pan again. By this process they hopefully mix and turn from one side to the other. For all larger meat and seafood cuts, the regular chef's fork, the pallet knife, or a spatula is used to turn the cooked foods. A good working cook will never attempt to flip a pan with half a dozen chicken breasts or several orders of fish fillet. Therefore, sautéing must be accepted to mean cooking in only a little fat which then becomes an ingredient of the finished dish.

Prawns a la Creole is, by its nature, a flip-fried dish. For practical reasons, it is the same dish as Supreme of Halibut Creole. The difference is that the boneless halibut fillet order can be sautéed, griddle-fried, or "baked". When transferred to the dinner plate, premade creole sauce finished with wine and butter could be sauced (spooned) over the fish.

Many more borderline preparations exist. An Entrecote (French name for a New York cut raw sirloin steak), could be broiled and served with premade Bordelaise in a sauce boat. This would be done to keep the eye-appealing grill marks visible. Or the same steak could be griddle-fried, placed on the dinner plate, and sauced with the Bordelaise sauce.

Looking again at table 19-1, it should be understood now, that in this *true* sauté preparation, the sauce will reflect the brandy flavor, the meat drippings, and the aroma of the finely chopped shallots sautéed in browned butter. Also important is the fact that the ingredients are raw until used and that they could be stored or put in a different preparation. This is where the advantage of sautéing lies. At the same time, this process needs the know-how of a skilled and responsible cook.

The understanding and mastery of basic cooking processes allows the cook to analyze the ingredients of an unknown dish and recreate it without difficulty. By applying the sautéing process, the cook can, as a bartender mixes new drinks, create many new and unusual dishes based on his own ideas of taste and artistry.

## SUMMARY

Sautéing, one of the most used processes of today's cookery, is one of the simplest things to do. The principles of tender foods, uniform cutting, use of good fats, high heat without burning or overcooking, and the addition of good premade sauces must be applied exactly and with understanding. The fact that the good fats which are used become a part of the preparation controls the amount that can be added. Deglazing adds the finishing touch to many dishes, and even gives them their specific taste and appearance. All sautés are made in the same way. They are some of the most elegant, tasty and appealing dishes prepared in the "Luxury Dinner Houses" of today. In sautéing, the texture and flavor of fresh fried food is preserved and mixed with the quality of premade sauces and garnishes.

### DISCUSSION TOPICS

1. What are suitable skillets for sautéing?
2. In cooking, what is the relation of skillet size, heat source, and food quantity?
3. What is the difference between griddle use and sauté cookery?
4. How are a sauté cook and sauce cook related?

### SUGGESTED ACTIVITIES

1. Define: griddle, deglazing, Newburg, scampi, prawn, pasta, G.R.A.S.
2. Demonstrate chicken disjointing and boning.

3. Practice chicken disjointing and boning.

4. Sauté preboiled vegetables.

5. Make a chicken sauté with mushrooms.

6. Sauté a "Fillet of Sole a la Meuniere".

## ACHIEVEMENT REVIEW

A. Complete the following:

1. A griddle must be visualized as a large _____.

2. Sauté cooking has the characteristics of luxury _____.

3. Sautéed potatoes are an example of sautéing without _____.

4. The immediate deglazing is done with some _____.

5. Sautéing meat is a waste of taste if it is done without _____.

6. Sautéed fish "Meunier" is dipped first in _____.

7. The Entrecote Bordelaise is a steak which translates as _____.

8. Shellfish sautés can be made from seafood that is either cooked or _____.

B. Read each question carefully and completely before answering it. Select the *best* answer.

1. Sautéing is ideal for vegetable cookery because

    a. it retains more vitamin C
    b. it retains taste and nutritional value
    c. it saves the cutting up of vegetables
    d. it is liked better by customers

2. Sautéing without deglazing is customary for the following dishes with the exception of

    a. Beef Stroganoff          c. Buttered Almonds
    b. Buttered Egg Noodles      d. Home Fried Potatoes

3. A griddle should be considered a large stationary skillet most efficient for the

    a. frying of fish            c. cooking of luxury cuisine
    b. broiling of steaks        d. cooking of breakfast hotcakes

4. The sauté cooking of luxury cuisine does not consider one of the following a suitable fat:

    a. pork fat                  c. olive oil
    b. shortening                d. butterfat

5. Sauté chickens which are disjointed and semiboned weigh an average each of

    a. 3/4 to 1 1/4 lb.          c. 1 3/4 to 2 1/4 lb.
    b. 1 1/4 to 1 3/4 lb.        d. 2 1/4 to 2 3/4 lb.

6. Entrecote Bordelaise and Crab Legs Bordelaise have the following in common

    a. both are served in dinner houses
    b. both are sauté dishes
    c. both are served with the same sauce
    d. both are served undercooked

7. The difference in cooking time for disjointed chicken legs and breasts is

   a. zero minutes
   b. two and a half minutes
   c. five minutes
   d. seven and a half minutes

8. Sautéing gains wider acceptance slowly but constantly for all these reasons, except

   a. meat quality is getting better
   b. costs less to produce it
   c. retains greater nutritional values
   d. does away with leftover food

9. The sauce which makes up the sauté preparation Bordelaise is composed of

   a. white wine and creole sauce
   b. white wine, dill, cream and brown sauce
   c. red wine, shallots, brandy and brown sauce
   d. red wine, sherry, cayenne pepper and cream

10. "Newburg" is a most popular preparation for

    a. fried fish fillets
    b. sautéed oysters
    c. veal scallopine
    d. shelled lobster meat

C. Answer in your own words:

   1. Explain the principle of sautéing.
   2. List the suitable sauté fats.
   3. Describe the cooking of sautéed, deglazed foods.
   4. List the names of 4 different chicken sauté preparations.

# Unit 20  The Boiling of Meat and Fish

## OBJECTIVES

After studying and practicing this unit, the student should be able to

- List the reasons for the boiling of protein food.
- Explain the principles of boiling.
- Boil a corned brisket of beef.
- Boil a turkey breast for sandwich use.
- Prepare Sole a la Bonne Femme.

It was pointed out in units 1 and 7 that boiling may serve the purposes of tenderizing , rehydrating, and desalting. Also it can be a taste preference, especially with fish preparations. There is a difference between the simmering of boiled foods and the extraction of liquefiable foods into stock.

## PROCESS REVIEW

For food cooked by boiling, the leaching out of nutrients and taste must be prevented. Observing these rules will make the task easy:

- Use only enough liquid (water) to cover the food.
- Bring cooking liquid to a strong rolling boil first; then slip food into liquid and bring quickly to the boiling point again.
- Simmer until done.
- Saturate the liquid with flavor-giving herbs, spices, and salt so as to prevent unnecessary leaching through osmosis.
- Simmer food until nearly tender, if it is to be served hot.
- For food to be used cold, carry-over heat (additional tenderization during the cool-off) must be considered.
- Cooling of boiled protein foods in their own cooking liquid improves their taste.
- Cooling of fresh cooked foods in cold water results in loss of taste and nutritional values.
- Simmering of protein food in flavor-saturated stock gives it a better taste than food cooked in water only.

## BOILING CHARACTERISTICS AND SHRINKAGE

In roasting, heat and time can be regulated to achieve the desired result; but in boiling the heat degrees are set. Food kept below the simmering point will not tenderize. Food cannot be heated above the rolling boil. Pressure cooking of meat or fish is not done since there is no control by inspection, and also broth is not created. Steam cannot be flavor-saturated in the way a liquid can. Pressure steamed meats have less flavor and may be overcooked. Many people believe that steam leaches less than liquid, but this is true in unsaturated water only. It must also be considered that the outside of food exposed to 250°F. moist heat overcooks much more than when it is only heated to 190°F. Overboiling in liquid results in just the same shrinkage and dryness as overcooking by a dry method. When the liquid content of the meat cells is brought to the boiling point, these cells burst open and the natural juices flow into the boiling liquid. Therefore, overcooked protein food, cooked by any method, will be dry and tasteless.

### Boiling of Meats

All boiled meats are cooked by the same principles. Herbs and spices include salt, peppercorns, cloves, bay leaves, thyme, basil, and parsley. The flavor-giving vegetables are the same as those used in sauce cookery.

These are celery, carrots, onions, leeks, parsnips, and sometimes cabbage. The cooking time always depends on the kind of meat, its quality, and the size of the piece to be cooked. Boiled meats, when served hot, are often eaten plain, or with mustard and grated horseradish. They may be served in broth or on a plate, covered with sauces of contrasting taste. Boiled meat should be carved to the order, across the grain like a roast. It is kept hot in its own broth.

*Fresh Boiled Beef.* Fresh boiled beef is popular in cold and wintery areas. Pieces used are chuck meat, short ribs, brisket, and rump cuts from grades which are lower than good. The cuts should not be too large. The best size is an 8-12-pound average. Boiling a whole bottom round, for instance, is impractical because the heel (shank) and the eye need longer cooking than the sirloin tip (culotte) end. Larger pieces are also hard to handle when cooked. They may break or tear apart when taken out of the broth. Cooking time for short ribs could be 1 1/2 hours, for a brisket about 2 hours, and for some heavy chuck or round pieces, as long as 2 1/2 - 3 hours, or more. Lots of soup vegetables, parsley, bouquet garni, peppercorns, a few tomatoes, and a little cabbage should be added to the boiling liquid. The meat should be defatted before serving.

*Corned Beef.* These are the same beef cuts as those used for fresh boiled beef. They might be of a lower grade, because of the tenderizing characteristic of the curing. Curing means pickling in brine. This is a salt solution, in which Chile Saltpetre (potassium nitrate) has been added. A well-known dish is Corned Beef and Cabbage, usually served to the Irish on St. Patrick's Day. Most of the corned beef used in restaurants goes into sandwiches or corned beef hash.

**Pastrami.** Pastrami is the same as corned beef, except that the cured salted beef is also smoked. Pastrami is beef that has been prepared like ham. Its uses are similar to corned beef, but more is used for sandwiches than anything else.

*Pickled Fresh Pork.* Pickled fresh pork is made and handled the same way as corned beef. Since it always comes from younger animals, it has a shorter cooking time than corned beef.

*Boiled Leg of Lamb.* Boiled leg of lamb is an English dish where a whole leg of lamb, or mutton, is boiled instead of roasted. The procedure is the same as for beef, but with a shorter cooking time. The broth is used for a sauce, (capersauce, mustard sauce, etc.) or finished into a Scotch Broth (Consomme Eccossaise). (See Soups, unit 21.)

*Boiled Chicken.* Any size chicken can be boiled and served in a pot with vermicelli and vegetables if this is the dish one wants to make. Colored hens or fowl must be boiled as the only practical way to be used. After boiling, the hot chickens are skinned. When cool, they are boned. The meat is used for chicken a la king, creamed chicken, chicken pot pie, chicken salad, sandwiches, and other dishes.

*Boiled Turkey.* Boiled turkey is often used instead of chicken. Turkeys are large, need less handling, and give a better yield. This is especially true when the breast is sliced up for sandwiches. Just as for roast turkey, it is better to separate white and dark meat before cooking. This is for easier handling and better results. Twenty-eight- to thirty-pound turkeys, with legs separated from the breasts but in the same stock pot, simmer approximately 2 1/2-3 hours. When these are cooked, they should be turned so that the breast is down, and covered with aluminum foil while still hot and moist. This prevents needless drying out of the breasts.

### Boiling of Fish

Fish of a larger size is boiled whole only if it is to be used for a cold buffet. A fish cooker, for easier handling, must be available. The fish prepared in this way are usually salmon, smaller sturgeons, and large trout. The same principles apply as for the cooking of meat proteins, except, of course, that they have a shorter cooking time. Court Bouillon (stock made from fish bones and soup vegetables) should be used as the boiling liquid. A plain onion and pepper stock, which gives a very sharp taste, can be used for some preparations. Something slightly acid is very often added to fish stock to make it less bland. It should be remembered that vinegars and wines will firm up the flesh of the fish, but lemon juice will tenderize it even more. If a whole salmon is to be cooked for a cold buffet, it is a trick of the trade to add unflavored gelatine to the liquid after the fish is taken off the fire. The gelatine dissolves in the court bouillon, where the fish has to cool completely. When chilled, it will help to hold the fish in a better shape.

*Poaching.*  Poaching is used for portion cut fish pieces. It is very much like boiling, except that less liquid is used. Half the fish piece is in the poaching liquid, and the upper half cooks in the steam.

Poaching is done to have a stronger fish stock, which is then used to make the sauce which gives the preparation its name. Poached Fillet of Sole Bonne Femme, for instance, means that folded fillets of sole are covered with sliced raw mushrooms; then poached in half court bouillon and half white wine and finished with a very light cream sauce.

All the many fancy named poached fish dishes can be made the same way. Only the flavor-giving ingredients are changed. If the name and preparation stay the same, the kind of fish is changed. Poaching liquids are made of different wines, stock, water, milk, or beer. Roux, egg yolk, or starches change any liquid into sauce. The addition of spices, garnishes, special vegetables, cream, cheeses, and others accounts for the many hundred of varieties which are common. Following is a list of poached fish preparations made like "Sole Bonne Femme" except with a change of the mushroom garnish to something else. The new and different ingredient accounts for the different name:

- Sole Argenteuil – asparagus tips replace the mushrooms.
- Sole Duglere – chopped tomatoes and onions replace the mushrooms.
- Sole Nantua – crayfish tails replace the mushrooms.
- Sole Marguery – Olympia Oysters and bay shrimps replace the mushrooms.
- Sole Walewska – poached, then covered with a lobster slice and a piece of truffle, then glazed with a Mornay (cheese-fish sauce) under the broiler.

---

Sole Bonne Femme must be thought of as the basic preparation for poached fish dishes. As in most cooking, variations are made by changing some or all of the ingredients and the type of fish used. The principles and techniques remain the same. Poached fish can be made to the order just the same as a steak. Fillet always implies skinned and boned fish. A la bonne femme means cooked after the fashion of the homemaker.

*Materials Needed:*

A fireproof platter or portion casserole
One 8-inch aluminum skillet with cover
A whisk, rubber spatula, pastry bag, and star tube
Some Duchess potatoes (optional)
Heavy cream
Hollandaise sauce, veloute sauce

Fresh Fillet of Sole
Mushrooms
Butter
White wine (dry sauterne)
Lemon
Salt

*Procedure:*

1. Select 8-10 ounces of sole fillet in 2 or 4 pieces.
2. Score, trim and salt them; portion into 2 uniform packages (paupiettes).
3. Place paupiettes in a buttered skillet, cover fish with about 2 ounces of sliced fresh mushrooms, well washed.
4. Add one bay leaf and a little lemon juice.
5. Pour 3-4 ounces of dry sauterne over fish and cover.
6. Put on low heat; poach for 4-5 minutes.
7. While fish poaches, pipe Duchess potatoes
   a. onto a fish platter as a border, or
   b. into fireproof casserole as a divider
8. Brown the potato border (divider) under the broiler.
9. When poached fish is done, transfer it and the mushrooms to the freshly prepared platter and keep warm.
10. Remove the bay leaf; add 2 ounces of veloute sauce and 2 ounces of heavy cream to the fish stock.
11. Simmer well together, reduce a little; taste, and salt if necessary.
12. Take sauce off the heat, cool for a few seconds, then fold in 2-3 tablespoons of Hollandaise sauce.
13. Pour sauce over fish and mushrooms, set platter under broiler for about 30 seconds, until the sauce is golden glazed.
14. If a casserole with the duchess divider was used, fish goes into the larger space. The small space can be filled with buttered peas or parsley parisian potatoes.
15. Serve immediately either as a fish course or a main course.

NOTE: The Duchess potato border is not essential to a poached fish preparation and may be omitted.

---

**TABLE 20-1  FILLET OF SOLE BONNE FEMME**

It is obvious that sole can be replaced by any fine flaked fish, such as Dover, sole, halibut, turbot, or whatever local specialty is available.

### Crustaceans

Crustaceans, such as lobster, langustes, prawns, scampi, crabs, and crayfish are all boiled by the same boiling principles as outlined earlier. For fish, salt is of the first importance. A bouquet garni, vegetables, and spices are optional to the region. The cooking time for live lobsters, crabs, or spiny lobsters of a 1 to 1 1/2-pound size, is a total of 10-12 minutes of simmering after the liquid has been brought back to the boiling point. Scampi, langustinos, and prawns, depending on their size, may have a 2-3 minute simmering time after they have been brought back to the boiling point.

### Blue Trout

Blue trout is a fresh, unfrozen trout, simmered in fish stock with some white vinegar, parsley, onions, bay leaf, and salt. The freshly cleaned trout is slipped into the court bouillon which is again brought to the boiling point. Then the trout is taken off the range and steeped. Eight to twelve-ounce portions steep 3-4 minutes. Twelve to sixteen-ounce portions steep 5-6 minutes. Trout for this true gourmet preparation should weigh 6-8 ounces. They are served with clarified butter, lemon wedge, and parsley potatoes only.

### Finnan Haddie

Finnan Haddie is cured, smoked haddock available as fillet or with the bones still in. It is usually blanched in boiling water for a minute or so, drained, then poached in half and half or rich milk. It can be served plain, covered with a light cream sauce, or flaked and mixed with a light cream sauce. Finnan Haddie is most popular in the Eastern USA and Canada.

### SUMMARY

The cooking of protein foods in clear liquids is known as boiling, simmering, or poaching. Essentially these are the same since only the stage of simmering should be used to reach best results. Poaching is a term applied mostly to fish dishes or to poached eggs. For fish dishes, poaching means simmering in as little liquid as possible, but for the poaching of eggs (discussed in unit 28), simmering in a rather large quantity of liquid is essential.

Meat and fish, called in this unit protein food, react to boiling in the same way as to other cooking methods. Moisture prevents caramelization. Overboiling, unlike overfrying or roasting, will not burn food. Overboiling does make protein food dry and tasteless and could turn food into pulp.

All plain boiling or poaching uses the same principle. Food is put into boiling liquid; the heat is then reduced to simmering until the food is done. Liquids must have a flavor of their own to prevent needless taste loss of the protein food cooked. Salt is a most important addition to any boiling liquid for fresh protein food. Only those foods which may have been preserved by the curing or salting process may be cooked in plain water. Boiled meat dinners are simple in their presentation. When the boiling liquid is changed into sauces, a large variety of especially poached fish dishes comes into existence. Boiling as a meat preparation is applied to large or whole pieces only; but for fish, because of its tenderness and difficult handling, portion cuts are more popular. The logical continuation of boiling is the changing of the broth into sauces. This is explained in the following unit.

### DISCUSSION TOPICS

1.  How is a cooking method selected which is related to need?
2.  How does boiling compare to other cooking methods?
3.  Can poached fish dishes be made to order?

### SUGGESTED ACTIVITIES

1.  Define: Duchess potatoes, pipe, court bouillon, pastrami.
2.  Make a list of meats and meat cuts best suited for boiling.

3. Compose as many poached fish variations as possible, based on the step-by-step preparation of "Sole Bonne Femme".

4. Prepare Sole Bonne Femme according to the step-by-step outline.

5. Select and boil a chicken for chicken salad. Skin and cool it properly.

6. Compose a formula of boiling liquid to cook a leg of lamb. (Approximate pot size, water quantity, salt and amount of vegetables and seasonings to be added.)

7. Boil a corned brisket of beef.

8. Boil a turkey breast for sandwich use.

## ACHIEVEMENT REVIEW

A. Complete the following:

1. All boiled meats are cooked by the same _____.

2. When food is boiled, the leaching out of taste must be _____.

3. The amount of liquid used must be balanced to the amount of _____.

4. All boiled protein foods are started with the liquid brought to a rolling _____.

5. Saturated liquids prevent taste losses by _____.

6. For boiled, just as for roasted food, carry-over heat must be _____.

7. Cooling off protein foods in their cooking liquids improves their _____.

8. Cooling off fresh cooked foods in cold water is a waste of _____.

9. Steam cooking of meats is wasteful since there is no _____.

10. Pressure steam cooking means taking the risk of _____.

B. Read each question carefully and completely before answering it. Select the *best* answer.

1. Boiled fresh meats will taste better if
   a. salt is not added to the liquid at all
   b. salt is added after the meat is tender
   c. salt is added to liquid before meat is immersed
   d. salt is sprinkled on the sliced meat after cooking

2. To get food boiled properly, the cook adjusts the
   a. temperature of the boiling liquid
   b. time of cooking
   c. time and temperature
   d. size of the meat pieces to be cooked

3. A common cut of fresh beef for boiling is the
   a. rib roast          c. knuckle
   b. top sirloin        d. brisket

4. Pastrami, a favorite boiled sandwich meat, is actually a
   a. smoked, cured beef brisket    c. pickled pork shoulder
   b. corned beef round             d. smoked lamb leg

5. Colored hens or fowl are boiled first, then made into the following preparations except
   a. Chicken a la King    c. Southern Fried Chicken
   b. Creamed Chicken      d. Chicken Salad

6. Poached fish preparations use less boiling liquid for

   a. a stronger fish and sauce flavor
   b. less shrinkage
   c. being served dry
   d. a shorter cooking time

7. The correct cooking time for live lobsters or crabs of 1 to 1 1/2-pound size is

   a. 6-8 minutes     c. 10-12 minutes
   b. 8-10 minutes    d. 12-14 minutes

8. Poaching preparations intended for fine fleshed fish, like fillet of sole, should not be made with

   a. halibut     c. dover sole
   b. smelts     d. turbot

9. For the boiling of fish, the most important addition to the boiling liquid is

   a. celery     c. pepper
   b. salt     d. bay leaves

10. When boiling large or whole pieces of protein food, it is best that

   a. the boiling is started with cold liquid
   b. the full boil is maintained for the first 20 minutes
   c. the cooking vessel is well covered
   d. the cooking liquid only simmers

C. Match the garnish of the "Sole" preparations in Column I with the corresponding name in Column II.

| *Column I* | *Column II* |
|---|---|
| 1. Lobster slices | Argenteuil |
| 2. Oysters | Bonne Femme |
| 3. Crayfish tails | Duglere |
| 4. Asparagus tips | Marguery |
| 5. Mushrooms | Nantua |
| 6. Tomatoes | Walewska |

D. Answer in your own words:

1. Briefly explain the principles of boiling.

2. List the reasons for boiling protein food.

# Unit 21  Stocks, Sauces, and Soups

## OBJECTIVES

After studying and practicing this unit, the student should be able to

- Make all mother sauces based on roux.
- Extract brown stock from beef bones.
- Make a sauce Hollandaise.
- Make composition sauces by formula.
- Make the clarification of consommé.
- Make a de luxe vegetable cream soup.

Stocks, sauces, and soups are foods made from nutrients dissolved in water. Milk is liquid food produced by an animal. Soup is liquid food made by the cook.

## PROCESS REVIEW

The extraction of liquefiable foods is the fifth method of cooking. Its theory and technological background was discussed in unit 10. For the cook, it is a very important skill which must be understood and mastered.

Liquid foods are known under the names of stocks, broths, soups, sauces, and gravies. All these have their food parts dissolved in water. They may be proteins, carbohydrates, or fats and are distinguished by taste, texture, or color. Stocks and broths are clear liquids composed of proteins and fats. Soups, sauces, and gravies are made from stocks or broth by the addition of starch and more fat.

In unit 20, the paragraph titled Boiling of Meats explains that the boiling liquid for meat or fish is called broth. For making stock, the same procedure is used. Bones, sinews, and gristles are simmered in cold water to make stock. Cold water is used to start the stockpot, since cold water has a greater dissolving power. When all proteins and fats are dissolved and leached out, the water is called stock. The stock is drained off. The leached out sinews, bones, and gristles which remain are discarded. Stock is either white or brown and has the flavor of the bones used. Stock is white when the bones and trimmings are raw. Stock is brown if the bones and trimmings are roasted at high heat in the oven before they are boiled. Chicken and fish stock is kept white. Fish is never mixed with meat while cooking. Chicken bones are sometimes kept separate for pure chicken stock only, but they may be mixed in with the general meat stock. Beef, veal, and pork bones are used either for brown stock or for white stock. Lamb bones, because of their strong and unpopular flavor, are seldom used in the western hemisphere.

## STRUCTURE OF SAUCES

Nearly all warm sauces common to western luxury cuisine start from five "mother" or basic sauces. They are

- VELOUTE – *Ivory colored* meat or fish sauce from white stock.
- ESPAGNOLE – *Brown*, heavy meat sauce made from brown stock.
- TOMATE – *Red* vegetable sauce, made from tomato juice.
- BECHAMEL – *White* cream sauce made from milk.
- HOLLANDAISE – *Yellow* egg sauce made from yolks and butter.

Today, fewer basic sauces are recognized than in the past. All sauces except the Hollandaise are made the same way. They consist of one of the stocks and roux.

154

Stock is similar to broth. It is made of by-products such as bones, sinews, and gristle, as well as meat and vegetable trimmings. These by-products are simmered in water and the result of this extraction is called stock.

*Materials Needed:*

Large roasting pan
Steam kettle or stockpot, about 96-quart size
30-40 pounds beef and veal bones, trimmings, bacon rind, etc.
3 pounds each of rough cut onions, celery, carrots, parsnips

2-3 bunches of parsley
2 tablespoons each of thyme, pickling spices, peppercorns
Additional garlic, bay leaves, cloves
2 pounds tomato paste
15 gallons cold water

*Procedure:*

1. Put chopped bones into a roasting pan.
2. Put pan into preheated 475°F. oven.
3. Stir bones about every 1/2 hour to brown them evenly.
4. When brown, sprinkle the vegetables over the bones.
5. Roast 1/2 hour more, then add the tomato paste.
6. Continue roasting for 1/2 hour more.
7. Take pan out of oven, transfer contents of pan to steam kettle, but reserve the fat.
8. Fill kettle with 15 gallons of cold water.
9. Add all spices and parsley.
10. Bring to a slow boil, then simmer 5-6 hours.
11. Strain stock, cool off, unless used immediately.
12. Refrigerate overnight, skim fat off before use.

——— ATTENTION: KEY POINTS ———
- Brown stock can be made from beef, veal, or pork bones.
- Keep stock free of salt.

**TABLE 21-1  BROWN STOCK**

*Materials Needed Per Gallon of Water:*

2 to 3 pounds of raw bones or trimmings of meat, chicken or fish
Approximately 1 to 1 1/2 pounds of mixed soup vegetables (parsley, parsnips, celery, carrots, onions, leeks, scallions)
Spices

*Procedure:*

1. Cover bones, vegetables and spices with cold water.
2. Bring to a slow boil, then simmer

   bones from young chickens, not more than 2 hours.
   bones from hens or turkeys, 3 to 4 hours.
   veal or pork bones, 4 to 5 hours.
   beef bones, 5 to 7 hours.
   fish stock; cook vegetables 1 hour first, add fish trimmings and only cook for 1/2 hour more, then strain.
3. Strain stock, cool off fast, use, or refrigerate
4. Remove fat next morning before use.

——— ATTENTION: KEY POINTS ———
- Always simmer only. Do not salt stock while simmering, because unsalted water will leach out better.

**TABLE 21-2  WHITE MEAT, CHICKEN, OR FISH STOCK**

**Fig. 21-1  Sauce pot for roux-based mother sauces.**

## ROUX

Roux is a French word for a mixture of one weight part cooking fat and one weight part all-purpose flour. This mixture is fried for a short time on low heat. When added to a liquid and brought to a boil, it thickens the liquid immediately.

- White meat stock with roux becomes veloute.
- Chicken stock with roux becomes chicken veloute sauce,
- Brown meat stock with roux is named espagnole sauce.
- Tomato juice with roux makes tomato sauce.
- Hot milk with roux is called bechamel sauce.

By adding to these four basic roux sauces various garnishes and refinements, nearly all sauces of the Western type cuisine are made. Only for a few special preparations is roux omitted and white wash (plain cornstarch dissolved in water) used.

---

Roux consists of flour, lightly browned, in edible fat. Since starch burns easily under heat, it is best to use a heavy sauce pan or "sauteuse" which diffuses heat. Constant watching and stirring over a low fire is necessary.

Any good fat can be used. Chicken fat to make a chicken supreme sauce is acceptable, but neutral oils or butter are more common. All-purpose flour is preferred. The finished roux can be kept warm close to the stove, and used all day or be kept under refrigeration for weeks without spoiling.

Roux cannot be eaten by itself. It must always be mixed into a liquid and be brought to a rolling boil to be sure that all starches have *gelatinized* (meaning the starch granules have absorbed liquid to their fullest capacity). For this reason, roux is called a thickening agent.

*Materials Needed:*

| | |
|---|---|
| 1/8-inch heavy aluminum "sauteuse" sauce pan | 1 1/2 cups sifted, all-purpose flour |
| 1 cup clear fat | 1 wooden spatula or a whip |

*Procedure:*

1. Put fat into casserole on low heat.
2. When warm, stir flour in and keep stirring.
3. Depending on the type of sauce needed, roux is taken off when
   a. still white (4 to 5 minutes) or
   b. light golden brown (6 to 10 minutes).
4. Take from the heat and cool to about 175°F.
5. Now, little by little, the roux is added to the liquid to be thickened, which should be about 185°F. to 195°F. Whisk liquid constantly while adding the roux. Stop adding it when the thickness has the desired look.
6. Bring to a full boil. Beware of scorching, but keep boiling at least for 10 to 20 minutes.
7. Check texture of the sauce. Change it if necessary by adding more roux or more liquid.
8. Strain sauce into fresh container and keep uncovered in the steam table, or cool for storage under refrigeration.

—————————————— ATTENTION: KEY POINTS ——————————————

- The best way of using roux is to add warm roux by eye measurement to nearly simmering liquid, stirring with whisk until smooth. Why by eye measurement? Because of the difference in liquids, sauce pans used, heat sources, ideas, habits, and desired textures. This is one of the instances where the cook becomes the artist. He is the professional who uses his own standards, his own sophistication and understanding to determine how the expected end product should be.
- Do not use sizzling hot roux or cold water; in either case, it may cause a lumpy sauce.

**TABLE 21-3 HOW TO MAKE AND USE ROUX**

## HOLLANDAISE SAUCE

Hollandaise is a rich, warm, mayonnaise-like sauce made from egg yolk and butter, seasoned with lemon juice and salt. It is served with fish, vegetables, or eggs. Some of its more spicy variations, such as Sauce Bearnaise or Sauce Choron are served with meat. Hollandaise is also used to improve various sauces made with roux, especially when they are used for gratinated dishes. Egg sauces have a limited holding ability and should be made as close to serving time as possible. Egg sauces will curdle if kept too hot, and when cold, the butter will stiffen, making rewarming very difficult. Egg yolks contain sulfur, and lemon

*Utensils Needed:*

One 12-inch stainless steel bowl

One 12-inch stainless steel whip

One 8-inch tapered sauce pan (to improvise double boiler)

One rubber spatula

*Ingredients Needed for Approximately 20 Orders:*

6 extra large egg yolks

2 tablespoons lemon juice

4 tablespoons cold water

8 ounces clarified warm butter, about 100°F.

*Procedure:*

1. The tapered sauce pan is half filled with hot water.
2. Yolks, water, and lemon juice are mixed in the bowl.
3. The bowl is set on top of the sauce pan with water.
4. The improvised double boiler is put on the range.
5. The yolk mixture is whipped over heat to a fluffy custard.
6. Double boiler and bowl are taken off the heat.
7. The clear butter is whipped into the custard in a thin, steady stream. Too much butter at once will curdle the sauce.
8. The sauce is tested for texture and tasted for salt and lemon flavor. If it is too thin, more heat is needed. If it is too thick, water or more lemon juice can be added.

——————————————— ATTENTION: KEY POINTS ———————————————

- The finished sauce should not be kept too long.
- A suitable warm place must be found. The steam table is too hot. Storage must be in a temperature zone from 100°F. to 120°F.
- All utensils used must be of nonoxidizing materials.

**TABLE 21-4  SAUCE HOLLANDAISE**

juice contains acid. Thus, only stainless steel, glass, or china can be used in the making of this sauce. A stainless steel whisk must also be used.

## *MOTHER SAUCES AND SOME DERIVATIONS*

Brown meat stock, especially when made from veal and pork bones, can be reduced to a strong meat essence called Glace de Viande. This is done by slow simmering of the stock in a flat sauce pan. Most chefs today buy commercial meat bases or meat essences to save labor. Meat essence is used to give extra flavor to other sauces or dishes.

**ATTENTION:  KEY POINTS OF SAUCE COOKERY**

- The quality of a stock simmered slowly with proper ingredients.
- The quality of the fat used for a roux.
- The care extended to this roux.

Sauce texture in itself is a value judgement differing with cuisine and from chef to chef. The amounts given in this unit are approximations only! It must be understood that two quarts of any sauce, simmering in a five-quart sauce pan for five minutes will have a different texture (thickness-thinness) than two quarts of the same sauce simmering for five minutes in a nine-inch tapered sauce pan.

**Fig. 21-2  Sauce pan, for faster reduction and mixing of small amounts of sauce.**

```
┌─────────────────────────────────────────────────────────────────────────┐
│                       ATTENTION: KEY POINT                                │
│  • Sauce cookery will be successful when the proper size commercial       │
│    casseroles of a heavy gauge material are used. Casseroles with thin    │
│    bottoms which are made of material which does not diffuse heat         │
│    uniformly will usually result in scorched or burned sauces.            │
└─────────────────────────────────────────────────────────────────────────┘
```

### Meat, Chicken, or Fish Veloute

About one gallon of the desired stock is simmered with two cups of golden roux for about 30 minutes, then strained.

- *Sauce Supreme* — 2 quarts of chicken veloute and 2 quarts of manufacturing cream are simmered to a desired texture.
- *Sauce Allemande* — 3 quarts of meat veloute sauce are brought to a boil. One pint of white wine is added. One pint of heavy cream and 10 egg yolks are whipped together. The simmering veloute is poured over this mixture, while it is still being whisked. Season with nutmeg and salt.
- *Sauce Normande* — 3 quarts of fish veloute, 1 pint clam juice and the juice of half a lemon is brought to a boil. Then it is finished with 10 egg yolks and one pint of heavy cream, as in Sauce Allemande.

### Espagnole

About one gallon brown meat stock, one-half cup of caramelized tomato paste and one cup red wine are simmered with two cups of brown roux for at least 30 minutes, then strained.

- *Sauce Bordelaise* — 1 cup of chopped shallots is sautéed in 2 ounces of olive oil, deglazed with 3 quarts of heavy claret type wine and reduced by one-third. This is seasoned with thyme, bay leaf and black pepper. Then it is blended with 2 quarts of espagnole and half a cup of meat essence. It is then strained. This sauce is often served with poached beef marrow as a garnish.
- *Sauce Poivrade* — 2 cups vinegar, 2 cups burgundy, 1 cup onions, 1 cup parsley, several garlic cloves and 3 tablespoons of crushed pepper are simmered until reduced to half. This is strained and then blended with 3 quarts of espagnole and one pint of tomato puree.
- *Sauce Robert* — 2 cups chopped onions are sautéed in butter, deglazed with 1 cup of tarragon vinegar and 1 cup of stock. It is simmered until reduced to half. Then 1 cup of prepared french mustard is whisked in and blended with 1 1/2 quarts of supreme sauce and 1 quart of espagnole.
- *Brown Mushroom Sauce* — 2 1/2 pounds (1 basket) of fresh mushrooms are sliced and sautéed, then blended with 3 quarts of espagnole and 1/2 cup of dry sherry wine.
- *Sauce Demi-glace* — 4 quarts of brown stock are slowly reduced to half, then blended with 2 quarts of espagnole and simmered for 30 minutes more. To finish the sauce, 4 tablespoons of cornstarch are dissolved in 1/2 cup of dry port wine and added to the simmering sauce.

### Bechamel

One gallon of fresh milk (or substitute) is heated in the steam table or a double boiler to about 140°F. Two cups of chopped onions are sautéed in 2 ounces of bacon fat. These are blended with the milk and 2 cups of roux made from clarified butter. It is simmered for 20 minutes (scorches easily) and strained.

- *Sauce Mornay (Cheese sauce, plain)* — 3 quarts of bechamel are brought to a boil; 1/2 pound of grated parmesan and 1/2 pound of grated swiss cheese are whisked in. It is then taken off the heat, and 1/4 pound of fresh butter is worked in. Then it is seasoned with salt and cayenne.
- *Sauce Mornay (Cheese sauce, for gratinating)* — for each quart of Mornay, as described above, 1/2 to 1 cup of rich Hollandaise is blended in when needed.

### Tomato Sauce

Tomato sauces can be made in many varieties. Every combination will have a slightly different flavor. Spices, garlic, sugar, onions, bacon, or ham can be added at will. The tomato concentration of the sauce in itself allows for many variations. Tomato juice, puree-paste or fresh tomatoes can be used with stock, fish stock, chicken stock, or water to dilute the tomato concentrates.

- *Creole Sauce* — 2 cups each of the following are cut into a coarse julienne: onions, bell peppers, celery, mushrooms, and tomatoes. They are lightly sautéed in 3 ounces of olive oil, deglazed with 3 quarts of light tomato puree, spiced with sautéed garlic, salt, sugar, cayenne, and oregano. This is simmered for 4-5 minutes (the vegetables must remain crunchy), then thickened with cornstarch dissolved in cold water.

Fig. 21-3 Sauce pan, intermediate size

- *Hungarian Lesco Sauce* — 3 cups of onions, 2 cups of bell peppers and 3 cups of peeled, deseeded tomatoes are cut in a coarse julienne and sautéed in 3 ounces of bacon fat. Then 2 tablespoons of finely chopped garlic and 2 tablespoons of fancy paprika are added. Then 2 quarts of sour cream and 1 quart of tomato sauce are blended into it. It is brought to a full boil and reduced if necessary.

---

The following table lists the compositions and names of sauces, popular in luxury cuisine. No measurements or working methods are given. A chef who creates a sauce does it much the same way as an artist painting a picture. The ingredients are known but the rest is up to the individual. If quantities were standard it would not help too much, since the size, thickness, shape of the casserole, the heat source, and the food are different. Understanding comes through repeated practice.

The sauce names listed could be of regional origin, reflecting the specialty of a certain area. Other names indicate the flavor of the sauce. Some sauces have been dedicated to famous persons or historic events.

─────────── ATTENTION: KEY POINTS ───────────

- All sauces can be blended with other sauces, cream, sour cream, wine, juices, reductions, purees, eggs, cheese, butter, condiments and so on.
- Sauces should be blended in small quantities at the time of serving.
- Garnishes must be sautéed in butter or heated before they are added.
- Garnishes must be edible and eye appealing.
- Sauces are reduced (concentrated) by simmering, sometimes diluted with stock, or taken off the heat to prevent curdling.

This table will also familiarize the student with French-influenced culinary terminology.

| Sauce Bearnaise | Hollandaise — shallots, pepper, tarragon in vinegar reduction, chopped parsley. |
|---|---|
| Sauce Bourguignonne | Espagnole — Burgundy wine, dash of sugar. |
| Sauce Cardinale | Bechamel — fish stock, mushroom essence, lobster puree, butter, cayenne pepper. |
| Sauce Champignon | Espagnole — sautéed mushrooms, Madeira wine. |
| Sauce Chasseur | Espagnole — mushrooms, tomatoes, white wine. |
| Sauce Choron | Hollandaise — tomato paste concentrated. |
| Sauce Bigarade | Espagnole — orange zeste and juice in red wine reduced, lemon juice, sugar, currant jelly. |
| Sauce Duxelles | Espagnole — chopped onions, mushrooms, parsley sautéed, tomato paste. |
| Sauce Estragon | Veloute — tarragon reduced in white wine, fresh butter. |
| Sauce Godard | Espagnole — mushrooms, white wine, chopped ham. |
| Sauce Indienne | Veloute — fresh cream, curry paste, cooked potato cubes. |
| Sauce Madere | Espagnole — Madeira wine reduced. |
| Sauce Meyerbeer | Espagnole — chicken livers, mushrooms, onions, sherry wine. |
| Sauce Raifort | Veloute — horseradish, vinegar, dash sugar, fresh butter. |
| Sauce Tortue | Espagnole — tomato sauce, reduced clear turtle soup. |
| Sauce Nantua | Bechamel — fish stock, cream, white wine, crayfish, paprika, cayenne, brandy. |
| Sauce Newburg | Bechamel — paprika, cream, cayenne, sherry. |
| Sauce Perigueux | Espagnole — demi-glace, mushrooms, truffles, red wine, Madeira wine. |

**TABLE 21-5 SAUCE COMPOSITIONS OF THE LUXURY CUISINE**

- *Cacciatore Sauce* — 1 quart of espagnole is blended with 2 cups of red wine, reduced a little, then 2 1/2 quarts of creole sauce are added.

## PAN GRAVY OR "JUS DE VIANDE"

Pan gravy has been discussed in detail in unit 10. Gravy is made from roast drippings, diluted with brown stock, then lightly thickened with roux and cornstarch. The word gravy is often misused to describe liquids which should be called a sauce. To give the student a better understanding of how to make gravy, table 21-6 is provided.

Fig. 21-4 Chinoise, china cap style strainer used in sauce cookery.

---

*Materials Needed:*

Roast drippings                                          Brown stock
Mirepoix (roughly cubed equal parts of onions,           Flour
   celery, carrots)

*Procedure:*

1. Remove roast from pan; place pan with all the drippings on the top of the stove or range.
2. If mirepoix was not added before, then it is added now.
3. Reduce drippings over slow fire, until remaining fat is clear.
4. Drain off most of the fat. Leave just enough to absorb flour for roux.
5. If paprika is desired, it is added now. The flour, to absorb the fat, is stirred in and mixed well.
6. Fill up with the minimum amount of hot stock needed, which matches the roast.
7. Bring back to simmering point, stir constantly, and simmer for at least 10 minutes or to desired consistency.
8. Finish to taste and color.
9. Strain through china cap; keep warm in bainmarie.

--- ATTENTION: KEY POINT ---

- Gravy or pan juice must have a strong flavor. It should not be diluted unnecessarily.

---

**TABLE 21-6 HOW TO MAKE GRAVY**

## STRUCTURE OF SOUPS

Food in a more liquid than solid state, eaten with a spoon, is called *soup*. Soups are well liked by the public because they are easy to eat and digest. They are filling, nourishing, and not costly. The nature of soups has been discussed in unit 10. Soups probably began as kettle stews. Many of today's regional specialty soups clearly indicate such a development.

For the cook, soups are easy to make when modern equipment is used with an understanding of the structure of soups. Soups can be grouped into clear soups or thickened soups.

### Clear Soups

Clear soups may be unclarified plain broth or clarified consomme. Broth is leftover liquid from the boiling of protein foods. For a better flavor, vegetables are added to the broth. Vegetable broth is used too, but seldom as a single flavor. Other flavor-giving ingredients are even added to tomato soup. In home cookery, vegetable soups are made without meat additives. Commercial cookery boasts even vegetable flavors with some kind of protein stock.

**Consommé.** Consommé is clarified broth or stock; its strength is improved with extra vegetables and proteins. It is served either clear or with a garnish. The garnish may be cooked with the soup, as in "Consommé Julienne", or prepared completely extra and added to the finished soup at the last minute, as in "Consommé Celestine".

*Thickened Soups*

Thickened soups are grouped by 1) the addition of plain starch or roux for better flavor and texture, 2) the addition of a vegetable, meat or fish pulp (puree) for thickening, 3) the combining of puree, roux and, for absolute refinement, cream. Thickened soups, just as clear soups, can be served strained and plain, or they may have a garnish prepared in the same way as for the consommé.

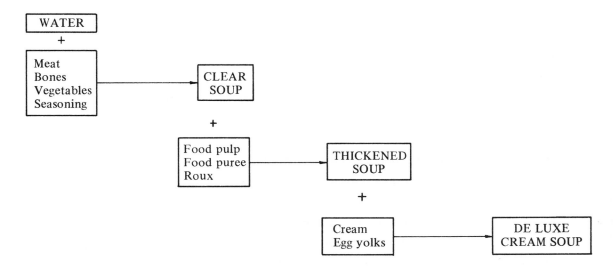

**TABLE 21-7 FLOWCHART OF SOUPMAKING**

---

*Utensils Needed:*

16-quart soup pot, china cap, 2 clean linen towels, large dipper, whip                    1-2-gallon stainless steel soup inset

*Materials Needed for Approximately 1 1/2 Gallons of Consommé:*

5 lbs. coarse lean ground beef                    10 cloves
10 egg whites and shells                    5 bay leaves
10 cups mixed onions, parsnips, leeks, celery, carrots                    1 tablespoon salt
4 bunches parsley                    2 1/2 gallons of strong beef bouillon or stock

*Procedure:*

1. Ground raw lean beef is mixed with 10 egg whites and shells.
2. Add 2 quarts cold stock, mix again.
3. Add 10 cups chopped-up vegetables, cloves, parsley, and bay leaves.
4. Add the remaining cold stock, 1 tablespoon salt. Mix well again.
5. Bring to a very fast boil while stirring, then turn heat down and simmer. (Watch out, egg white might scorch!)
6. Simmer, without stirring or shaking for 2 hours.
7. Carefully take it off the stove. Do not stir up broth.
8. Strain with large dipper through double towels. Do not stir up.
9. Season to finish, reheat to boiling point and serve.

───── **ATTENTION: KEY POINTS** ─────

- Egg whites must be half-whipped and completely mixed with clairage and mirepoix.
- If lukewarm stock is used, the two quarts stock of step 2 must be iced.
- A few onion peels can be included for a darker color.
- The boiling point must be reached under constant supervision and stirring to prevent overboiling or scorching.
- Shaking of pot will cloud clarification.
- Rinse linen towel with hot water and squeeze dry before using. (Emphasis: sanitation, better conduction.)
- The degreasing of strained consommé can be done with pieces of butcher paper.

**TABLE 21-8 THE CLARIFICATION OF CONSOMMÉ**

This is a variation of the well-known Scotch Broth made from lamb stock. When it is made from lamb stock, the soup is also a French specialty named Consommé Eccossaise.

*Materials Needed for 30 Orders:*

1 1/2 gallons beef stock
4 cups finely chopped vegetables consisting of:
  celery, onions, parsnips, carrots, parsley

6 cups pearl barley
1/2 cup butter
1/2 cup flour

*Procedure:*

1. Bring stock to boil, add barley.
2. Let simmer for 1 1/2 hours.
3. Sauté all the vegetables in butter, add flour, improvise a roux.
4. Stir into barley stock.
5. Simmer for 1/2 hour more or until barley is completely tender.
6. Season with salt, pepper.
7. Sprinkle with fresh chopped parsley and serve.

**TABLE 21-12  BEEF AND BARLEY SOUP**

This delightful soup is also known as New England Clam Chowder. It is completely different from soups called Manhattan or Coney Island Clam Chowder, which are not chowders by definition. Clam chowder is served with oyster crackers.

*Materials Needed for Approximately 30 Orders:*

1 cup diced salt pork
1 cup bell pepper, diced
2 cups celery, diced
2 cups onions, diced
5 cups peeled, cubed potatoes
3 quarts milk plus 1 quart whipping cream
6 cups cooked chopped clams and their juice

Thyme
Salt
Pepper
Tarragon
1/2 cup butter
1/2 cup flour

*Procedure:*

1. Cover potatoes with cold water, bring to boil and simmer for 15 minutes. Add thyme and tarragon.
2. Sauté pork, cubed celery, pepper and onions in butter. Add flour.
3. Blend the sauté, the potatoes, the boiling milk, and the clams in their own juice.
4. Season with pepper and salt and bring to boiling point again.
5. Let steep for twenty minutes, at about 185°F.
6. Transfer to bainmarie and add 1 quart of hot whipping cream.

───── **ATTENTION: KEY POINTS** ─────

- Keep soup hot in bainmarie only.
- Do not exceed a bainmarie temperature of 150°F.

**TABLE 21-13  BOSTON CLAM CHOWDER**

*Materials Needed for Approximately 30 Orders:*

6 cups dried yellow peas, soaked overnight in 3
   quarts of stock
1/2 pound bacon or salt pork
3 cups of mixed root vegetables (celery, onions, carrots)
Bay leaf

Thyme
Salt
1 1/2 gallons ham or meat stock (includes the 3 quarts
   used to soak the peas)
2 tablespoons chopped garlic

*Procedure:*

1. Bring stock to boil, add peas (presoaked) and simmer.
2. Add bay leaf, thyme, and some salt.
3. Dice bacon or pork fine and sauté. Add finely diced vegetables, garlic.
4. Fry until glassy, then add to soup.
5. Continue simmering 1-2 hours, until peas are completely tender or mashed up.

**ATTENTION: KEY POINTS**

- In the province of Quebec and Eastern Canada, whole yellow peas are used instead of split ones and the name used is Habitant soup.
- Dried green split peas can be used interchangeably.
- With slight variations, this soup is known under many names. Well known is the French version, Potage St. Germain, in which green split peas are used. The soup is served strained or blended with fried bread croutons as a garnish.

**TABLE 21-14 CANADIAN PEA SOUP**

This soup is of Creole origin. It has become an American favorite and one can find its variations under names like Creole Chicken Soup, Chicken Gumbo, etc.

*Materials Needed for Approximately 30 Orders:*

6 cups okra
1 cup onion
1 cup parsnips
2 cups celery
1 cup bell pepper

6 cups peeled, deseeded and cubed tomato
1 1/2 cups rice
1 cup chicken fat
3 cups cooked, chopped, left-over chicken meat
1 1/2 gallons chicken stock

*Procedure:*

1. Cut onion, parsnips, pepper, and celery into 1/2-inch square slices.
2. Saute them in chicken fat.
3. Add hot stock. Bring to boil. Add uncooked rice.
4. Add tomatoes, with their own juice.
5. Simmer for 1/2 hour. Add sliced, cleaned okra (1/4-inch wheels).
6. Continue simmering until tender. Add chicken meat and season to taste. Serve.

**ATTENTION: KEY POINT**

- To achieve an eye-pleasing soup, vegetables have to be neatly cut and small.

**TABLE 21-15 CHICKEN OKRA SOUP**

This soup can be considered an American specialty. If these steps are followed, this is a very simple preparation.

*Materials Needed for 30 Orders:*

6 cups creamed corn
1 gallon hot milk
1/4 lb. butter
3 ounces flour

1 cup finely chopped onions
1 cup finely chopped celery
Salt
Pepper

*Procedure:*

1. Sauté onions in butter until glassy. Add celery.
2. Sauté a little longer, then add flour to make into roux.
3. Pour hot milk on; bring to boil.
4. Add corn; reheat *to* boiling point. Season and serve.

——————— ATTENTION: KEY POINTS ———————

- Keep soup hot in bainmarie.
- Do not exceed a bainmarie temperature of 150°F.

**TABLE 21-16 CORN CHOWDER**

This soup, a true regional specialty, is relatively unknown outside of good Italian restaurants.

*Ingredients Needed for about 30 Orders:*

1 1/2 gallons of good beef stock
15 slices of sourdough French bread, crust cut off
1/2 lb. butter

1/2 lb. grated parmesan cheese
4 whole eggs and 6 egg yolks
1 pint whipping cream

*Procedure:*

1. Pan fry the bread slices in butter to a golden brown.
2. Bring the beef stock to a boil.
3. Put fried bread into the stock and simmer at least 10 minutes.
4. Use whisk to whip the bread into small particles.
5. Continue to simmer 10 more minutes.
6. Put eggs and yolks into a bowl to mix with the whipping cream.
7. Whip this mixture over a double boiler to a custard.
8. Sprinkle the parmesan over the custard and fold in.
9. Pour the boiling soup-bread mixture into the custard while continuing to whip.
10. Serve immediately with finely chopped parsley sprinkled on top.

**TABLE 21-17 MILLE FANTE (THOUSAND FLOWERS SOUP)**

This is a homestyle soup and also a regional specialty. This soup is easy to make, tasty, and nourishing. Many different combinations with other vegetables can be made.

*Materials Needed for 30 Orders:*

12 cups cubed potatoes
8 cups sliced mushrooms
1 1/2 gallons beef stock

1 cup roux, made with butter
1/4 cup fresh butter
1/2 cup chopped parsley

*Procedure:*

1. Bring stock to a boil, add the potatoes, then simmer for 15 minutes.
2. Wash and sauté mushrooms in 1/4 cup of butter.
3. Add to the simmering potatoes and cook 15 minutes more.
4. Add warm roux; mix in well. Boil fully for 5 minutes.
5. Add parsley; finish with salt and pepper. Serve.

——————— ATTENTION: KEY POINT ———————

- If thickness of soup while in bainmarie is to be kept, soup should never be fully covered.

**TABLE 21-18 MUSHROOM AND POTATO SOUP**

The most popular specialty soup in the San Francisco Bay area is an Italian vegetable soup called Minestrone. There are a few varieties, but its main flavor consists of fresh vegetables in season, tomatoes, garlic, Italian herbs, and olive oil. For starch content, beans and pasta are added. Grated parmesan cheese is sprinkled on top before eating.

*Materials Needed for 30 Orders:*

4 cups tomatoes
1 cup carrots
1 cup celery
1 cup parsnips
1 cup leeks
2 cups fresh spinach or chard
2 cups zucchini
1 cup peas
1 cup string beans

1 cup cabbage
1 cup mushrooms
2 cups kidney beans or garbanzos, soaked and precooked
1/2 lb. cut macaroni
1 1/2 gallons beef stock
2 ounces olive oil
Salt, rosemary, oregano, or basil
Grated parmesan cheese
6 tablespoons finely chopped garlic

*Procedure:*

1. Cut all vegetables in uniform 1/3-inch slices or cubes.
2. Add stock and spices.
3. Bring to a boil, then simmer for 25 minutes.
4. Add macaroni and the finely chopped garlic sautéed in olive oil.
5. Simmer 1/2 hour more; finish with salt and spice.
6. Serve with parmesan sprinkled on top or, even better, on the side.

─────────── **ATTENTION: KEY POINTS** ───────────

- For real flavor, the stock must be strong and clear. The soup must simmer only.
- Garlic must be finely chopped and sautéed golden brown in olive oil.

**TABLE 21-19  ITALIAN MINESTRONE**

Despite its French-sounding name, this soup is a new invention by a chef from a leading New York hotel. It has become a favorite all over the United States.

*Materials Needed for 30 Orders:*

Commercial blender or speed cutter
3 bunches of leeks, cut up
1/2 cup shallots
5-6 pounds raw peeled potatoes, thinly sliced

1 gallon beef stock
1 cup finely chopped chives
1 cup olive oil
2 quarts fresh, unwhipped cream

*Procedure:*

1. Bring beef stock to a boil. Add thinly sliced potatoes.
2. Sauté cut-up leeks in olive oil.
3. Add leeks and potatoes to the simmering stock.
4. Simmer for about 3/4 hour, then blenderize well. Taste.
5. Force blended soup through a fine china cap.
6. Refrigerate until completely cold. Then stir in the cream.
7. Adjust taste and texture to your liking.
8. Serve in iced cups with chopped chives as garnish on top.

─────────── **ATTENTION: KEY POINTS** ───────────

- The consistency of this soup could become too thick or too thin, depending on the size of the casserole used. A wide, flat one will evaporate more liquid than a narrow, high one.
- If the cold soup appears too rich and too thick, it can be diluted with cold, defatted bouillon and milk.

**TABLE 21-20  COLD VICHYSSOISE**

An inexpensive soup from various kinds of fresh vegetables, made in a blender. A mixture of pureed vegetables is called Potage Carbure. Otherwise it is called Cream of Cauliflower, or Celery Puree Soup, and so on.

*Materials Needed for 30 Orders:*

12 cups various vegetables such as cauliflower, celery, broccoli, peas, asparagus, potatoes, parsnips, leeks
4-6 ounces butter roux

2 gallons beef stock
1 pint whipping cream
1/2 cup butter

*Procedure:*

1. Cut the clean vegetables to be blended roughly, but reserve 1/3 as garnish.
2. Cut reserved 1/3 into eye-appealing shape, cover with stock and cook.
3. Sauté the blended vegetables in butter.
4. Add beef stock and bring to a boil.
5. Simmer until tender, but crunchy.
6. Add warm roux. Use wire whip to stir smooth.
7. Boil again, simmer for at least 5 minutes.
8. Puree in the blender. Reheat.
9. Add cream and the crunchy cooked 1/3 of the vegetable as garnish. Take off stove.
10. Finish to taste and serve.

**TABLE 21-21  FRESH VEGETABLE PUREE SOUP**

This is a popular winter soup from the northeastern region of the United States. Variations of this preparation are well known all over the world.

*Materials Needed for 30 Orders:*

3 pints of navy beans, soaked in cold stock overnight
2 cups chopped onions
2 cups chopped celery
2 cups drained, chopped tomato pulp

2 cloves finely chopped garlic
4 ounces bacon or ham fat
2 gallons stock from smoked meat
2 cups chopped ham or bacon

*Procedure:*

1. Bring the beans in their own soaking stock to a boil.
2. Add the remainder of the 2 gallons stock, and simmer until beans are nearly tender. This may take 2 - 2 1/2 hours.
3. In the meantime, sauté onion and celery in ham fat. Add garlic. They should puree easily.
4. Add this mixture to the tender beans.
5. Add chopped tomatoes and ham.
6. Bring to boil again and simmer for at least 5 minutes.
7. Whip well with wire whisk to break up some of the beans.
8. Season with salt, pepper. Serve.

**TABLE 21-22  NAVY BEAN SOUP**

## SUMMARY

Extracting liquefiable foods is the basis of stock, sauce, and soup cookery. The difference between a sauce or a soup very often lies in its texture only. The principles of making cream soups are like the ones of making sauces. Sauces have a more intense flavor than soups, if sauces and soups of the same raw ingredients are compared. The addition of starch changes a clear liquid to a thickened one. For the sake of quality, Western cuisine uses a starch-fat combination, cooked for a little while, called roux. Sauces are classified into four basic roux sauces and one egg yolk-butter sauce called Hollandaise. Sauce cookery can be compared to bar mixing. The five basic sauces are changed with the addition of different wines, liquors, cream, cheeses, herbs, spices, condiments, and special cut garnishes into a hundred different sauces. These are highly cherished by Western luxury cuisine. Sauce Hollandaise, the fifth of the basic or mother sauces, is the only one not based on starch. The texture of this sauce comes through the emulsification of fat and egg yolks, which enclose fine air bubbles, instead of the saturation of starch granules with liquid. Sauces based on eggs have a limited holding time and must be made fresh whenever needed.

Sauce and soup cookery have a definite structure. Thus, they are easy to master and practice. Most important are the personal standard of understanding how a sauce should look and taste, the use of fresh quality ingredients, and careful, systematic work. Just as in all the other fields of cookery, the same principles are used over and over again.

## DISCUSSION TOPICS

1. Why is it necessary to learn all the foreign names of sauces and other dishes?
2. What purpose do sauces actually serve in Culinary Art?
3. What is the origin of specialty soups and why do they have emotional appeal to customers?

## SUGGESTED ACTIVITIES

1. Define: gristle, consistency, puree, potage, steep, mother sauce, clarify.
2. Make all of the sauces based on roux.
3. Make a small quantity of Sauce Hollandaise.
4. Blend some composition sauces as listed on the preceding pages.
5. Clarify 2 gallons of broth into a strong consommé.
6. Make a Potage a la Reine, the de luxe French chicken puree cream soup.

## ACHIEVEMENT REVIEW

A. Complete the following:

1. Brown stock mixed with roux makes _____.
2. White stock is made from bones which have *not* been _____.
3. Lamb bones have a strong flavor and are not used for a general _____.
4. Espagnole, one of the mother sauces, has a color of _____.
5. Tomato sauce can be made from tomato juice or _____.
6. Bechamel is the French name for _____.
7. Plain white meat stock sauce is called _____.
8. Roux is the ingredient which makes a thin liquid _____.
9. The quantities of fat and flour used for roux must be equal in _____.
10. For a roux, the flour is fried to achieve a better _____.
11. Blending of roux into a liquid is done best with a _____.
12. True gravy must contain meat _____.
13. The best flavor of meat broth is achieved by adding _____.
14. The emulsification of egg yolks and butter is called sauce _____.
15. Veloute sauces can be made from meat of _____.

B. Read each question carefully and completely before answering it. Select the *best* answer.

1. To change broth into consommé, it is essential to use

   a. sherry wine          c. onions
   b. egg whites           d. beef extract

2. A double consommé is

   a. 2 cups of consommé
   b. an extra large cup of consommé
   c. strong consommé in a cup
   d. tomato consommé

3. A cauliflower cream soup is best described as a

   a. broth with cauliflower and cream
   b. cauliflower puree with roux and cream
   c. consommé with cauliflower garnish
   d. broth with roux and cauliflower

4. Mille fante, an Italian soup, is made of

   a. vegetables, cream, cheese, roux, stock
   b. chicken puree, cream, roux, parmesan
   c. bread, butter, cheese, eggs, cream, stock
   d. fish stock, roux, shrimps, onions, cheese

5. Minestrone, the popular Italian soup, also contains

   a. cracked wheat                 c. dumplings
   b. polenta (corn grits)          d. garbanzo beans

6. Sauce Bearnaise is a derivation of the mother sauce,

   a. veloute                       c. supreme
   b. bechamel                      d. hollandaise

7. Brown stock made from beef bones should simmer

   a. 3 to 4 hours                  c. 5 to 6 hours
   b. 4 to 5 hours                  d. 6 to 7 hours

8. To make Hollandaise sauce, it is important that all utensils are of

   a. nonoxidizing material         c. polished aluminum
   b. copper, lined with tin        d. good heat conduction material

9. For the blending of composition sauces, it is best to have a

   a. stock pot                     c. sauté pan (sauteuse)
   b. soup casserole                d. flip fry pan

C. Match the sauce names in Column I with the corresponding ingredients in Column II.

| *Column I* | *Column II* |
| --- | --- |
| 1. Allemande | Espagnole, mushrooms, red wine, truffles, madeira wine. |
| 2. Bigarde | Bechamel, parmesan, cream, egg yolks, white pepper. |
| 3. Bordelaise | Veloute, tarragon, butter. |
| 4. Champignon | Veloute, horseradish, cream, sugar, vinegar. |
| 5. Estragon | Espagnole, red wine, beef marrow, shallots. |
| 6. Chasseur | Veloute, cream, egg yolks, white wine. |
| 7. Mornay | Espagnole, orange and lemon peel and juice, red wine, sugar. |
| 8. Newburg | |
| 9. Raifort | Espagnole, mushrooms, madeira wine. |
| 10. Perigueux | Bechamel, paprika, cream, sherry. |
| | Espagnole, mushrooms, white wine, tomatoes. |

# Unit 22  Pot-Roasting, Fresh or Marinated

*OBJECTIVES*

After studying and practicing this unit, the student should be able to

- Devise a formula for cooking a plain pot roast.
- Marinate and cook a basic Sauerbraten.
- Select a cooking method for a game animal.

Pot-roasting, as discussed in section 2, unit 9, is a part of the cooking process called Caramelizing and Tenderizing Combined. It is detailed here in a separate unit because many people have wrong ideas about roasting and pot-roasting. Pot-roasting belongs in the preparation group which is commonly called braising or stewing.

## *PROCESS REVIEW*

Pot-roasting, as implied by its name, stands for a large piece of meat, (several portions in one), "roasted" in a covered pot (dutch oven, casserole, brassiere) on top of the range. It means cooking with moisture, unlike the true roast where moisture evaporation is the heart of the process. Pot-roasting is a moist cooking process like steaming or boiling, with the difference of browning the meat first. This changes, or caramelizes, the carbohydrates present and creates a different flavor and appearance. Since as little moisture as possible is used, just as in poaching fish, a maximum sauce flavor is the result. Although pot-roasting is a commonly accepted expression, the term *Braised Roast* would be better.

It is not necessary to use a dutch oven or covered casserole for this process. A high-walled roasting pan in the oven and some liquid added at the beginning will give the same results. The term roast always implies a large piece of meat, at least more than three portions in one.

## *BASIC POT ROAST*

Pot roast in general is beef meat, but any edible meat that is basically tough can be prepared in the same manner. Beef cuts that are used come from the round or the chuck. Brisket and flank can also be used. Outside round, sometimes called bottom round, is the best cut. It is free of gristle and ingrown fat. It slices nicely, but is too tough to be used for steak or roast. It is also too lean for ground meat or stew. But there are chefs who like chuck, knuckles, and even triangle roasts.

Pot roast, not having the name of a special preparation, is served with a plain but concentrated brown sauce. Flavors and names are changed through the addition of wine, cream, garnish, herbs and spices. In short, the same principles of cookery are applied as discussed previously for sauté and sauce cookery.

- *Jardiniere Pot Roast* — a garnish of some separately cooked garden vegetables such as peas, cauliflower, mushrooms, artichokes, carrots, broccoli, asparagus; parsnips, turnips, is added to the brown sauce served over the meat.

- *Burgundy Pot Roast* has a garnish of diced mushrooms, fried bacon cubes, and pearl onions added

Fig. 22-1  Bottom or outside round, heel removed. The eye of the round can be recognized on the upper right side of the meat cut.

The cooking of a pot roast, or pot-roasting in general, is one of the important skills of a Chef or Second Cook. It is one of the basic skills of cookery and the processes involved cover a great part of general cooking.

*Materials Needed for About 25 Orders:*

| | |
|---|---|
| Heavy casserole with matching cover | 1 teaspoon thyme |
| 10 lbs. bottom round in one piece | Salt |
| 1 quart mirepoix | Pepper |
| 1/2 cup tomato paste | 2-3 quarts of stock |
| 3-4 cloves garlic | Approximately 3 ounces roux |
| 5 bay leaves | 3 ounces oil |
| 2 bunches parsley | |

*Procedure:*

1. Wash and season meat.
2. Place into oiled, hot casserole, no cover.
3. Put into 475°F. oven to start browning.
4. After 15-20 minutes, or when meat is browned, add mirepoix and garlic.
5. Roast 10 more minutes.
6. Add tomato paste. Stir well. Roast a few more minutes.
7. Add all remaining ingredients except roux, and only 1/2 of the stock. Cover.
8. Put back into oven. Reduce heat to 350°F.
9. Leave in oven for about 2 1/2 hours or until tender.
10. Add roux. Cook for 5 minutes more.
11. Remove meat from sauce. Cool off, then keep warm.
12. Finish sauce with remaining stock, season to taste, strain and keep sauce in bainmarie. Slice meat to the order, or preslice in the portion control manner.

**TABLE 22-1 HOW TO MAKE POT ROAST**

to the brown sauce, which has been finished with a heavy burgundy type red wine.

- *Western Pot Roast* has a garnish of dried prunes and pitted olives added to the brown sauce.

- *Yankee Pot Roast* or *American Pot Roast* is a name sometimes used instead of plain pot roast.

- *Boeuf a la Mode* is the French version of a larded pot roast. Bacon or salted pork strips are inserted through the middle of the raw piece of meat, which then is cooked in the same way as a plain pot roast, with added red wine.

- *Braised Leg of Veal Marengo* is made from heavy veal legs, not tender enough for scallopine, or even whole or seamed baby beef legs, which can be handled like pot roasts. *A la Marengo* (as in chicken Ma-

Fig. 22-2 The separated eye of the round, a lean but dry meat cut easy to keep portion controlled.

rengo) means that the sauce consists of one part tomato sauce with sliced mushrooms as a garnish. The original classic version also included crayfish tails in addition to the mushroom garnish.

- *Sauerbraten* is the German word for a marinated pot roast. There is a mistaken belief that a marinade containing tartaric acids (wine, vinegars) tenderizes meat. If anything, it toughens food while cooking. In the past, marinade was used to preserve meat for a few more days. The tenderizing effect came from the enzyme action during "aging" or storing the meat. Modern food technology believes that aging is in fact, decaying. While the loosening of the fibres through aging tenderizes, it also changes flavor and possibly nutritional values. The acid of a marinade slows the growth of some bacteria in the meat and therefore prolongs its storage life. Very little of the marinade flavor really penetrates the meat. The flavor stays in the sauce which is to be served over the meat. Thus, marinating for over 4 to 5 days as it was done in the past is not necessary. It is only important that all the marinade, which was poured over the meat, is used to braise and make the sauce.

Fig. 22-3 Brazier with cover, good for pot roasts.

Sauerbraten, a German word, translates as marinated pot roast. Due to its specific piquant flavor, it has become a popular dish. Its preparation is only slightly different from the making of a regular pot roast.

*Materials Needed for Approximately 25 Orders:*

A stainless steam table insert, big enough to marinate
A braising casserole with a cover
10 pounds of bottom round, eye of the round or
   silver side, in one or two pieces
1 quart of mixed root vegetables: celery, onions,
   parsnips, carrots, cubed (mirepoix)
6 cloves of garlic, smashed
20 juniper berries, crushed
5 bay leaves
2 bunches of parsley

1 teaspoon of thyme
1/2 teaspoon whole pepper
1/2 teaspoon whole pickling spice
6 cloves, whole
2 teaspoons of salt
2 quarts of water
2 cups of white vinegar
3 ounces of sautéing fat
2 ounces of roux
2 cups of rich sour cream

*Procedure:*

1. All the spices are put into a cheesecloth bag.
2. Water, vinegar, salt, and all the spices and herbs are brought to a boil, simmered for 2 minutes, then cooled off.
3. The meat is placed in the stainless container with some of the root vegetables, (garlic and parsley), underneath and on the sides.
4. The cooled marinade is poured over the meat with all the meat well covered.
5. Container is covered with plastic wrap and refrigerated from 8 to 72 hours (minimum-maximum).
6. Meat in the container is turned around every 12 hours.
7. Oil is poured into the braising casserole and heated.
8. The drained roast is dipped into flour and browned evenly on all sides.
9. Garlic and the marinated vegetables are added to the sautéing meat.
10. The bay leaves and the spice bag are removed.
11. The remaining liquid and content are added to the roast, then it is covered and simmered for about 1 1/2 hours.
12. The roast is separated from the sauce but continues to cook, covered, over a low fire.
13. A blender is used to osterize the vegetables in the braising liquid.
14. The coarse pulp after osterization is strained out and the liquid is added to the roast.
15. When sauce starts to simmer, enough roux is added to create a heavy texture.
16. Cook at least 10 more minutes, to assure smoothness of sauce, or until the meat seems to be tender. Consider the carry-over heat!
17. When tender, roast is removed from the sauce, the sour cream is added to the sauce, which is to be seasoned and brought again to a full boil.
18. It is best to handle meat and sauce separately in the steam table.

──────── ATTENTION: KEY POINTS ────────

- Selection and quality of the meat cut is decisive for the final quality of the preparation.
- The marinade must not be too sour. It can be diluted with water. No sugar can be added.
- Cooking time depends entirely on the shape of the meat and its quality. Two hours of total cooking time could be too much.
- In the USA, German Sauerbraten is often served with potato pancakes (Kartoffelpuffer) and red cabbage. In the German speaking countries of Europe, noodles, Spaetzle, dumplings, Gnocchi or any pasta is preferred. Red cabbage as a vegetable is not acceptable to this dish either; a sour flavor on the same plate twice is gastronomically wrong.

**TABLE 22-2 HOW TO MAKE GERMAN SAUERBRATEN**

A sauerbraten is a pot roast, cooked with the addition of acid (wine, vinegar, or lemon juice) and finished in a white brownish sauce, which for better class cookery is finished with sour cream. Table 22-2 gives the step-by-step preparation of a true high class German Sauerbraten.

### Game

Game can also be pot-roasted fresh or in a marinade. Some parts of game animals, when they are young enough, can be prepared as roasts or steaks. Regional cookery of venison or other game prefers to marinate and braise most of the game meats. Game meat in Europe is very well aged, 4 to 8 weeks if the temperature conditions permit it. The meat is also marinated. The marinade, which can be spiced well, takes some of the gamey flavor away. Even if a marinade is not used at all, wine, lemon juice, buttermilk, or sour cream is often a part of the preparation. Since game meat cannot be sold in the USA, the average cook has little chance to prepare these specialties. They are sometimes prepared in private clubs for some of their hunting members. All pot-roasting methods can be applied to prepare wild hare, venison, moose, elk, reindeer, wild ducks, geese, and wild boar.

## CONCLUSIONS

Pot roasts, marinated or fresh, are a basic meat preparation where the flavor of the sauce and the garnish are related to the name of the preparation. All pot roasts can be and should be made in one way only, regardless of their names. The selected preparation method must be fast and simple to fit the production of modern professional cookery. Today, more than ever, "time is of the essence", both for economic reasons and because overcooking is seen as the destroyer of nutritional food value and quality. Students are encouraged to think about the tremendous similarity of pot-roasting as compared to sautéing and sauce making.

## SUMMARY

The pot-roasting of fresh or marinated meats, commonly named stewing or braising, is a part of the cooking process called "Caramelizing and tenderizing combined".

The word roast stands for a large piece of meat, at least more than three portions in one. Roasted in the pot implies that originally a covered pot was used to retain all moisture, which in turn tenderizes tough meats. Later, when baking ovens became more common, roasting in the oven with the addition of liquid, thereby creating steam, replaced the roasting in the pot. It is better to use the oven for pot-roasting because heat is diffused better and there is less danger of scorching, despite continuing browning of the meat. The small quantity of liquid used at one time guarantees the maximum sauce flavor.

Although pot roast is regarded as beef roast, the preparation method is used for all tough meats, regardless of the species of the animal. Therefore, pot-roasting or braising as it is sometimes called, is one of the basic cooking methods in use.

Marinades in the past were used as meat preservatives, but are used today for the distinctive flavor they give to food. Most popular is the German Sauerbraten, a preparation also favored for game meats. Marinating does not change the basic pot-roasting process. Care has to be taken that the marinade is not too spicy or too sour, since for full flavor of the sauce, the marinating liquid must be used as the braising liquid.

### DISCUSSION TOPICS

1. What are the types of meats for which pot-roasting is the best cooking method?

2. Do different braising methods have different merits?

3. Why is marinating a flavoring device?

### SUGGESTED ACTIVITIES

1. Define: marinate, seam, enzyme, braise.

2. Pot-roast a beef eye of the round under supervision.

3. Prepare a Sauerbraten.

4. Demonstrate the preparation of a game animal.

## ACHIEVEMENT REVIEW

A.  Complete the following:

1.  Pot-roasting actually means cooking with the retention of _____.

2.  Pot-roasting can be done on top of the range in a pot which is _____.

3.  Pot-roasting can be done in the oven with the addition of _____.

4.  In pot-roasting, it is essential that the raw meat is first _____.

5.  The meat used for pot-roasting can be fresh or _____.

6.  The meat marinade started as a method of _____.

7.  Marinades are useful to reduce the wild flavor of _____.

8.  Although the term pot-roasting is commonly accepted, a better word would be _____.

B.  Read each question carefully and completely before answering it. Select the *best* answer.

1.  The pot-roasting process is mostly applied to
    a. young and juicy meats        c. tough and lean meats
    b. boneless and trimmed meats   d. large chunks of beef meat

2.  In pot-roasting, meat is caramelized and tenderized, which means that the meat is practically
    a. boiled first then browned    c. roasted first then boiled
    b. browned first then poached   d. baked in its own juice

3.  A pot roast without a specific name should be served with
    a. tomato sauce and mushrooms
    b. cream sauce and vegetables
    c. prunes and olives
    d. plain strong brown sauce

4.  A strongly spiced marinade is good to use on a
    a. braised leg of venison       c. roasted sirloin strip
    b. veal leg "Marengo"           d. braised large turkey

5.  German Sauerbraten in the USA is sometimes served with a side dish which is unacceptable to true gastronomic art. This dish is
    a. potato pancakes              c. bread dumplings
    b. buttered noodles             d. braised red cabbage

C.  Match the ingredient listed in Column I with the corresponding preparation in Column II.

| Column I | Column II |
|---|---|
| White vinegar | 1. Burgundy Pot Roast |
| Red wine | 2. Veal leg "Marengo" |
| Cauliflower, peas | 3. Boeuf a la Mode |
| Tomato sauce | 4. Braised Moose Leg |
| Bacon or salt pork | 5. Western Pot Roast |
| Mirepoix | 6. German Sauerbraten |
| Olives & Prunes | 7. Jardiniere Pot Roast |
| Buttermilk | 8. American Pot Roast |

# Unit 23 Braising of Portion-Cut Meats

*OBJECTIVES*

After studying and practicing this unit, the student should be able to

- Explain the difference between Swiss steak and Potted steak.
- Demonstrate the making of veal roulades.
- Apply a modern working sequence to the braising of steaks.

The braising of portion-cut meats falls into the same group of cooking methods as pot-roasting. Here, it is discussed in a separate unit to explain distinctly that it is the same preparation which this text calls Caramelizing and Tenderizing Combined.

*PROCESS REVIEW*

Braising is a term often used in place of pot-roasting and stewing. Why, then, are different words used to describe the very same process? The difference is in the size of the piece of meat that is cooked. Pot-roasting means the cooking of a large piece of meat only. *Braising* means that portion-cut meat, usually called a steak or chop, is prepared by the "combination process". It should be seen that a braised Swiss Steak a la Jardiniere is made of the very same meat cut and ingredients as a pot roast Jardiniere. The Swiss steak is cut to its portion size and then cooked. The pot roast is cooked in one whole piece, then carved for serving.

*SWISS STEAKS*

The term Swiss steak means that a beef steak from a less tender meat cut than usually used for steaks has been prepared by the combination process. Just as in other preparations, the different names given to these dishes only describe the garnish or a variation of taste ingredients. Otherwise, a Swiss steak is always a braised portion-cut piece of beef meat.

- *Potted Steak a la Esterhazy* is a special flavored Swiss steak, served in an individual fireproof casserole which should have been used to braise the meat in individual portions. Again, new words are used to create the impression that this is not a stew. By following the procedure in Table 23-1, but changing some of the ingredients and using a different shape for the cutting of vegetables, many different formulas for Swiss steaks can be created.
- *Beef Roulades* are made from raw steak pounded with the flat side of a cleaver to a thickness of about 1/8 inch. The meat is *scored* (cut in parallel lines) to prevent shrinking, seasoned, and spread with

Fig. 23-1 Steaks for braising, eye of the round, portion-control cut.

Fig. 23-2 Steaks for braising, full outside round cut.

Fig. 23-3 Steaks for braising, outside round split for portion cut.

Braised beef steaks, often called Swiss steak or potted steak, consist of one piece of beef meat, steak-size per order, prepared like a stew or pot roast. The meat may weigh from 6-12 ounces and could be any cut (but is usually from the round or chuck) suitable for braising. To use a regular steak cut, such as New York, Fillet or even Top Sirloin would be a waste of quality, since these cuts are too tender for stewing. This steak is usually served with noodles or some other form of pasta.

*Ingredients Needed for 6 Orders:*

6 bottom round steaks, about 8 ounces each
Salt/pepper to taste
1 cup flour
1/2 cup pork fat
1 pound onions, celery/carrots, equal parts cut
  into julienne strips
1 teaspoon garlic, chopped fine

1 tablespoon tomato paste
3 cups of beef stock or broth
2 tablespoons french mustard
1 cup sour cream
1 teaspoon anchovy paste
1 tablespoon capers chopped

*Procedure:*

1. Salt and pepper the steaks, drench them in the flour.
2. Brown them in a skillet in 1/2 of the fat but keep them rare.
3. Transfer to a suitable casserole, in shingle fashion.
4. Sauté the raw vegetable julienne and garlic in the remaining fat to golden brown. Drain surplus fat.
5. Add the tomato paste. Sauté for a few more minutes.
6. Add two cups of hot beef stock. Bring to boil.
7. Stir in the mustard, capers and anchovy paste.
8. Pour this sauce over the steaks, then cover the casserole.
9. Braise in 350°F. oven for about 50-60 minutes or until tender. Do not overcook and lose meat texture.
10. If necessary, add some of the remaining cup of stock.
11. When tender, place meat on a serving dish and keep warm.
12. Stir 2 tablespoons of flour into the sour cream.
13. Bring the leftover meat braising liquid to a boil.
14. Stir in the sour cream. Reboil and bring to desired consistency by using all the remaining beef broth.
15. Sprinkle the pickle julienne on top and serve.

**TABLE 23-1  POTTED BEEFSTEAK A LA ESTERHAZY**

mustard or catsup. A small amount of any filling, plain or combined, is placed close to the long side of the pounded steak. These fillings could be anything, such as pork sausage meat, ground beef, fried onions, chopped pickles, sliced or chopped ham, cheese, mushrooms, sauerkraut, bread dressing, or rice. The meat is rolled, fastened with toothpicks or string, and handled in the same way as any other Swiss steak preparation.

This method can be applied to veal, pork, and poultry as well. There are hundreds of regional preparations based on this same principle, and there are just as many different sounding foreign names.

*Pork Chops*

Savory pork chops are often prepared from chops which are tough and taste fattier than usual. The individual portion-sized chops are pounded lightly for tenderization, salted, dipped in flour, and browned on both sides. They are laid out flat, next to each other, on a rimmed bake sheet. Each pork chop center is covered with 2 tablespoons of spicy, but not starchy, tomato sauce. The sauce is topped with two thin slices of fresh lemon, overlapping, and the lemon slices are topped with one teaspoon of brown sugar. They are baked slowly at 300°F. to 325°F. until done (30 to 45 minutes).

*Chicken*

Coq au Vin a l'Ancienne translates as old-fashioned chicken in wine sauce. Half a chicken, trimmed the same as for a chicken sauté, is seasoned, dipped in flour, and browned in a skillet. It is then covered with one part strong chicken stock and three parts heavy red wine, seasoned with onions, garlic, a bouquet garni, allspice, and cloves. After about 25 minutes of braising, the sauce is finished by adding half roux and half cornstarch dissolved in red wine. A garnish of mushrooms, pearl onions, and bacon lardons is added. Chickens today are so tender that sautéing should be preferred to braising. All those chicken sauté preparations in section 3, unit 19, can be cooked by the braising method if the cook feels that a special degree of "fork" tenderness is needed.

### Braised Shanks

Lamb shanks, veal shanks, and pig knuckles must be considered portion-controlled meat cuts, and braising would be one of the best preparations for them. They are handled exactly the same way as any other portion-cut meat, served with the bone.

## CONCLUSION

It is expected that by now the students see and understand the very simple structure of cooking and the constant and repeated similarities of work phases. A different approach to working procedures has to be learned now. In the restaurant business, the old adage "Time is Money" is a truism. Cooks could continue to make, for instance, Swiss steaks in the same way as Escoffier and other great culinarians. By taking advantage of the technical progress of our equipment, a modern manner of work sequences can be used, without any loss of quality or flavor. This saves about 25 percent of the time and labor. As a comparison example, two ways in the step-by-step sequence of braising portion-cut meats are given in table 23-2.

## SUMMARY

The braising of portion-cut meats explains the similarity of this process to pot-roasting. The only real difference is the size of the meat pieces prepared. Braised steaks, when served in individual casseroles or even braised in them, are called potted steaks. Again, there is no difference in the basic preparation. Swiss steak is the term used to describe a braised steak made like the plain or American pot roast. Steak a la Esterhazy, which is of Hungarian origin, has fancier ingredients, but the preparation method is the same. Roulades are a variety of braised steaks, made from beef or veal, in any desired way. Pork chops and chickens, two basically tender meats, are better tasting and more economical when sautéed only but for special reasons they can be braised. Savory pork chops and Old-Fashioned Chicken in Red Wine are examples.

| *Conventional* | *Modern* |
|---|---|
| 1. Mirepoix is sautéed in a casserole, remaining ingredients and stock are added. | 1. Meat is browned, then placed shingle-fashion and dry, into flat steam table pan. The pan is covered tightly with aluminum foil. Pan is placed in oven at 350°F. and baked until tender. |
| 2. The meat is browned and added to the sauce in the casserole. | |
| 3. Meat and sauce are simmered together until tender. | 2. Mirepoix and additional sauce ingredients are sautéed in a skillet, covered with a little cold stock, osterized coarsely and simmered for 30 minutes. Roux is added; seasoning checked; sauce simmers 10-15 minutes more before straining. |
| 4. Meat is separated from the sauce, kept in warmer while sauce is finished with roux, then seasoned and strained. | |
| 5. Strained sauce is combined with the separately cooked garnish and poured over the meat. A part of the sauce is kept separate in the steam table. | 3. The drippings from the tender cooked meat are blended with the strained sauce, the garnish is added. A part of the sauce is poured over the meat, the rest is kept separate in the steam table. |

─── ATTENTION: KEY POINTS ───

- Braising meat in the unfinished sauce causes additional time loss when the tender meat is moved from the casserole to the steam table.
- If starch is added from the beginning, there is danger of scorching, the breakup of meat is easier due to stirring or shaking. If the starch is added to the unfinished sauce after meat has been removed, when tender, at least 10 more minutes of simmering are needed to fully homogenize the sauce.
- Osterized vegetables yield more flavor in a shorter time; in many instances even the straining can be omitted when the sauce has been osterized.
- The browned meat braises in its own juice without evaporation loss due to the tight cover. The recondensed drippings (flavor) are blended into the sauce, before it is served.
- By the new method, meat is handled only once before serving. By the old method it is handled twice with a greater possibility of breaking up the meat orders.

**TABLE 23-2 STEP-BY-STEP SEQUENCE OF PORTION-CUT MEAT BRAISING**

Most important to the student cook is the understanding of how to save time and labor. Modern equipment must be used to the fullest. By using the Swiss steak procedure as an example, many working processes can be considerably streamlined.

## DISCUSSION TOPICS

1. What is the new culinary terminology for braised meat portion cuts? Why is it important?
2. Should tender pork or chicken be braised?
3. Does technical progress imply a need for constant re-evaluation of working processes?

## SUGGESTED ACTIVITIES

1. Define: roulade, shingle, osterize.
2. Prepare a potted steak a la "Esterhazy".
3. Demonstrate the preparation of beef or veal roulades.
4. Prepare plain Swiss steaks in the modern sequence.

## ACHIEVEMENT REVIEW

A. Complete the following:

1. To better understand the making of a Swiss Steak, it should be seen as a miniature _____ .
2. A Potted Steak is similar to a braised one except it is served in a _____ .
3. Meat roulades, as the name implies, are stuffed meat rolls cooked in the manner of _____ .
4. Pork chops or chicken, being very tender nowadays, are rarely _____ .
5. To save time and flavor it is advisable to use the available modern _____
_____ .

B. Read each question carefully and completely before answering it. Select the *best* answer.

1. The name Potted Steak is a term used to describe the cooking of a
   a. top sirloin steak
   b. Swiss steak
   c. baked chuck steak
   d. fried round steak
2. What all beef roulades have in common is that the meat is
   a. spiced with mustard
   b. served in brown sauce
   c. pounded thinly
   d. fastened with toothpicks
3. Savory pork chops, because of their slow cooking and sweet-sour flavor, are ideal for the preparation of
   a. young shoulder pork chops
   b. regular center cut pork chops
   c. lean loin pork chops
   d. fat pork chops from older animals
4. For the efficient young cook, it is important to familiarize himself with a modern method of making
   a. Coq au Vin a l'Ancienne
   b. a filling for beef roulades
   c. braised steaks or portion-cut meats
   d. a good Swiss steak sauce
5. When making Swiss steak the raw meat is cooked on the griddle or in the pan until it is
   a. charred and medium well
   b. brown and well done
   c. brown and tender
   d. well browned but rare

# Unit 24  Stews of Meat, Seafood, and Vegetables

*OBJECTIVES*

After studying and practicing this unit, the student should be able to

- Cook a burgundy beef stew.
- Cook a veal and mushroom stew.
- Cook a plain beef goulash.
- Prepare a prawn curry.
- Prepare a lobster stew.

Stewing is another word to describe cooking by the combination method of caramelizing and tenderizing. The term, *stew,* as a noun, describes cut-up pieces of meat and vegetables braised in their own sauce. Stews, much more so than steaks or roasts, can become dishes of poor quality. Cutting food small can tempt cooks to use up all leftovers. There is some concern on the part of patrons about ordering stew in a restaurant. Chefs and restaurateurs have looked for new names and terms that avoid the word stew as much as possible. Stews, if properly prepared and cooked, can be some of the best creations of a chef.

## PROCESS REVIEW

Stew meat is cut from the less tender parts of any food animal. All the meat cubes in one kettle of stew must have the same size and come from the same meat cut to assure uniform tenderizing. The better the meat is trimmed of fat, sinews, skin, veins, and bones, the better the stew will be. It should be remembered that each cube of beef meat must be thought of as a small pot roast. The same procedure is used for making stew as was used for pot roast and Swiss steak. The reason beef meat is used for stew is that a beef carcass has many more not-so-tender meat parts than veal, pork, lamb, or poultry. Stews are made from all the protein foods that are edible. Stew is an economic dish because it uses inexpensive, tougher meat cuts. These small meat pieces can be mixed and extended with vegetables and starches. This stretches the nutritional value.

### Burgundy Beef Stew

Burgundy Beef Stew is called Ragout de Boéuf Bourguignonne in some luxury restaurants. It is made from the same ingredients as a Burgundy pot roast. As the basic preparation for all stews, table 24-1 shows a step-by-step procedure for Burgundy Beef Stew. Just as for pot roast and Swiss steak, to know how to make one stew is to know how to make all stews. The only changes are the kinds of meat, flavors, garnishes, shapes of the food cut, and the corresponding cooking time.

### Beef Stew with Vegetables

Beef Stew with Vegetables is made like a basic Burgundy stew. The red wine is omitted and the garnish is changed to a selection or mixture of carrots, celery, parsnips, onions, turnips, string beans, potatoes or other vegetables as chosen by the chef. The vegetables used must have the same eye-appealing shape. They are added at such times in the cooking process that they are just crunchy-tender at the same time that the meat is ready.

### Veal Stew with Mushrooms

Veal Stew with Mushrooms uses lean veal shoulder or knuckle meat. Since veal is a white meat, the finished dish is a light brown color. Sauce ingredients are finely chopped onions, some parsley, and mushroom trimmings. If the sauce is to be blended or strained, some celery and carrots can be added. A small amount of tomato puree or freshly diced tomatoes and some wine can be used, if desired. The mushrooms for the

This Burgundy Beef Stew is an institutional adaptation from the classic French cuisine. It is a regional creation from the Burgundy area, but other wine-growing areas have had the same ideas. The stew must be made with red wine to deserve this name.

The quality of any stew depends on meat quality (trim, tenderness, fat). Its eye appeal depends on consistency and color of the sauce. TASTE in itself is disputable. More or less garlic, spices, herbs, or wines do not make the real chef. Amateurs emphasize spice. Professionals try to please many different tastes and have to be careful. Only salt has to be in the dish. The chef who does not salt (except for a salt-free diet), regardless of his reason, is never a real chef.

The color of the stew should be a rich, reddish brown. The consistency of the sauce should be on the light side. A heavy, thick sauce is neither appetizing nor sophisticated. The peas should be added shortly before serving in order to keep their nice green color. The best meat size is large, lean chunks, evenly cut, about 1 - 1 1/2 ounces each, with 5-6 pieces to the order.

*Materials Needed for About 25 Orders:*

10 pounds trimmed beef chuck, cut for a stew
3 pounds onions, chopped
2 ounces fresh garlic, chopped
1 cup carrots, cubed
3 cups chopped celery
1 cup parsnips, cubed
1 cup chopped parsley
6 single pieces bay leaf
1-2 teaspoons thyme

18 ounces tomato paste
1 quart dry, heavy red wine
2 pounds pearl or small boiling onions, pre-sautéed
One 2 1/2-pound package frozen green peas, defrosted
1 1/2 pounds mushrooms, cut in quarters, pre-sautéed
4 ounces oil
4 ounces roux
2-3 quarts brown stock

*Equipment Needed:*

Heavy stewing casserole with lid
Range and baking oven

Large skillet or sauteuse

*Procedure:*

1. Set oven temperature to 500°F. Place empty casserole in it and pre-heat.
2. Mix salt, pepper, and oil into the meat.
3. When casserole is very hot, the oiled meat is put in it, evenly spaced.
4. The meat is cooked, while being stirred often, for 15 to 20 minutes, until well browned.
5. The fat is drained into a skillet or sauteuse and saved for later.
6. The tomato paste, thyme, and bay leaves are stirred into the meat.
7. When the tomato paste has browned, the stew is deglazed with the red wine and simmered for a few minutes. Oven heat is reduced to 350°F.
8. About a quart of the brown stock is added. The casserole is covered and simmered in the oven until nearly tender.
9. While the stew simmers, the onions, garlic, and remaining vegetables are sautéed in the fat to golden brown.
10. These vegetables are deglazed with a quart of stock and then osterized.
11. The osterized sauce is returned to the top of the range. The stock and the roux are added and simmered for at least 30 minutes.
12. When the meat is about tender, the pre-sautéed mushrooms, onions, and the defrosted raw peas are added to the stew in the oven.
13. The sauce, which is simmering on top of the range, is strained over the stew.
14. The finished stew is brought to a full boil, checked for taste and sauce consistency. It is then transferred to the steam table for holding and serving.

--- ATTENTION: KEY POINTS ---

● Watch total cooking time. For good meat, about 60 minutes could be enough. Consider the time the meat has to be in the steam table. MEAT MUST NEVER BE OVERCOOKED.

● Serving may be best in individual, fireproof casseroles or silver dishes. Be sure that each order gets an equal amount of meat, pearl onions and mushrooms. This is a deluxe preparation of a fine restaurant or a hotel dining room.

**TABLE 24-1  BURGUNDY BEEF STEW**

garnish are cooked in butter separately. Small ones are cooked whole or halved. Medium or large mushrooms are cubed.

### Lamb Stew Provincale

Lamb Stew Provincale uses lamb meat which has much indigestible fat. Well-trimmed and defatted lamb leg is the best choice. Again, the basic Burgundy Stew preparation is used. The garlic should be increased three to five fold, then chopped fine and sautéed separately in olive oil to a golden brown before it is added to the sauce. Wine use is optional. The garnish for the sauce is about three pounds of peeled, de-seeded, cubed tomatoes and one cup of finely chopped fresh parsley.

### Meat Sauce Bolognese

Meat Sauce Bolognese is a typical meat sauce dish. All meat sauces must be thought of as meat stews, where the ingredients are chopped small with the help of a meat grinder. In the grinder, a medium to large plate is the best size for meat coarseness. For one weight part of mixed root vegetables, 1 to 2 parts of good quality lean beef chuck should be used. The preparation of the Burgundy Beef Stew can be used as a guide. Again the red wine and the garnish are omitted. The onions of the mixed root vegetables should be chopped with a knife for better sautéing. The rest of the mirepoix can be ground. The vegetable juice from the grinding is saved and used later for the sauce. A Bolognese style meat sauce should taste like plain pot roast, strong in garlic flavor and very light on the tomatoes.

### Goulash

Beef Goulash is probably the oldest form of stew. The difference between the other stews and goulash is as follows:

a. the raw meat is not browned separately, but is added to the sautéed onions and spices;

b. the sauce base for any goulash is made of onions, tomatoes, potatoes and paprika. No other vegetables are used. Marjoram is sometimes added, but garlic and caraway seeds are used generously. Paprika is a spice like chili powder. It is made from various kinds of dried and ground red peppers (Capsicum annum). This paprika spice gives the goulash its flavor and color.

Depending on the country which has adopted it, goulash can be spelled Gulyas, Goulash or Gulasch. Hungarian variations, due to the ingredients used, have more names. A goulash made without tomatoes is called Paprikas. A goulash finished with sour cream in the sauce is called "Poerkoelt". Goulashes are very important to central European cuisine. They are very popular. Many cookbooks are written for goulash only.

---

Hungarian Beef Goulash is a beef stew, prepared as in Central Europe, especially Hungary, Czechoslovakia, and Austria. It can be served with buttered noodles, boiled rice, boiled potatoes, or any other starch.

*Materials Needed for About 25 Orders:*

| | |
|---|---|
| 10 pounds cubed lean beef chuck, about 1 1/2-inch size | 6 fluid ounces Hungarian paprika |
| 5 pounds chopped onions | 1 pound pork fat |
| 6 ounces tomato paste | 1/2 cup flour |
| 2 tablespoons chopped caraway seeds | About 3 quarts of hot stock |
| Zeste of two lemons, grated | Salt |
| 2 tablespoons fresh chopped garlic | Large sauteuse for onion frying |
| 1/2 tablespoon of marjoram | Casserole with lid for stewing |

*Procedure:*

1. Fry the onions in the fat until light golden brown. Drain and keep fat.
2. Add all spices and tomato paste to the onions. Leave on heat for a minute and stir well.
3. Add two quarts of hot stock. Mix well, and let simmer for a few minutes.
4. Add salted raw meat. Mix well.
5. Cover pan tightly. Transfer to preheated oven of about 350°F. Stew slowly for about one hour.
6. Check stew for tenderness and taste. Mix flour into accumulated fat on top of stew like a roux.
7. Mix everything very well. Add remaining stock if necessary, and cook meat to finish.
8. Check again. BEWARE OF OVERCOOKING. Serve when ready.

--- ATTENTION: KEY POINTS ---

- Any stew loses most of its eye appeal and taste when overcooked. Meat should be chewable. It should have the consistency of a tender New York cut steak.

- Onions must be chopped and fried uniformly to a golden brown. When the onions are brown, the fat, onions, and pan must be separated by draining. Otherwise, the carryover heat will burn the onions.

**TABLE 24-2 HUNGARIAN BEEF GOULASH**

- *Pork Paprikas* — is a basic goulash made with pork meat. The tomatos are omitted. As a garnish, 3 to 4 pounds of peeled, cubed, raw potatoes are added, just in time to be tender together with the meat. Depending on meat quality and cube size, the braising may take from 35 to 60 minutes.

- *Szekeley Poerkoelt* is a basic pork goulash in which a No. 10 can of drained, chopped sauerkraut is stewed with the meat. The sauce is finished with one quart of rich sour cream, just before serving.

### Various Curries

Curry is the name for a mixture of spices commonly used in the Far East. It has a hot, pungent flavor and yellowish-greenish color. It comes in many different blends and brands, but its taste is always specific curry. From 7 to 50 different spices may be used to blend it. Some of the following are indispensable: cumin, cayenne, fennel, fenugreek, ginger, garlic, nutmeg, turmeric, pepper, cloves, cinnamon. Nearly all dishes spiced with this mixture are called curries. There are Indian, Malayan and Chinese curries. The chefs of India have created hundreds of different curry varieties. Most curries, especially the Indian ones, are made like stew. Raw cut-up meat, chopped onions, some other vegetables and curry powder or paste are mixed together and cooked over low heat. They are made in the same way as the goulash, with curry instead of paprika. Real Far Eastern curries are too hot for Western cuisine. The amount of curry which is used must be changed for Western acceptance. Curries are made from all protein foods and vegetables. They are served with plain white cooked rice.

---

*Basic Curry Sauce for Meat and Seafood Stew*

For making about 2 quarts of a basic curry sauce, 3 to 4 cups of finely chopped onions and 2 tablespoons of chopped garlic are sautéed lightly in clear butter. Depending on the quality of curry powder, 1/4 to 1/2 cup is added and stirred in. One cup of tomato puree, 1 quart of white meat or fish stock, 1 pound of peeled, diced, raw potatoes is added. The sauce is then simmered for at least a few minutes before the raw protein food is added. Then it is stewed until done. The curry flavor can be made stronger by adding cumin, all-spice, cloves, and some fresh herbs such as basil, oregano, or marjoram. A curry can be finished by stirring in 2 cups of yogurt or buttermilk, thickened with 2 tablespoons of cornstarch.

---

- *Prawn, Crab, or Lobster Curry* should have the unfinished sauce simmered at least 30-45 minutes. Then the seafood, either shelled or unshelled, is added. This is done because the fish should only stew for 3-5 minutes.

- *Lamb, Pork, Beef, and Chicken Curry* can be made with the cut-up meats added from the beginning so that sauce and meat will stew together.

### Osso Buco

Osso Buco is a true Italian specialty stew, made of veal knuckle slices with the bones and bone marrow still in. It is a basic stew in the French manner. Since its ingredients are slightly different, the step-by-step procedure of this dish is found in table 24-3.

### Seafood Stews

Seafood, which is almost pure protein, does not stew well. Fish is too brittle. Shellfish are not practical to stew, and overcook easily so that they become tough and tasteless. Bouillabaise or Cioppino are sometimes called fish stews. They are not. They should be called soups. One shellfish preparation which can be considered a stew is the Lobster a l'Americaine.

- *Lobster Americaine,* sometimes called Amoricaine, is a basic preparation for crustaceans. When made from live lobster, it is called Lobster Stew Americaine. It can be made into basic lobster sauce (sauce Americaine) or Lobster soup (Bisque). The same procedure is used for the stewing of crabs, prawns, crayfish, and languste. A step-by-step method for this classic preparation is found in table 24-4.

This popular Italian dish translates roughly as braised veal knuckles. Unlike lamb shanks or ham hocks, which are left whole and used as one piece for one portion, these veal knuckles are sawed into about 1 1/2 - 2-inch round slices with the marrow intact and the meat still around the bones. They are then handled like any other stew. It must never be forgotten that all stews are prepared the same way, no matter how fancy or foreign sounding are their names.

*Ingredients for 4 Persons:*

| | |
|---|---|
| 4-5 pounds veal knuckles, sawed 1 1/2 - 2 inches thick | 1 tablespoon chopped garlic |
| 2 cups finely diced, equal parts of onions, celery and carrots | 1 bouquet garni |
| | Zeste and juice from 1-2 oranges and lemons each |
| About 1/2 cup flour | 3-4 fillets of anchovies |
| 1 1/2 pounds peeled, de-seeded, cubed tomatoes | 1/4 cup chopped parsley |
| 1 cup dry wine | 1/2 cup olive oil |

*Procedure:*

1. In a casserole with lid, sauté the 2 cups of vegetables and the garlic, in half of the fat. Set aside.
2. Salt meat, roll in flour, and brown on all sides in remaining fat in another skillet.
3. Transfer meat from the skillet into the casserole with the vegetables on the bottom.
4. Deglaze skillet with the wine. Scrape residue loose and pour liquid over the meat.
5. Add the tomatoes, the bouquet garni, and half of the citrus juices to the meat.
6. Cover casserole and stew on low heat in the oven until meat is crunchily tender. This will depend entirely on the meat quality and could be from 3/4 of an hour to 2 hours.
7. In the meantime, chop anchovies and zeste together. Add the anchovies, oil, parsley, and 1/4 of the remaining citrus juice.
8. Stir into this mixture about 2-3 tablespoons of flour.
9. When they are tender, remove veal knuckles to warmed platter.
10. Stir the chopped anchovies mixture into the simmering sauce.
11. Check sauce for consistency and taste.
12. Finish as needed with salt, the citrus juice, and stock or bouillon.
13. Depending on the raw material used, size of the casserole, and heat, it could be that the sauce is too watery. In this case, it should be reduced on high heat under constant stirring, until desired consistency is reached.
14. Remove the bouquet garni. Pour sauce over the meat and serve.
15. To qualify for the name a'la Milanaise, Risotto Milanaise, (section 5, unit 27) is served as a side dish.

**TABLE 24-3  OSSO BUCO MILANESE**

## CONCLUSIONS

Stews are made mostly to tenderize tough meats. These meats are often not presentable as whole pieces since they are not the same size. They are also not lean nor free of gristle. Thus, the cutting and trimming of the meat to the same size so it will tenderize equally in the same time, is a must. When this cutting and trimming is not done the way it should be done, poor quality stews result. Customers reject poor quality. If stews are made with tender meats only for the purpose of creating a flavor blend, overcooking can be the greatest problem. Fish stews are outdated for modern and even classical cookery, because the sauté method of cooking has been developed to a fine point. Customers like their fish and crustaceans as clean and boneless as possible. Fish stews in the shells are not convenient. Fresh sautés are superior to warmed up or even fresh stews. The essentials of a stew are that small-cut food is cooked in its own sauce, with all ingredients blended together, served together, and eaten together. Stewing should only be applied to the use of tough foods. Sautéing replaces stewing for tender foods.

## SUMMARY

Stewing is another word for braising. The noun stew describes meat and vegetables cut into small pieces, braised in their own sauce. The public is often concerned about stews in food service establishments because too many patrons have been disappointed too often. Restaurateurs know this and are trying to avoid the term *stew* on their menus. The only reason for stewing is for its economy. Tough meat cuts, which are not so expensive, can only be boiled, ground or braised. If the basic rules of making a stew are followed, it can become the chef's best creation. The chef must have pieces of meat which are the same in size and quality, free from fat, gristle, and sinews. Overcooking causes mushy meat, which is not a taste delight. When food freshness is combined with knowledge of cooking and careful salting and seasoning, stews may again find greater acceptance.

Amoricaine is probably the original name for this dish and many experts are still arguing which of the spellings should be used. The preparation of a l'Americaine, for handling live lobsters and other edible crustaceans, is basic. It may be served as a made-to-the-order dish, like other lobster preparations, or the same procedure can be used to make lobster sauce (Sauce Americaine) or lobster soup (Lobster Bisque). The preparation is only effective when live crustaceans are used. The stewing process extracts from the shells extra flavor and color.

Already shelled, edible crustaceans are tender enough to be sauteed in a few minutes. Long stewing of shelled meat is the cause of poor quality in the final dish. Old-fashioned cookbooks often directed long stewing or boiling times. The authors were not aware of the effect overcooking has on protein foods.

*Ingredients Used per Lobster:*

1 live lobster
1/3 cup dry white wine
1 1/4 ounces brandy
1/4 cup white stock (fish)
2 tablespoons shallots, finely chopped
3 tablespoons tomato sauce, light starch
1/2 cup tomatoes, peeled, de-seeded, diced

2 tablespoons meat glaze (glace de viande)
1/2 teaspoon garlic, finely chopped
2 tablespoons herbs, finely chopped (parsley, coriander, tarragon)
2 ounces fresh butter
2 ounces clear butter, liquid
2 ounces oil

*Procedure:*

1. Split live lobster in half, lengthwise.
2. Separate tail and claws, crack claws open.
3. Clean the remaining shell, reserve the coral (lobster roe and liver).
4. Rinse shell. Boil it in salt water to bright red. Reserve for later.
5. Remove the black vein (gut) from the tail.
6. Cut each tail half in two or three pieces.
7. Salt the exposed flesh of tail and claws.
8. Heat oil in a sauteuse to very hot. Add all the lobster meat.
9. Sauté, shake pan, and cover for 1-2 minutes. Shell is still red.
10. Drain off the sauté oil.
11. Add the *fresh butter*, garlic, shallots and herbs.
12. Keep on sautéing for one or two minutes.
13. Add the brandy and flame.
14. Deglaze with wine, white stock and tomato sauce. Cover, reduce heat, and simmer 3 to 4 minutes.
15. Remove from heat. Steep with cover for another few minutes. Cool.
16. When cool enough to handle, take meat out of the shell.
17. Reserve the shells for later use (to make lobster butter).
18. Place the meat on a service platter and keep warm.
19. Return sauté pan with sauce to heat. Add tomatoes and meat glaze.
20. Bring to a full boil.. Then reduce heat and simmer to desired consistency.
21. Mix the coral with the clear butter and stir into the simmering sauce. Taste, season, and bring to a full boil.
22. Pour the sauce over the lobster meat. Use the boiled lobster head as decoration.
23. Serve immediately. If it is a first course, serve with toast. If it is a main course, serve with buttered steamed rice.

─── ATTENTION: KEY POINTS ───

- Whole lobsters for individual orders weigh an average of 1 1/4 to 1 3/4 lbs., although larger lobsters can be used.
- Beware of overcooking. This is an expensive a la carte preparation. A high food cost is combined with skilled handling. These preparations are found only in real luxury restaurants.

**TABLE 24-4  LOBSTER A L'AMERICAINE**

Student cooks must learn that the difference between meat sauce, meat stew, braised steak, and potted roast is only in the size of the meat cuts and not in the preparation method. The process called Caramelization and Tenderization Combined includes all, no matter what term is used.

Probably the oldest form of stewing started in one kettle. The Indian curry and the Hungarian Goulash are still made in this way. In ancient preparations, the browning of the meat is omitted, but more care is taken to handle the sauce, vegetables, and spices. There are other specialty stews like the Italian Osso Buco. The ingredients are a little fancier than in general, but the French-influenced preparation method still remains the same.

## DISCUSSION TOPICS

1. What are the historical links of Curry and Goulash?

2. Why is there a need to improve the stew's image?

3. What are the key points to quality stews?

## SUGGESTED ACTIVITIES

1. Define: stew, bisque, curry, zeste, sauerkraut.

2. Cook a plain beef stew.

3. Cook a burgundy beef stew.

4. Cook a Szekeley Pork Poerkoelt.

5. Cook a veal and mushroom stew.

6. Cook a lamb curry.

7. Cook a plain beef goulash.

8. Demonstrate the making of Osso Buco.

9. Prepare a prawn curry.

10. Explain the preparation and application of Lobster Americaine.

11. Make a lobster stew.

## ACHIEVEMENT REVIEW

A. Complete the following:

1. The noun, stew, stands for braised food in a size that is _____.

2. Beef stews in restaurants are not too _____.

3. When tender foods are stewed, the cook has to prevent _____.

4. Hungarian Goulash and Indian Curry are made by the same _____.

5. Knowing the best suited meat cuts and how to trim them is of the greatest importance in _____.

6. Adding wines or fancy ingredients does not change stewing's basic _____.

B. Read each question carefully and completely before answering it. Select the *best* answer.

1. A Hungarian meat stew finished with sour cream is called a

   a. Gulyas          c. Poerkoelt
   b. Paprikas        d. Gulash

2. Indian stews are food preparations seasoned with a mixture of spices called

   a. turmeric        c. paprika
   b. chili powder    d. curry

3. To call a mixture of small-cut food stew, it must

   a. have browned meat in it
   b. be spiced with paprika or curry
   c. be served with a sauce
   d. be cooked in its own sauce

4.  If the cooking time for a stew is short, the additional sauce vegetables have to be

   a. ground coarse
   b. adjusted to the cooking time
   c. cut uniformly large
   d. osterized

5.  Curries are a wide field of preparations but what they all have in common is

   a. a rather hot taste        c. the yellow color
   b. the stewing process       d. the addition of potatoes

6.  Osso Buco is an Italian stew with tomatoes and wine, made from

   a. lamb shanks        c. beef chuck
   b. veal knuckles      d. pork shoulder

7.  Fish or shellfish are rarely made into stew because they

   a. are tender foods by nature
   b. have too many bones
   c. do not brown well
   d. do not blend with the vegetables

# Unit 25  Fricassees, Blanquettes, and Casseroles

*OBJECTIVES*

After studying and practicing this unit, the student should be able to

- Prepare Chicken Brunswick Fricassee.
- Make a Blanquette de Veau with Cauliflower.
- List a variation of "baked beans" of his own creation.
- Prepare a beefsteak and kidney pie by the second method.

Stews are often served under different names. This unit explains variations, which may have fancy names, but are still stews.

## Fricassees

A fricassee is a stew made from white poultry meats, such as chicken or turkey. This remains white during preparation. The meat for a fricassee must not be browned. It is handled in the manner of goulash or curry, except that the colorful spices are omitted.

In some dishes the white meat is lightly sautéed. In most cases, the meat is poached in a little liquid, which is then changed into sauce by adding a thickener. The thickener could be plain starch, roux, cream, or egg yolks. Vegetables are added. This may be only chopped parsley in the sauce. It may be a selection or combination of asparagus, artichokes, cauliflower, broccoli, peas, beans, mushrooms, carrots, or others.

*Brunswick Chicken Stew.* This is a fricassee, with corn and often other vegetables added as a garnish.

## Blanquettes

*Blanquette de Veau.* This is a term used for stews of white meats, such as veal, kid, or goat. It is prepared just like a fricassee.

Blanquettes, like fricassees, have sauces based on starch, egg yolks, or a combination of both. Onions, herb bouquets and mirepoix are used to season the poaching liquid and are removed before the liquid is changed into sauce.

*Irish Stew.* Irish stew is a white lamb blanquette with onions, lamb meat cubes, sliced raw potatoes and cabbage, seasoned, salted, and arranged in layers in a casserole. Then enough boiling liquid is added to cover the meat. The covered casserole is simmered without stirring until the meat is tender. The thinly sliced potatoes completely cook to a pulp and make the thickening for the sauce. At the same time the liquid is reduced. Before serving, the stew is stirred and then sprinkled with chopped parsley.

*Baked Beans.* Dried navy beans are soaked in cold water overnight, then boiled in their soaking water until very tender. They are drained, if necessary. Many styles are made by using spices, syrup, molasses, sugar, salt, bacon, franks, smoked sausages, or smoked meats. This mixture is placed in a bean pot or any flat casserole and baked for several hours. If it gets too dry, stock or water must be added, a small amount at a time.

Baked bean dishes are known all over the world and many varieties exist. They can be made like stews, with onions or other vegetables which have been sautéed first. The beans must always be soaked and boiled first.

*Cassoulet.* A French term for a dish like baked beans is *cassoulet.* It is made with lamb, goose, duck, pork (smoked or fresh) and different seasonings. Cassoulets, like baked beans, are winter dishes served mostly in cold areas or where food poverty demands more economy.

*Casseroles*

A casserole can be any stew which is cooked and served in the same container. Casseroles may be of single-portion size or larger. They are made of china, ceramic, earthenware, glass, copper and others. Combining food, layer by layer, as in Irish Stew, is a popular way of making them. Casseroles can be made meatless if a starch (pasta or potatoes) replaces the protein.

*Beefsteak Pie.* Beefsteak pie is a plain beefsteak variation in which the meat is often sliced instead of cubed. This stew is put into a pot pie dish, covered with a pie crust and baked until the crust is done. The second, rather home style, version of this dish is slightly different. The raw seasoned meat mixed with presautéed vegetables is put into the pie dish, covered with a slightly thickened gravy, topped with the pie crust and baked until the meat is tender. The baking time depends on the meat cuts and quality used.

*Beefsteak and Kidney Pie.* This is made like the beefsteak pie, with sliced presautéed veal or beef kidneys added to the meat. The proportions should be not more than one part kidneys to two parts of meat.

*Chicken Pot Pie.* A small-cut chicken fricassee, usually boneless, with vegetables, is handled like the beefsteak pie.

*Shepherds Pie.* Lamb meat is used instead of beef in the beefsteak pie. The pie crust cover is replaced by a cover of piped potatoes or spread on mashed potatoes (Duchess potato mixture).

## CONCLUSIONS

To explain the processes of caramelizing and tenderizing combined, the preparations were subdivided for better understanding into units 22, 23, 24 and 25. All of them have in common that the liquids used to tenderize become a major part of the preparation. Most of them have in common the fact that some or all of the ingredients are browned to obtain the changed flavor. To distinguish the dishes listed in these units as completely different from boiled, poached or steamed foods, it must be recalled that in cooking with moisture only (boiling, etc.), the food and liquid are separated as soon as the food is tenderized. In braising, a mixture of proteins, starch and liquid is created. The intent is to serve it exactly this way.

The larger number of fancy names comes from the regional origins of the dishes. Some other names were accepted in place of the word stew.

From a nutritional viewpoint, dishes with a long cooking time are not as good for diets as those which cook fast and retain more vitamins. From a customer's viewpoint, long-cooked dishes do not have the same freshness as sautéed, fried or broiled foods. From the restaurateur's viewpoint, long-cooked dishes do not allow for proper portion control. The highly skilled chef who is needed for this type of cooking is not found in the average restaurant.

## SUMMARY

Braised dishes have many different names and flavors but they are still basic stews. This point is stressed often to make the student see how simple stews are. Cookery must accept the constant technical and science-nutritional progress of our time. Cooks, in order to provide competitive products, must always look for more economic methods to achieve better, or at least equal, quality creations. The better the young student cook can see through this maze of terms, procedures, and individual side developments, the more effective a chef he will become.

Fricassees are white stews of poultry. Blanquettes are white stews of white meats. Cassoulets are baked beans, old world style. Casseroles are stews, cooked and served in the same dish. Meat pies are stews served in a pot pie dish, covered with pie crust or mashed potatoes.

It is no longer true that restaurant cuisine in the USA can show greater profit by serving braised foods. The reasons are food waste and the lack of trained cooks. For the truly skilled cook who has taste and artistic talents, the process called Caramelizing and Tenderizing Combined provides an excellent stage for presenting his skills.

## DISCUSSION TOPICS

1. Is the confusing terminology of names necessary?
2. What are some of the important considerations of fricasseeing which would be similar to stewing?
3. Are *true* casserole dishes practical to make for a restaurant?

## SUGGESTED ACTIVITIES

1. Define: fricassee, poultry, cassoulet, blanquette.
2. Make a Chicken Brunswick Stew.
3. Make a Blanquette de Veau with Cauliflower.
4. Select and compare various recipes of baked beans.
5. Create an original recipe for baked beans.

## ACHIEVEMENT REVIEW

A. Complete the following:

1. A fricassee is the name of a stew made from _____.
2. Blanquette is a French name for a white veal _____.
3. Baked bean dishes are, in a technical sense, _____.
4. Cassoulet is the French name for a form of _____.
5. A stew cooked and served in the same container can be called a _____.
6. Irish Stew could be classified as a lamb _____.
7. Meat pies are similar to casseroles or _____.

B. Read each question carefully and completely before answering it. Select the *best* answer.

1. A white stew can be called fricassee when it is made of

   a. goose meat
   b. wild duck
   c. boneless chicken
   d. domesticated white ducks

2. Blanquettes are unbrowned meat stews from

   a. beef
   b. turkey
   c. venison
   d. veal

3. A beef stew served with a pie crust is called a

   a. casserole
   b. beefsteak pie
   c. shepherds pie
   d. cassoulet

4. Irish Lamb Stew which contains onions, potatoes and cabbage is made in the method of the

   a. casserole — blanquette
   b. "Lamb a la Provincal"
   c. shepherds pie
   d. chicken fricassee

5. Cassoulet is the French term for a casserole made with

   a. beef meat
   b. lamb meat
   c. fried onions
   d. dried beans

6. A beef goulash served in a pot pie dish with a pie crust has become a

   a. Beef pie
   b. Goulash Casserole
   c. Hungarian Beef Pie
   d. Beefsteak pie

# Section 5 Vegetable and Egg Cookery

## Unit 26  Progressive Vegetable Cookery

*OBJECTIVES*

After studying and practicing this unit, the student should be able to

- Prepare Artichoke Antipasto.
- Cook Asparagus Princess.
- Make Carrots Vichy.
- Sauté Cabbage a la Mode.
- Prepare Cauliflower a la Polonaise.
- Make a Mushroom Duxelles.

Vegetables are cooked by the same principles as all the other foods described in the other units. In the past it was thought that vegetables had to be cooked for a long time to become digestible. Newer studies have shown that this is not true.

*PRESERVATION OF VITAMINS AND FLAVORS*

It has been stated that the preservation of food values is a most important cooking objective. Long heat exposure destroys most of the vitamins, minerals, and other nutrients in vegetables and all other foods.

Progressive vegetable cookery means the preserving of the vegetable nutrients. For nutritious, tasty vegetables, the cooking must be done just before serving. They must have the shortest possible cooking time in order to become just tender.

*VARIOUS COOKING METHODS*

Two methods have been proved best for the cooking of vegetables. One is exact time-controlled pressure steaming with additional sautéing. The other is plain sautéing started from the raw stage.

---

*Vitamins* are chemical compounds which are necessary to nutrition. They occur in the normal diet in very small amounts, and are most necessary for good health. They also help in the use of other healthful food factors.

Vitamin A is needed for growth, functioning of the body's internal and external surfaces, and for vision in dim light. It also aids the body in resisting infection.

*Carotene,* a yellow pigment substance formed in green plants, can be changed into Vitamin A within the body. The green coloring matter of plants covers it to make it invisible, but it is found in leafy vegetables. Because of this carotene content, many green leafy and yellow vegetables are known as sources of Vitamin A. Some of the best sources of Vitamin A are kale, chard, collards, broccoli, spinach, green lettuce, turnip tops, green peas, green beans, yellow squash, carrots, sweet potatoes, and tomatoes.

Vitamins $B_1$, $B_2$, and $B_3$ are also found in vegetables, but not in large enough amounts to be discussed at this time.

The greatest concern of chefs is ascorbic acid or Vitamin C. It is found in most fresh vegetables and fruits. Members of the cabbage family have a very high C content. It oxidizes easily, is destroyed through cooking, and is water soluble. Even raw vegetables, soaked in cold water, will lose their Vitamin C value. The more water that is used for processing, the more vitamins are lost.

Humans need Vitamin C in large quantities constantly. Therefore, cooks must preserve it in cooked vegetables by using progressive cooking methods. They should try to add as many fresh raw fruits and vegetables as possible to regular menus.

---

**TABLE 26-1  VITAMINS FOUND IN VEGETABLES**

The baking of vegetables is very good from a nutritional point, but most can not be baked very successfully. Deep frying, a fast process which is quite tasty when done right, adds too many calories to the restaurant diet. Boiling, in which the food is separated from the cooking water after it has been cooked, is the least suitable process. Most nutrients are leached out of the vegetables, dissolve in the cooking water, and the boiled vegetables are left much less nutritious.

Vegetable cookery must be seen and practiced in the same way as meat cookery. For example, cut-up cauliflower can be covered with a minimum of boiling, salted water, and simmered to near doneness. Then by adding a little butter roux to the cooking liquid (the cauliflower water), it will become a white sauce. The dish is then served, just like a veal blanquette. But the same amount of raw cauliflower should *not* be boiled in a large pot of water until tender, then drained, with the vegetables being rinsed in cold water to prevent overcooking. The vegetable would then have to be heated when needed, and finished for serving. It is much better to pressure steam cook fresh cauliflower (2-3 minutes) and serve immediately with brown butter sauce Hollandaise, or in some other conventional way. For keeping the most taste and food value at the same time, the freshly washed and cut-up vegetable should be sautéed with butter in a covered skillet. A little stock or water is added for about five minutes. This changes the sautéing into stewing. Other vegetables, such as mushrooms, contain so much water of their own that strict sautéing without any additional liquid is enough to produce a tasty and nutritious dish.

### Boiling

Boiling, or steaming, is the simplest and most widely used vegetable cooking method in the English speaking world. Unfortunately, vegetables in some establishments have become pulp with little or no food value. Faulty cooking methods and handling principles have caused this. Too much unsalted, lukewarm water for cooking, followed by draining and cold rinsing causes loss of value. The use of soda bicarbonate to keep the green color is another poor practice. Pressure steaming often results in overcooking since the chef is not able to look at the food while it is cooking. However, strictly time-controlled pressure steam-cooking of vegetables, as they are needed, is the answer to quality vegetable cookery for hospital tray lines and other institutions. *Time-controlled* means to use a timer and to remove the vegetables from the heat immediately after cooking. Shutting off the pressure automatically is not enough. The carry-over heat will do the damage. It also means that the same load and kind of vegetable must be cooked for the same time with the same amount of heat each time, after the cooking norms have been established by tests. It must be realized that a pressure steamer is a powerful heat source in which one or two minutes of overcooking or exposure to carry-over heat will completely destroy whatever food values were left in the vegetable.

Restaurant chefs do not like to use pressure steamers for green vegetables, since it is difficult to keep the fresh color which is eye appealing. Cooks too often think only about the eye appeal of their vegetables. The loss of taste and nutrients through faulty cooking methods is covered up by adding herbs, spices, and sauces. On the other hand, institutional cooks under the supervision of dieticians are often concerned only about keeping vitamin values, but care very little for eye appeal and taste. In this unsatisfying vacuum of vegetable cookery, the consumer is definitely shortchanged.

---

Clean, cut and wash vegetables thoroughly.

Bring as much salted water to a boil as needed to cover the vegetables.

Make sure water is salted enough to prevent the leaching out, or washing away, of the vegetable's natural minerals.

When water boils vigourously, put vegetables in, then bring water to boiling point again, fast. Then turn down heat and let simmer until vegetables are crunchy.

Cooking time will vary for different vegetables. Cooking time will also vary for the *same* vegetables at different times of the year.

Cooking times may range from 1 minute for young peas or flat Italian beans to twenty minutes for late season Kentucky Wonder beans, cauliflower, carrots, etc.

Never cook vegetables longer than necessary. They should be crunchy.

Butter, season, or finish vegetables according to chef's ideas or recipes, and serve.

*Never* rinse freshly cooked vegetables with cold water. This washes away flavor and important vitamins and minerals.

**TABLE 26-2  BOILING VEGETABLES IN WATER**

Frozen vegetables are food products of great convenience to the chef. They have replaced canned vegetables in most places where there is a deep freezer.

Before they are frozen and packed, the vegetables are cleaned, cut, and blanched. They need less labor and less cooking time than fresh vegetables. In general, they may be boiled or steamed the same way as fresh vegetables. Dietitians recommend cooking them while still frozen in order to retain full vitamin and mineral content. This is not always possible. When a 2 1/2-pound block of vegetables is frozen solid, it must be pre-thawed and separated. If it is not, the outside will overcook while the inside will stay raw.

New time tables for cooking each kind of vegetable have to be established whenever a different brand is bought. To be sure of exact timing, a timer must be used. Overcooked vegetables are bad, both for eating and for dietetic values.

Pressure or live steam cooker models vary from maker to maker. The manufacturer's guidelines should be a starting point for the establishment of cooking times. It is also important to consider carry-over heat and steam table holding times when making these guidelines. Vegetables that are also sautéed in a skillet can be salted and mixed in the skillet, but vegetables which are only steamed, then served plain or with a cover sauce, should be salted before they are steamed.

A pressure steamer is a machine. The quality of the vegetables cooked in any machine depends entirely on the intelligence and attentiveness of the cook who is standing behind it.

**TABLE 26-3  THE STEAMING OF FROZEN VEGETABLES**

### Methods to be Followed

For the student who wants to become an excellent vegetable cook and chef, the following guidelines are of the greatest importance. Nutrients, eye appeal, and taste in vegetables are kept by strictly time-controlled pressure steaming to the order, then sautéing in the skillet with butter and seasoning. It is even better to cut or slice vegetables into certain shapes and sauté or short-stew them in the skillet to the order. Coated deep frying may be used if the quality principles in units 15 and 18 are observed. Students must realize that taste and nutrients are both kept or both lost.

### SPECIFIC PREPARATIONS

Boiling and steaming are outlined in tables 26-2 and 26-3. Following are some less common but important vegetable preparations.

### Artichokes

American Globe Artichokes are thistle-like plants, grown mostly in California, near Castroville. They are fresh or frozen. For luxury cookery, the de-leafed artichoke bottom, or sometimes the whole small artichoke (also called heart) is used.

Cleaning artichokes is the difficult part of the cooking. The leaves are tough and have thorns. Artichokes discolor easily when cut; nonoxidizing bowls or casseroles are a must.

**THE CLEANING OF ARTICHOKES**

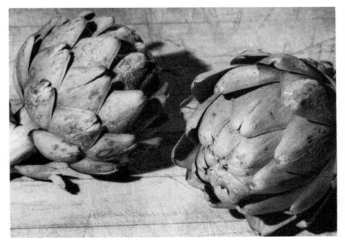

Fig. 26-1  California Globe Artichokes, as purchased

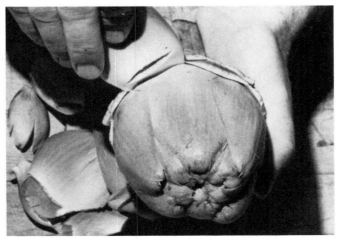

Fig. 26-2  The tough, stringy outer leaves are pulled off.

After it is cleaned and washed, asparagus can be cut into one-inch long sticks and sautéed in a pan for a few minutes until done. Asparagus must never be overcooked. Like spaghetti, it should always be crunchy "al dente", whether it is hot or cold, sautéed or boiled.

Asparagus tips are used to garnish many sauces, meat preparations, or even other vegetables.

## Beans

Fresh green beans can be boiled, steamed, sautéed, or stewed. There are many regional bean varieties which each need a different cooking time to be tenderized.

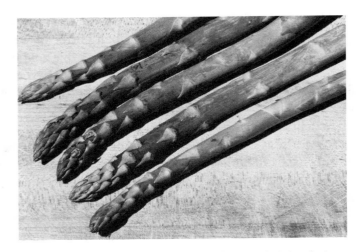

Fig. 26-9  Fresh asparagus spears (large or jumbo size).

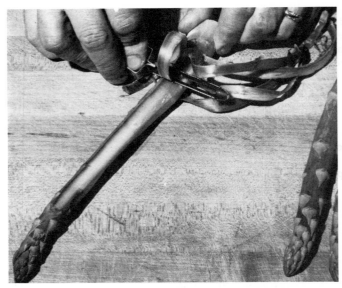

Fig. 26-10  Using a potato peeler to peel asparagus spears.

Fig. 26-11  Pulling back the stringy peel.

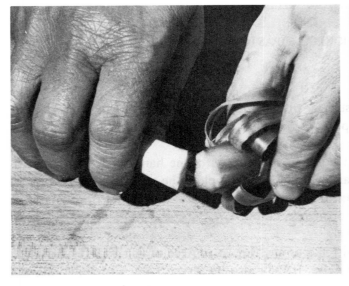

Fig. 26-12  Breaking off the end with peels still attached.

Fig. 26-13  The peeled and washed asparagus is now cut, if desired, for sautéing.

A sauté dish can be made within 5 minutes. This is an excellent preparation served as an a la carte vegetable in luxury restaurants.

*Ingredients:*

2 pounds peeled, washed asparagus (fresh, raw)
About 4 ounces tiny frozen green peas
2 ounces butter
2-ounce ladle of veloute sauce

Salt
Sugar
About 2 ounces chicken stock

*Procedure:*

1. Cut asparagus oriental style (diagonally).
2. Melt butter in skillet, add asparagus, salt and a little sugar.
3. Sauté on hot fire 1-2 minutes.
4. Moisten the bottom of the skillet with chicken stock, then cover.
5. Reduce heat and simmer one or two more minutes.
6. Add green peas, flip and mix, replace cover.
7. Wait one more minute, remove cover, add sauce, flip and mix.
8. If necessary, dilute with more chicken stock. Serve.

─────────────── ATTENTION: KEY POINT ───────────────
● This vegetable should not be saucy, but barely held together with some thin, light sauce.

**TABLE 26-5 ASPARAGUS PRINCESS FOR FOUR**

*Flat Italian Beans.* The beans which need the least cooking time are flat Italian beans. If sautéed in the skillet without preboiling, they may need only two to three minutes. In a pressure steamer at fifteen pounds of pressure (250°F.), thirty to forty seconds is enough. If boiled in water, bringing them up to the reboiling point usually cooks them. Flat Italian beans are never "French" or Julienne cut. They are left whole or in halves. They taste best with brown butter only.

*Blue Lake Beans.* Blue Lake beans are round and fleshy, of excellent taste, but have a slightly longer cooking time than the flat Italians. They are prepared whole or only cut in half.

*Kentucky Wonder Beans.* Most often used is the Kentucky Wonder bean. This is a large meaty bean, which must be destringed before cutting. It can be french or plain cut. It has a longer cooking time than the Blue Lakes.

*Lima Beans.* Fresh or frozen, lima beans are better precooked in moisture, then sautéed in butter and seasoned by choice.

### Red Beets

Red beets are boiled first, then sautéed plain, or served sweet-sour in a little cornstarch-thickened sauce of their own juice. To keep the red color they must be boiled, unpeeled and uncut. This prevents the leaching out of the juice. The salted cooking water should also be made a little acid, especially in hard water areas.

### Broccoli

Broccoli is handled like cauliflower, but may have to be peeled, like asparagus.

### Brussels Sprouts

Brussels Sprouts look like small cabbage heads, which they are. Outer leaves and stems are removed before they are steamed or boiled, then sautéed in butter or served a la "Polonaise". The Polonaise preparation is listed in table 26-6.

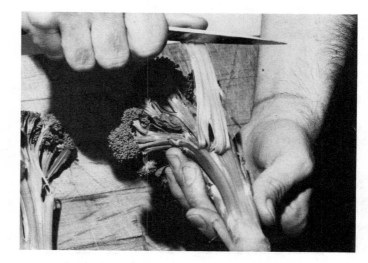

**Fig. 26-14 Peeling broccoli with a paring knife.**

"A la Polonaise" is the name of a preparation for various vegetables, first steamed or boiled, then served with the following covering:

1 weight part of fine bread crumbs, sifted, fried in an equal weight part of butter, like a roux, to a golden brown.

This bread crumb-butter is kept hot and spooned over the freshly cooked vegetables before they are served. The fried bread crumbs on the vegetable are topped with a mixture of chopped hard boiled eggs and parsley.

Egg yolk, egg white and parsley can be kept separate and used in a color pattern for better eye appeal.

The vegetables most often served a la Polonaise are cauliflower, asparagus, broccoli, brussels sprouts, wax beans, and string beans.

This preparation can be served as a side dish or as a separate vegetable appetizer.

**TABLE 26-6 PREPARATION A LA POLONAISE**

## Cabbage

*Curly Cabbage.* This is also called Savoy Cabbage and tastes best stewed with raw grated potatoes, garlic, pepper, and beef stock. It should be *short,* which means it should have only a little sauce to hold it together.

*White Cabbage.* When boiled for 30-45 minutes, white cabbage loses its vitamins. It also causes a smelly kitchen. Released sulphur is the cause of indigestion for many people. Boiling the same cabbage for only 3 to 5 minutes does not release sulphur, nor does it destroy the many vitamins in cabbage. Undercooking of cabbage for many preparations is the answer, but the best solution is the sauté method. Table 26-7 gives a step-by-step process for sautéed Cabbage a la Mode.

The fastest, tastiest and most nutritious preparations of cabbage are made by the sauté method.

### Cabbage Sautéed a la Mode

*Ingredients per Person:*

1/3 pound large, cubed, cleaned cabbage
1 ounce of suitable sauté fat (olive oil, oil, butter, etc.)
Salt, pepper, sugar for seasoning
Choice of herbs: thyme, basil, marjoram, dill, oregano
Other additional choices: onions, garlic, tomato paste, shallots, sour cream

*Procedure:*

1. A large enough sauté pan, with cover, is heated with the chosen fat.
2. If onion or garlic is used, it is sautéed first.
3. The cabbage is added to the pan, seasoned by choice, and the pan is covered.
4. On medium high heat, the cabbage is sautéed for 2-3 minutes, then flipped.
5. It is covered for another minute of sautéing.
6. All other ingredients are added, and heat is increased, especially when sour cream or tomato puree is used.
7. Without the cover, pan is flip-fried until the liquid is reduced. Now it is tasted and served.

### Cabbage Sautéed a la Russe

*Ingredients for 6 Persons:*

3 pounds white, cleaned and cubed cabbage
1 teaspoon of dill weed
1/3 pint of sour cream
2 tablespoons of finely chopped onions
Salt, dash of sugar, lemon juice when needed
2 ounces of pork fat or oil for sautéing

*Procedure:*

1. Heat fat. Add onions. Sauté for a few seconds.
2. Add cabbage and salt. Cover.
3. Sauté for 2 to 3 minutes.
4. Add sour cream and dill (sugar and lemon juice as needed).
5. Uncover, increase heat, flip-fry until dish becomes fully mixed. Serve.

### Cabbage Sauté California

*Ingredients for 6 Persons:*

3 pounds white, cleaned and cubed cabbage
2 teaspoons of thyme
1 cup of tomato puree
2 tablespoons of finely chopped onions
2 ounces of olive oil
Salt, pepper and sugar

*Procedure:*

1. Heat the oil, add onions and sauté for a few seconds.
2. Add cabbage, salt, sugar, and thyme. Cover.
3. Sauté for several minutes, then add the tomato puree.
4. Uncover, increase heat and flip-fry until dish becomes fully mixed. Taste, add pepper, and serve.

**TABLE 26-7 MODERN PREPARATION OF CABBAGE**

*Red Cabbage.* This is often prepared as Wine Cabbage or Bavarian Cabbage. Any of these preparations is a basic stew. The raw shredded cabbage is mixed with salt and kept under weight pressure for at least 20 minutes. Then the water is squeezed from the softened cabbage by hand and thrown away. The drained cabbage is braised with onions, shredded apples, red wine, vinegar, and sugar until tender. Vinegar is added immediately to prevent change in color and crispness of cabbage. Spices, such as cloves, allspice, or cinnamon may be added.

### Carrots

Carrots are usually cut, preboiled or steamed, then pan sautéed or mixed with a veloute or bechamel sauce. They can be glazed with butter and sugar only. They can be made like beets with extra liquid and cornstarch to produce a shiny coat. One of the best preparations is Carrots Vichy as shown in table 26-8.

### Cauliflower

Cauliflower is usually preboiled in salt and lemon water, then either sautéed in butter or served with Hollandaise or Cheese Sauce. It can also be creamed, mixed with other vegetables, or refried, either breaded or dipped in batter, as cauliflower fritters. Excellent and unusual is sautéed cauliflower mixed with raw eggs and some cream. For each pound of cauliflower, two ounces of butter, two eggs, and one-third cup of half and half cream are used. It is sautéed and finished like scrambled eggs in the skillet.

### Celery

Celery needs only sautéing, but it can also be braised. Sometimes it is gratinated with cheese (a la Milanaise). Usually it is creamed, or served as a filler with mixed vegetables.

### Celeriac

These large celery roots are excellent when preboiled or steamed to crunchy, then sliced into 1/4-inch discs, breaded, and refried.

### Chestnuts

Chestnuts must be peeled raw first. A cut is made against the fibers across the top. Small amounts of the chestnuts are placed in a 550°F. oven for a few minutes, until the shells pop open. They must be shelled immediately, while still hot. They are parboiled for a few minutes, and drained. Then they are finished by stewing with butter, salt, sugar, some of the boiling juice and some dry sherry wine.

---

The same preparation can be used for the cooking of parsnips, broccoli, asparagus, and many other vegetables. The sugar may be omitted.

*Ingredients and Utensils Needed for about 6 Orders:*

| | |
|---|---|
| 2 pounds raw carrots | 1/4 teaspoon salt |
| 3 ounces butter or margarine | 1 ten-inch skillet |
| 3-4 tablespoons of sugar | 1 ten-inch cover |

*Procedure:*

1. Peel and wash carrots.
2. Slice crosswise into uniform wheels, approximately 3/32 inch thick.
3. Heat butter in ten-inch skillet.
4. Add carrots, sugar, and salt.
5. Put a tight-fitting cover on the skillet.
6. Keep on a low-medium heat for about 4 minutes.
7. Remove cover and mix carrots well.
8. Continue to stew for 2 minutes more.
9. Check for doneness, and taste. If carrots are too soupy, remove cover and leave them on a hot fire for the remainder of the time.
10. If carrots are too crunchy, continue cooking 2-3 more minutes.
11. When done, remove from stove and serve.

**TABLE 26-8 CARROTS VICHY**

### Eggplant

This internationally well-known vegetable is called Aubergines in French, Melanzani in Italian, and Eieirfruechte in German. It can be sautéed, deep fried or baked, but never boiled in water. One basic preparation is to peel, cut, then stew with onions, garlic, tomatoes, etc. They may be left unpeeled, cut in half, scored around the rim and across the cut surface, then baked in a hot oven at 475°F. for about 50 minutes. If seasoned from the beginning they can be served just this way. The flesh may be scraped out, chopped, mixed with other precooked meat or vegetables, and put back into the peel for serving. They can be gratinated by sprinkling parmesan cheese over the refilled tops and browning them.

### Green Peas

Green peas or pea pods, also called sugar peas, should only be sautéed in butter with salt and sugar. Boiling is not necessary at all.

### Lentils

A lentil is a dried legume. It should be thought of as a starch like dried beans. Lentils have a much shorter cooking time than beans. This is a Continental vegetable, served often with game meat. The clean lentils are boiled in a little beef stock with thyme, bay leaf, and salt, until tender. The stock should be completely reduced. Diced smoked bacon is sautéed to a golden brown and added, with its fat, to the lentils. The dish is seasoned with a jigger of red wine vinegar and some white pepper. It should be creamy without any extra starch.

### Mushrooms

One of the edible mushrooms, called *Champignon,* is a domestic cultured vegetable. It is highly regarded in culinary art.

Many wild mushrooms are also edible. Near each wild edible one, there also grows a poisonous one. They look very much alike. This makes eating wild mushrooms dangerous; people all over the world have died from mushroom poisoning. Wild mushrooms are thought to be better tasting than cultured ones. In most European countries, they are sold in the markets. They are government inspected. The people who gather them know the difference between good and bad ones.

Since just one poisonous mushroom can kill a person, only cultured, safe mushrooms are handled in the USA. Fresh mushrooms have a fine flavor, smell, appearance, and consistency. After a few days, they lose these qualities rapidly. In general, mushrooms are precooked. They are not often put into a stew or preparation while still raw.

Fig. 26-15 The eggplant is cut in half, lengthwise.

Fig. 26-16 An incision is made around the rim.

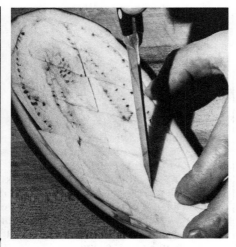

Fig. 26-17 Scoring the eggplant across the surface for better heat penetration and easier scooping-out of the flesh when baked.

Steps in precooking mushrooms, cut or uncut:

- The mushroom is washed well, but quickly, in a deep container of cold water which has been soured slightly with lemon juice, ascorbic acid, or vinegar. Deep water is necessary since the mushrooms are lighter than water and float to the top. Sand, earth, and dirt will sink to the bottom.

- The floating mushrooms are lifted out of the water, drained, and put into a frying pan already on the stove, containing hot butter.

- The pan is covered to preserve as much of the natural mushroom juice as possible, and simmered from 3-10 minutes, according to the size of the mushrooms. When taken from the heat, they are left in their own juice until needed. If handled and stored properly under refrigeration, they should keep for a few days.

*Duxelles.* A stew of chopped mushrooms called "Duxelles" is an important part of French luxury cuisine. Duxelles has been adopted by cooks all over the Western World. For the step-by-step procedure of making Duxelles, see table 26-9.

*Creamed Mushrooms.* These are used as a filling for such dishes as egg omelettes, pancakes, and patty shells. Sliced, precooked mushrooms are mixed with a small amount of heavy white sauce, then improved with fresh cream, egg yolk, or hollandaise sauce. Creamed mushrooms may be served on toast as appetizers or a light snack.

---

Duxelles is a vegetable paste made mainly from mushrooms and used to add to the flavor of other preparations. Its applications are many, not only in vegetable cookery, but also for meat and seafood preparations.

*Materials Needed:*

| | |
|---|---|
| 2 1/2 pounds mushrooms | Salt |
| 1 pound onions | Pepper |
| 1 cup tomato paste | Garlic |
| 1 cup chopped parsley | 1 cup olive oil |

---
**ATTENTION: KEY POINT**

- All the procedures for the handling of mushrooms are to be observed.
---

*Procedure:*

1. Chop onions fine. Sauté in oil 5-8 minutes.
2. Add finely chopped, cleaned mushrooms. Sauté 5 minutes more.
3. Add garlic, tomato paste, salt and pepper. Sauté 5 minutes more.
4. Add chopped parsley. Cover casserole. Stew 5 minutes more.
5. Take from the fire, stir well. Cool off and use.

*Uses of Duxelles:*

Duxelles, the mushroom paste, could also be used as a sauce:

Sauce Duxelles: An optional amount of duxelles is mixed into brown sauce, veloute sauce, or tomato sauce.

For stuffing mixes:

- 1/2 Duxelles and 1/2 chopped, sautéed eggplants.
- 1/2 Duxelles and 1/2 chopped, cooked ham.
- 1/2 Duxelles and 1/2 chopped or ground leftover roast or cooked meat.

These stuffings are used to fill refried pancakes, turnovers, meat rolls, other vegetables, or combinations of them.

The most common use of Duxelles in vegetable cookery is for the stuffing of tomato halves, zucchini, cucumbers, summer squash, artichokes, and others. Grated parmesan cheese is then sprinkled over the top, and the dish is fast browned under the broiler.

For fancy meat preparations such as "Filet de Boeuf Wellington", veal chops or pork links in puff paste or pork tenderloins colbert, Duxelles is used as a flavoring spread on the dough before the meat is wrapped in it.

**TABLE 26-9  HOW TO MAKE AND USE DUXELLES**

*Breaded Deep-fried Mushrooms.* Whole, fresh, raw mushroom buttons (stem cut off) are washed and immediately breaded. Then they are deep fried like prawns or scallops for 5-6 minutes. They are served immediately, as an appetizer or vegetable. For appetizers, serve with tartar sauce or mayonnáise.

### Onions

Onions may be the oldest known vegetable. The ancient Egyptians worshipped onions as a god symbol. It is believed that onions came from Asia. Today, Oriental cookery uses onions even more than our own Western cuisine.

Onions are bulbs of the lily family and grow well in all moderate climates. Their vitamin, mineral and caloric content is about the same as other vegetables, but they contain an element irritating to the eyes. When the outer dry skin of the onion is removed, this gas is freed.

Onions are used mainly as a flavoring ingredient, more like garlic, herbs, or spices, and less as a vegetable dish. Sometimes menus have baked onions or onion salad. They may be used raw, sautéed (half fried), crisp fried (Viennese Fried), stewed, baked or boiled. Medical research shows that onions in any form are hard to digest. For ulcer patients and "soft hospital diets" they must be avoided completely. Raw onions in salads are some of the offenders causing heartburn, gas and indigestion. The experienced cook knows when to use them and when not to use them. They should be used sparingly, just as any other flavor ingredient. If a dish contains a lot of onions, it should be named accordingly to warn those who have to avoid them.

There are several ways to reduce the eye irritation (tearing) caused by peeling of onions.

- Onions may be cooled to near freezing, 32°F., before they are peeled. The gas will remain liquid and escape only later when the temperature has risen again.

- Use a draft which blows onion gases away from the peeling person. Ventilators are very helpful.

- Onions may be peeled 2-3 days before being used. The gases will evaporate slowly and no irritation of the eye will be caused when they are chopped or cut later. The use of modern plastic wraps makes it possible to store chopped or peeled onions under refrigeration for days without affecting other food in the refrigerator with the penetrating smell.

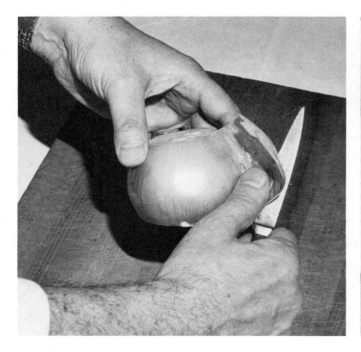

Fig. 26-18 Peeling onions. For the speediest onion-peeling the top and the bottom of the onion is cut off first. The outer skin is then pulled away sideways, if possible, in one movement.

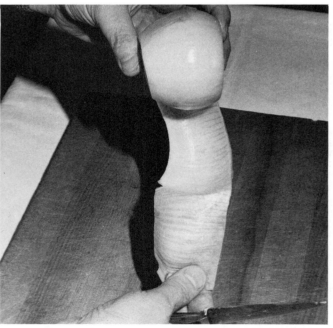

Fig. 26-19 If this is done properly, the peeling of one onion should only take seconds.

Onions must always be cut with stainless steel knives. Carbon steel (ordinary) knives will oxidize immediately on contact with onion juice. This causes a gray color of the onion later, as well as a bad iron taste. The carbon knife itself turns black, becomes very smelly, and has to be cleaned thoroughly before it can be used again. This oxidation factor is very important, if a mechanical tool is used.

Onions are often used to top meats or vegetables as a garnish. French fried or breaded onion rings are popular in steak houses. All that concerns the deep frying of onions has been discussed in units 15 and 18.

### Romaine

Romaine is mostly known as green salad. The outer leaves can also be cleaned and steamed or blanched. When they are chopped, they can be sautéed with onions, butter, some white sauce, and green peas.

### Spinach

Spinach is a green leafy vegetable with a slight mouth-constricting taste. It used to be thought of as highly nutritious for its vitamin and iron content. Newer research shows that this tartness comes from oxalic acid, which is poisonous in pure form or strong concentrations.

Spinach, freshly washed and still wet, can be sautéed in the usual manner. More often it is blanched in larger amounts of water. This reduces the oxalic acid content, but also causes a loss of vitamins. Then it is buttered or creamed. When spinach is creamed with milk, some of the acid is neutralized and the mouth-constricting tartness disappears.

### Squash

Several varieties of both large and small squashes are common. Most popular of the large ones are banana and spaghetti squash. They can be baked or stewed, but need strong seasoning since they are very bland.

**Summer Squash.** Summer squash is attractively small and round. It can be sautéed or stuffed with meat, duxelles or some other filling, and then baked.

**Italian Squash.** Small and young Italian squash is popular under the name of "Zucchini" or "Zuchetti". It is served as a sautéed vegetable. Sauté preparations are made with garlic, onions, tomatoes, and bell peppers. The cabbage a la mode preparations (a la Russe & California) are excellent, also, used for zucchini. Zucchini Souffle Custard is an unusual and practical zucchini dish.

### Tomatoes

Tomatoes are a very soft fruit-vegetable, used for sauces or as a flavor addition to stews. Tomato halves, cut lengthwise and seeds removed, can be grilled, sautéed, baked, or stuffed with another vegetable. Because of their bright color and piquant taste, they are commonly used in cooking. Tomatoes should be considered a garnish rather than a filling vegetable.

**Tomato Concasse.** This tomato stew is used to fill egg omelettes or garnish other dishes, for its color and taste. The ripe tomatoes are dipped into boiling water for 30 seconds, then into ice water. Then they are peeled, halved, de-seeded, and uniformly cubed. When needed, they are quickly sautéed in butter or olive oil on high heat. They should just get hot. If cooked too long, they will turn into sauce. Tomato concasse is seasoned by choice with finely chopped onions, shallots, garlic, or herbs, salt, and sugar.

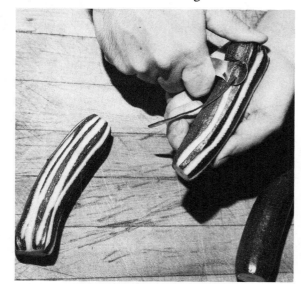

Fig. 26-20 The decorative lemon peeler, (scorer, strip peeler) can be used to make sliced zucchini more attractive.

## CONCLUSIONS

Cooking vegetables is like the cooking of all other foods. Methods are chosen for the same reasons as in meat and fish cookery. Cooking has progressed with tech-

This Italian squash dish is a practical and presentable vegetable creation, well suited as a local specialty. Its true origin is unknown, but it is probably a regional Northern California dish, since all its ingredients are very popular in the San Francisco Bay area.

*Ingredients Needed:*

5 pounds zucchini, approximately
8 large eggs
3/4 cup grated parmesan cheese
1/2 cup bread crumbs
2 cloves garlic, finely chopped

2 tablespoons of dill weed
1 teaspoon of salt
1 ounce of butter (for the baking dish)
3 ounces of olive oil
White pepper, if desired

*Procedure:*

1. Slice squash like potato chips, sauté in oil until half done.
2. Spread on a cookie sheet and cool completely; drain off surplus liquid.
3. Break eggs, add spices and whip them well.
4. When squash has cooled off, add it to the eggs.
5. Add cheese and bread crumbs. Mix well with rubber spatula.
6. Taste for proper seasoning.
7. Fill into buttered crumb-coated and dill-dusted 2-quart Pyrex or similar flat baking dish.
8. Bake at 325°F. for about one hour. Let set another 20 minutes before serving.

This dish can be kept warm for hours if necessary, and if left over could be easily rewarmed without loss of quality.

**TABLE 26-10  ZUCCHINI SOUFFLE CUSTARD**

nology and medical knowledge. Old habits must be put aside for newer cooking methods. Since the objective of cookery is to provide tasty sustenance, the nutritional values of vegetables must be used as much as possible. Better taste is a welcome by-product of the progressive way of cooking. It must also be understood that most preparations are interchangeable, just as in meat cookery. Most vegetables have the same carbohydrate and water content. For example, the preparation of carrots vichy is excellent for parsnips, celeriac, kohlrabi, and white radishes. Cabbage is very versatile and tastes good in any flavor combination, if no overcooking occurs. Nearly all vegetables, except the watery ones like tomatoes and eggplants, can be creamed. Students who understand these principles of the basic similarity of cookery will have no difficulty in creating the most interesting, nutritious, and tasty vegetable combinations.

## SUMMARY

The cooking of vegetables is the same in principle as the cooking of all other foods. For vegetable cookery more than any other cookery, vitamin retention must be the cook's main objective. If nutrients are saved, the taste of vegetables will be better, since minerals and flavor salts in vegetables are identical. Vegetables contain mostly Vitamin C and carotene, which helps the body to convert its own Vitamin A. Vitamin C, being water soluble and affected by the heat, is destroyed easily during the cooking process. Time-controlled pressure steaming, sautéing, and baking are better vegetable preparation methods than boiling in water. All vegetables are tender enough to be prepared in one of the preferred ways.

In English speaking countries, boiling vegetables in water is a popular preparation. Students should realize that vegetable cookery in the USA has a long way to go before the vegetables served to the public in most eating establishments have the standard of quality and nutritional value they should have.

### DISCUSSION TOPICS

1. What should cooks know about vitamins and how to keep them?
2. What are the vegetable cooking methods of different cuisines?
3. Since taste is an accepted habit, should cooks try to influence the taste judgement of the general public?

### SUGGESTED ACTIVITIES

1. Define: vitamin, nutrition, 'al dente', carotene, ascorbic acid.
2. Make Artichoke Antipasto.

3. Cook Asparagus Princess.

4. Prepare Carrots Vichy.

5. Saute Cabbage a la Russe.

6. Make Cauliflower a la Polonaise.

7. Prepare a mushroom duxelles.

## ACHIEVEMENT REVIEW

A. Complete the following:

1. Vegetable cookery and meat cookery are _____ .

2. Retention of nutrients is vegetable cookery's first _____ .

3. Vitamin C is water soluble and therefore affected by _____ .

4. Taste salts react to cooking in a manner that is just like the reaction of _____
_____ .

5. Time-controlled pressure steam-cooking of vegetables is most common in
_____ .

6. For a la carte cooking, one of the best vegetable preparation methods is
_____ .

7. Color retention in cooked vegetables is important but more important is the
retention of _____ .

8. Deep frying of coated raw vegetables is acceptable but it adds to the diet many
_____ .

9. Baking is a good vegetable cooking method but it can not be used for all
_____ .

10. Asparagus is peeled with a _____ .

B. Read each question carefully and completely before answering it. Select the *best*
answer.

1. Sliced carrots, sautéed with butter, salt, and sugar are called

   a. Buttered Carrots          c. Vichy Carrots
   b. Glazed Carrots            d. Creamed Carrots

2. Bavarian Red Cabbage uses all the following ingredients *except*

   a. red wine                  c. green apples
   b. white cabbage             d. yellow onions

3. Tender green peas, fresh or frozen, can be sautéed and need a cooking time of

   a. 2-5 minutes               c. 8-11 minutes
   b. 5-8 minutes               d. 11-14 minutes

4. Onions can be peeled with little eye irritation when the onions are

   a. fresh                     c. cold
   b. old                       d. wet

5. When preparing fresh jumbo asparagus for cooking, it has to be first

   a. blanched                  c. trimmed
   b. peeled                    d. split

6. Tomato Concasse is a

a. tomato sauce                     c. tomato stew
b. tomato salad                     d. tomato dressing

7. Duxelles has, in addition to mushrooms, the following ingredients *except*

a. parsley                          c. tomato paste
b. onions                           d. red wine

8. A la Polonaise is a popular preparation for

a. asparagus                        c. parsnips
b. carrots                          d. mushrooms

9. Cabbage Sauté a la Russe is distinguished by the following ingredients

a. tomato paste and thyme
b. sugar and vinegar
c. sour cream and dill
d. garlic and shallots

10. For clean, table-ready artichokes, it is important that the artichoke

a. has all leaves removed
b. is boiled in lemon water
c. has the hairy inside removed
d. is cooked very soft

# Unit 27  Starches

*OBJECTIVES*

After studying and practicing this unit, the student should be able to

- Explain the need for starches.
- Bake Potatoes a la Pushkin.
- Identify the shapes and names of four "Pasta" varieties.
- Make a Spinach Lasagne.
- Write a detailed recipe for a Cannelloni preparation.
- Cook a Risotto a la Milanese.

In nutritional science, starch is a tasteless, odorless, white substance, classified as a complex carbohydrate. Culinary art uses the term, starch, as a collective name for all foods that contain a large amount of flour. They may be processed foods in the form of paste, noodles, spaghetti or bread, made from wheat starch (flour). They may be the original vegetable, from which starches are extracted. These vegetables are corn, rice, potatoes, beans, cereals and others.

## THE NEED FOR STARCHES

Starches are inexpensive, nourishing, and filling. Man could live by meat and vegetables alone, as he did in early times. Today's man could not afford it. This is why every country of the world has its own starchy staples. All starches are used in every country, but in different amounts. Mexico is well known for its use of beans, Italy for pasta, China for rice, Ireland for potatoes, and Germany for bread. The Western world uses more wheat and potatoes. The Oriental world uses more rice and beans.

## POTATOES: STAPLE OF THE WESTERN WORLD

Potatoes are fruits from a tuber-bearing plant which grows in the dry soil of a cool climate. There are several hundred varieties which differ in shape, skin color and taste. The nutritional value is very high. There is about 70 percent water. The rest is mostly starch, some sugar, minerals and vitamins, including Vitamin C.

Western cuisine uses potatoes from the beginning to the end of a menu. They are found in soups, salads, casseroles, vegetable dishes, desserts and snacks. In many poor areas, potatoes may be the main dish of the day. Deep-fried potatoes are the most popular in the USA. Healthiest, from a dietetic viewpoint, is the baked potato, since all the minerals are preserved. Other nations prefer potatoes fixed in other ways. The Germans, for example, like theirs boiled.

Potatoes are cooked in many different ways. Some of them are simple, but others are fancy. For the croquette potato, much manual skill and experience is needed.

The same preparations often have different names because they come from different countries, perhaps even at different times. In every potato eating country, American fried potatoes are known as home fried potatoes, sauté potatoes, or German fried potatoes. There are almost identical preparations, such as home fried potatoes and hashed browned potatoes. When just one different ingredient is added, the name changes again. Home fried potatoes with onions are called Lyonnaise Potatoes.

A classification of potato preparations:

- Processed before peeling:
  a. in dry heat
  b. in moist heat

- Processed after peeling:
  a. in fat
  b. in moist heat
  c. combined

## Cooking Methods

The same basic cooking principles are used.

*Baked Potatoes.* These are more popular in the USA than in any other country. This is due to the quality of the American Russet potato. Washed and scrubbed potatoes are scored with a fork, to prevent them from exploding in the oven, and baked at 475°F. for 45 to 55 minutes according to size. They will taste excellent for the first 25 minutes after baking. Then they slowly become soggy. A good baked potato has a dry, fluffy texture. Plain baked potatoes are cut and split open before serving, and are eaten with butter or sour cream. Baked Potatoes a la Pushkin (Table 27-1) is a basic preparation for stuffed baked potatoes. Various combinations are possible. All are made by the same principle.

---

*Ingredients Needed for 4:*

5 single No. 1 baking potatoes, 10-12 ounces select          1 cube fresh butter (4 ounces)
Little oil

*Procedure:*

1. Wash and brush potatoes.
2. Pierce a few holes with a two-prong fork into the top of the skin.
3. Oil the potatoes.
4. Bake in a preheated oven at 475°F. for 50 minutes.
5. Select the 4 best looking ones. Cut upper one-third off, lengthwise.
6. Hollow them out with a spoon or melon ball cutter but leave enough potato so shell won't collapse.
7. If 5th one was not needed, peel it, and add it to the scooped-out potato of the four others.
8. Press all the potato through a potato ricer.
9. Brown butter and pour over the riced fluffy potatoes.
10. Mix together very well. Salt if needed and refill the potato shells. Replace cover. Reheat in oven for a few minutes and serve.

---

**TABLE 27-1  BAKED POTATOES A LA PUSHKIN**

*Boiled or Steamed Potatoes.* Raw potatoes are peeled first, then boiled in salt water or steamed. Water-boiled potatoes are more difficult to handle, and steaming of potatoes is the better way of cooking them. Depending on their size, they will need from 5 to 60 minutes cooking time (6-8-ounce whole potatoes will steam in about 45 minutes). They can be served plain or with melted butter, chopped parsley and butter, chives, caraway seeds or in other combinations.

*French Fried Potatoes.* Raw potatoes are cut into sticks and deep fried. They are available pre-fried and frozen. Most establishments today buy them this way, for convenience. The names depend on the shape of the cut potatoes. Americans call them, in addition to french fries, crinkle cuts, long branch, shoe strings, and chips. French terms are Pommes frites, Pommes Pont Neuf, Pommes Allumette, Pommes paille, Pommes chips, Pommes Geofrette, Pommes Parmantier, Pommes Parisienne, and others.

*Home Fried Potatoes.* These are steamed in the skin, peeled while still hot, then cooled and sliced into 1/4-inch discs. When needed, they are sautéed in butter to a golden brown, then served.

*Hashed Browned Potatoes.* The potato is chopped or grated instead of sliced, but made like home fries.

*Hashed Creamed Potatoes.* Cold, boiled, peeled potatoes are grated. They are reboiled in half and half cream with some salt and spices (nutmeg, ginger, pepper), to a very heavy pulp. This is put in a gratinating dish, brushed with butter, and browned under the broiler. This is also the principle of a potato casserole and variations are made by using potatoes in different shapes, mixed with sauces, eggs, cheese, meats, vegetables, and seasoning.

*Mashed Potatoes.* Mashed potatoes can be made from freshly peeled steamed potatoes or from baked and peeled potatoes. In both cases, the cooked dry potato is mashed or pressed through a potato ricer. It is then whipped up with hot milk, butter and salt. Duchess Potatoes (Table 27-2) is a variation of mashed potatoes. Potato croquettes are made like Duchess potatoes, but formed into rolls or balls. They are cooled, breaded and deep fried to the order.

These potatoes are a sophisticated version of mashed potatoes but far more attractive to look at, with a much greater ability to "stay warm". They are made in advance, and can be handled very easily in a short time when needed.

*Ingredients Needed for 6-8 Orders:*

| | |
|---|---|
| 3 pounds baking potatoes | 3 egg yolks |
| 3 ounces butter | Salt, nutmeg, or ginger to taste |

*Procedure:*

1. Clean and bake potatoes as usual (475°F. for 50 minutes).
2. While still hot, peel or scoop them out, then press through a potato ricer or wire mesh sieve.
3. Add butter, yolks, salt and spices. Mix well with wooden spoon or whip.
4. Put mixture into a pastry bag with a No. 5 star tube.
5. Pipe them onto a buttered cookie sheet with a spiral-circular motion into little pyramids. Usually they are about 1 1/2 inches across the bottom and about 1 inch high.
6. They can be refrigerated or frozen until further use.
7. When needed, they are baked at 400°F. for not longer than 10 minutes, or until brown.
8. They taste best when baked fresh and served with sauce or gravy.

**TABLE 27-2  DUCHESS POTATOES**

---

**RAW UNPEELED POTATOES**

| **Dry Heat** | **Moist Heat** | |
|---|---|---|
| *Baked* | *Steamed, Peeled and Cooled* | *Mixed with Cream or Sauces* |
| Baked Plain Potato | Potato Salad, Cold or Warm | Creamed Potatoes |
| Baked Pushkin Potato | *Refried in Pan (Sautéed)* | Creamed Hashed Potatoes |
| Baked Stuffed Potato | Home Fried Potatoes | Gratinated Potatoes |
| Mashed Potatoes | American Fried Potatoes | Potato-cheese Casserole |
| | German Fried Potatoes | Potato-ham Casserole |
| | Hashed Browned Potatoes | Potato-egg Casserole |
| | Lyonnaise Potatoes | |

**RAW PEELED POTATOES**

| **In Fat** | **In Moisture** | **Combination** |
|---|---|---|
| *Sautéed* | *Steamed* | *Stewed* |
| Cottage Fried Potatoes | Plain Steamed Potatoes | New Potatoes |
| Ana Potatoes | Pommes Vapeur | |
| Parisienne Potatoes | Buttered Potatoes | |
| Noisette Potatoes | Parsley Potatoes | |
| Olivette Potatoes | Dill Potatoes | |
| Chateau Potatoes | Mashed Potatoes | |

**Deep Fried**

| | | |
|---|---|---|
| Sticks | Cubes | Discs |
| Fries | Parmentiers | Chips |
| Crinkle Cuts | O'Briens | Pommes Souffle |
| Long Branches | | |

**MASHED POTATOES**

| *With Milk and Butter* | *With Egg Yolk and Butter* | *With Cream Puff and Paste* |
|---|---|---|
| Mashed Potatoes | Duchess Potatoes | Dauphine Potatoes |
| Pommes a la Neige | Croquette Potatoes | (deep-fried, uncoated |
| Puree Potatoes | Croquette Berny (almond coated) | croquettes) |

**TABLE 27-3  CLASSIFICATION OF POTATO PREPARATIONS**

*Conclusion of Potato Cooking Methods.* The boiling of potatoes, peeled or unpeeled, is done best in a pressure steamer. All rules of vegetable cookery apply. When steamed 'in the jacket' (unpeeled), it is easier to peel them while they are still hot. When they cool off with the skin on, the peeling takes much more time and is wasteful. Raw peeled potatoes must be kept in cold water until used so that they will not change color. Potatoes which are going to be sautéed after boiling should be a little undercooked. Every cooking method can be used on potatoes since they are very versatile and adaptable. Steamed and baked potatoes cannot be rewarmed without loss in quality. When left over, they can be pan-fried successfully.

## PASTA

Pasta, from the Italian word Pasta, is the collective name for all kinds of noodles. The most often used ones are: spaghetti, macaroni, vermicelli, shells, and other Italian names for different shapes. All pasta must be boiled in lots of salted water first. After boiling, it may be buttered, mixed with sauces, fish, meats,

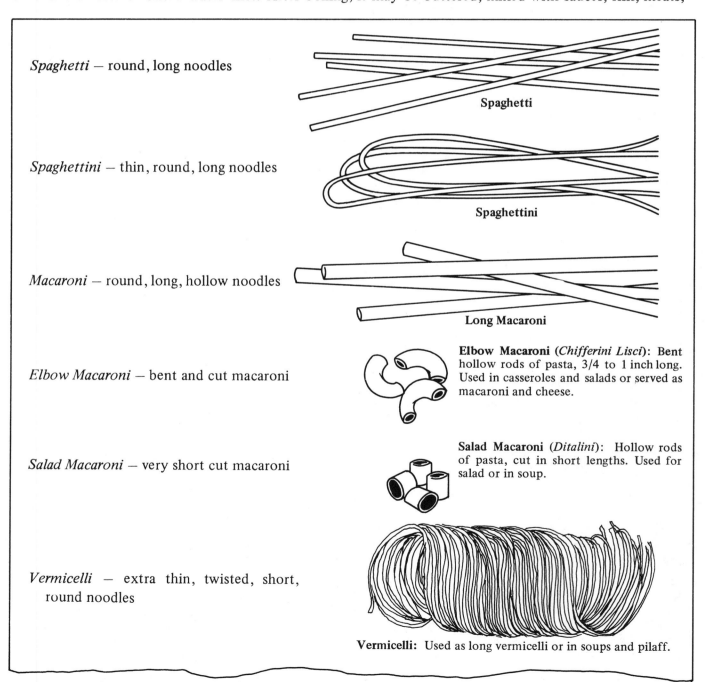

*Spaghetti* — round, long noodles

**Spaghetti**

*Spaghettini* — thin, round, long noodles

**Spaghettini**

*Macaroni* — round, long, hollow noodles

**Long Macaroni**

*Elbow Macaroni* — bent and cut macaroni

**Elbow Macaroni** (*Chifferini Lisci*): Bent hollow rods of pasta, 3/4 to 1 inch long. Used in casseroles and salads or served as macaroni and cheese.

*Salad Macaroni* — very short cut macaroni

**Salad Macaroni** (*Ditalini*): Hollow rods of pasta, cut in short lengths. Used for salad or in soup.

*Vermicelli* — extra thin, twisted, short, round noodles

**Vermicelli:** Used as long vermicelli or in soups and pilaff.

**TABLE 27-4 IDENTIFICATION CHART OF SHAPES AND NAMES OF ITALIAN PASTA**

(continued)

**Small Sea Shells** (*Marruzzelle*): Small, shell shaped pasta. Used in soup or seafood casseroles. Can be used for salads.

*Shells* (large and small) — shell shaped pasta, machine molded

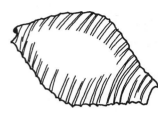

**Large Shells:** Large shell shaped pasta. Served with sauces, usually those containing large pieces of meat and/or vegetables. Can also be stuffed.

*Mostaccioli* — diagonal cut macaroni

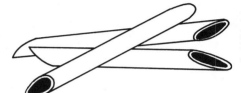

**Mostaccioli:** Hollow rods of pasta, cut diagonally, about 2 inches long. Served with specialty sauces.

*Manicotti* — giant stuffing macaroni, like cannelloni

**Stuff-a-Roni** (*Manicotti*)

*Tagliatelle* — long, flat noodles

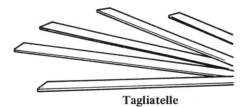

**Tagliatelle**

*Lasagne* — extra wide noodles, rippled at rim

**Lasagne**

*Fettucine* — wide, short, egg noodles

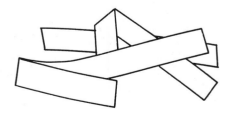

**Fettucine**

**TABLE 27-4  IDENTIFICATION CHART OF SHAPES AND NAMES OF ITALIAN PASTAS**

vegetables, cheeses, cream or others. Italians eat plain pasta as their full meal without meat or meat sauce. They use just butter, olive oil, grated dry cheese, and perhaps a little fresh cream.

The best pasta, made from durum wheat, needs longer cooking time than a cheaper pasta. It will fluff up considerably more, and will keep its crunchy texture for a much longer time, while in the warmer.

Italians are not the only pasta eaters. All of the Western cultures have adopted pasta with great delight.

Pasta eaters are very particular about the softness of their noodles. *Pasta has to be crunchy*

**Fig. 27-1 Colander used for pasta and vegetable straining.**

*(al dente)* to be perfect. Overcooked pasta is one of the worst things to be served. In many of the better Italian restaurants, all pasta is cooked to the order. Customers gladly wait 15 to 20 minutes just to get their orders right.

### Spinach Lasagne

Lasagne noodles, precooked and cooled, are laid in a buttered, square gratinating dish alternately with buttered chopped spinach, grated parmesan cheese and melted butter. Between 3 layers of lasagne noodles, 2 layers of spinach are sandwiched in. The top layer of noodles is covered with slices of Mozarella cheese. This casserole is covered, and baked for 30 minutes at 350°F. Then it is uncovered and finished at 375°F.

---

Spaghetti or similar shaped pastas are supplied in the form of very long noodles. They are not shortened before, nor after boiling. When finally on the dinner plate, they are not cut, but are rolled onto a fork and eaten that way. Short shaped pasta can be cooked in a little less water than the spaghetti shapes.

*Utensils and Materials Needed:*

2 1/2-gallon stockpot          2 pounds spaghetti
Colander                       1 1/2 tablespoons salt
Chef's fork                    6 ounces butter or olive oil
12-inch skillet

*Procedure:*

1. Fill stockpot 3/4 full of water. Add salt and bring to a boil.
2. When water bubbles, push in spaghetti and bend them around the stockpot as soon as they soften.
3. Use the chef's fork to keep them moving while waiting for the reboiling of the water.
4. When reboiling, reduce heat to prevent overflow, and keep stirring to prevent sticking together of pasta.
5. Check the tenderness of the pasta after about 5 minutes, then continue to cook by "inspection".
6. When considered done (al dente), drain through colander.
7. Rinse quickly with cold water to stop the carry-over heat and to wash off loose starch.
8. Shake off excess moisture.
9. Heat the skillet with the butter or olive oil.
10. Sauté the drained spaghetti until well mixed and hot.
11. Serve with any desired sauce.

───────────── **ATTENTION: KEY POINTS** ─────────────

- The manufacturer's suggested cooking time on the pasta package is usually too long. Cook the first lot of a given pasta brand or kind by inspection. Then establish the exact cooking time for repeat cooking.
- Boiling time always varies according to the shape and wheat quality of the product.
- Unbuttered cooked pasta, kept warm in the steamtable, will stick together.
- For economy's sake, it is better to keep pasta and pasta sauce separate in the steamtable until serving.

**TABLE 27-5 THE COOKING OF SPAGHETTI OR SIMILAR PASTA**

for 10 to 15 minutes more. When baked, the lasagne should set at least 15 minutes before it is portion cut and served. It is served with or without tomato sauce underneath.

### Cannelloni

In the true Italian style, cannelloni are made from noodle paste rolled paper thin and cut into 3" x 4" squares. For restaurant cannellonis, the paste square is often replaced with a large pancake (crepe). Mixture for the noodle paste: 3 cups of flour, 4 whole eggs and one yolk, 1/4 teaspoon salt. Knead 10 to 15 minutes until satin smooth, roll out and cut or shape immediately. When dried they can be kept for a few days in a dry place.

The cannelloni are boiled like pasta, carefully drained, cooled, filled, and rolled. The rolls are arranged in a buttered gratinating dish in which the bottom has been covered with about 1/2 inch of spicy tomato sauce. They are laid in rows, one next to the other. Then each cannelloni roll is covered with a slice of mozarella cheese, and baked at 375°F. for 15 to 20 minutes.

The fillings are varied, depending on the regional origin of the dish and the inventiveness of the chef. A good standard filling is 1 lb. chopped, cooked, drained spinach, 1 lb. uncreamed cottage cheese (ricotta), 1/2 cup thick bechamel sauce, 3 egg yolks, 1 cup parmesan cheese, salt, pepper, fried garlic, basil, etc., mixed together. The spinach can be replaced with presautéed zucchini. Various amounts of ground cooked meats can be added. The ricotta cheese always remains in the mixture.

### RICE AND OTHER CEREALS

Rice is the staple for the largest group of people in the world. These are the Orientals, who eat rice three times a day. The rice used in that area is unpolished (brown). Thus, it has not lost its vitamin value. American grown and processed rice has no vitamins, but does not need washing and has a shorter cooking time. All rice should be cooked by the original Chinese principle that all the cooking water should be absorbed. Flavor or remaining nutrients are not lost. Average American long grain rice needs two volume parts of water for each part of rice. Good rice cooking is done only in a casserole with a tight-fitting cover. The casserole should be flat and wide. Rice should not fill the casserole higher than 1 1/2 inches. The rice is never stirred during cooking. As soon as rice and water have come to a strong boil, the heat is reduced and the rice, according to type and quality, is simmered for a given time. When the rice is ready, it should be uncovered and loosened up to let the steam and extra heat escape. This will prevent overcooking.

---

On the menu, it may be called Buttered Rice, Steamed Rice, or White Rice. There are several ways of cooking, but the Chinese way is best. No water is left over, and the rice is never too mushy or still uncooked.

*Materials and Utensils Needed:*

One heavy 5-quart flat casserole with cover     1 teaspoon salt
1 quart long grain rice                         2 quarts boiling water

*Procedure:*

1. Put casserole with rice, salt, and the measured, boiling water on heat. Bring to a fast boil.
2. Stir with fork or ladle once, to mix thoroughly. Reduce heat to simmering.
3. Cover casserole. Simmer for 30 minutes.
4. Turn heat off. Let rest for 10 more minutes.
5. When ready to serve, loosen rice with fork only, to fluff it up without smashing the grain. Keep it warm until used.

**TABLE 27-6 COOKING OF PLAIN WHITE RICE**

### Risotto

Europeans have improved their rice cookery by adding fat and sometimes vegetables. This mixture is called a risotto. For a risotto, a small amount of fat is put into the casserole first. Then finely cut onions or whatever vegetable is giving its name to the risotto are added and sautéed. The rice is added, sautéed a little, then covered with the measured hot liquid (water, soup, or stock). The Chinese process is then used.

*Ingredients Needed:*

2 cups long grain rice
4 1/4 cups chicken or meat bouillon
15-20 Saffron stems (stigmas)
1 large chopped onion

3 ounces butter
1 cup parmesan cheese
1/4 teaspoon salt

*Procedure:*

1. Select a suitable casserole with lid and sauté the onions in the butter.
2. At the same time bring chicken bouillon to a boil. Add the Saffron stigmas and salt.
3. When the onions are translucent, add the rice and heat thoroughly.
4. Pour simmering chicken bouillon over the rice. Bring to a boil. Stir or shake rice for even distribution.
5. Reduce heat to simmering. Place cover on casserole.
6. Move the casserole into an oven about 325°F. Leave it there for 30 minutes. Do not stir rice while in the oven.
7. When it is taken out of the oven, sprinkle parmesan over rice, and stir in with a kitchen fork.
8. Taste, checking for salt and softness. Keep warm until serving.

**TABLE 27-7  RISOTTO MILANESE**

Risottos can be made with meat, fish, or vegetables. Anything added to the raw rice must have the same cooking time as the rice.

Risottos can be made with zucchini, eggplants, green peas, celery, shrimps, prawns, fish fillets cubed, boneless chicken, chicken livers, tender lamb, veal, pork, and beef meat or in any combination of these. Saffron, chili, paprika, turmeric, and cumin are some of the seasonings used.

***Tomato Risotto.*** Tomato Risotto is prepared like a Risotto Milanese with the ingredients changed to: 4 cups rice, 4 cups chopped tomato pulp with juice, 4 cups meat stock, 4 ounces of butter or oil, one teaspoon of salt, and a small onion. The use of parmesan is optional.

***Mushroom Risotto.*** Mushroom Risotto is prepared like a Risotto Milanese with the ingredients changed to: 4 cups rice, 6 cups beef stock, 2 cups diced precooked mushrooms in juice, 4 ounces butter or oil, a teaspoon of salt, and a small onion. The use of parmesan is optional.

***Paella.*** This Spanish national risotto consists of a stew in which the liquid is measured and adapted to the rice quantity. Half an hour before the stew is tender, the raw rice is added. The dish is finished by the same general steps for risotto. Only the ingredients for the stew are unique. This is a mixture of chicken, pork, seafood, saffron, onions, tomatoes, peas and others.

### Cereals

The word cereal comes from the Latin word "Ceres" which was the name of the Roman goddess of agriculture. Cereal includes all edible grains or grasses, but the name is applied mostly to breakfast foods. Cereals are not often served with main dishes. In the USA they are mostly breakfast foods such as oats, farina, cream of wheat, and cornmeal. Some are used as a starch in the ethnic-regional cookery. These include bulgur (cracked wheat), barley, grits, cornmeal grits or mush (Polenta), and buckwheat. The packer's instructions should be followed for cooking.

### SUMMARY

Starches make man's diet less expensive and more filling. Potatoes, flour in the form of paste and bread, rice, beans, and cornmeal are the staples of some ethnic groups and cultures. Potatoes can be adapted to any cooking process. Baking is the healthiest one, but deep frying is the more popular. Potatoes are usually found in some form on a western menu. Paste, or pasta as it is called by the Italians, has been adopted by the rest of the world. Paste is a processed,

**Fig. 27-2  Heavy sauté pan with fitting cover, if needed. Ideal for rice cooking or stewing.**

dehydrated food made from starch and water. It has to be boiled in water to become edible. This is also true for all the other cereals and beans. All dried grains are reconstituted by the addition of water. Great care has to be taken to use only as much water as the grain can absorb. This avoids mushiness or, worse, loss of nutrients. Orientals eat rice plain, just cooked in water. Other groups have improved their rice cookery with risottos and paellas. Today's choice of starch is a wide one for Western man. In the past, people had to be satisfied with those starches they were able to cultivate, due to the climatic conditions of their countries.

## DISCUSSION TOPICS

1. Why are starches the cheapest food source to man?

2. Trace the history of pasta. Where did it come from?

3. Trace the history of potatoes.

4. Why is starch known as the filler?

## SUGGESTED ACTIVITIES

1. Define: risotto, ricotta, cannelloni, paste, paella.

2. Make Duchess Potatoes from baked potatoes.

3. Make Croquette Potatoes from Duchess Potatoes.

4. Prepare Cannelloni.

5. Prepare Potatoes a la Pushkin.

6. Make Zucchini Lasagne instead of Spinach Lasagne.

7. Create a "mixed meat vegetable" risotto.

8. Experiment with baking of potatoes; use two equal-sized potatoes, bake one at 475°F. for 50 minutes, the other at 350°F. for one hour. Compare.

## ACHIEVEMENT REVIEW

A. Complete the following:

1. In science, starch is seen as a complex _____ .

2. In Culinary Art, starch is the same as _____ .

3. Pasta is the collective name for different shaped _____ .

4. Plain rice is cooked best by the methods of the _____ .

5. Europeans have improved rice cookery and call it _____ .

6. Paella is a meat-fish-vegetable risotto, native to _____ .

7. Pasta is best when cooked to the stage of _____ .

8. Spaghetti are always cooked and served _____ .

9. Potatoes are versatile and adapt to all _____ .

10. Restaurant Cannelloni are made not from paste but from _____ .

B. Read each question carefully and completely before answering it. Select the *best* answer.

1. A 10-ounce size baked potato will be fluffy and dry when baked for

   a. 40 minutes at 475°F.          c. 60 minutes at 400°F.
   b. 50 minutes at 475°F.          d. 70 minutes at 325°F.

2.  Baked potatoes can be transformed into all these listed preparations *except*

    a. Chateau Potatoes          c. Pushkin Potatoes
    b. Duchess Potatoes          d. Lyonnaise Potatoes

3.  One pound of raw pasta is cooked best with salt and

    a. 1 quart of boiling water   c. 3 quarts of boiling water
    b. 2 quarts of boiling water  d. 4 quarts of boiling water

4.  When pasta has cooked to the "al dente" stage, it is drained and

    a. rinsed with hot water      c. cooled off in ice water
    b. rinsed with cold water     d. not rinsed off at all

5.  Cannelloni are rolls from thin pasta dough, filled with

    a. ground meat and tomatoes   c. spinach and dry cottage cheese
    b. ground meat and spinach    d. mashed potatoes and parmesan

6.  American grown and processed rice has a cooking time of

    a. 20 minutes                 c. 30 minutes
    b. 25 minutes                 d. 35 minutes

7.  Risotto, which is rice mixed with other foods, is always

    a. spiced with saffron
    b. baked for at least 2 hours
    c. sautéed in fat while still raw
    d. cooked by the Chinese method first, then mixed in with the meats.

8.  Plain mashed potatoes, made from freshly riced baked potatoes, are mixed with

    a. boiling stock              c. warm cream
    b. scalded hot milk           d. browned butter

C.  Match the basic preparations of Column I with the terminology used in Column II.

    *Column I*                    *Column II*

    Baked                         1.  Duchess
    Refried                       2.  Gratinated
    Creamed                       3.  Parsleyed
    Steamed                       4.  Lyonnaise
    Stewed                        5.  Pushkin
    Sauteed                       6.  O'Brien
    Deep Fried                    7.  New Potatoes
    Mashed                        8.  Cottage

D.  Answer in your own words.

    1.  Name and describe 4 kinds of pasta.

    2.  Compare the amounts of water used for pasta and for beans. Why are they so different?

# Unit 28  Various Egg Preparations

*OBJECTIVES*

After studying and practicing this unit, the student should be able to

- Describe the seven basic egg preparations.
- Poach and serve plain poached eggs on toast.
- Explain the combination of Eggs Benedict.
- Make a Parmesan Cheese Omelette.
- Demonstrate the preparation of a Sabayon.
- Prepare plain French pancakes.

There is hardly any other food as verstaile and commonly used as the egg. Western cuisine uses only chicken eggs, but other areas of the world also use some other kinds of bird eggs. Eggs have nourishing proteins. They probably were an important food source to early man.

Eggs are prepared by all the basic cooking methods: moist, dry, and in fat. Each of these methods gives a different characteristic to the cooked egg. Western cookery, as it is practiced today, depends largely on the use of eggs.

## BASIC EGG DISHES

There are seven different ways of cooking eggs by adding only fat. Hundreds of variations have come from these seven basic forms.

*1. Soft boiled eggs.*  Their cooking time is related to egg size or weight. An extra large egg is put in boiling water for 6-7 minutes. A medium large egg will only take 5 minutes. Some people like eggs very soft and ask for three-minute eggs. This applies to medium eggs only. Large ones would still be too raw. Soft boiled eggs are served unpeeled in an egg cup or peeled in a glass. They are eaten plain.

*2. Poached eggs.*  Raw eggs are dropped into simmering vinegar water for two to three minutes. This results in the egg white wrapping itself around the yolk, shaping the egg into a large raindrop. When done, these eggs are rinsed in boiling salt water, drained, and served in various ways.

*3. Scrambled eggs.*  Raw eggs are cooked over a slow fire in butter and a little cream. They are stirred with a whip until they have a creamy consistency. Then they are served plain, over toast, or other ways.

*4. Egg omelette.*  The beaten eggs are cooked on a hot fire with constant stirring and shaking of the pan until they are nearly done. The eggs are folded into the shape of an omelette. Omelettes are served plain or with a filling.

*5. Plain fried eggs.*  The eggs are carefully cracked open, to keep the egg yolk whole. They are put into a hot skillet and cooked slowly until the egg white is completely set and stiff. The eggs are put on a plate and served. Shirred eggs are served in the same heat-proof dish in which they are cooked.

*6. Eggs in casserole.*  One or two eggs are poured into individual little buttered casseroles (pots). These are set in a skillet, filled with 1/4 inch of water and put into a moderate 350°F. oven. They are baked for a few (2-4) minutes until softly cooked. Do not overcook. Yolk has to stay soft.

*7. Deep fried eggs.*  Eggs are dropped individually into deep hot oil (similar to poaching) and the splattering, frying egg white is wrapped around the yolk with the help of a spatula. One egg should be done in one minute. They are degreased on blotting paper, and served with ham, bacon, grilled tomatoes, toast, or tomato sauce.

In the USA, eggs are considered breakfast dishes. Omelettes and poached eggs are also excellent for lunches and light dinners. All egg dishes can be served for brunches and snacks.

## POACHING

Poached egg is a poor name for this preparation. *Poaching* means to simmer, usually fish, half submerged in liquid. The rest of the food cooks in its own steam. But poached eggs have to be simmered in lots of water, with white vinegar in it. A perfect poached egg has the shape of a large drop. It is a soft boiled egg, cooked without shell. The vinegar in the water prevents the egg from dissolving. Poached eggs are served hot on meat, starch, or vegetable, bases, and covered with a sauce. There are also cold poached egg varieties, served in a similar way and covered with a mayonnaise sauce.

For poaching, a high sauce pan or pot of unsalted water is brought to a boil. For each quart of water, 1/2 cup of white vinegar is added. A second pot with simmering salt water is kept nearby. One egg at a time is cracked open and dropped into the simmering vinegar water. A fast cook can easily drop 6-8 eggs into one casserole within 30 seconds. The eggs, depending on their size and desired softness, are steeped in the water from two to three minutes. They are tested by light finger pressure. If done, they are moved from the vinegar water into the salt water. This washes off the sour taste and leaves a salty one. It must be done quickly, since too much time in the hot water will overcook the eggs.

Before serving, they are dried of any cooking water. A paper napkin is held in one hand, while the other hand skims the egg out of the water with a slotted spoon. The spoon is dipped onto the napkin and the egg is dried. For breakfast, these poached eggs are often served on buttered toast. They may be finished in other ways.

For efficient restaurant service, the poached egg, after it is cooked in the vinegar poaching liquid, is completely cooled in salted ice water. It will stay soft and can be kept under refrigeration at least 36 hours for later use. When needed, they are warmed in simmering salt water for one or two minutes, then handled as if they were freshly made.

### Eggs Benedict

Two halves of a toasted English muffin are buttered and covered with a slice of grilled Canadian bacon. A poached egg is placed on each muffin half. Each egg is covered with 2-3 tablespoons of Hollandaise. The top of the Hollandaise is decorated with a truffle slice. Watercress is used for garnish. This dish is ideal for being served under glass.

### Poached Eggs Florentine

A buttered, shirred egg casserole is filled with a serving of buttered chopped spinach. Two hot poached eggs are set on top of it. Four to five tablespoons of Mornay sauce are poured over the eggs and spinach. One tablespoon of parmesan and a teaspoon of melted butter is sprinkled over the sauce, and the dish is browned under the broiler.

### Poached Eggs Halevy

Arrange on a round service platter, a circle of six or eight small chicken hash patties. Top each one with a poached egg. Cover every second egg with heavy white chicken sauce. Cover the other eggs with tomato sauce. Serve one egg of each color per person. Use watercress for garnish. (This dish is only attractive if three or four orders are served together on one platter.)

### Poached Egg Parmentier

A small, well formed baked potato is hollowed out, then filled with ham hash. (Ham hash is chopped ham, onions, parsley, and the scooped-out potato meat.) A poached egg is set on top of it, covered with Sauce Mornay and browned under the broiler.

Many different foods can be used as a base. Fillings can be hashes, fine ragouts, or vegetables, and any cover sauce can be adapted to suit. Creative cooks may make as many different combinations as they have imagination.

## FRENCH EGG OMELETTE

No other dish is as simple in ingredients as the plain omelette. But it needs much skill and experience to be cooked right. Professional cooks and chefs use their omelette-making skill as a measure of achievement and gastronomic sophistication.

A parmesan cheese omelette can be made on the spur of the moment. All ingredients should be in any well organized kitchen.

*Utensils and Ingredients Needed per Order:*

| | |
|---|---|
| One 8-inch commercial restaurant skillet. A regular skillet used for reheating sauces will make omelette stick | 3 extra large eggs |
| | 1 tablespoon clear butter |
| | 3-4 tablespoons of grated parmesan cheese |
| 1 wood or rubber spatula | Parsley for decoration |
| 1 dinner plate | |

*Procedure:*

1. Break eggs into a non-oxidizing bowl and whip well (for parmesan cheese, salt can be omitted).
2. Heat the dry omelette pan to approximately 325°F. Then pour in clear butter.
3. Pour in the whipped eggs.
4. Let them set for a few seconds. Sprinkle cheese into eggs.
5. Loosely shake pan over hot fire with one hand. Use the other hand with the spatula to control the egg movement inside the pan. Shake until omelette appears to set, then stop shaking and stirring.
6. Tap omelette pan on the handle until the eggs tilt into the omelette shape.
7. Reverse hand grip on the handle, and turn omelette onto the prewarmed dinner plate.
8. Decorate with parsley and serve.

**TABLE 28-1 OMELETTE AU PARMESAN**

Omelette-making cannot be learned by only reading about it. The student must see omelette demonstrations and practice it himself. The ingredients are whole, lightly beaten eggs, a dash of salt, and a small bit of butter. An omelette skillet of the right shape is important. Teflon, a modern convenience, can also help.

Key factors are heat, timing, and the whipping of the raw eggs. The actual process is very much like the fast scrambling of eggs. The chef must know when to stop scrambling, and how to do the right flipping of the wrist for the perfect mold.

Omelettes can be served plain, with a variety of fillings, covered with sauce, or with both a filling and a sauce. They are always made to order and must be eaten immediately. Omelettes can be served at any time of the day: breakfast, lunch, dinner, or supper. They may be a full meal, an appetizer, or a snack.

### Common Fillings

These are sometimes stirred into the omelette while in the making. Sometimes they are filled into the nearly cooked one. Sometimes they are poured over the top of an omelette already cooked and turned out on a plate.

A fresh mushroom omelette is carried on the menu of many restaurants and coffee shops. In a high class establishment, omelettes are not often listed on the menu, but it is understood that they can be served any time of the day.

*Utensils and Ingredients Needed per Order:*

| | |
|---|---|
| One 8-inch commercial restaurant skillet. A regular skillet used for reheating sauces will make omelette stick | 1 tablespoon clear butter |
| | 1/4 cup presautéed, sliced mushrooms |
| | 1/4 teaspoon chopped fresh parsley |
| 1 wood or rubber spatula | Salt |
| 1 dinner plate | Pepper |
| 3 extra large eggs | |

*Procedure:*

1. Break eggs into non-oxidizing bowl, add pinch of salt (white pepper optional) and whip well.
2. Heat dry skillet to approximately 325°F., then pour in clear butter.
3. Add the presautéed mushrooms (omit any liquid).
4. Pour in all the whipped eggs.
5. Loosely shake pan over the hot fire with one hand. Use the other hand with the spatula to control egg movement inside the pan. Shake until omelette appears to be set.
6. Tap omelette pan on its handle until the eggs tilt into the omelette shape.
7. Reverse hand grip on the skillet handle and turn omelette onto the prewarmed dinner plate.
8. Decorate with parsley and serve.

**TABLE 28-2 MUSHROOM OMELETTE**

Cheese, ham, bacon, fine herbs, tomatoes, mushrooms, Spanish sauce, spinach, Chicken a la King, Shrimp Newburgh, and others can be used. Some of the fancy, luxury cuisine fillings are asparagus, foie gras, chicken liver, veal or lamb kidneys, calf brains, seafood, and ragouts.

### COOKING OF HARD BOILED EGGS

The boiling of hard cooked eggs is one of the simple procedures anyone can master. The professional cook is concerned about certain facts in regard to hard boiled eggs. First, there must not be any green or blue ring around the yolk. Second, the egg must peel easily, in seconds. A cook with high hourly wages can not waste half an hour to peel two dozen hard boiled eggs. The knowledge and skill of the cook must be used in the best possible way.

*Instructions:*

1. Fill casserole half full with cold water.
2. Place eggs, two by two, carefully into water without cracking shells.
3. Be sure eggs are well covered with cold water.
4. Put lid on casserole. Bring to boil.
5. Turn heat low, to simmer.
6. Cook for 10 to 14 minutes, according to egg size.
7. Drain off all hot water.
8. Add ice cold water immediately, if possible with ice, to shock the hot eggs and cool them fast. This will avoid the green rings around the yolks.
9. Start peeling by hitting egg lightly and rolling it against hard surface to crack the shell.
10. Peel off shell and membrane.
11. Rinse under tap and remove shell particles.
12. Store eggs in salt water under refrigeration until used.
13. If used for chopping or salads, they can be stored without water.

---

### ATTENTION: KEY POINTS

- Select large eggs with thin shells.
- Remove eggs from refrigerator 2-3 hours before cooking. It is important that they have room temperature.
- Always use timer. Twenty percent overcooking will discolor yolk.
- Starting in cold water cooks them faster.
- Proper shocking with cold water makes it easy to peel the eggs.

---

Hard boiled eggs are not served warm. They have their place in the sandwich and salad pantry. Units 29 and 30 discuss further uses of hard boiled eggs.

### EGG CUSTARD

An egg custard is a pudding-like dish made from eggs and milk. Some custards are used salty, as a garnish in consommes and clear soups. Custards are more often served as desserts. They may be plain or flavored, such as caramel or a coffee custard.

#### Egg Sabayon

This must also be considered a custard-like preparation. It is a warm dessert made by cooks to the order. Table 28-4 gives the step-by-step process.

### PLAIN PANCAKES (CREPES) AND SOME USES

This paragraph does not consider the American breakfast pancakes, made from raised dough. The Continental pancake, or crepe (in French), resembles a Mexican tortilla. They have many applications, such as side dishes, garnishes, and snacks. The most popular use is as a dessert.

*Ingredients for Approximately Twelve 6-ounce Custards:*

1 pound caramelized sugar

1 quart milk

8 whole eggs

8 egg yolks

3/4 cup sugar

Dash of salt

Vanilla flavor, optional

Butter for custard molds

*Procedure:*

1. Butter the insides of the custard molds.
2. Pour the caramelized hot sugar into each mold to cover the bottom with a thin layer of caramel.
3. Break all the eggs and the yolks into a non-oxidizing bowl. Whip together lightly.
4. Mix in the salt, vanilla, sugar (3/4 cups) and milk.
5. Fill the prepared molds about 4/5 full.
6. Improvise a double boiler by setting molds into a cake pan and fill the pan with hot water.
7. Bake at 350°F. until custard appears to be set. Test by inserting clean paring knife halfway between center and rim of the mold. If dry, custard is done.
8. Cool. Unmold by cutting edge of custard loose with paring knife, when needed. Pour caramel collected in the mold over the custard.
9. This can be served with whipping cream or different sauces for a fancier appearance.

─────────────── ATTENTION: KEY POINTS ───────────────

- Egg proteins are easily overcooked. At step 7, the test is not made in the center. If the center is cooked, the carry-over heat will overcook the custard.
- The custard-making principle is used to make Bread and Butter Pudding or Diplomate Pudding as well.

**TABLE 28-3 CREME RENVERSE (Unmolded Caramel Custard)**

Sabayon, also known as Zabaione, or Zabaglione, is a frothy, custard-like cream. It is often served hot in a champagne glass. It can also be used as a sauce for a suitable dessert.

It is made with wine as a base, but there are many regional varieties. The custard can be served chilled, even frozen.

*Utensils and Ingredients Needed for Four:*

Copper or stainless steel bowl

Stainless piano wire whisk

Casserole, to improvise a double boiler for the bowl

2 whole eggs

4 egg yolks

2/3 cup dry white wine

3/4 cup granulated sugar

1 teaspoon lemon juice

Lemon zeste

1 ounce brandy or liquor (optional for additional flavor)

*Procedure:*

1. Break eggs and yolks into bowl. Add wine and lemon juice and whip together.
2. Add sugar, lemon zeste.
3. Place on top of casserole half filled with simmering water, (improvised double boiler).
4. Whip vigorously over heat until mixture becomes a thick, frothy, custard. This may take from 5-10 minutes. (The custard temperature, if measured, would be about 130°F.)
5. Take from heat and whip in brandy. Serve immediately, if it is to be used as a hot custard or dessert sauce.
6. If to be used as a cold or frozen custard sauce, put mixture into the bowl of the electric mixer. Whip on medium speed until completely cooled.

**TABLE 28-4 SABAYON**

For the proper pancake batter consistency, the following could be tried:  8 ounces milk, 3 whole eggs, 1/4 teaspoon salt, and 6 ounces flour. Sometimes water is also added. These ingredients are whipped or osterized together without lumps. A suitable skillet is heated. Clear butter is poured in and poured out right away. A small amount of batter, just enough to cover the bottom, is poured into the skillet. The skillet is turned up and down in all directions to make the batter paper thin. The skillet goes back on the heat to bake the first side golden brown. The crepe is turned and baked on the other side for only half the previous time. Then the crepe is ready for further use.

### Stuffed Italian Pancakes

Large, cold pancakes are filled with a mixture of 1/2 Duxelles and 1/2 chopped ham, then rolled like a jelly roll. They are flattened a little to make them oblong when cut, and then put in the cooler for several hours. When completely cold and firm, they are cut into diamond or other shapes, rebreaded in flour, eggs, and bread crumbs. These are deep fried to the order and served with a creamed vegetable, or a hot or cold sauce. They are used as an appetizer, side dish, or main dish.

### Russian Piroshkis

Small pancakes are stuffed with meat hash or fried cabbage, folded like a package, dipped in batter, and deep fried to a crisp brown. They are eaten as snacks or appetizers, without sauce. For batter and deep frying processes, see units 15 and 18.

### SUMMARY

The egg is a versatile popular food, one of the more important ingredients to cooking in general. All by itself, it can be prepared in seven different basic ways which do not resemble each other. Egg dishes can be served at every meal and are ideal as in-between snacks, due to their short cooking time.

Omelettes and poached eggs are some of the more difficult egg preparations. The proper techniques for scrambling eggs just right also result from experience. The handling of hard boiled eggs is important. The quality of a boiled egg and the time used to handle it can be wasted if the proper procedures are not understood. Omelette-making is a skill performance which student cooks should try to perfect.

Eggs are used in batters, for custards and fast desserts such as Sabayon. French pancakes, crepes, have many uses in culinary art, either as a dessert in itself, or as a shell to hold different fillings (example: cannelloni, unit 27). The making of omelettes, poached egg variations, crepes, custards and Sabayon are tasks of the skilled cook and future chef. It is important to do it well.

### DISCUSSION TOPICS

1. What is the theory of omelette-making?

2. Why are egg dishes so popular for Sunday brunch?

3. What are some of the dessert crepes which can be made easily?

4. Why is Sabayon the specialty of Italian restaurants?

### SUGGESTED ACTIVITIES

1. Define: crepe, Sabayon, omelette, shirr, custard.

2. Watch a demonstration of making poached eggs.

3. Watch at least three demonstrations of omelette-making.

4. Watch a demonstration of making creamy scrambled eggs.

5. Watch a demonstration on deep-fried eggs.

6. Practice all the above demonstrations.

### ACHIEVEMENT REVIEW

A. Complete the following:

1. The versatile egg can be prepared by all cooking _____.

2. Egg dishes are not necessarily served for _____.

3. The number of different basic egg dishes is _____.

4. Sloppy egg boiling procedures will result in _____.

5. No other dish is as simple in ingredients but as difficult to execute as the
   _____.

6. In culinary art, a crepe serves very often as a _____.

7. A Sabayon is a different form of a _____.

8. The principle of custard-making is used for many _____.

B.  Read each question carefully and completely before answering it. Select the *best* answer.

1. Medium-sized eggs, to be soft boiled, need to simmer
   a. 3 minutes        c. 5 minutes
   b. 4 minutes        d. 6 minutes

2. Poached eggs are first simmered in water to which
   a. salt has been added        c. lemon juice has been added
   b. vinegar has been added     d. oil has been added

3. Poaching of eggs needs speed and experience. A good cook can poach at once in one casserole
   a. 2 - 4 eggs       c. 6 - 8 eggs
   b. 4 - 6 eggs       d. 8 - 10 eggs

4. The doneness of a poached egg is checked by
   a. thermometer check        c. paring knife insertion
   b. finger touch             d. exact timing

5. Freshly made omelettes can be kept warm for
   a. 1 - 5 minutes       c. 10 - 15 minutes
   b. 5 - 10 minutes      d. 15 - 20 minutes

6. A visible sign of an overcooked hard boiled egg is a
   a. gray shell       c. soft yolk
   b. cracked shell    d. greenish yolk

7. Egg custard is baked best at
   a. 300°F.       c. 400°F.
   b. 350°F.       d. 450°F.

8. Poached eggs "Florentine" are poached egg combinations with
   a. bacon and tomatoes     c. spinach and cheese sauce
   b. ham and hollandaise    d. ham hash and cheese

9. A parmesan omelette can stay true to its name when made with
   a. Fontina        c. Ricotta
   b. Mozzarella     d. Romano

10. Extra large hard boiled eggs should simmer for
    a. 8 minutes      c. 12 minutes
    b. 10 minutes     d. 14 minutes

11. Sabayon is a whisked egg custard with a base of
    a. milk       c. water
    b. wine       d. orange juice

12. Eggs Benedict are topped with a
    a. Bechamel Sauce     c. Hollandaise Sauce
    b. Veloute Sauce      d. Supreme Sauce

# Section 6
# The Salad Pantry

## Unit 29  Cooked Salads, Fruit Salads, and Sandwiches

*OBJECTIVES*

After studying and practicing this unit, the student should be able to

- Prepare potato salad in a professional manner.
- Prepare and arrange plain Waldorf Salad.
- Cut and set up a melon ball cocktail.
- Make a three-decker club sandwich.
- Prepare a garnished steak sandwich.
- Explain the popularity of the Hofbrau Sandwich.

*PANTRY WORK DESCRIPTION*

The preparation of cooked salads is the work of the pantry cook. Cooked salads were first made to use up leftover cooked foods. Professional chefs, who really are food managers, know the pantryman's importance to the guarding of food. Hence, he has the name Garde-manger, as he is called in the French kitchen brigade (review unit 2, Table 2-4, Skill Levels and Ranks). Since the Garde-manger has the skill level of a master chef, the job description for pantry cooks in American restaurants does not include all of the Garde-manger's work. The work outlined in units 29 and 30 is included.

Some pantry cooks cook their own meats, fish and vegetables. Others will get them from the chef or second cook. Garde-mangers will do their own cooking if they feel that special preparation of raw food is the only way to get the desired results for buffet work.

Pantry cooks working lunch shifts are in charge of salads, dressings, and sandwiches. Some hot sandwiches are made by short order cooks, but the garnish comes from the pantry. The pantry cooks in dinner houses set up and prepare all salads for a la carte and dinner service. They also prepare the dressings, appetizers, and hors d'oeuvres.

*COOKED SALADS*

Cooked salads are made from cooked foods, whereas "Tossed Green Salads" are made from raw vegetables with the occasional addition of cooked food. Cooked salads are made of vegetables, seafood or meat. Sometimes they are mixtures of several main ingredients, several flavor additions, and the dressing. Salad combinations are endless and exact group classification is impossible. Nearly all foods which can be eaten warm can be eaten as cold salads.

The protein and starch foods used for salads are boiled, steamed, baked, or roasted. Rarely are they sautéed, deep fried, or stewed. The pantry cook uses his own cold sauce in the form of a mayonnaise or a dressing.

*Combination Salads*

Cooked salads are divided by their ingredients, the way these ingredients are cut or shaped, and their table presentation. Vegetables are cooked whole, so as not to lose their flavor. They must be cooked fresh, then cooled off, cut, and blended with the dressing. Potato salad, if made from potatoes in the refrigerator for a day, will taste like old potato salad. Protein foods are not as sensitive as starch foods. They can be used as long as they are still wholesome. Fresh prepared and mixed salads can be stored under refrigeration for a few days.

*Potato Salad.* Some people think it is easy to make a good potato salad. There are tricks of the trade which are the difference between a good salad and an excellent one. Table 29-1 gives a detailed description of making potato salad and it is suggested that every step be followed.

---

Many varieties of potato salad and methods of making it exist. The best potato salad is made by one basic method. Students should try and taste different methods, then taste, judge, and select what they consider best.

*Materials Needed:*

| | |
|---|---|
| Approximately 5 pounds white or red rose potatoes | Salt |
| 1/4 cup fine chopped parsley | Pepper |
| 1 cup chopped dill pickles | Vinegar or pickle juice |
| 1/2 cup onions | 1 - 1 1/2 cups mayonnaise of heavy texture |
| 2-3 tablespoons prepared mustard | |

*Procedure:*

1. Slice potatoes thin. Put them into bowl. Add the pickles.
2. Osterize onions with 1/4 to 1/2 cup of vinegar or pickle juice.
3. Mix mustard into the osterized onions.
4. Salt, pepper the sliced potatoes. Add parsley and onion pulp.
5. Mix all together carefully and check for the taste.
6. Add mayonnaise in just a sufficient amount gradually. Taste again, and add what may be needed.

─────────────── ATTENTION: KEY POINTS ───────────────

- Potatoes are boiled in the jacket, peeled, and cooled about two hours before mixing.
- All flavors and spices have to be mixed with the potatoes first. After potatoes are coated with mayonnaise, or any oil, they will not absorb the flavoring.
- For salad making, white or red rose potatoes are preferred.
- Since natural grown foods are seldom uniform, and processed foods vary from maker to maker, a recipe can never be handled like a chemical formula. The cook must make allowance for these differences and mix the ingredients with personal judgement.

**TABLE 29-1  POTATO MAYONNAISE SALAD**

---

*Macaroni Salad.* It is an inexpensive, filling salad for Smorgasbords and coffee shop mass production. It is made like potato mayonnaise salad, with short, cooked macaroni or other pasta in the place of the potatoes.

*French Vegetable Salad.* This salad is often used for buffet work. It differs from potato salad by the cut and variety of the vegetables used. The main ingredients are diced, about green pea-size. The vegetable ratio is 3 parts green peas, 3 parts cooked celeriac (root celery), 3 parts carrots, 6 parts potatoes, 2 parts pickles, and 1/2 part finely chopped onions. Mustard, mayonnaise, and extra vinegar are used for the dressing.

*Italian Frascatti Salad.* All of the meats in this mixed salad are cut short julienne: 2 parts ham, 2 parts veal, chicken or turkey, 2 parts well-done beef, 2 parts green peas, 2 parts celery, 2 parts carrots, 2 parts pickles, and 6 parts potatoes. Mayonnaise, catsup, mustard and some basil-vinegar are used for the dressing.

*Tuna Fish Salad.* Table 29-2 gives detailed instructions for making tuna fish salad. The tuna fish could be replaced by cooked salmon or any other coarse, flaked fish.

*Shellfish Salads.* Prawns, shrimps, lobsters, crabs, crayfish, abalones, or even squid can be used in a shellfish salad. The principles of general salad mixing are applied.

*Egg Salad.* This salad from hard boiled eggs is common as a sandwich filling or garnish. How to make it is given in table 29-3.

Tuna fish salad can be used as a sandwich filling or a luncheon meal. It is one of the most popular fish salad dishes in America. In many areas it is the number one Friday lunch special.

*Materials Needed:*

One 60-ounce can chunk tuna fish in light oil
2 cups finely diced celery
3 hard boiled eggs
Chopped onions
1/2 cup pickle chips
Salt

Pepper
Juice of lemon
1-2 cups mayonnaise
Salad bowl
Osterizer
Rubber spatula

*Instructions:*

1. Drain tuna. Save the oil.
2. Chop drained tuna fish, place in salad bowl. Mix with celery.
3. Take 1/2 cup liquid from tuna, pickles, onions, eggs, lemon juice, and osterize.
4. Pour osterized pulp over tuna. Add salt and pepper.
5. Add mayonnaise gradually. Mix well. Taste and finish accordingly.

—— ATTENTION: KEY POINTS ——

- For salad bowls, the tuna can be chopped coarsely.
- For sandwich filling it should be chopped fine or run through the meat grinder using a fine or medium plate.

**TABLE 29-2 TUNA FISH SALAD**

Egg salad is best known as a sandwich filling. It is a basic salad which can be used as part of a salad plate or to stuff tomatoes or other vegetables.

*Materials Needed:*

2 dozen hard boiled, shelled eggs, chopped or grated
2 cups finely chopped celery
1/4 cup finely chopped parsley
1/2 - 1 cup mayonnaise
Salt

Pepper
Tabasco sauce
Dry mustard
Salad bowl
Large rubber spatula

*Procedure:*

1. Place all dry ingredients into salad bowl and mix together.
2. Add mayonnaise gradually. Taste, and finish accordingly.

—— ATTENTION: KEY POINT ——

- Hard cooked cold eggs can be chopped by hand, with the egg slicer, shredded with a coarse grater, or the meat grinder.

**TABLE 29-3 EGG SALAD**

### Combinations with Fruits

Peaches, apples, raw or cooked pineapples, and other hard fruits are sometimes mixed into combination salads.

*Chicken Waldorf Salad.* This is a mild-tasting luncheon salad of cubed chicken meat, celery, green apples, walnuts, and mayonnaise, with only salt used for seasoning. Plain Waldorf Salad is the same mixture without the chicken.

*Fruit Salads.* Fruits can be mixed into many combinations, using raw fruits, compote fruits (canned), or a mixture of both. All of them are served as salads. Different cuts or shapes are used. A melon ball salad (cut with the melon ball cutter) made of different colored melons can be very attractive. These salads are also served as cocktails, such as fruit cocktail, melon ball cocktail, avocado and citrus cocktail, and others. Dry sherry can be used to macerate (marinate) them.

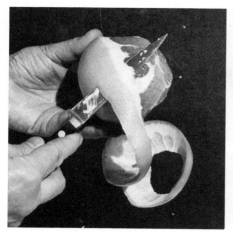

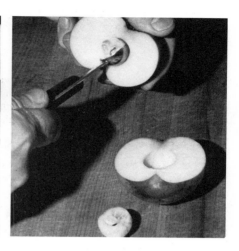

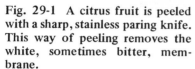

Fig. 29-1 A citrus fruit is peeled with a sharp, stainless paring knife. This way of peeling removes the white, sometimes bitter, membrane.

Fig. 29-2 The peeled citrus fruit is cut in sections, by removing the fruit flesh with the paring knife from the membrane shell.

Fig. 29-3 For fruit salad preparation, the fastest way of removing the core of an apple is by using the stainless potato ball cutter.

Fruit salads are often served with dressing on the side. It could be whipped cream, Mousseline Sauce, mayonnaise with lemon juice, a Honey-Olive oil-Lemon dressing or others. Fruits with cottage cheese are an American creation. They can be served with a good dressing, such as sour cream or whipped cream, or just plain. Fruit salads, like other combination salads, are appetizers, luncheon dishes, or in-between snacks. In the fruit-growing regions of America they are made especially attractive.

## SALAD DISHES AND THEIR GARNISHES

The way salads are presented depends on the style of the establishment. In the USA, lettuce leaves are used to underline nearly every salad or cocktail. This practice is not used all over the world. Parsley, watercress, lemon wedges for seafood, hard boiled eggs, olives, tomatoes, cucumbers, pickles, and pimentos are some of the other garnishes used. For an elegant looking salad, it is important to have the right service dish. Absolutely clean work, a sense of spacing or symmetry, and a sense for color is needed. The more artistic talents a cook has, the better his pantry creations will look. There are many wrong ideas about the use of additional colors. Only colors which appear naturally on edible foods can be used. The exceptions are non-poisonous flowers without any smell. They are used as a food garnish in some unique specialty restaurants. Artificial coloring in culinary art is only used to bring out the natural colors of the food. Pale reds, yellows, browns, and greens are the only colors possible. Blues have no place in food except in blueberries and plums.

## SANDWICHES

The Earl of Sandwich, a well-known horse racing fan and gambler, asked his butler to place a steak between two slices of bread and wrap it up. He took it along to the races to eat for lunch, thus, not missing any action. This, as the story goes, was the birth of the sandwich, named after its inventor.

### Plain or Toasted Sandwiches

Sandwiches serve many purposes, from a snack to a filling meal. They are eaten at any time of the day. They are available in many price ranges. The sandwich is made of two slices of bread with a filling between them. It is cut in halves or quarters, to be eaten with bare fingers. A sandwich was never intended to be eaten with knife and fork and, therefore, should not be served that way.

The composition, the work process, and the presentation of the plain sandwich is explained here for all of these plain or toasted sandwiches.

*Breads.* The bread may be shaped regular, square, round, oval, stub, or as rolls. White, wheat, rye, french, black, and sweet bread are used.

The making of a plain sandwich is as simple as it looks. However, both knowledge and skill are required to own a sandwich shop.

*Materials Needed:*

| | |
|---|---|
| Sandwich station setup | Sandwich bread |
| Cutting board | Spread |
| 10-inch cook's knife | Filling |
| Spatula | |

*Procedure for a Plain Ham Sandwich:*

1. Spread one slice of bread with mayonnaise.
2. Put on it from 1 1/2 - 3 ounces of cooked ham and a trimmed lettuce leaf.
3. Spread second slice of bread as the first one.
4. Put on sandwich, spread side down.
5. Trim all four sides carefully to remove crust, or leave crust as it is.
6. Cut either diagonally or straight into 2 or 4 equal sections.
7. Arrange pleasantly on a plate.
8. Garnish with parsley (minimum).

*Procedure for a Plain Cheese Sandwich:*

1. Spread sliced bread with butter or margarine.
2. Place slices of cheese (1 - 2 1/2 ounces) on it.
3. Spread second slice of bread as first one.
4. Put on sandwich, buttered side down. Trim crust if desired.
5. Cut diagonally into two equal triangles.
6. Arrange neatly on a platter.
7. Add the garnish.
8. Serve.

A plain ham and cheese sandwich is made with two slices bread as above, but ham and cheese (one slice each) are used for a filling. A ham and cheese on rye is the same sandwich as the one described here, but on rye bread.

As soon as a student is able to make one sandwich, he is able to make any sandwich, if the customer specifies what he wants in it.

A toasted sandwich is made like the plain one, but the bread (2-3 days old) is toasted first. Toasted sandwiches are better when spread with soft butter instead of mayonnaise.

**TABLE 29-4 HOW TO MAKE PLAIN OR TOASTED SANDWICHES**

*Spreads.* Butter, margarine, fat, cream cheese, spiced butter, peanut butter, mustard, mayonnaise, and all varieties of spreads are used.

*Fillings.* Cooked meats, cold cuts, cheeses, salad vegetables, meat, fish or combination salads, jams or marmalades, cured, smoked, marinated or canned food specialties, or any suitable combination may be used.

*Working Process.* The four crusts *may* be trimmed off. The sandwich *may* be cut into special forms, such as triangles, squares, rectangles, or strips, but should be small enough to be eaten with one hand.

### Presentation and Garnish

Sandwiches served on plates are usually garnished. The garnish may be lettuce, raw or cooked vegetables, fruits, vegetable combination salads, fresh whole parsley, watercress or mint. Fancy toothpicks, swordpicks, paper frills and other small niceties are often used with colorful and decorative foods to create an appetizing and eye-appealing appearance. Garnishes must be a taste compliment to the sandwich and their eye appeal should improve its sales.

*Toasted Club Sandwiches.* The sandwich called Club or Clubhouse is a generous luncheon dish. When served at its best, it has three slices of buttered toast filled with sliced chicken breast, lettuce and mayonnaise on one layer, and crisp, fried bacon, with tomatoes, on the other. A club sandwich is cut into four triangles which are held together individually by a toothpick through the middle. To keep it warm, it is half wrapped in a prewarmed linen napkin and served on a warmed plate. The food cost of a real club sandwich has gone so high that many average-priced establishments cannot afford to keep them on their menus.

Just like any sandwich, a toasted Three Decker can be made with a variety of fillings on different breads. Fried ham, eggs, onions, avocados, and many meats can be used. The garnishes are often french fries, potato chips, or coleslaw. A garnish should not repeat any ingredient already in the filling.

*Steak Sandwiches.* Steak sandwiches, according to culinary history, are the original sandwiches, and are still very popular. It is logical that the American hamburger started as the poor man's steak sandwich. Steak sandwiches can be made at every quality and price level, depending on the size and cut of meat used. Least

For many years the club (or clubhouse) sandwich has been a specialty preparation of coffee shops or luncheon rooms.

*Materials Needed per Order:*

Sandwich station setup
3 slices white sandwich stub bread, stale
1 lettuce leaf
4 center slices of tomatoes
4 cooked, warm, bacon strips, cut in half
2 ounces sliced chicken or turkey breast
2 tablespoons mayonnaise
Butter for toast

Salt
Pepper
4 toothpicks and olives or 4 frilly canape picks
Boston lettuce
Watercress
Gherkins
Coleslaw or chips as a garnish

*Procedure:*

1. Toast three slices of bread.
2. Butter toast. Lay it on sandwich board.
3. Place sliced chicken on bread.
4. Spread half the mayonnaise on the chicken.
5. Place flattened lettuce leaf on chicken.
6. Put second buttered toast on. Butter toast on second side.
7. Put bacon on top of toast.
8. Put sliced tomatoes on bacon, salt and pepper.
9. Spread remaining mayonnaise on buttered side of third toast. Cover tomatoes, buttered side down.
10. Square sandwich. Press together lightly.
11. Stick picks into sandwich, straight down in the middle of each of the four rims about one and a half fingers away from the outside.
12. Cut diagonally twice, into four triangles.
13. Transfer with the cutting knife used as a lifter or pallet to the serving dish lined with an opened napkin.
14. Finish platter with garnish and serve immediately.

──────────── ATTENTION: KEY POINTS ────────────

- Most important for a sandwich man is his preparation or mis-en-place. If he also knows his menu, keeps calm when the orders are piling in, and pays attention instead of talking, he will be a valuable employee.

**TABLE 29-5  HOW TO MAKE A CLUB SANDWICH**

## STEPS FOR CUTTING AND SETTING UP A THREE DECKER (CLUBHOUSE TYPE) SANDWICH FOR SERVICE

Fig. 29-4  Placing toothpicks or sword picks into the sandwich.

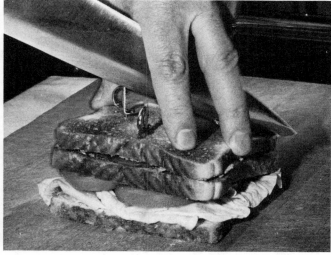

Fig. 29-5  Using all fingers to hold sandwich in place while slicing.

(continued)

Fig. 29-6 Lifting of the first two sections with the chef's knife.

Fig. 29-7 Align with the second two sections to a diamond shape.

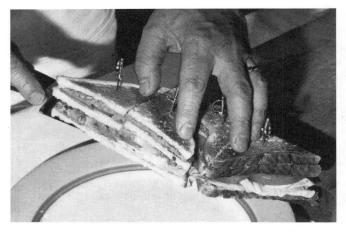

Fig. 29-8 Lift up all four sections with the flat side of the knife blade.

Fig. 29-9 Transfer to the service plate.

expensive is the ground meat patty or hamburger. Next in order are the tenderized rump steak, the cubed steak, the club steak, top sirloin, sirloin, and tenderloin steak. A steak larger than 6 ounces would be difficult to eat in a sandwich. Steaks, like burgers, should be cooked to the order, rare, medium, or well. The finishing of a steak sandwich is the same as any other sandwich.

---

The Steak, or Bookmaker, Sandwich is made in various price ranges, depending on the meat cut and portion size. As a late evening snack it is ideal. It is also a lunch favorite of men who prefer to eat at the bar.

*Materials Needed (for Four Orders):*

4 pieces, 4-5 ounces each, flattened, tenderized steaks
4 French rolls, sour dough
16 medium cherry tomatoes
16 small, sweet sour gherkins
1 bunch cleaned watercress

4 butter lettuce leaves
Mixture of 1 ounce French mustard, 1 ounce soy sauce, 2 ounces catsup, 1/2 ounce dry English mustard, salt and pepper

*Procedure:*

1. Salt and pepper steak.
2. Cook medium rare on broiler or grill.
3. At the same time, split roll.
4. Toast on the inside only (salamander, broiler, etc.).
5. Butter roll.
6. Dip both sides of the medium rare steak into sauce mixture.
7. Place between roll.
8. Cut in half.
9. Transfer to warm dinner plate.
10. Serve with garnish of 4 tomatoes, 4 gherkins and watercress in butter lettuce cup. French fries are usually added.

**TABLE 29-6 HOW TO MAKE A STEAK SANDWICH**

Here is a different steak sandwich. Basically it is made as any other steak sandwich.

*Materials Needed (for Six Orders):*

6 sesame seed hamburger buns
Six 4-ounce cubed steaks
2 cups diced onions
French type prepared mustard
1/2 cup butter or oil

6 tomato halves, seeds removed
12 dill pickle sticks
3/4 cup canned or fresh sauerkraut
1/2 bunch watercress
3 pitted, ripe olives

*Procedure:*

1. Arrange sauerkraut on top of salted and peppered tomato halves; decorate with 1/2 ripe olive.
2. Divide cleaned watercress into 6 bouquets and place on 6 plates large enough to hold the sandwich and garnish.
3. Place stuffed tomato halves over the watercress stems on plate. Garnish with pickle stick and keep refrigerated until needed.
4. Sauté onions to brown. Keep them warm.
5. Dip inside of sesame bun into butter. Place it on hot griddle and toast it.
6. At the same time, salt and pepper steaks. Fry them to desired doneness.
7. Spread mustard on the toasted buns. Place one steak each on bottom part.
8. Divide fried onions on top of steaks.
9. Cover with mustard-spread top bun. Cut sandwich in half.
10. Serve on garnished plate immediately.

**TABLE 29-7  THE SARATOGA**

## THE DELICATESSEN SANDWICH

The word delicatessen is from the German language. It means something fine to eat. A delicatessen shop is a gourmet shop and sandwich restaurant in one. It has gourmet food items for sale. Counter-assembled fine foods may also be eaten here. Some of the delicatessen items used as sandwich fillings, appetizers, or hors d'oeuvres are:

• All cold cuts: Italian salami, cooked salami, German salami, Hungarian salami, Danish salami, Kosher salami, beef salami, summer sausage, liverwurst, met wurst, mortadella, bologna, galantina, head cheese, Parma ham, prosciutto, Westphalian ham, Virginia ham, Bundnerfleish, pastrami, corned beef, smoked tongue, ham, bacon, pork.

• All cheeses, vegetable preserves: all pickled cucumber varieties, mixed pickles, olives, artichokes, melons, kumquats, beans, sauerkraut, chilis, peppers, tomatoes, asparagus.

• All caviar and canned fish: tuna, salmon, oysters, sardines, kippers, matjes, mackerels, anchovies. All marinated fish in barrels or jars, herrings (all varieties: bismarck, rollmops, cream, tomato), eels, smoked fish: salmon, sturgeon, eel, herring, mackerel, cod, oysters, tuna, carp, white fish, and many more.

A large assortment of breads, condiments, and spreads are also found in a delicatessen shop.

Delicatessen sandwiches are made in a delicatessen shop. They may also be sandwiches filled with the food the delicatessen shop specializes in. Delicatessen sandwiches are a little more expensive than those from a coffee shop. They have a better amount and quality of filling than the average sandwich. Delicatessen shops are most often ethnic oriented, serving German, Italian, Jewish, Hungarian, Armenian, Greek or other specialties.

## THE HOFBRAU SANDWICH

Hofbraus are restaurants serving limited food in a distinct way. They are a type of cafeteria with a selected menu. Hofbraus feature huge cuts of meat, such as steamship rounds of beef, baked hams, roast turkeys and corned beef. All these meats are kept warm during the time the hofbrau stays open. The hofbrau carvers stand behind the food on steam table counters. They are ready to make sandwiches as ordered. The customers in front of them choose the meats they like, select the bread and pick up the orders just as in a regular cafeteria.

This service is popular because the customer can see what sandwich he will get. If the ham looks too fat or the beef too rare, he does not need to order it. The fresh cut from the big roast is psychologically appealing, since the quality appeals to the eye and there is no dealing with a middle man or server. The customer can tell the cook directly what he wants to eat.

The hofbrau sandwich in itself is rather simple. It has the fresh cut meat on a split roll or bread of choice, with self-service condiments. Most hofbraus serve their few main dishes with as many side dishes as they can produce. They try to present as large a variety as possible. To cook the food, cooks and a chef work in a kitchen in the back. The carver deals with the customer.

## SUMMARY

The preparation of cooked salads is the work of the skilled cook. Salads came into being as a use for leftovers. The Garde-manger of the French kitchen brigade is an important person for his ability to recycle leftovers without any loss. Pantry cooks are not truly garde-mangers. Those who work luncheon shifts fix only sandwiches, salads, and dressings. Those in a dinnerhouse, where sandwiches are seldom served, handle all salads, appetizers, and hors d'oeuvres.

Salads can be grouped loosely into tossed greens and mixed cooked salads. These are, in principle, quite alike. The dressings are the same. Salad dressings must be seen as cold sauces holding salads together, much like warm sauces holding stew together. Although dressings are creamy and thick, their texture is not based on the starch of hot sauces, but on the mixing of oil and liquid. Pantry work and serving need more artistic expression than plain cooking. Student chefs will do well to learn as much as possible about the guiding principles of pictorial and graphic art.

Sandwich-making becomes a more important skill as the popularity of sandwiches increases. They are served most often as light luncheon dishes. Any food served in a roll or two slices of bread can be called a sandwich. Three deckers are warm combination sandwiches fashioned after the worldwide well-known club sandwich (in some areas called clubhouse sandwich). Americans prefer light snacks such as the poor man's steak sandwich, called the hamburger. Its popularity is making it known to the rest of the world. Delicatessen sandwiches overwhelm by sheer quantity and quality of their fillings. They can be considered the sandwich man's sandwich. Hofbrau sandwiches are simple, but solid and fresh in content. They are made before the watchful eyes of the customer.

## DISCUSSION TOPICS

1. Analyze buffet work. How difficult is it?

2. Match foods for salad combinations.

3. Why do American fruit salads have such wide acceptance?

4. Is there a place for an inexpensive, good sandwich house?

5. What are some of the new steak sandwich variations?

6. How can the coffee shop sandwich image be improved?

## SUGGESTED ACTIVITIES

1. Define: delicatessen, hofbrau, sandwich, salad, garde-manger.

2. Make about 2 1/2 pounds of potato salad.

3. Compute the food needed for 10 pounds of Italian Frascatti Salad.

4. Prepare 2 pounds of Frascatti Salad.

5. Make, serve, and garnish 2 orders of plain Waldorf Salad.

6. Make and set up a melon ball cocktail.

7. Make a three decker with fried eggs, bacon, and tomatoes.

8. Prepare the Saratoga Sandwich step-by-step from the recipe.

9. Visit a hofbrau and watch the carvers perform.

*ACHIEVEMENT REVIEW*

A.   Complete the following:

1.   American fruit salads are often served with _____.

2.   Preparing cooked salads is the work of the _____.

3.   Cooked salads are held together with _____.

4.   Garde-mangers have the skill of a _____.

5.   A salad of apples, celery, walnuts and mayonnaise is called _____.

6.   Club Sandwiches are filled with bacon, tomatoes, lettuce, mayonnaise and _____.

7.   French Vegetable Salad is commonly used for _____.

8.   Salad vegetables are cooked whole, in order not to lose _____.

9.   Cooked, peeled potatoes left refrigerated too long make potato salad taste _____.

B.   Read each question carefully and completely before answering it. Select the *best* answer.

1.   Potato salad will be at its best when the potatoes are cooked

   a. the day before               c. about 3 hours before mixing
   b. without peel                 d. after having been peeled and cut

2.   When cooked potatoes are mixed into the salad, it is important to add the mayonnaise

   a. in one lot                   c. before the seasoning
   b. mixed with the seasoning     d. after the seasoning

3.   Salad and sandwich garnishes are intended to

   a. make the order appear larger   c. repeat and show the filling
   b. supplement taste and boost sales  d. justify a higher price

4.   Sandwiches, when ordered toasted, should be spread with

   a. butter                       c. peanut butter
   b. mayonnaise                   d. cream cheese

5.   According to culinary history, the first sandwich made was

   a. the Club Sandwich            c. the Steak Sandwich
   b. the Hofbrau Sandwich         d. the Hamburger

6.   Italian Frascatti Salad has the ingredients cut into

   a. small dice                   c. short julienne
   b. large cubes                  d. thin slices

7.   A Chicken Waldorf Salad is dressed with

   a. French dressing              c. Waldorf dressing
   b. sour cream                   d. mayonnaise

8.   Tuna fish, for large quantities of salad, should be chopped with the

   a. meat grinder                 c. osterizer
   b. chef's knife                 d. fish knife

9. Fruit salads served as a luncheon dish are popular with

   a. sugar and lemon juice
   b. french dressing and whipped cream
   c. cottage cheese and sour cream
   d. bourbon and Mousseline dressing

10. Delicatessen stores are likely to make more interesting sandwiches than coffee shops because they

   a. employ garde-mangers to make sandwiches
   b. have a larger assortment of fillings
   c. use a special spread on the bread
   d. take more time to make them

# Unit 30 Green Salads and Salad Dressings

*OBJECTIVES*

After studying and practicing this unit, the student should be able to

- Mix a basic French dressing.
- Make mayonnaise with the electric mixer.
- Prepare and toss Romaine with Roquefort dressing.
- Make a commercial onion dressing.
- Set up a Green Goddess salad.
- Explain in detail the mixing of a Caesar Salad.

Some of the finest, most luscious and sophisticated salads are served in America. They are very popular on the West coast, in the warmer regions, and in the large, metropolitan areas. Salads are served as first courses, side dishes to meat, full meals, or snacks. The reasons for this popularity are the right climate, the right ingredients, and promotion.

*HOW TO SERVE SALADS*

Most luxury restaurants promote the serving of green salads through elaborate and elegant salad carts, salad bars, or other serving setups. They also employ trained personnel to serve the salads in style.

Ingredients of salads and the serving plates and implements should be ice cold when presented. Salads must be served immediately after the greens have been tossed. All salad mixing should be done in front of the patrons. Salads must look fresh, fluffy, clean, appetizing, tempting, and dainty. The tossing must be made into a performance of skill and showmanship. The salad server (tosser) should know that good salads are never too oily, too sour, or over-spiced. He also knows that a full platter filled over the rim is never served. Salad ingredients must match in flavor. The next course of the meal must also be considered. In France and other wine-drinking countries, salads are served after the main course. This does not interfere with the wines served at the meal. Salads and wines do not match and, in general, are not served together.

---

*Vegetable and Protein Ingredients for Salad Compositions*

*Lettuce:* Romaine, Iceberg, Chicory, Escarole, Endive (Belgian and domestic), Limestone, Boston, Butter, Chinese Cabbage, and many regional varieties. The choice depends on the season and growing area.

*Vegetables, Raw:* tomatoes, avocadoes, cucumbers, celery, radishes, cabbage, mushrooms, bell peppers, chilis, onions, scallions, zucchini.

*Vegetables, Cooked:* artichokes, beets, bamboo, palm hearts, water chestnuts.

*Proteins:* shrimp, crab, lobster, seafood, eggs, ham, beef, chicken, cheese.

*Herbs:* parsley, chive, dill, cilantro, watercress, sorrel, tarragon, basil, rosemary, garlic, shallots, and others.

---

*SALAD DRESSINGS*

The most important part of the salad, for flavor, is the dressing. Most lettuce is eaten for its texture, crunchiness, and vitamin content. A salad dressing is a cold sauce which helps to digest the raw vegetables, and adds taste to the salad. Human beings can live on raw meat, but not on raw unprocessed vegetables or grains. Raw salads without oil are hard to digest. Oil by itself is not too tasty, because of its richness.

A mixture of oil, acid (to make the oil more palatable), and spices was created to be used as a salad dressing.

### Basic Salad Dressings

Dressings are a blended mixture of fat, acid, liquid, herbs, and spices. They are divided into three basic groups: 1) Oil and Vinegar Emulsion, 2) Mayonnaise, and 3) Sour Cream. These bases, as in sauce cookery, reflect the culinary taste of the chef. Catsup, mustard, avocado or any other vegetable pulp, hard-boiled eggs, cheeses, anchovies, capers, onions, garlic, peppers, olives, pickles, and pimentos are some of the ingredients the chef may add.

Two chefs rarely make the same dressing, even when using the same names. For instance, Roquefort, or Blue Cheese dressing, is accepted in many different variations. The true French Roquefort dressing has four parts: Roquefort, 1 part fresh cream, and six to eight parts plain French dressing. It should be mixed fresh on the table whenever it is ordered. Other variations use blue cheese for the roquefort, with sour cream as a base. This allows greater dilution of the cheese. The name Roquefort or Roquefort Dressing is a trademark. It can be used only if true French imported Roquefort cheese is served or used.

Some dressings with a specific name, like Roqefort, Russian or Thousand Islands, can be served over any salad. Others, such as Green Goddess or Caesar dressing, should be served over a specific kind or lettuce only. Garlic is optional, but if used in a subtle way, enhances the flavor and digestibility of every salad.

Due to dressings, salad combinations are practically endless. They truly show the cook's sense of beauty and taste.

*French Dressing.* The oil and vinegar emulsion is called French dressing. It is made by mixing two or three parts oil with one part vinegar. Salt, pepper, and sometimes mustard are added. The mixing is done in a salad bowl or a bar shaker. The use of a blender gives a better result. French dressing will separate after some time. It has to be made fresh, or at least reblended, whenever it is needed. If more spices or other ingredients are added, the basic French dressing is changed to a dressing of another name.

*Mayonnaise.* Mayonnaise is a creamy mixture of egg yolks, oil, acid, liquid and spice. The egg yolk acts as emulsifier to the process of whipping with a wire whisk. The yolks, while whipped vigorously, absorb the

---

*Equipment and Materials Needed:*

| | |
|---|---|
| Electric mixer | 3 cups salad oil |
| Stainless bowl and utensils | 3-4 tablespoons vinegar |
| 5 egg yolks | Salt |
| 1 tablespoon prepared mustard | White pepper |

*Procedure:*

1. Clean bowl with a towel.
2. Separate yolks into the bowl.
3. Add the mustard.
4. Start mixer on low, then switch to high speed.
5. Add very thin flow of oil. Watch emulsion occuring. Stop after one cup of oil is used.
6. Reduce to slow speed. Add half the vinegar.
7. Continue on high speed. Add the remaining oil.
8. Slow mixer again. Add salt, pepper, and remaining vinegar.
9. Mix all and taste. Remove mayonnaise to storage container and store in a 45° - 60°F. area.

### ATTENTION: KEY POINTS

- Mayonnaise, like the Hollandaise discussed in a previous unit, is sensitive to metal oxidation. Only stainless, non-oxidizing utensils must be used.
- Be sure that all ingredients are at room temperature (65°F.-75°F.) before mayonnaise is started.
- Keep mixer in clean condition.
- Stop mixer before tasting.
- Separate yolks and egg whites neatly. Too much egg white will change the consistency of the finished mayonnaise.

**TABLE 30-1 HOW TO MAKE BASIC MAYONNAISE**

oil in very small amounts at a time. All the ingredients used must be in a temperature range of 65°F. to 75°F. If they are colder than that, emulsion will not take place and the mixture will curdle. The same will happen if the oil is added too rapidly. Mayonnaise may also be made in a blender. For real commercial amounts a centrifuge is used.

*Cold Sauces or Dressings Based on Mayonnaise.* Mayonnaise, the base for salad dressings and cold sauces, is also a sandwich spread. It has been known since the beginning of the 18th century in Bayonne, France. Like hot sauces, cold sauces start from a base. Fruit purees are one base, and mayonnaise is the other. The only difference between a mayonnaise sauce and a mayonnaise dressing is the consistency. The sauce or spread is kept at a stiffer or heavier consistency. Sauces can be used as dressings. Dressings can be used as sauces.

Combinations based on mayonnaise are endless and it is left to the cook to blend what he considers best. To start with a better understanding of what is accepted, some of the more popular combinations are listed in table 30-2. Measurements are not given, since neither the consistency of the mayonnaise nor the strength and taste of the condiments are standardized. All the garnish ingredients must either be chopped, osterized, or cut very small. The basic mayonnaise (table 30-1) is used. As a guide to amounts, it is suggested that for Tartar Sauce, 2 cups of freshly made mayonnaise are diluted with 2 tablespoons of mustard, 1 tablespoon of chopped capers, and 3 tablespoons each of finely chopped dill pickles, raw onions, and parsley. Salt, additional lemon juice, or vinegar are added to taste.

These dressings are commonly used for dinner salads, included on the dinner, and served from the pantry instead of the salad cart. These dressings are also available from commercial sources. The skilled cook will always find that he is able to make dressings not only with a personal touch but also of a better quality at a cheaper price.

## SPECIALTY SALADS TOSSED AT THE TABLE

Specialty salads tossed at the table are served for two, and are a la carte dishes. They are comparatively expensive. Sometimes the emphasis is on the quality of the lettuce, at other times the emphasis is on the preparation of the dressing. Belgian Endive or Limestone Lettuce are very delicate and expensive salad greens which are themselves the attraction. These should be served with a mild plain dressing, based on quality ingredients only. The dressing must be mixed at the table. The olive oil, vinegar, mustard, etc. should be in the original containers so that there is no doubt about quality.

---

*Sauce Verte* – cooked spinach, parsley, and chives are osterized with lemon juice and worcester sauce, and mixed with mayonnaise.

*Sauce Remoulade* – parsley, chives, capers, pickles, anchovies, and mayonnaise.

*Sauce Tyrolienne* – remoulade sauce, mixed with catsup.

*Sauce Andalouse* – catsup, chopped bell peppers, and mayonnaise.

*Sauce Verdi* – sour cream, pickles, chives, and mayonnaise.

*Sauce Mousseline* – whipped cream and mayonnaise, in equal parts.

*Sauce Suedoise* – reduced apple sauce, horseradish, lemon juice, and mayonnaise.

*Sauce Ravigotte* – cooked egg whites, anchovies, shallots, parsley, and mayonnaise.

*Sauce Aurore* – reduced tomato chutney, lemon juice, and mayonnaise.

*Sauce Indienne* – apple sauce, sour cream, curry, and mayonnaise.

*Thousand Island Dressing* – pimento, bell pepper, chili, catsup, French dressing, and mayonnaise.

*Indienne Dressing* – mayonnaise, sour cream, curry, mango, chutney, sugar, and lemon.

*Chiffonade Dressing* – French dressing, chopped herbs, and beets.

*Russian Dressing* – tartar sauce with catsup and caviar.

*Roquefort Dressing* – Roquefort cheese, cream, and French dressing.

*Blue Cheese Dressing* – blue cheese, sour cream, and mayonnaise.

*Avocado Dressing* – French dressing, avocado pulp, and lemon.

*Onion Dressing* – French dressing, raw onion pulp, parsley, sugar, and pepper.

*Mustard Dressing* – French mustard, mayonnaise, sour cream, dry mustard, and pepper.

**TABLE 30-2 COMBINATION DRESSINGS**

Less expensive combinations on the menu are Romaine, Boston, or Butter Lettuce, and Tossed Greens. A soft salad like butter lettuce must have a light dressing. If it were to be mixed with mayonnaise, the dish would become a gluey, unappetizing dish. Many times a restaurant lists two or three lettuce combinations and then offers a choice of dressings. Following are some of the more elaborate combinations which are well known.

### Green Goddess

A California salad specialty, this was first made at the Palace Hotel in San Francisco. Many years ago, a famous actor stayed at this well-known hotel while playing the title role in *Green Goddess,* which was a hit play. He loved salads, so the chef created this one for him and culinary history was made.

### Salad Maximilian

This is a combination of bay shrimps, sour cream-avocado dressing, and artichokes. For banquet service a salad like this could be set up in advance by filling the bay shrimps into artichokes, with the dressing as a cover.

### Caesar Salad

This very popular salad has to be made very mild so that the anchovies, garlic, and parmesan do not destroy the taste sensitivity of the palate for the rest of the meal.

### Tomato and Watercress

This salad is made without lettuce. For an appetizer, this is not unusual. Other preparations can also be made this way.

No matter where salads are set up, if in the pantry or tossed at the table and finished by the headwaiter, the chef bears the responsibility for the initial and partial preparation. If the chef fails to keep the salad pantry on a high quality level, the best headwaiter will not be able to make a worthy salad.

### SUMMARY

The American public is well aware of the importance of salads as a part of their diets. Many salad ingredients, the right climate and excellent promotion have made salads important in restaurants. They are often presented in elaborate settings.

---

Green Goddess is a favorite for ladies' luncheons and it can be made with different seafoods or cooked chicken.

*Materials Needed:*

| | |
|---|---|
| 1 head of Romaine, cleaned, washed, drained, cut to 2-3-inch lengths | 1 tablespoon finely chopped anchovies in oil |
| 1 avocado, ripe, peeled, and sliced | 1/2 lemon, juiced |
| 6 ounces Alaska King Crab, shrimp, lobster, or similar cooked, cold shellfish | 5-6 tablespoons sour cream |
| | 5-6 tablespoons mayonnaise |
| *For Dressing:* | Additional olive oil and wine vinegar, if needed |
| 1 tablespoon grated onion | Salt |
| | Pepper |

*Procedure:*

1. Have all dressing ingredients arranged in large bowl. Mix well.
2. Add all romaine, avocado, and shellfish.
3. Salt and toss lightly. Taste.
4. If necessary, add more of the ingredients to achieve desired taste, and toss again. Serve.

──────── ATTENTION: KEY POINTS ────────

- All rules for salad in general have to be observed.
- Watercress should be used to garnish the table-ready plate.
- Two tomato wedges can be used to add color to the plate.
- Freshly ground pepper is added last.

**TABLE 30-3 GREEN GODDESS SALAD WITH SHELLFISH**

This salad, although one of the finest and true California creations, is relatively unknown. Many similar or slightly varied salads are served under different names all over California. It may be used as a dinner appetizer or a summer lunch with French bread.

*Materials Needed for 2-3 Orders:*

1 head Romaine
4 sliced, cooked artichoke bottoms
1/2 bunch watercress
6 ounces cooked, tiny Bay shrimps

*Dressing:*

1/4 avocado
1 lemon

2 ounces buttermilk
2 ounces sour cream
Dash of dill
Salt
Pepper
1 teaspoon chopped onion

*Procedure:*

1. Blend avocado with buttermilk, onion, and half the lemon juice.
2. Put in sour cream, and season to taste with the remaining ingredients.
3. Adjust consistency by adding or diluting.
4. Have all salad ingredients except watercress properly cut up in a large salad bowl.
5. Pour enough dressing on, but not too much. Toss slightly.
6. Taste, and add what is necessary.
7. Put on dinner plate or large salad plate.
8. Garnish with watercress, sprinkle a little dill on top. Use pepper mill.
9. Serve immediately.

**TABLE 30-4 SALAD MAXIMILIAN**

This salad comes from Southern California and was created by a headwaiter named Caesar. It may be served as a luncheon to some people or a dinner appetizer to others.

*Materials Needed Per Order for 2:*

2 measured portions of clean, cut-up Romaine
4 tablespoons grated parmesan cheese
Juice of 1/2 lemon
1 large coddled egg (blanched in boiling water
    for one minute)
1/3 cup garlic croutons

2-3 mashed-up anchovies
Watercress and two tomato wedges for decoration
1 tablespoon red wine vinegar
4 tablespoons olive oil
Salt
Freshly ground pepper

*Procedure:*

1. Observe all rules in regard to salad preparation.
2. Place salad in mixing bowl.
3. Add remaining ingredients except pepper, tomato, and watercress in any order.
4. Toss lightly and taste.
5. Finish. Put on plate. Add garnish and pepper. Serve immediately.

**TABLE 30-5 CAESAR SALAD**

This salad is made and served without any kind of lettuce, but is still considered a salad. It is eaten as an appetizer before dinner and can be served like cold artichokes, hearts of palms, or asparagus. Tossing is not absolutely essential. The tomatoes should be sliced and arranged with the watercress on a plate, and the marinade or dressing spooned or basted over this layout. This is very convenient for party service on individual plates.

*Materials Needed:*

| | |
|---|---|
| 2 medium tomatoes | Tarragon |
| 1/2 bunch watercress | Garlic |
| Red wine vinegar | Salt |
| Olive oil | Pepper |

*Procedure:*

1. Peel and wedge tomatoes. Clean watercress. Place into salad bowl.
2. Add salt and pepper, a dash of tarragon, garlic, about one tablespoon vinegar, and 2-3 tablespoons oil.
3. Toss quickly, taste, and serve.

─────── ATTENTION: KEY POINT ───────

- This is not a bulky salad or appetizer and can be served on a small plate or glass dish.

**TABLE 30-6 TOMATO AND WATERCRESS SALAD**

Salads have low food cost, but need skilled labor for their presentation. The variety of salad combinations makes them fit to serve at every occasion. Lettuce and vegetables used in preparations are important, but more so is the dressing. Salad dressings are cold sauces based on oil or fat as the thickener. The oil is needed to make salads easier to digest. The acid and seasoning of the dressing enhances the blandness of the greens and the richness of the oil. A plain oil and vinegar emulsion is called French dressing. It serves as a base for many dressing variations. Mayonnaise and sour cream are the other two bases for cold and salad sauces.

Salads for dinner are generally prepared in the pantry, but specialty salads are a la carte orders tossed at the table, the salad cart, or the salad bar. Although mayonnaise and mayonnaise dressings are available on a commercial basis, every skilled cook must know how to make them. Making his own dressing provides the chef's personal touch to his cookery. It also has a better food cost. The public sometimes expects the chef to toss a salad at the table for his favorite guests. The young cook will do well to practice salad making in the dining room.

### *DISCUSSION TOPICS*

1. Do salads reflect a restaurant's "Gourmet" image?

2. How do food cost and quality of dressings compare with convenience?

3. Is there a difference between Roquefort and Blue Cheese?

4. What equipment is necessary for salad promotion?

### *SUGGESTED ACTIVITIES*

1. Define: appetizing, emulsion, oxidation, wedge, mousseline.

2. Review Table 13-2, Cleaning of Romaine Lettuce.

3. Identify different kinds of lettuce.

4. Make a plain French dressing with whip and bowl.

5. Make onion dressing with the blender.

6. Make mayonnaise with the mixer.

7. Prepare romaine with Roquefort dressing.

8. Set up for a Green Goddess Salad.

*ACHIEVEMENT REVIEW*

A.  Complete the following:

1.  Salads and salad utensils must be visibly _____ .

2.  Salads are tossed just before serving in order to assure _____ .

3.  Good salad dressings should always be _____ .

4.  Belgian Endive is a salad which is very _____ .

5.  For Boston or Butter Lettuce the dressing must be _____ .

6.  Without dressing, lettuce is not _____ .

7.  Homemade French dressings, after standing a while, have to be _____ .

8.  Mayonnaise is not only a sauce-dressing, but also a _____ .

9.  Specialty salad portions are usually for _____ .

B.  Read each question carefully and completely before answering it. Select the *best* answer.

1.  Mayonnaise, a cold, basic sauce contains mostly

   a. vinegar                    c. oil
   b. cornstarch                 d. egg yolks

2.  A mayonnaise is an emulsion where the egg yolks absorb oil

   a. unlimited                  c. rapidly
   b. gradually                  d. not at all

3.  Salad dressings may be composed of many different ingredients, but must always contain

   a. fats                       c. proteins
   b. starch                     d. sugar

4.  The lettuce base of the Green Goddess Salad is

   a. Iceberg                    c. Endive
   b. Butter Lettuce             d. Romaine

5.  For plain French dressing, the oil to vinegar ratio is

   a. 1 part oil to 3 parts vinegar     c. 3 parts oil to 1 part vinegar
   b. 2 parts oil to 2 parts vinegar    d. 8 parts oil to 1 part vinegar

6.  The dressing of the Salad Maximilian has a base of

   a. sour cream                 c. olive oil
   b. mayonnaise                 d. salad oil

7.  For the Tomato Watercress Salad, a la carte, the tomatoes should be

   a. large                      c. peeled
   b. soft                       d. marinated

8.  A good Roquefort cheese dressing can be made with

   a. Roquefort and buttermilk          c. Blue Cheese and sour cream
   b. Roquefort and French dressing     d. Blue Cheese and mayonnaise

9.  For making mayonnaise by hand, it is essential to have a

   a. hand beater                c. wooden fork
   b. stainless whip             d. rubber spatula

10. The French people, like the Americans, are great salad eaters. The French serve salads

    a. as the appetizer
    b. after the soup
    c. with the main course
    d. after the main course

C. Match the name of the preparation in Column I with the ingredients listed in Column II.

| *Column I* | *Column II* |
|---|---|
| Sauce Tartare | 1. Mayonnaise, catsup, bell pepper, pimentos, chilis |
| Sauce Remoulade | 2. Oil, vinegar, cream, roquefort |
| Sauce Suedoise | 3. Oil, vinegar, herbs, beets |
| Sauce Aurore | 4. Mayonnaise, capers, pickles, mustard, onions, parsley |
| Sauce Ravigotte | 5. Mayonnaise, parsley, chives, capers, pickles, anchovies |
| Chiffonade Dressing | 6. Mayonnaise, tomato chutney, lemon |
| Russian Dressing | 7. Mayonnaise, apple sauce, horseradish, lemon |
| Roquefort Dressing | 8. Mayonnaise, sour cream, dry and prepared mustards, pepper |
| Thousand Island Dressing | 9. Mayonnaise, egg whites, anchovies, shallots, parsley |
| Mustard Dressing | 10. Mayonnaise, capers, mustard, pickles, onions, parsley, catsup, caviar |

# Glossary

| | |
|---|---|
| *a la* | In the manner of |
| *a la carte* | Single, fresh made food order; not included in dinner |
| *a la mode* | In a modern way |
| *Agar-Agar* | Seaweed gelatin |
| *Albacore* | White tuna |
| *Allumettes* | French Fries thin as matches; regular matches |
| *Antipasto* | Appetizer; marinated vegetables in tomatoes, Italian |
| *Aspic* | Meat jelly, used in buffet work |
| *au gratin* | Gratinated, browned under broiler or Salamander |
| *au jus* | With natural pan gravy |
| *Bain-Marie* | Wet steam table; steam table |
| *Bar-le-duc* | Large, seedless currants |
| *Barbecue* | Meat cooked over open fire |
| *Bayonne Ham* | French raw ham, like prosciutto, or Westphalian ham |
| *Bechamel* | White cream sauce made with milk |
| *Bellevue* | Well decorated (beautiful to look at) |
| *Bien Cuit* | Medium well-done |
| *Bigarad* | Bitter oranges |
| *Bisque* | Shellfish soup made with rice puree |
| *Bistro* | Small bar or tavern |
| *Blanche, to* | To submerge under boiling water for a short time |
| *Bloater* | Smoked herring |
| *Boil* | Cooking of foods in liquids; simmer; steam |
| *Bordure* | A border of mashed potatoes on a service platter |
| *Bouquet garni* | Herbs in a bunch, for seasoning of soups, sauces |
| *Braise* | To cook slowly in fat, with a little added moisture |
| *Brigade* | Crew of chefs, cooks, bakers, butchers and helpers who work under the executive chef |
| *Brochettes* | Skewers, food cooked and served on skewers |
| *Broil* | To cook by the radiation of the open fire |
| *Broth* | By-product of foods which have been simmered in liquids |
| *Buffet* | Food counter, table with cold foods on display |
| *Buffetier* | Buffet Carver Cook |
| *By-product* | Something produced in addition to the principal product |
| *Camembert* | Fermented soft French cheese |
| *Canapes* | Small, fancy, open-faced sandwiches |
| *Cannelloni* | Wide, short, Italian noodles for stuffing |
| *Capers* | Buds from the caper bush, marinated |
| *Caramelize* | Change color to brown |
| *Carbohydrates* | Compounds of carbon, hydrogen, and oxygen (as sugars, starches and cellulose) |

| | |
|---|---|
| *Carbonize* | Burn |
| *Cassoulet* | French term for a dish like baked beans, but made with lamb, goose, or pork |
| *Caviar* | Salted sturgeon roe |
| *Cayenne* | Very hot red pepper |
| *Cellulose* | Fibers of plant food |
| *Chablis* | White Burgundy wine |
| *Chambertin* | Red Burgundy wine, expensive |
| *Champignon* | Cultured mushroom |
| *Chantille Cream* | Whipped cream |
| *Char* | Burn, carbonize |
| *Chateaubriand* | Double tenderloin steak |
| *Chef de Cuisine* | Master Chef and Administrator |
| *Chef de Partie* | Master Chef or Skilled Chef |
| *Chef Entremetier* | Vegetable and Egg Station Cook |
| *Chef Garde-manger* | Cold Pantry Cook |
| *Chef Rotisseur* | Roast and Broiler Station Cook |
| *Chemical Change* | A change in the substance |
| *Chili* | South American red, green, or yellow pepper |
| *Chowder* | Soup made with milk, American Style |
| *Clarified Butter* | Clear butter |
| *Clarify* | To filter, strain, or make clear by use of egg whites |
| *Cocotte* | Small, individual casserole |
| *Combination Method* | Food is exposed to some or all of these: cooking in dry heat air, in liquid, or browning. Food is first caramelized by frying or roasting, then tenderized by adding liquid. |
| *Conductor* | Carrier of heat |
| *Connoisseur* | An expert who is competent to act as a critical judge |
| *Consistency* | Degree of firmness; density |
| *Convection* | Heat is carried by warm air |
| *Cooking* | Heating of food to a certain temperature to make the food edible; preparation of food in general |
| *Coral* | Lobster roe and liver |
| *Court-bouillon* | Fish stock |
| *Crepe* | Small, thin French pancake |
| *Crouton* | Toasted or butter-fried white bread cut in shapes |
| *Cuisine* | Style of cooking |
| *Culotte* | Top part of a bottom round |
| *Curing* | Pickling in brine |
| *Curry* | Stew spiced with curry powder |
| *Curry Powder* | Indian spice combination, pungent, yellow-greenish |
| *Deglazing* | A small amount of liquid is added to caramelized juices to cook them loose after sauteing of food |
| *Dejeuner* | French for breakfast or brunch |
| *Dehydrated* | Dried; the water has been evaporated |
| *Delmonico* | Once famous New York restaurant |

| | |
|---|---|
| *Deuxieme Commis* | Skilled cook with 1-5 years of experience |
| *Devilled* | Strongly spiced or served with brown butter |
| *Disjointed* | Poultry pieces separated at joints; partly boned |
| *Drippings* | Roast or sauté residues left in the pan |
| *Dust* | Sprinkle with flour |
| *Dress* | Truss, make oven ready for poultry |
| *Dressing* | Salad sauce, marinade; or a stuffing for a roast |
| *Duchess Potatoes* | Mashed potatoes with egg yolk and butter, through pastry bag |
| *Edible* | Suitable for eating; eatable |
| *Eggwash* | Beaten eggs with water or milk |
| *Emulsify* | A liquid mixture suspended in another (usually eggs and oil to prevent separation) |
| *Entrée* | Main course |
| *Entrecote* | New York cut sirloin steak |
| *Escoffier* | Famous French chef (1846-1935) |
| *Essence* | Extract of meat flavors |
| *Fillet* | Boneless slice of meat or fish |
| *Fines Herbes* | Selected herbs, minced |
| *Fond* | Natural juices; or bottom |
| *Frappé* | Iced |
| *French* | The meat from the flank end of the rib is completely removed |
| *Fritter* | Deep-fried, batter-coated food |
| *Gastronomy* | The art and science of good eating |
| *Gelatinize* | In making of roux, this means the starch granules have absorbed liquid to their fullest capacity |
| *Gigot d'Agneau* | Lamb leg, whole |
| *Gnocchi* | Italian dumplings |
| *Gratin* | Gratinated, browned on top |
| *Gratinate* | To cook with a covering of buttered crumbs or grated cheese until a crust or crisp surface forms |
| *Grill* | Broiler |
| *Grillade* | Broiled meat |
| *Ground Meat* | Minced meat |
| *Herbs* | Aromatic greens for seasoning, dry or fresh |
| *Hollandaise* | Yellow egg sauce made from yolks and butter |
| *Homogenize* | Break up fat globules into very small particles |
| *Hors d'oeuvres* | Appetizers; opening course |
| *Hofbrau* | Beer cellar, with open food buffet |
| *Hofbrau Style* | Buffet with carver and assembler of sandwiches |
| *Hot Slaw* | Warm coleslaw |
| *Keel Bone* | Breastbone |
| *Kipper* | Smoked, processed herring |
| *Lamb Noisette* | A boneless loin eye, looks like filet mignon |
| *Larding* | Inserting strips of salt pork into meat to add flavor and prevent drying |
| *Leaching* | Extraction of nutrients and flavor from a food through the use of water |

| | |
|---|---|
| *Liquefy* | To make into a liquid |
| *Liquefiable* | Foods which may be made into liquid form |
| *Maraschino* | Sour cherry liquor |
| *Marble* | Visible fat veins |
| *Marinade* | Similar to salad dressing, used also as food preservative and flavoring device |
| *Menu* | Bill of fare; sequence of food served at a meal |
| *Mirepoix* | A mixture of cut vegetables |
| *Mis en Place* | Work station setup |
| *Mock Turtle* | Turtle soup imitation |
| *Navarin* | French, generic name for lamb stew |
| *Osterized* | Blended to a liquid |
| *Oyster* | Bivalve mollusk with a rough, irregular shell closed by a single muscle. Also, a small mass of muscle in a concavity of the pelvic bone on each side of the back of a fowl |
| *Parmentier* | French health inspector (1737-1813) who popularized potatoes in France |
| *Pastrami* | Cured, smoked, beef plate; beef-ham |
| *Patissier* | Pastry Station Cook |
| *Perigord* | Capital of the French truffle district |
| *Petits Fours* | Small, bite-sized pastry |
| *Physical Change* | A change only in the appearance, not in the substance |
| *Poach* | To cook in acidulated water that is simmering |
| *Poissonier* | Fish Station Cook |
| *Polenta* | Cornmeal, grits |
| *Polonaise* | Polish manner or style |
| *Potager* | Soup Station Cook |
| *Premier Commis* | Skilled cook with a minimum of 5 years' experience |
| *Prosciutto* | Italian raw cured and dried ham, eaten raw |
| *Pungent* | Biting or sharp taste or odor |
| *Radiation* | Exposure of food to direct rays from an open flame |
| *Reconstituted* | Water is added to food in order to return it to its original form |
| *Reduce* | Boil off extra liquid to make the dish thicker |
| *Rissole* | Well fried and browned |
| *Roast* | A cut of meat ready to cook or already cooked; for more than three persons, at least |
| *Roasting* | Dry heat cooking with the intent to evaporate some of the water content that all meats have |
| *Roulade* | A slice of meat rolled with or without a stuffing and braised or sauteed |
| *Roux* | Mixture of equal parts by weight of fat and all-purpose flour. It is used as a thickening agent |
| *Rump Steak* | Round steak |
| *Saffron* | Orange-yellow colored pungent spice |
| *Sago* | Tapioca |
| *Saignant* | Medium rare or bloody |
| *Salamander* | Small broiler for toasting and gratinating |
| *Satay* | Indonesian skewer specialty |

| | |
|---|---|
| *Sauté* | Flip fry, pan fry with little fat |
| *Score* | To make superficial cuts in parallel lines, to prevent contractions |
| *Sear* | Score or burn |
| *Seminola* | Farina; cream of wheat |
| *Shashlick* | Lamb brochette, Russian |
| *Shish Kebab* | Lamb brochette, Armenian |
| *Short* | The dish should have only a little sauce to hold the cooked food together |
| *Simmer* | Cooking in liquid below the boiling point |
| *Skewer* | Spit of metal or wood (brochette is French term) |
| *Sous Chef* | Master Chef, Second in Command |
| *Spit-Roasting* | Food is cooked with the heat radiating from an open fire; same as broiling |
| *Steam* | Cooking of foods in liquids; simmer, boil |
| *Sterilize* | Heating of food to a certain temperature to prevent infections by bacteria |
| *Stew* | Cut-up pieces of meat and vegetables braised in their own sauce |
| *Stock* | Liquid containing nutrients and flavor that have been extracted from food |
| *Tenderize* | To make tender by dissolving connective tissues. This causes food to become more digestible |
| *Tomate* | Red vegetable sauce, made from tomato juice |
| *Tournant* | Relief (swing shift) Cook |
| *Tournedo* | Half of a filet mignon |
| *Troisieme Commis* | Skilled cook — first year after apprenticeship |
| *Truffle* | Pungent mushroom, aromatic, growing below the soil |
| *Truss* | Tie together for a better shape |
| *Veloute* | Ivory-colored meat or fish sauce from white stock |
| *Whitewash* | Flour or cornstarch in water; primitive way of thickening liquids |
| *Zeste* | Citrus (lemon or orange) peel |

# Acknowledgments

*CONTRIBUTORS*

J. A. Henckels, Twinworks, Inc., Elmsford, New York

Hobart Manufacturing Company, Troy, Ohio

National Live Stock and Meat Board, 36 S. Wabash Ave., Chicago, Illinois

Miss Barbara Schultz, Albany, New York — Photographer

Silo Restaurant, Albany, New York — Ed Newman, Chef

U. S. Department of Commerce, National Oceanic and Atmospheric Administration, National Marine Fisheries Service, Washington, D.C.

Waring Products Division, Dynamics Corporation of America, New Hartford, Connecticut

Wear-Ever Aluminum, Inc., Chillicothe, Ohio

Mr. Robert H. Wright, Pinole, California — Photographer


This edition of *COOKING FOR THE PROFESSIONAL CHEF: A STRUCTURED APPROACH* was classroom tested at the following schools:

Albany High Adult School, Albany, California

Contra Costa College, San Pablo, California

Contra Costa College, Extended Day Program

Diablo Valley College, Pleasant Hill, Evening School, California

L'Ecole Culinaire, San Francisco, California

Mount Diablo Adult School, California

Mount Diablo Vocational Occupation Center, California

Pleasant Hill Recreation Center, California

And many independent lectures and demonstrations


The staff at Delmar Publishers:

*Director of Publications* — Alan N. Knofla

*Source Editor* — Barbara S. Mohan

*Director of Manufacturing and Production* — Frederick Sharer

*Production Specialists* — Alice Schielke, Jean LeMorta, Sharon Lynch, Patti Manuli, Betty Michelfelder, Debbie Monty, Lee St. Onge

*Illustrators* — Anthony Canabush, George Dowse, Michael Kokernak

# Index